The Holy Land
in History and Thought

Papers Submitted to the International Conference
on the Relations Between the Holy Land
and the World Outside It

JOHANNESBURG 1986

Edited by

MOSHE SHARON

E.J. BRILL
LEIDEN · NEW YORK · KØBENHAVN · KÖLN
1988

Library of Congress Cataloging-in-Publication Data

International Conference on the Relations between the Holy Land and
the World Outside It (1986 : Johannesburg, South Africa)
  The Holy Land in history and thought : papers submitted to the
International Conference on the Relations between the Holy Land and
the World Outside It, Johannesburg, 1986 / edited by Moshe Sharon.
      p.   cm. — (Publications of the Eric Samson Chair in Jewish
civilisation ; no. 1)
  ISBN 9004088555
  1. Palestine—History—Congresses.   2. Palestine—Description and
travel—Congresses.   3. Palestine in Judaism—Congresses.
4. Palestine in Islam—Congresses.   I. Sharon, Moshe.   II. Title.
III. Series.
DS101.5.I57 1986
956.94—dc19   88-14502
                                                          CIP

Distributed outside the Republic of South Africa by E.J. Brill,
Leiden, The Netherlands.

Distributed in the Republic of South Africa by Southern Book
Publishers, Johannesburg, under the title *Pillars of Smoke and
Fire.*

ISBN 90 04 08855 5 (E.J. Brill)
ISBN 1 86812 048 1 (Southern Book Publishers)

Publications of the Eric Samson Chair in Jewish Civilization,
No. 1.

Set in 10 on 12 pt. Times by Unifoto, Cape Town

Printed and bound by CTP Book Printers, Cape

BD8465

Foreword

No single fraction of the world's surface is linked to our history, to our beliefs, to our emotions, as strongly as the Holy Land, a relatively small and unspectacular tract of country between the eastern shores of the Mediterranean and the surrounding deserts.

There were born two of the most important religions to have shaped the destiny of mankind. To the Jewish diaspora and to the citizens of the State which emerged again in 1948 after an eighteen-century eclipse, Eretz Yisrael is not only a holy land but the eternal Zion, a gift of God to His people. To Christians all over the world, the birth of Jesus in Bethlehem, the Galilean village of Nazareth, the Christ's preaching at Capharnaum and the final tragedy of the Crucifixion at Jerusalem make up a deeply moving picture book, an integral part of their sensibility. The history of Europe cannot be understood without the pilgrimages, without the Crusades.

Moreover, the third and most recent of the monotheistic religions, Islam, although it possesses its own holy places in the Arabian peninsula, considers "Al-Quds" as one of the cities sanctified by its Prophet. The beautiful mosques of Jerusalem are among the most renowned monuments of worship of the Muslim world.

The Holy Land has been a country at crossroads since the Palaeolithic era and the theatre of the Empires' expansion and wars from antiquity right up until today. Its history bears the seal of tragedy. All the peoples who have invaded it or dwelt in it have abundantly shed their blood on its soil.

The International Conference on the Relations between the Holy Land and the World Outside it, thanks to the University of the Witwatersrand in Johannesburg, under the chairmanship of Prof. Moshe Sharon, has given an opportunity to specialists from Israel, Great Britain, Germany, Denmark, the United States of America and South Africa to discuss such themes as the early history of the Holy Land, its relations with Christian theology and the attraction it exercised upon so many people, including the Falashas from Ethiopia as well as the medieval pilgrims. The papers submitted to that Conference are a worthy contribution to one of the most fascinating subjects of human science. Such a symposium not only clarifies a certain number of problems; it also raises meaningful questions which should be addressed in further meetings. It is therefore to be hoped that the example set by the Conference on the Holy Land will be followed by other initiatives of the same kind, and with the same success.

Dr Jacques Soustelle
Member of the French Academy
Paris, May 1987

Preface

The International Conference on the Relations between the Holy Land and the World Outside it brought together some 40 scholars from major centres of scholarship in the world. They convened at the University of the Witwatersrand at the beginning of December 1986 to mark the introduction of Jewish Studies into the University. Most of them contributed papers to the conference and studies for this volume.

The choice of the Holy Land as the theme for the conference seemed most appropriate because of its relevance to all three monotheistic religions and to the civilisations which they produced.

"The Holy Land is at the centre of the development of great civilisations" wrote Karl Tober, Principal and Vice Chancellor of the University of the Witwatersrand. "It was in the Middle East that mankind made the initial advance from the conditions of pre-historic life to the formation of urban communities. These sizeable and complex communities represented in their development a shift of such dimensions that in the whole of the subsequent history, perhaps, only the changes wrought by industrialisation and, in this century, the technological revolution can be compared with it. Modern historians have developed, to an unprecedented degree, an awareness of the relevance of the past for contemporary society. By systematically exploring the past, scholars may perhaps be able to develop insights which will illuminate the obscurities of the future."

The studies presented in this volume represent these ideas. They belong to a wide range of disciplines: history, general and Hebrew literature, archaeology, theology, Bible studies, Islamic studies and modern politics; and they cover an extraordinarily long period which stretches from the depth of pre-history some 70 000 years ago to our present time.

It is with much gratitude that I wish to thank all my colleagues who contributed to the success and the high standard of the conference.

The establishment of the Chair in Jewish studies would have been impossible without the generous donation of Mr Eric Samson, the Chairman and Chief Executive of Macsteel, South Africa, and without the dedication of Mr I. Greenstein, the Chairman of the South African Committee for Tertiary Jewish Education, and the members of this committee. Thanks are due to Professor K. Tober, the Vice Chancellor, and Professors L.A. Suzman and N. Garson, the successive Deans of the Faculty of Arts, for the crucial parts they played in bringing to fruition the idea of Jewish Studies at the University.

The convening of the conference would have been impossible without the unusual commitment and professionalism of Ms Sharon Wolman, the conference co-ordinator.

Special gratitude belongs to Mrs M.M.M. Blackbeard (van Wyk) and to Mrs M.J. du Toit for their contributions to the professional preparation of the manuscript. Mr C. Cohen has not only seen to the legal matters connected with the publication of the book but has always been a source of encouragement on all matters concerning the establishment of the Chair.

The conference was also supported by The Anglo American and the De Beers Chairman's Fund, Anglo American Corporation of South Africa Ltd, De Beers Consolidated Mines Ltd, Mr R. Ackerman, Mr N. Nossel and the Adcock-Ingram Laboratories Ltd, South African Airways and Snap Print.

May they all be blessed.

M.S.
Johannesburg, July 1987

Contents

Introduction xii
Moshe Sharon, Hebrew University, Jerusalem

PART 1: ARCHAEOLOGY AND EARLY HISTORY

1. Modern-type, intelligent behaviour prior to 70 000 years ago 3
   Avraham Ronen, University of Haifa

2. The holiness of the Holy Land in the light of a new document from
   Qumran 9
   Elisha Qimron, Ben Gurion University

3. The commercial relations of Canaan in the second millenium BC –
   a discussion of the cuneiform texts from Mari and Ugarit 14
   Izak Cornelius, University of Stellenbosch

4. The administration and the army in Judaea in the early Roman period
   (from Pompey to Vespasian, 63 BC–AD 79) 33
   Denis Saddington, University of the Witwatersrand

PART II: CHRISTIAN THEOLOGY

5. The contribution of the Holy Land to a theology of Church and State 43
   Godfrey Ashby, University of the Witwatersrand

6. The significance of the capacity of God as Creator for His relationship to the
   Land in the Old Testament 48
   Jacob Helberg, Potchefstroom University for Christian Higher Education

PART III: ASPECTS OF ATTRACTION TO THE HOLY LAND

7. Medieval pilgrims, the Holy Land and its image in European civilisation   65
   Aryeh Grabois, University of Haifa

8. Nineteenth-century travelogues and the Land of Moab   80
   Hannes Olivier, University of Stellenbosch

9. Mark Twain in the Holy Land   96
   Reingard Nethersole, University of the Witwatersrand

10. The connection between the Falashas and the Land of Israel   105
    Tudor Parfitt, University of London

PART IV: THE HOLY LAND IN HEBREW AND JEWISH LITERATURE

11. The attitude towards the Land of Israel in Spanish Hebrew poetry   117
    Ezra Spicehandler, Hebrew Union College

12. "Here" and "There" in modern Hebrew poetry   141
    Glenda Abramson, Oxford Centre for Hebrew Studies, Oxford University

13. Israel as redemption in S.Y. Agnon's *A Guest for the Night*   150
    Zilla Goodman, University of Cape Town

14. The gates of Zion and the dwellings of Jacob: Zion and Zionism in the work
    of Isaac Bashevis Singer   163
    Joseph Sherman, University of the Witwatersrand

PART V: REALISM AND MYSTICISM

15. The fantasy of theology and the reality of power: Zionism in the thought of
    Richard L. Rubenstein   175
    Jocelyn Hellig, University of the Witwatersrand

16. An iconographical analysis of Duchamp's Bride image in the *Large Glass* ...   187
    Rory T. Doepel, University of the Witwatersrand

PART VI: THE HOLY LAND IN ISLAM

17. The birth of Islam in the Holy Land   225
    Moshe Sharon, Hebrew University, Jerusalem

18. Jerusalem and Mecca, the Temple and the Kaaba. An account of their inter-
    relation in Islamic times   236
    Heribert Busse, University of Kiel

19. Islam versus Christian Europe: the case of the Holy Land   247
    David Ayalon, Hebrew University, Jerusalem

20. New discoveries in Islamic archaeology in the Holy Land 257
    Myriam Rosen-Ayalon, Hebrew University, Jerusalem

PART VII: MODERN HISTORY AND POLITICS

21. The United States and the Holy Land in the nineteenth century 273
    Jacob M. Landau, Hebrew University, Jerusalem

22. The Jews of Baghdad and the Holy Land 281
    Sylvia G. Haim

23. Judaism and Zionism in the Holy Land 287
    Elie Kedourie, London School of Economics

Introduction

Moshe Sharon

The Holy Land is more than a geographical name; it is a concept, it is a focus of identity, it is a source of inspiration, it is legend and reality intermingled and interchanged. Although there are millions who would not know its exact location, there is no other place on the surface of this planet which has had such a tremendous impact on human history, human culture, on the spirit and life of man, as has this piece of land, which is not much bigger than the Kruger National Park. The term Holy Land does not have to be explained for almost half of the human race. For Jews, Christians and Muslims it is self explanatory; none of them would ask "Which Holy Land?" and this is exactly the reason for the choice of name for the conference which resulted in this collection of studies.

Since we speak about a concrete geographical location, it is important to note immediately that in spite of, or probably because of, its extreme importance, the Holy Land is not a very well-defined piece of real estate.

In the Bible, it appears under various names, but never as the Holy Land. It is defined by various borders, some of which extend its territory from the Upper Euphrates to Sinai; and some of which confine it more to the land which lies between the Mediterranean and the Jordan. In post-biblical literature the doctors of Jewish law had long debates whether the city of Acre, bordering on the Galilee, should be included in it.

For all practical purposes history has decided on the modest size of some 24 000 km² between the Mediterranean and the deep cleft of the Jordan and the Dead Sea. Yet it was only in a very few periods in history that the Holy Land was really a distinct name on the map. During most of its history it was part of a greater area, and only when it was an independent or semi-independent state, its name, whichever it was, had a defined political or geographical meaning.

Early biblical tradition designates the Holy Land according to the peoples that lived in it before the appearance of the Israelites. It is called the Land of Canaan after the Canaanites, the principal people that occupied most of it. This is also the name which it has in one of the earliest extra-biblical sources, the Tel el-Amarna tablets from the fifteenth century BC. It was only after the Israeli tribes conquered the land that the name of Israel became associated with it.

From the beginning of the first millenium BC, the name Israel designated specifically the northern Kingdom of Israel as a separate political entity from the Kingdom of Judaea in the south; and after the destruction of the two kingdoms between the end of the eighth and the beginning of the sixth centuries BC, the name Judaea became the name *par excellence* of the Second Temple Jewish State.

The coastal plain which, during most of the First Temple period, was occupied by the Philistines was called after them, the Land of the Philistines or *Peleshet*. In the fifth century BC the great Greek historian Herodotus was probably the first to describe this territory by the name *Syria hé Palaistine,* "The Palestinian Syria", and from then onwards the name Palaestina became the name for the coastal plain and then for the whole country to the west of the Jordan.

The Romans were responsible for this final change. Eager to obliterate the name of the rebellious Judaea, they turned, in 135 CE, the whole former territory of Israel into a Roman province which they renamed *Palaestina* or *Syria Palaestina.*

When the Eastern Roman Empire, better known as the Byzantine Empire, reorganised its administration in 429 CE, the territory to the west of the Jordan was made into two provinces, *Palaestina Prima* (first Palestine) and *Palaestina Secunda* (second Palestine), the former comprising the Galilee and the latter comprising Judaea and Samaria.

When the Arabs took over Syria in the seventh century, they followed the Byzantine administrative arrangements and used the same place names. The Roman and Hebrew names acquired an Arabic pronunciation but, on the whole, were rarely changed. Thus, for instance, Neapolis became *Nābulus* in Arabic and Aelia Capitolina, the Herodian name for Jerusalem, became *Ilyā.* Not being able to cope, however, with two provinces that had the same name, Palaestina, they conferred the name *Filastīn,* which is the Arabic form of Palaestina, only on Judaea and Samaria, whereas the Galilee was renamed *Urdunn,* namely, the Province of Jordan. In time this Arabic-Islamic administrative division became a geographical division and it appears in all the Arabic geographical works until modern times.

It was only after the First World War and the British occupation of Syria and the Holy Land that the name Palestine became the official name of the country under the British mandate. The Arab Nationalists made this Arabicised Roman name the main focus of their political aspirations, whereas the Jews fought to add to the official mandatory name the Hebrew letters EY in brackets, that is to say, Eretz Yisrael, "the land of Israel".

In the Qur'ān, the country is mentioned only once, in Sura 5 verse 21, when Moses speaks to the people of Israel and says to them: "O my people enter the Holy Land (*al ard al-muqaddasah*) which Allah hath written down as yours, and turn not back to your rearward so as to be rendered losers" (trans. R. Bell).

The designation of *Terra Sancta* or the Holy Land is of Christian origin. It became the most common name in Christian literature and thereafter influenced both Jewish and Islamic usages in the Middle Ages. In spite of this, the term Holy Land remained very much the designation of the Church. As time passed, neither Jews nor Muslims regarded the name as representative of their respective cultures. The Muslims continued to call it *Filasṭin* and the Jews Eretz Yisrael, but for the rest of the world it is remained the Holy Land.

Part I
Archaeology and Early History

1 Modern-type, intelligent behaviour prior to 70 000 years ago

Avraham Ronen

In the convenient, three-fold division of human evolution into the Early, Middle and Upper Palaeolithic periods, anatomically modern man, *Homo sapiens sapiens* ("Intelligent Man"), gained world-wide dominance in the latter phase, which began about 35 000 years ago. Clues indicating a different behavioural pattern than before appeared simultaneously in the archaeological record. The new pattern shows more sophisticated methods of tool manufacture, a wider and more thorough utilisation of resources of both alimentary and raw materials, and a different — and higher — mental capacity than before. The appearance of this modern-type, intelligent behaviour has naturally been connected with the anatomical form of *Homo sapiens sapiens*. Recently, however, this causative link has been disproved by the discovery that in the Levant, anatomically modern man co-existed with Neanderthals as early as 80–70 000 years ago (Vandermeersch: 1981) and yet no sign of a "modern-type" behaviour was seen in his cultural remains which are, on the contrary, very similar to those of his Neanderthal neighbours.

We would like to draw attention to another problem associated with identifying certain types of human behaviour with anatomical development, namely, the appearance of a "modern-type" behaviour long before the classical Upper Palaeolithic one. Which human type was associated with this episode is as yet uncertain, but the episode clearly lasted for a relatively short time (Butzer *et al.,* 1978; Clark, 1982; Jelinek, 1982; Volman, 1984) during Isotope Stage 5 a–b (about 90 000–70 000 years ago). It then completely disappeared from our known archaeological record until its classical appearance 35 000 years ago. Here then is a unique case in human history in which an "advanced" form of behaviour is subsequently "forgotten", and reappears about 40 000 years later.

MODERN-TYPE BEHAVIOUR

Compared with the preceding, roughly 2-million-years-long cultural remains left by man, the traits of the modern, intelligent behaviour of the Upper Palaeolithic are as follows:

3

- Objects of art and decoration are manufactured.
- The environment is more widely exploited than before. Special, and better, raw materials are sought for stone tools, and aquatic alimentary resources are added to the diet.
- Bone is used for tool making.
- Raw material is "recycled", old stone tools are re-used for the making of new ones.
- A new, sophisticated method of blade manufacturing appears, probably requiring the use of a punch. This technique is used in addition to·(and sometimes replaces) the traditional flake technique.
- Composite tools are manufactured through a highly sophisticated binding of various elements (stone, bone, antler, wood). Residues of binding resin have been found preserved on stone artefacts.
- An extremely long tradition (1,5 million years or more) of handaxes and racloirs as major tool types is replaced by grattoirs, burins, knives and microliths, variously associated.

The above traits are not merely technical innovations; they mirror another level of concepts and abilities, a different mental state, and, we may deduce, a new social organisation and a higher intelligence than before. The significance of this "modern-type behaviour" is not yet fully known, but it is enough at this point to realise what its symptoms may signal.

THE EARLIEST OCCURRENCE OF MODERN BEHAVIOUR

The earliest unmistakable occurrence of some of the traits of modern-type behaviour described above surprisingly came to light in the Syrian site of Yabrud (Rust, 1950), in a much earlier stratigraphical position than would have been expected. The claimed early date was accepted initially with scepticism by the scientific community (Bordes, 1962). Other assemblages with very similar characters and in an identical stratigraphical situation were subsequently discovered and finally gained general acknowledgement. They were termed "Pre-Aurignacian" (Rust, 1950; McBurney, 1967) or "Amudian" on grounds of different tool composition (Garrod and Kirkbride, 1961). The Pre-Aurignacian and Amudian assemblages are known only in the Levant and, until now, have been discovered in six sites (see Figure 1.1), either sandwiched between Lower Palaeolithic layers or underlying Middle Palaeolithic. They have nothing in common with the layers which directly underlie or overlie them; on the contrary, they bear a striking resemblance to Upper Palaeolithic assemblages, and hence they represent a similar type of behaviour. We shall refer to these early "untimely" assemblages as "Pre-Upper Palaeolithic" (PUP).

A similar phenomenon exists in Southern Africa, surprisingly originating from the same time (Volman, 1984). It is termed the Howieson's Poort phase, and is found sandwiched between Middle Stone Age layers, with which it has little in common. Its characters and deduced behaviour pattern are strongly similar to those of the Late Stone Age, as in the Levant. Hence, we include the Howieson's Poort phase with the PUP group of assemblages. It was recognised certainly in 15, perhaps in 20 sites in Southern Africa. (Figure 1.1).

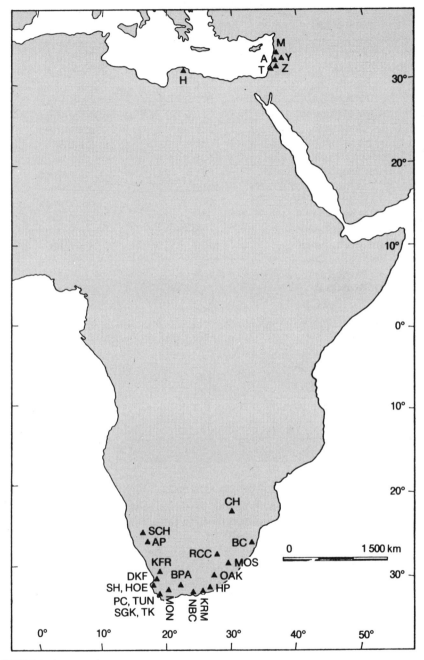

FIGURE 1.1 Approximate location of PUP occurrences in the Levant and Southern Africa
(Southern African data from Volman, 1984)

Name of Site	Abbreviation	Country
Adlun	A	Lebanon
Apollo 11	AP	Namibia
Boomplaas	BPA	South Africa
Border Cave	BC	South Africa
Cave of Hearths	CH	South Africa
Diepkloof	DKF	South Africa
Haua Fteah	H	Libya
Hoedjies Punt (?)	HOE	South Africa
Howieson's Poort	HP	South Africa
Klasies River Mouth	KRM	South Africa
Klipfonteinrand	KFR	South Africa
Masloukh	M	Lebanon
Montagu Cave	MON	South Africa
Moshebi's Shelter	MOS	Lesotho
Nelson Bay Cave	NBC	South Africa
Oakleigh Farm	OAK	South Africa
Peers Cave	PC	South Africa
Rose Cottage Cave	RCC	South Africa
Schlangengrotte(?)	SCH	Namibia
Sea Harvest(?)	SH	South Africa
Skildergatkop	SGK	South Africa
Tabun	T	Israel
Trappieskop	TK	South Africa
Tunnel Cave	TUN	South Africa
Yabrud	Y	Syria
Zuttiya	Z	Israel

PUP assemblages have the following characteristics which denote "modern-type" behaviour (see Table 1.1): a sophisticated blade technology (Ronen *et al.,* in press); grattoirs, burins, knives and microliths are the dominating tools, the latter especially in Southern Africa; engraved objects exist in South African sites and the Haua-Fteah in Libya; elaborate bone tools are also found in these two localities; exploitation of marine resources is demonstrated in the Libyan site (McBurney, 1967), but it is also possible, in our opinion, that the oldest shell middens currently known in the world, the 70 000 year-old middens in the Cape Province of South Africa (Volman, 1978), belong to the Howieson's Poort Phase. There is a preference for some fine-grained stone for tool making in the Southern African PUP, like in the Late Stone Age and unlike the Middle Stone Age layers among which the PUP is situated. Finally, a smart reutilisation of old tools as raw material is attested in the Levantine sites of Yabrud and Tabun (Rust, 1950; Jelinek, pers. comm.).

TABLE 1.1   Cultural and Behavioural Traits Compared

	Lower and Middle Palaeolithic	Upper Palaeolithic	PUP Assemblages
Art	Absent	Present	Absent
Engraving	Absent (?)	Present	Present
Environmental exploitation	Narrow-range	Wide-range	Wide-range
Re-use of raw material	Absent	Present	Present
Bone tools	Absent	Present	Present
Technology	Flake production	Blade production	Blade production
Composite tools	Absent	Present	Present
Stone tools	Handaxes, racloirs	Grattoirs, burins, knives, microliths	Grattoirs, burins, knives, microliths

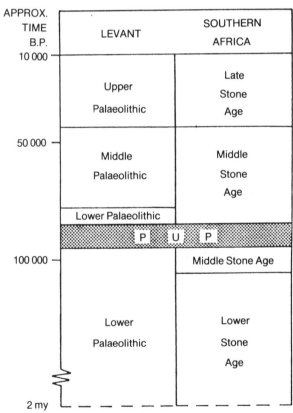

FIGURE 1.2   Schematic chronological diagram

7

DISCUSSION

What caused this episode of early modern-type behaviour, of "high standard precision work" in McBurney's words (1967:99)? A partial answer may lie in the possible, still disputed, association of *Homo sapiens sapiens* with PUP remains at Border Cave, South Africa, dated to about 95 000 years ago (Butzer *et al.*, 1978). But even if this is confirmed by future research, the mere presence of anatomically modern man does not in itself imply a modern-type behaviour, as we have learned from the Levantine Middle Palaeolithic example. Some sort of environmental trigger is to be sought for the advanced behaviour of Stage 5. By way of a largely generalised hypothesis, we would stress the geographical location of the known PUP occurrences: between latitude 24° and 34° South, and 32°–34° North. This parallel setting is in ice-free latitudes, and has to be viewed in the transgressive conditions of Stage 5. There followed a loss of large fertile coastal plains without a compensating deglaciated territory. The ensuing stress may have been at the root of the earliest appearance of intensified environmental exploitation and modern-type behaviour. In our opinion, similar conditions in a much later time may have triggered the Neolithic Revolution in the Levant (Ronen, in press).

REFERENCES

F. Bordes, "Sur la Chronologie du Paléolithique au Moyen Orient", *Quaternaria* 5, 1962, pp. 57–69.

K.W. Butzer, P.B. Baumont, and J.C. Vogel, "Lithostratigraphy of Border Cave, Swaziland, South Africa: a Middle Stone Age Sequence Beginning ca. 195,000 B.P." *Journal of Archaeological Science* 5 1978, pp. 317–41.

J.D. Clark, "The Transition from Lower to Middle Palaeolithic in the African Continent", in A. Ronen, (ed.), *The Transition from Lower to Middle Palaeolithic and the Origin of Modern Man*, B.A.R. S151, Oxford, 1982, pp. 235–55.

D.A.E. Garrod and D. Kirkbride, "Excavation of Abri Zumoffen, a Palaeolithic Rock-shelter near Adlun, in South Lebanon, 1958", *Bulletin Musée de Beyrouth* 16, 1961, pp. 7–46.

A.J. Jelinek, "The Middle Palaeolithic in the Southern Levant with Comments on the Appearance of Modern *Homo sapiens*", in A. Ronen, (ed.), *The Transition from Lower to Middle Palaeolithic and the Origin of Modern Man*, B.A.R. S151, Oxford, 1982, pp. 57–101.

C.B.M. McBurney, *The Haua Fteah (Cyrenaica) and the Stone Age of the South-East Mediterranean*, Cambridge, 1967.

A. Ronen, "Man and Pest: Another Narrative of the Origin of Agriculture" (in press).

A. Ronen, M. Lamdan, L. Shmookler, "Pre-Upper Palaeolithic Occurrences of Isotope Stage 5", (in press).

A. Rust, *Die Hohlenfunde von Jabrud (Syrien)*, Neumunster, Karl Wachholtz, 1950.

B. Vandermeersch, *Les Hommes Fossiles de Qafzeh (Israel)*, CNRS, Paris, 1981.

T.P. Volman, "Early Archaeological Evidence for Shellfish Collecting", *Science* 201, 1978, pp. 911–13.

T.P. Volman, "Early Prehistory of Southern Africa", in R.G. Klein, (ed.), *Southern African Prehistory and Palaeoenvironments*, A.A. Balkema, Rotterdam/Boston, 1984, pp. 169–395.

2 The holiness of the Holy Land in the light of a new document from Qumran

Elisha Qimron

Eretz Yisrael is holy to the Jews, the Christians and the Muslims. But its holiness has almost no practical implications. For the Jews it is holy because God dwells in it, because it is the land which God has chosen for His people, and because He gave certain commandments which are applied only within its borders. For the Christians it is holy because it is the birthplace of Jesus. The reasons for its holiness in Muslim eyes are more complex and need not be dealt with here.

In Jewish law there are some commandments — mostly relating to agriculture — which apply only in Eretz Yisrael. This fact may give Eretz Yisrael some degree of holiness, but, strictly speaking, the holiness of a place implies something different: it means that impurity must be kept away from that place.[1] As we shall see, the Holy Land as a whole is not holy in this sense; only certain places in it are holy. From which places must impurity be kept away? Or in other words: what was the scope of the purity laws of the Torah? This question was a subject of much controversy during the Second Temple period. Before discussing the problem, we shall consider the background and some of the ancient sources at our disposal.

As is well known, what characterised Judaism in the Second Temple period was sectarianism.[2] Thus Josephus states[3] that the Jews in that period were divided into three groups: Pharisees, Sadducees and Essenes. In fact most people did not belong to any of these leading groups, whose membership was confined largely to the élite. They were what the Hebrew sources call עם הארץ. But the עם הארץ generally followed the position of the Pharisees.[4] Josephus briefly characterises the beliefs and way of life of these three groups. He does not, however, tell us when these groups were created, or what brought about their creation. Nor does he specify the *halakhic* views of these groups.

Fortunately, much information is now available owing to the discovery of the Dead Sea Scrolls. Most scholars tend to identify the group that used these documents as the Essenes.[5]

The most explicit data about the origins of the three groups are to be found in a new document from Qumran which Professor Strugnell from Harvard University and I are publishing. I give here a short description of this document.

The new document is a letter discovered in cave 4 at Qumran. It includes *halakhoth* (rulings) which manifest the author's sectarian *halakhic* views. These differ from the normative practice of Judaism. Six manuscripts of the work have been discovered, all of them incomplete. Taken together, the manuscripts provide a composite text of 120 lines.

The composite reconstructed text seems to indicate that the letter originally had four sections:
- An opening formula — now completely lost.
- A calendar of the sect. The year they used consisted of 364 days.
- A list of more than 20 *halakhoth,* all of which are peculiar to this group.
- An epilogue discussing the separation of the group.

The issues dealt with in the letter are regarded by its author as of the utmost importance, since they are the ones which caused the separation of the group. Practically all of them concern the Temple, and specifically its purity.

From the content of the letter we may infer that it was written by the leader of the Essenes and addressed to the leader of Israel, apparently Jonathan the Prince.[6] It specifies the reasons for the separation of the Essenes from the rest of Israel, the main reason being a controversy over certain *halakhoth* relating to the purity of the Temple and its cult.

Even before the discovery of the document, it was well known that the purity laws were regarded as of the utmost importance.

The fact that the letter consists of controversial *halakhoth* is of great importance, because we may learn from it not only the *halakha* of the Essenes but also that of their opponents. Examining the *halakhic* views of the opponents we find that they are always identical with those of the Rabbis, which proves that the opponents were the predecessors of the Rabbis. It further proves that the Rabbinic *halakha* in those areas discussed by the letter was established at a very early date. This disproves the theory of Abraham Geiger that the Pharisaic *halakha* is a "new *halakha";* the Pharisaic *halakha* rather contains both old and new rulings, Its roots are very old.

We may further learn from the letter that the *halakhoth* of the Essenes were more strict than those of the Rabbis. The Essenes always took the biblical law literally, whereas the Rabbis adapted the biblical law to the needs of the time.

We now return to our main subject, the holiness of places in Eretz Yisrael. As is well known, most of the purity laws of the Torah involve places. A Jew should be pure mainly when entering a holy place. Otherwise he may be impure.[8] For example, according to Jewish law, a person is made impure by proximity to, or contact with, a corpse. The only way to become pure is by means of a remarkable and archaic procedure: a red cow must be slaughtered, its corpse burnt, and the ashes mixed with water. The contaminated person is made pure again when this water is sprinkled on him.[9] But for all practical purposes we can dispense with this proceeding, since the purity which it creates is necessary only in order to enter the Temple, and the Temple, of course, was destroyed 2 000 years ago.

The Rabbinic view of the scope of the laws of purity is set out in Mishna Kelim 1:6–9.

There are ten grades of holiness: The Land of Israel is holier than all other lands. And what is the nature of its holiness? That from it are brought the *omer*, the first fruits and the two loaves, which may not be brought from any of the other lands. Cities that are walled are holier, for lepers must be sent out of them and a corpse, though it may be carried about within them as long as it is desired, may not be brought back once it has been taken out. The area within the wall (of Jerusalem) is holier, for it is there that holy things of a minor degree and second tithe may be eaten. The Temple Mount is holier, for neither *Zavim* nor *zavoth* nor menstruants nor women after childbirth may enter it. The Rampart is holier, for neither idolaters nor one who contracted corpse uncleanness may enter it. The Court of Women is holier, for no *tevul yom* may enter it, though no sin-offering is thereby incurred. The Court of the Israelites is holier, for a man who has not yet offered his obligatory sacrifices may not enter it, and if he enters he incurs thereby a sin-offering. The Court of the Priests is holier for no Israelites may enter it except when they are required to do so in connection with the laying on of hands, slaying or waving. The area between the *ulam* and the altar is holier, for men afflicted with blemishes or with a wild growth of hair may not enter it. The *Hekal* is holier, for no one whose hands or feet are unwashed may enter it. The holy of holies is holier for only the high priest on the day of atonement, at the service may enter it . . . .

Commentators of the Mishna observed that the holiness ascribed here to Eretz Yisrael as a whole is different from the holiness ascribed to certain specific places within Eretz Yisrael, in that there is no mention of the need to keep impurity away from Eretz Yisrael as a whole (see Rav Hay Gaon and Maimonides).[10] Furthermore, one may see that the real holiness centres around the Temple, while the other places, including Jerusalem, may be entered by most kinds of impure people. One may conclude that according to the Rabbis, real holiness centres around the Temple, and that in other places in Eretz Yisrael there is hardly any holiness in the narrow sense of the word.

The main problem in establishing the scope of holiness involves the interpretation of the word *maḥane*, "camp", that appears in the Torah. As is well known, most of the purity laws in the Torah are confined to the *maḥane*.[11] This camp existed only during the generation of the desert wanderings, while the purity laws were to be observed for all generations. How should one apply these rules later in the land of Israel?

As we have seen, the Rabbis restricted the force of most of the purity laws to the Temple alone. They were able to do so by giving the word *maḥane* various meanings, declaring that there were three camps in the Torah: the camp of God (the Tabernacle), the camp of Levites (the area around the Tabernacle in which the Levites lived) and the camp of Israelites (the area in which the other tribes lived). Similarly, there were three sections in Jerusalem: the Temple (the camp of God), the Temple Mount (the camp of Levites) and the rest of Jerusalem (the camp of Israelites).[12] According to the Rabbis, most of the purity laws applied to the Temple alone and not to the rest of Jerusalem (and, of course, not to other places in the Land of Israel).[13]

Why did the Rabbis give the word *maḥane* various meanings? The significance of their attitude can now be evaluated in the light of our new document, which presents the attitude of the Essenes towards the question. In our document we find the following statement:

כי ירושלים היא מחנה הקדוש היא המקום שבחר בו מכל שבטי ישראל כי ירושלים היא דראש מחנות ישראל

For Jerusalem is the holy camp, it is the place which He chose from among all the tribes of Israel. For Jerusalem is the chief of the cities *(maḥaṅot)* of Israel.

Here all Jerusalem is identified with the camp *(maḥaneh)* of the Torah while the other cities are called "camps" and also have purity, albeit to a lesser degree. (Their degree of purity according to the Essenes will not be discussed here.[14])

order that people might live with them. That is why they gave the word *maḥane* three different meanings. Unlike the Essenes, they would not make life in Jerusalem intolerable. holiness as that of the camp had to observe in Jerusalem the purity laws which were to be observed in the camp. Thus they did not bring their wives to Jerusalem, since sexual relations were forbidden in the camp,[15] and they were not allowed to defecate in Jerusalem, since this had to be done outside the camp.[16] We have evidence that the Essenes who lived in Jerusalem were unmarried[17] and that they did not defecate on the Sabbath, since they were forbidden to leave Jerusalem on the Sabbath.[18] This extreme law was rejected by the Rabbis, who maintained that the laws of the Torah were given in order that people might live with them. That is why they gave the word *maḥane* three different meanings. Unlike the Essenes, they would not make life in Jerusalem intolerable.

The outcome of this controversy was the exile of the Essenes from Jerusalem. The Essenes accused the Rabbis of defiling Jerusalem as well as the Temple. And since Jerusalem was being defiled they could not live in it, and they left for a place where they were able to keep the purity laws of the Torah. In this new place they kept the highest degree of purity — that of the camp.

In summary, the general orthodox view in the Second Temple period was that holiness in the strict sense of the word existed in the Temple alone, rather than in Jerusalem as a whole or in other places in the Land of Israel. The Essenes, however, who maintained a strict attitude towards the laws of the Torah, held that holiness existed in the whole of Jerusalem and to a much lesser extent in the other cities of the Land of Israel.

NOTES
1. Cf. *Encyclopaedia Biblica,* 7, Jerusalem, 1976, pp. 44–62 (Hebrew).
2. See S.J.D. Cohen, "The Significance of Yavneh: Pharisees, Rabbis, and the End of Jewish Sectarianism", *HUCA,* 55, 1984, pp. 27–53.
3. *Antiquities,* XIII, pp. 171–3.
4. D. Flusser, *Megilloth Midbar Yehda,* Jerusalem, 1967, p. 79 (Hebrew).
5. Geza, Vermes, *The Dead Sea Scrolls – Qumran in Perspective,* U.S.A., 1978, pp. 116–36.
6. We believe that the addressee is the Wicked Priest, and adopt the opinion of those who identify him with Jonathan, see Vermes, *id,* pp. 150–51, 161.
7. A. Geiger, *Hamiqra Vetargumav,* Jerusalem, 1972, p. 98 (Hebrew).
8. G. Alon, *Studies in Jewish History,* I, Tel-Aviv 1967, pp. 148–76 (Hebrew).

9. Numbers 19: 1–22.
10. See C. Albeck's commentary on the Mishna, order Teharoth, p. 508, and P. Kehathi's commentary on the Mishna order Teharoth, p. 21.
11. Y. Yadin, *The Temple Scroll,* Jerusalem, 1983, I, pp. 278–81.
12. See *Tosefta, Kelim, Baba Kama* 1:12.
13. Cf. the discussions by Alon and Yadin, op. cit.
14. The identification of Jerusalem with the camp may be seen also in the Temple Scroll. But the evidence there is not explicit — see L.H. Schiffman, "Exclusion from the Sanctuary and the City of the Sanctuary in the Temple Scroll", *Hebrew Annual Review* 9, 1985, pp. 301–20.
15. Lev 15:18; Temple Scroll 45:11; Damascus Covenant 12:1–2.
16. Deut 23:13–4; Temple Scroll 46: 13–16; Josephus, *Wars,* II, pp. 147–9.
17. Y. Yadin, *The Temple Scroll,* Jerusalem, 1983, I, pp. 288–9.
18. Josephus, *Wars,* II, pp. 147–9.

3 The commercial relations of Canaan in the second millennium BC — a discussion of the cuneiform texts from Mari and Ugarit[1]

Izak Cornelius

"The most visible element in Middle Eastern civilization is transport and the traffic in fine goods".[2]

INTRODUCTION

Before proceeding, some general remarks concerning the purpose of this study and definitions of terms should be given. The purpose is to discuss the commercial relations of Canaan in the second millennium BC, using as data textual material from Mari and Ugarit.

In the period under discussion "Canaan" is used as a term for the Holy Land in cuneiform texts *(kinaḫḫu)* when denoting the region between Egypt and the Syrian state of Amurru.[3]

The earliest reference to Canaan or rather Canaanites[4] in cuneiform texts is in an eighteenth century letter from the palace of Zimri-Lim (*c.* 1780–1758 BC) at Mari, published by G. Dossin.[5] Canaanites occupied a certain village but their immediate origin and purpose is unknown. This text predates Idrimi[6] (fifteenth century BC) who fled to the land of Canaan *(ki-in-a-nim)*, as well as various occurrences in the Alalaḫ texts,[7] Amarna letters[8] and Ugaritic texts.[9] According to G. Pettinato,[10] Canaan also appears in the third millennium texts from Ebla. To this may be added biblical references.[11] It is interesting to note that in some books of the Bible, *kĕna'ănî* does not only include the region of Canaan and its people, but refers to merchants or traders.[12]

"Commerce" is defined as referring to "foreign trade" or international trade, which was carried out "with countries outside this region" (Leemans),[13] in this case Canaan. In this chapter attention will be devoted to the following aspects of trade: the geography of the trade (interconnections), trading objects (commodities), trade routes, transport of commodities, the agents of the trade or carriers of commodities (merchants) and the organisation of the trade.[14]

The main sources utilised were cuneiform texts from Mari (Tell Ḥarīrī), from the eighteenth century or Middle Bronze Age iib and from Ugarit (Ras Shamra), from the fifteenth to thirteenth centuries BC or Late Bronze Age. Important evidence such as the Amarna letters is excluded[15] as well as Egyptian texts.[16] Likewise non-epigraphical or archaeological data, which may supply valuable qualitative[17] data and may indicate commercial links,[18] is also left out.

MARI[19]

The discovery of Tell Ḥarīrī and its subsequent excavation by A. Parrot (1933 ff.) and J. Margueron (1979 ff.) have revealed a mass of evidence, foremost the cache of cuneiform texts.[20] When the Mari texts were first published, the scholarly world was amazed that regions as far apart as Cyprus (Alašiya), Crete (Kaptarûm) and Bahrein (Telmun) formed part of the geographical horizon of these texts. These also included regions as far south as Canaan (Palestine).

The location that appears in various Mari texts is the city of Hazor (Hebrew *ḥāṣôr*).[21] A. Malamat[22] published a series of studies in this regard and this will not be repeated here. Attention will be devoted primarily to commercial aspects in these textual references.

There will be no discussion of the archaeological material which was brought to light by the labour of the late Yadin[23] at Tell al-Qadaḥ.

The textual evidence reflects that Hazor functions mainly in two contexts: that of trade in tin and of messengers. Attention will be devoted to both of these themes.

Messenger texts

ARM VI 23:9–23 refers to various messengers *(mār šiprī)* in transit *(etiqtim)* in Mari on their way to Hazor. It is assumed that they were involved in commerce, as *mār šiprī* is also used for traders or agents of international trade and commerce in various other texts.[24] The *mār šiprī* were involved in much more than only the dispatch of messengers.[25] The messengers originated from Babylon, Ešnunna, Karanā and Arrapḫa and were on their way to Aleppo, Qatanum and Hazor. These last three locations are identical with the cities of the *Assyrian Dream Book*:[26] Mari, Imār, Aleppo, Qatanum and Hazor and represent a well-known route in the Ancient Near East, presumably also used for international trading missions. The fact that relations existed with regions as far apart as Babylon and Hazor may indicate that an international trading mission was involved, as there would be no sense in messengers travelling so far for the sake of politics alone. Line 23 is broken and may refer to some other Canaanite toponym — perhaps Layiš (Dan)? Malamat proposed Megiddo[27] and Alt even Egypt,[28] but no evidence exists for relations between Mari and Egypt in the Old Babylonian period, as is also the case with relations between Babylonia and Egypt.[29]

In addition *ARM* VI 78 refers to messengers *(mār šiprī)* from Babylon who were also in transit in Mari on their way to Babylon (lines 13–16), escorted[30] by a man from Hazor (!) where they resided for a long time *(pa-na* in line 14).[31] Does this refer to the fact that Babylonians were engaged in business in Hazor?[23]

15

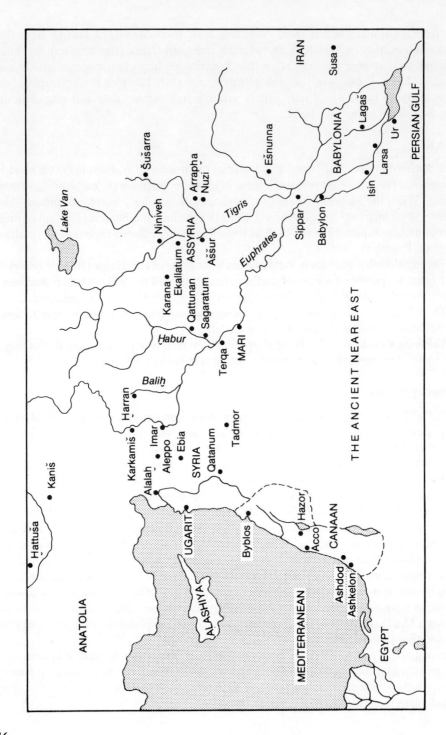

THE ANCIENT NEAR EAST

IRAN
Susa

BABYLONIA
PERSIAN GULF
Lagaš
Ur
Larsa
Isin
Ešnunna
Babylon
Sippar

Tigris
Euphrates

Šušarra
Arrapḥa
Nuzi
Nineveh
Ekallatum
ASSYRIA
Aššur
Lake Van

Karana
Qattunan
Sagaratum

Ḥabur
Terqa
MARI

Baliḥ

Harran

Karkamiš
Imar
Aleppo
Ebla
SYRIA
Qatanum
Alalaḥ
Tadmor

Kaniš

Ḥattuša

ANATOLIA

UGARIT
Byblos

ALASHIYA

MEDITERRANEAN

Hazor
Acco
CANAAN

Ashdod
Ashkelon

EGYPT

If this interpretation is correct, it means that commercial relations existed between Hazor and regions in Syria (Aleppo, Qatanum) and Mesopotamia (Ešnunna, Ekallātum, Karanā, Arrapḫa, Babylon and Qabra). The *commodities* that were traded are unknown, although the *carriers* were messengers *(mār šiprī)*. On account of the toponyms the *routes* can be constructed stretching from South Mesopotamia, along the Tigris and Euphrates rivers via Imār[33] to Syria and from there to Northern Canaan. *Transport* would have been by way of boat on the rivers[34] and on donkeys when leaving the river valleys at Imār and crossing over Syria into Canaan. As these messengers operated under the protection of the sovereigns, it seems reasonable to accept that they were not private entrepreneurs, but royal merchants,[35] operating in the sphere of international *diplomacy*. The way in which the trade functioned may have been by way of *gift trade*,[36] a matter well attested to in the Ancient Near East and closely related to diplomacy and royal messengers.[37]

The detail of *A.2760* (unedited) is unknown, but from references[38] to this text it seems that the matter is the same as in the preceeding two texts — messengers from Qatanum, Hazor and Amurru stayed in Mari. The messenger of the king of Qatanum (Išḫi-Addu) is to take care of them on their return journey via Qatanum. This text is even more important because it is sent by Šamši-Addu of Assyria (c. 1813–1781 BC) to his son Yasmaḫ-Addu, viceroy of Mari, and is thus far the oldest Mari text referring to messengers of Canaan.

To this can be added an administrative text, *ARM* XII 747. Messengers from various places (Babylon, Karkamiš, Imār, Ešnunna, Aleppo and Hazor) received cuts of meat while staying at the palace of Zimri-Lim. Although they are mentioned together with singers, a priest and artisans,[39] they might have been commercial agents as argued above with regard to other messengers. This also occurs in *ARM* XXIV 75:9 (text broken) — messengers from various locations including Hazor (?) received wine when meeting the king.

Tin texts

In one of the most recently discovered Mari texts (*ARM* XXIII 505:10) animals — and more important, tin — were delivered to Hazor. Canaanite destinations function in various texts from Mari dealing with the dispatch from this important transit centre and *entrepôt* of tin,[40] although the immediate origin of tin in the Ancient Near East still evades us.[41] In *ARM* VII 236:6[42] tin was exported to Hazor from Mari, carried in ingots *(le'um)*[43] It is interesting to note that a tin ingot was discovered at Haifa harbour.[44] Tin would have been carried by way of donkey trade (well known in the Old Assyrian Kaneš[45] texts) or by boat over water.[46]

In 1970 Dossin[47] published *A. 1270*,[48] a ledger which included the import of tin to Mari and its export to various destinations in the ṛeign of Zimri-Lim. The tin originated from an unknown location, was sent from Iran (Šeplarpak of Anšan) through Babylonia to various locations in Syria and even as far as the island of Crete in the Mediterranean. Line 22 refers to Hazor whose king Ibni-Addu[49] received a total of 4 200[50] sheqels of tin. Quite interesting is the fact that he is called LÚGAL (= *šarrum*) which is also used for

17

Ḥammurapi of Babylon (line 3), but not for Yarīm-Lim of Aleppo (line 12).[51] This provides important synchronisms and helps in dating the text, with the *terminus post quem c.* 1770 BC when Ḥammurapi of Aleppo took over from his father as sovereign of Aleppo.

Hazor (Tell al-Qedah) in Canaan can be identified with the *ḫa-ṣu-ra-a*(ki) of this text, but the identification of the other toponyms proves to be more difficult.

Line 21 mentions *la*-PI (= *yi/wi)-ši-im*(ki) which Dossin[52] and Malamat[53] identified with the Canaanite city Layis (= Hebrew *lēšēm*) or biblical Dan, situated at Tell al-Qā-ḍi/Tel Dan.[54] The name of its ruler is PI (= *wa/ya)-ri-ta-al-du,* a Hurrian name.[55] More recently Sasson[56] rejected this and located it in Syria between Ugarit and Aleppo. In line 19 *mu-zu-un-ni-im* (ki) is mentioned, which some locate in Syria,[57] but some in Canaan comparable to biblical *mādôn.*[58]

In order to identify these two locations the geographical horizon of this text has to be reviewed. At line 17 there is still mention of Syria (Aleppo), with line 22 mentioning Hazor in Canaan. Line 23 deals with the unidentifiable *ḫa-za-za-ar*(ki), perhaps near Hazor.[59] The text then returns to Amud-pī-El of Qatanum and to Ibni-Addu of Hazor before mentioning Caphtor in the Mediterranean. There seems to be no logic as far as geography is concerned and from the immediate context no conclusion can be made whether *Muzunnum* lay between Aleppo and Canaan or in Canaan itself, although a location on the Canaanite border is preferred. Only further textual and archaeological evidence will bring new light. For the matter of this discussion, however, it suffices to state that Canaan *is* the destination of tin exports via Mari.

Tin would have been transported in ingots (not mentioned here, but in *ARM,* VII 236:10), by boat or by donkey. As the route from Babylon went upstream, towers would have been needed in the form of human labour, well attested to in the Mari texts.[60] After embarkment at the Euphrates port of Imār it was carried by donkey[61] to Syria and Canaan, as was the case with the route from Iran to the river valleys of Mesopotamia.

The detail of the organisation of these commercial expeditions is unknown and the role played by the royal authorities is not stated explicitly. It seems nevertheless that they played a large role, especially as this text stems from the royal archives at Mari (but this can also distort the picture as *no texts* of private commercial enterprise have been found). Mention is made of kings (not individual commercial entrepreneurs) and their officials who organised and controlled the trade in tin between Mari and Canaan. Two merchants of Ugarit, Išḫi-Dagan and Yatar-Addu, played a paramount role in the trade as well as Sūmu-Eraḥ.

Silver, gold and precious stones from Hazor

In addition to these references, a new document mentioning Hazor *(SI15* 72–16)[62] should receive attention. This text dates from the reign of Zimri-Lim and is an epistle to his father-in-law, Yarīm-Lim of Aleppo.[63] He writes in connection with a "cupbearer"[64] who was accused of taking silver, gold and precious stones from Hazor without finalising the purchase (theft?) and made off to Mari. Because of this, the people of Hazor detained the donkeys and the *ṣābam ša ana tamkārūtim il-lu.* Zimri-Lim informs him that the truth of the matter is that he was seized, isolated and robbed in Imār of the goods which he was carrying as well as a *kunukkam* which he bought[65] (in Hazor?). He fled to Mari in order to save his life. The next legible lines indicate that Yarīm-Lim should give attention to the matter and see to it that the goods be returned.

No detailed discussion of all the philological and historical problems involved can be undertaken and attention will be limited to commercial aspects. The *commodities* involved — gold, silver and precious stones — were regular trading commodities, as is known from other texts from Mari. A short review of its function in Mari trade will be given. The archaeological material is excluded.   ·

Silver[66] was used in decoration, but also in payment, for tribute, as *terḫātum* (dowry), wages and salaries, as payment for various services, as toll and taxes, as fines, ransoms, redemption, as interest on loans and as gifts. Of all the metals, silver was used as a system of value *per se,* viz. as "money".[67] This was not only a standard of value, as A.L. Oppenheim[68] implied, but at Mari it served as a monetary metal.[69] Considerable amounts of silver were circulating in the kingdom of Mari, even in the hands of private individuals. According to Kupper[70] this was due to commerce that led to the influx of silver in the hands of merchants or traders. Silver was a means of financing foreign trade and was used to purchase foreign commodities such as other metals, timber and stones.

The origin of the silver in this text is unknown. Some Mari texts locate the origin of silver in the region west of the Baliḫ river[71] (near Mt. Bišri). The silver of Hazor might have originated from African sources (Algeria, Nigeria and possibly Zimbabwe), but this is pure conjecture. As no trade relations existed between Mari and Egypt in this period, it seems unlikely.

Gold[72] also had important uses in Mari, not only as decoration but also for commercial purposes. The use of gold as money[73] can be compared with customs in the Old Assyrian[74] and Amarna texts.[75] Gold was carried in ingots[76] *(lēʾum)* and sealed in sacks.[77]

The origin of gold in Mari is unknown. As far as Hazor is concerned the most logical source of origin would be Egypt,[78] where "the gold is like dust".[79] If the identification of Tema in the Sūmu-Yamam archives[80] is correct, it is possible that gold could have originated from gold mines in Arabia.[81] This is, however, conjectural, as is the case with Egypt. It is certain that the flow of gold was in the hands of the king of Mari, with the *bīt-maiālim* as the centre of the gold exchange.[82]

Precious stones were also important objects of international trade in Mari.[83] The famous *Treasure of Ur*[84] may have been manufactured in Mari itself as shown by the Moortgats[85] and not sent from Ur to Mari. Cylinder seals[86] were also objects of trade and such archaeological finds may reflect trade relations.[87] Seals also functioned in the sphere of "gift trade" between sovereigns. Zimri-Lim received a seal of lapis lazuli from his father-in-law Yarīm-Lim[88] and a silver seal was sent to his mother-in-law Gašera.[89] These seals had important functions in Ancient Near Eastern culture. In Mari they were used to seal containers, bags, wine jars, doors, storehouses, and documents for safekeeping.[90]

This last function, which was studied most recently by Leemans,[91] has led Malamat[92] to interpret the *kunukkam* in the text under discussion as a "sealed document" or some kind of "bill of sale". Both interpretations are possible in the light of the Near Eastern trade — seals were objects of trade and *kunukkum* may also refer to a document. However, the context of the letter under discussion seems to imply the last option. The "seal" is mentioned *separately* from the other objects of trade which he was carrying and his loss of this object led to his troubles. Because he lost this "bill of sale", he experienced trouble in Imār. Traders had to carry some kind of "passport"[93] when travelling through foreign regions or remaining in transit.

In spite of these difficulties, the text provides important evidence concerning commercial relations between Canaan and the outside world. Attention has been devoted to the objects of trade. These were carried by donkey caravans as reflected by the detainment of them in Hazor.[94] The use of donkeys *(imēre)* as animals of burden is well known from the Ancient Near East,[95] especially the Kaneš[96] trade and other Mari[97] texts. They could travel about 30 km a day[98] and carry about 90 kg of cargo,[99] covering distances of as much as 1 000 km.[100]

As far as the trade routes are concerned, the following definite toponyms can be established: Mari–Imār–Aleppo–Hazor. Comparative material, especially the Mari tin itineraries[101] and the Assyrian *Dream Book*[102] agree with this route.

Concerning these toponyms, the following short remarks can be made:

● *Imār:*[103] In the time of Yaḫdun-Lim (Zimri-Lim's predecessor who reigned in the period before the control of Mari by Assyria, *c.* 1830–1822 BC?), Mari controlled Imār,[104] but after his defeat by Assyria (Šamši-Addu) it became part of the realm of Aleppo. Imār played an important role in the foreign trade relations of Mari and was the port of embarkment of goods destined for Canaan. They were taken by boat to Imār and from there by donkey caravan through Syria to Canaan when the trade routes left the river valleys of Mesopotamia.

● *Aleppo:*[105] Relations existed between Aleppo and Mari both politically and commercially. Mari was bound to Aleppo through the diplomatic marriage of Zimri-Lim and Šiptu and through various commercial links. Aleppo was an important toponym in the tin itineraries.[106]

● *Hazor:* This Canaanite city has been dealt with above.

As far as the organisation of the commercial expeditions is concerned, the following carriers were involved: the "cup-bearer" or "butler"[107] who is the chief participator and the *ṣābam ṣa ana tamkārūtim illū*,[108] some officials involved in *tamkārūtim*,[109] "trading".

Most interesting in this letter is the fact that commerce functioned in the sphere of international diplomacy and politics of the Mari period.[110] According to international law, foreign merchants had to be protected,[111] a matter well known from Ugarit and Amarna. Zimri-Lim urged Yarīm-Lim to interfere on behalf of his merchants by appealing to their diplomatic relations.

The traders and their transport and merchandise were detained *(kalûm*[112]*)* in Hazor, a matter well known from Mari[113] and other Ancient Near Eastern texts. Merchants and caravans were under constant danger of attack by marauders and robbers.

In the light of this, the merchants involved could have been royal officials or could have stood under the protection of the royal authorities.

Conclusion

Commercial relations between Canaan and the outside world are reflected by:
(i)   Mari texts dealing with messengers (*mār šiprī*) of Hazor who might have been involved in foreign trade.
(ii) The export of tin via Mari to Hazor and possibly Dan.
(iii) The carrying of various commodities between Hazor and Mari via Imār.

It is assumed that this trade functioned in the sphere of international diplomacy and stood under the direct or indirect control of the royal authorities.

UGARIT

While much information has been available from the discoveries made at Mari, the second source, namely the data from Ugarit,[114] does not provide so much detail.

There are various references to Canaanite (i.e. Palestinian) toponyms in the Ugaritic texts. Ugarit is not regarded as part of Canaan and evidence from Ugarit is therefore included as denoting foreign commercial relations. This assumption is based on the interpretation of *RS*[115] 20.182[116] which refers to a dispute between "people of Ugarit" and "people of Canaan" ((mat) *ki-na-ḫi*) and thus differentiates between the region of Canaan and Ugarit.[117]

Merchants from Canaan *(knʿy)* are mentioned together with people from Egypt and Ashdod.[118]

The important harbour of Acco *(ʿky/Akku)*[119] which formed the gateway to Canaan and later the Holy Land from 2350 BC (general Uni) until AD 1918 (general Allenby) is mentioned in *RS* 18.31:25.[120] This text from *c.* 1300 BC is a letter from Tyre to the king of Ugarit, informing him that a ship[121] from Ugarit on its way to Egypt nearly sank[122] (literally, "died") in a storm off Tyre, but that the crew and boat were saved. He also assured him that a second ship was unloaded and stationed (literally, "naked") in Acco. This text reflects the fact that important maritime relations existed between the most important harbour of the East Mediterranean and Syria, Ugarit[123] (with its major part at Minet el-Beida = Leukos-Limên = Maḥadu)[124] and the most important harbour of Canaan (Palestine), Acco.

Acco is also mentioned in lists of foreigners in Ugarit.[125] There is mention of a man from Acco, together with people from towns in the kingdom of Ugarit and places such as Tyre and Arwad. It may be conjectured that they operated as foreign traders or commercial agents in cosmopolitan Ugarit.

Other Canaanite harbours that are mentioned are Ashdod and Ashkelon:
With regard to Ashdod *(Adddy/Ašdādu)*[126] there are texts referring to Ashdodites: (i) in lists of guilds,[127] (ii) foreign personnel,[128] and (iii) other professionals,[129] (iv) mentioned together with other merchants, attached to the royal economy *(gt)*[130] and (v) receiving quantities of oil.[131]

Astour identified these people from Ashdod as *merchants* who operated in the vicinity of the harbour of Maḥadu.[132] This seems probable as some of the texts referring to Ashdod reflect a definite commercial context. There is, however, no detailed evidence as

21

far as their social position and exact enterprises are concerned. It is conjectured that they stood under the control of the royal authorities.

In addition there are texts mentioning Ashdodite textiles *(ṣubātū Ašdādu/lbšm adddym)*.[133] This may refer to a type[134] (i.e. fashion) but also shows that textiles from Ashdod (i.e. origin) were exported to Ugarit, adding to the evidence of foreign commercial relations of Canaan and the outside world in the second millennium BC.

A most interesting use of Ashdod is as a weight measure *(kkr)* in one of the Claremont Ras Shamra texts.[135]

Some scholars (such as the prominent scholar C. Virolleaud)[136] rejected the identification of *Ạdd* with the well-known city of the Philistine pentapolis, but there no longer seems to be reason to doubt this. In one text[137] Ashdod is mentioned with Tyre, Arwad and Acco, which indicates that a toponym in Southern Syria (viz. Canaan) is concerned.

Ashkelon *(Ašqulunu)*[138] is mentioned in Akkadian lists of foreigners residing in Ugarit, together with people from places such as Acco and Arwad.[139]

Other Canaanite toponyms (perhaps Gezer,[140] Edom,[141] Jerusalem[142] and Yabne-Yam[143]) are excluded as the context and contents of these texts are unclear and they have very little relevance for the history of commerce.

The texts from Late Bronze Age Ugarit thus reflect that direct and indirect commercial relations existed between Canaan and Syria. These links were bound to the sea, between the harbour of Ugarit and important Canaanite harbours such as Acco, Ashdod and Ashkelon. Trade was thus mostly maritime. The method of transport[144] of trading merchandise would have been by ship or boat. Commodities may have included textiles and garments from Ashdod or in any case a type of garment of a style used in Ashdod. Foreigners from Canaan stayed in Ugarit, where they engaged in commercial enterprises and even did service in the *gt* (royal economy). The existence of Canaanite foreigners in Ugarit may have been due to political relations that existed, but they may even have been traders, merchants or commercial agents, primarily involved in trade with foreign countries such as Ugarit. With regard to their social position and organisation, very little is known.[145]

THE IMPORTANCE OF COMMERCE

The influence of the foreign merchant on Ancient Near Eastern civilisation and history has been amply illustrated by studies of the merchant and foreign trade. Merchants functioned not only as foreign merchants or commercial agents, but also as the carriers of culture and the communicators of customs. In an essay entitled "Colonies and Enclaves", Cyrus Gordon[146] argued about their influence, but emphasised that they also spread the tradition of written literature and language and writing. It may be that Babylonian Akkadian became the international *lingua franca* of the Amarna Age owing to the influence of trading enclaves and colonies. During this period Mesopotamian military power was not significant and the only reasonable solution to the spreading of Mesopotamian culture, manifested in its writing system, would have been by way of foreign trade and foreign merchants. An earlier example comes from the Old Assyrian period with the famous Assyrian trading colonies of Kaneš-Kültepe in Anatolia.[147] This also contributed to the spreading of Mesopotamian cuneiform into Anatolia,[148] to be used later in writing the non-Semitic language Hittite, although Assyria did not hold political control over Anatolia.[149]

The same may have been true for Canaan. Foreign writing systems were communicated by merchants doing business in Canaan, but vice versa by Canaanite merchants doing business abroad (e.g. the people from Ashdod in Ugarit) who brought it back to their homeland.

The list of cuneiform texts found in Canaan[150] has grown in recent years. This includes classical Akkadian cuneiform but since the identification of West-Semitic Ugaritic,[151] texts of this type have also been identified. A detailed catalogue of all these texts will not be given here and only a few examples will suffice:

- A copy of a fragment of the Epic of Gilgamesh was found at Megiddo.[152]
- Liver models from Hazor.[153]
- A Sumerian-Akkadian syllabary from Hazor.[154]
- A real-estate deed from Hazor.[155]
- Texts from Schechem.[156]
- Ta'anach tablets — letters and lists.[157]
- Tablets from Aphek, including a letter from Ugarit.[158]
- Cylinder seals with cuneiform inscriptions (Hazor, Jericho).[159]
- Fragment of envelope from Gezer.[160]
- A business note from Jericho (fourteenth century).[161]
- Personal name on a jar from Hazor.[162]

As far as texts in alphabetic Ugaritic are concerned, the following are noted:

- Knife from Nachal Tabor.[163]
- Tablet from Ta'anach.[164]
- Tablet from Beth-Shemesh.[165]

These examples illustrate the spreading of cuneiform writing in Canaan. It is interesting that most of these examples date from Old Babylonian or Middle Bronze and Late Bronze or Canaanite periods, from which the epigraphic evidence from Mari and Ugarit, discussed above, also stems. The proposed conclusion is that Canaan formed not only a landbridge in the Ancient Near East, connecting Egypt, Syria, Anatolia and Mesopotamia, but also a transit area for foreign merchandise and merchants who brought with them foreign customs such as writing systems. It is also possible that it could have worked the other way round, with Canaanite traders bringing customs from abroad to their homeland. To this may be added the transmitting of ideas[166] and concepts which may be reflected by the influence of foreign ideas in religion and ideology.[167]

The influence of trade on the history of this part of the world may have been even greater. In her dissertation Patty Gerstenblith[168] illustrated that trade and communication alone caused the development of Middle Bronze Age culture in the Levant.

Long before this, even before the advent of writing, Canaanite cities played an important role in commerce and trade, most amply illustrated by the example of Jericho, the first urban centre in world history whose origin may lie in trade and commerce.[169]

Conclusion

Commercial relations existed between Canaan or the Holy Land and the outside world in the second millennium BC. This had a profound influence on Canaanite civilisation and culture in the period before the people of Israel took control of the region which later became the "Holy Land" in Jewish, Christian and Muslim traditions.

NOTES

1 Paper read at the *International Conference, The Holy Land and the World Outside it,* University of the Witwatersrand, Johannesburg, 2 December 1986. The financial assistance of the University of Stellenbosch in attending this conference is acknowledged. However, opinions expressed and conclusions arrived at are those of the author and are not to be regarded as those of the University. Abbreviations are used as in "Keilschriftbibliographie", *Orientalia* 53 1984, 1*ff.

2 J. Coon, *Caravan. The Story of the Middle East,* 1961, 1.

3 Or roughly between Gaza and Byblos. For the borders of Canaan see A. Millard, "The Canaanites", D.J. Wiseman, *Peoples of Old Testament Times,* 1975, 29 ff; Y. Aharoni-M. Avi-Yonah, *The Macmillan Bible Atlas,* 1970, 50. Cf. Num. 34:1 ff. and *p.Anastasi* I (J.B. Pritchard, *Ancient Near Eastern Texts Relating to the Old Testament,* 1969 [abbreviated as *ANET*], 478).

4 See on this term M. Weippert, *Reallexikon der Assyriologie* V, 1980, 352 ff. and literature cited there; R. De Vaux, *The Early History of Israel* I, 1978, 125 ff.; O. Keel-M. Küchler, *Orte und Landschaften der Bibel* I, 1984, 240 ff.; Aharoni, *The Land of the Bible. A Historical Geography,* 1979, 67 ff.; W. Helck, *Die Beziehungen Ägyptens zu Vorderasien im 3. und 2. Jahrtausend v.Chr.,* 1962, 279 ff.; B. Mazar (Maisler), *Untersuchungen zur alten Geschichte und Ethnographie Syriens und Palästinas,* 1930, 54 ff. For cuneiform references see B. Groneberg, *Répertoire geographique des textes cuneiformes* 3, 1980, 139 and K. Nashef, *Répertoire* 5, 1982, 167.

5 "Une mention de Cananéens dans une lettre de Mari", *Syria* 50 (1973) 277–82: *A3552:* 6: (awēl) *ki-na-aḫ-nú(m)* (meš). Cf. A.F. Rainey, *Tel Aviv* 6 (1979) 161. But cf. also on *A.2760* below.

6 S. Smith, *The Statue of Idrimi,* 1949, 72–3: 18–23 and lately M. Dietrich and O. Loretz in *UF* 13 (1981) 201–69. See lines 18–19: *ki-in-nim* (ki) and remarks of Dietrich-Loretz, *op. cit.,* 251 and H. Klengel, *UF* 13 (1981) 274 and *Geschichte Syriens* I, 1965, 227 ff.

7 D.J. Wiseman, *The Alalakh Tablets,* 1953, nos. 48:5; 181:9; 154:2 *(ki-en/in-an-ni)* and *JCS* 8 (1954) 11.

8 Abbreviated as *EA*. For references see J.F. Knudtzon-Weber, *Die El-Amarna Tafeln* II, 1915, 1577 *(kinaḫḫu)* and A.F. Rainey, *El Amarna Tablets 359–379,* 1970, 32 (*EA* 367:8).

9 C. Gordon, *Ugaritic Textbook,* 1965, 421, no. 1272.

10 *The Archives of Ebla. An Empire Inscribed in Clay,* 1981, p. 272: (d)BÉ KÀ.NA.NA.

11 L. Koehler-W. Baumgartner, *Hebräisches und aramäisches Lexikon zum Alten Testament,* 1974³, 462 and Keel, *op. cit.,* 244 ff.

12 Keel, *op. cit.,* 240; Weippert, *op. cit.,* 355 and M. Elat in E. Lipinski (ed.), *State and Temple Economy in the Ancient Near East* II, 1979, 529–30.

13 W.F. Leemans, *Foreign Trade in the Old Babylonian Period,* 1960, 2.

14 See in this regard Leemans, *Reallexikon* IV, 76 who discerns the following: "Waren", "Vollzieher/ Händler", "Organization", "Handelswege" and "Recht".

15 See in this regard my paper read at the *Tell Amarna Centennial*, held in February 1987 at the Oriental Institute, Chicago (to be published): "Aspects of Foreign Trade in the Amarna Letters".

16 See e.g. W. Helck, *Die Beziehungen Ägyptens zu Vorderasien im 3. und 2. Jahrtausend v. Chr.*, 1962.

17 On this term see A.L. Oppenheim, "Trade in the Ancient Near East", *Fifth International Congress of Economic History*, 1970, 3. But note his (*op. cit.* 2–5) and Klengel's (*Handel und Händler im Alten Orient*, 1979, 8) warnings when this is used without taking into account the textual materials (quantitative date).

18 See G.A. Wright, *Archaeology and Trade*, 1974; P. Kohl, "The Archaeology of Trade", *Dialectical Anthropology* 1 (1975) 43–50, E. Porada, R.W. Ehrich (ed.), *Chronologies in Old World Archaeology*, 1965, 133–200 and G.A. Wright, *Obsidian Analyses and Prehistoric Near Eastern Trade: 7500–3500 BC.*, 1969.

19 This discussion forms part of my D. Litt dissertation: *Aspects of the Economy of Mari in the Middle Bronze Age. Foreign Trade in the Old Babylonian Period (c. 1830–1758 B.C.E.)*, Stellenbosch, 1985 (unpublished — summarised in "Mari, middelman in die Internasionale Handel van die Ou Nabye Ooste in die Ou-Babiloniese tyd (c. 1830–1758 v.C.)", which appeared in *Tydskrif vir Geesteswetenskappe* 27/1 (1987), 50–57). Financial assistance rendered by the Human Sciences Research Council of South Africa towards the cost of this research is hereby acknowledged. However, opinions expressed or conclusions arrived at are those of the author and are not to be regarded as those of the HSRC.

20 An estimated 20 000 have been found and up to date nearly 5000 have been published in the definite series *Archives royales de Mari* [abbreviated as *ARM*] and in various other publications, for a list see J.G. Heintz, *Archives Royales de Mari* XVII/1, 21*–39* and M. Birot, *ARMT* XVI/1, IX. Add to this *ARM* and *ARMT* XXI–XXIV. In this study *ARM* I–XXIV were utilised.

21 *Répertoire* 3, 93–4; D.O. Edzard and B. Hrouda, *Reallexikon* IV, 135; Helck, *Lexikon der Ägyptologie* II, 1074.

22 "Hazor the Head of all these Kingdoms", *JBL* 79 (1960), 12–17 (14–15); "Syro-Palestinian Destinations in a Mari Tin Inventory", *IEJ* 21 (1971), 36–37; "Northern Canaan and the Mari Texts", J.A. Sanders (ed.), *Near Eastern Archaeology in the Twentieth Century*, 1970, 164 ff.; "Silver, Gold and Precious Stones from Hazor. Trade and Trouble in a New Mari Document", *JSS* 33 (1982), 71 ff. and "Silver, Gold and Precious Stones from Hazor in a New Mari Document", *BibAr* 46 (1983), 169 ff. See also F.M. Tocci, "Hazor nell 'eta del medio e tardo bronzo", *RSO* 37 (1962), 59–64 and K. Galling, *Textbuch zur Geschichte Israels*, 1979, 12.

23 *Hazor I–IV*, 1958–1961, see also his *Hazor*, 1972 and *Hazor. The Rediscovery of a Great Citadel of the Bible*, 1975 and "Hazor", M. Avi-Yonah (ed.), *Encyclopaedia of Archaeological Excavations in the Holy Land* II, 1976, 747 ff. See also Mazar, "The Middle Bronze Age in Palestine", *IEJ* 18 (1968), 65–97 and K. Kenyon in I.E.S. Edwards *et. al., Cambridge Ancient History*³ II/I [abbreviated as *CAH*], 1978, 99 ff. On the literary tradition of Hazor which may indicate further (commercial) relations see below.

24 Cf. I. Cornelius, *Aspects*, 208 ff. – they escorted a trade caravan carrying commercial commodities such as timber (*ARM* II 123) and operated with other people involved in trade (*ARM* III 56; *ARM* VI 20:6; 23:13; 79:6; A3412 (= G. Dossin, *La voix de l'opposition en Mésopotamie*, 1973, 187–88)). Compare *Chicago Assyrian Dictionary* [abbreviated as *CAD*] M/1, 260–65; Edzard, *Reallexikon* V, 415; L. Holmes, *JAOS* 95 (1975), 376–81; Leemans, *Foreign Trade*, 142; *Reallexikon* IV, 80, 83; C. Zaccagnini, *Lo scambio dei doni*, 1973, 51–58,

25

89–93; *Iraq* 39 (1977), 171; A.D. Crown, *VT* 24 (1974), 366 ff.; *JESHO* 17 (1974), 244 ff.; E. Munn-Rankin, *Iraq* 18 (1956), 99–100; Edzard, *JESHO* 3 (1960), 48–49 and M.P. Maidman in M.A. Morrison and D. Owen, *Studies on the Civilization and Culture of Nuzi and the Hurrians in Honor of E.R. Lachemann*, 1981, 238–39 (n20) and *BO* 37 (1980), 187. In a letter from Amarna (*EA* 39) the term *mār šiprī* is equated with *tamkāru*, cf. line 14 where *mār šiprī are called amēlū annû tamkāria* = "these people are my *tamkāru*" (cf. for the translation of *tamkāru(m)* Diakonoff, *BO* 32 (1975), 225). For detailed discussion of this text see my "Aspects of Foreign Trade in the Amarna Letters".

25 J. Bottéro, *ARMT* VII, par. 112 called them "chárges des affaires".

26 A.L. Oppenheim, *The Interpretation of Dreams in the Ancient Near East*, 1956, 313. Cf. W.W. Hallo, *JCS* 18 (1964), 86, n 18.

27 *BibAr* 34 (1971), 12.

28 *ZDPV* 70 (1954), 130–34.

29 Leemans, *JESHO* 3 (1960), 21–22, 36. The archaeological evidence is excluded — cf. in this regard H. Yorkoff on the moulds found at Mari (*JANES* 4 (1972), 20–32, 81–84) and the famous *Tôd treasure* which according to E. Porada (M.A. Dandamajev *et al.* (ed.), *Societies and Languages of the Ancient Near East*, 1982, 289–90) may have originated from Mari. Contacts between Egypt and Byblos (Gubla), Ugarit and Alalah did occur in this period (Cornelius, *Aspects*, 275–76 with references).

30 *alik idišunu* (= "who goes by their side") refers to an escort; cf. *CAD* A/I, 343 and S. Dalley, *Mari and Karana*, 1984, 171 ff.

31 Cf. J.-R. Kupper, *ARMT* VI, 111 = "depuis longtemps"; Malamat, *JBL* 79 (1960), 14 = "long since"; W.F. Von Soden, *Akkadisches Handwörterbuch*, 1965–1981, 817b: *ištu-pāna* = "seit jeher". Cf. also *ARM* X 84:6.

32 Leemans, *Foreign Trade*, 141 admitted that *mār šiprī* were employed in trade (see 142, but saw no indication that this text refers to messengers doing trade.

33 Cf. the reference to this city in *SII5* 72–16, discussed below.

34 For detailed discussion see Cornelius, *Aspects*, 259–269. By boat over water: *ARM* I 7; I 98; XVIII 24; XIII 96; XIV 27; XIII 82; 96; 90, XIV 26–29; VII 233–25; IV 82:25ff.; XIII 34; 61–63; 70–75; XIV 33; IV 81.

35 On the social position of the merchant at Mari and the carriers of trade in Mari see Cornelius, *Aspects*, 203 ff.

36 See R. North, "Tin, Gift Mercantilism", *Or* 44 (1975), 290–91; M. Liverani, *Or* 42 (1973), 192; Liverani, "Irrational Elements in the Amarna Trade", *Three Amarna Essays*, 1979, 21–33; Edzard, *JESHO* 3 (1960), 47–49; Zaccagnini, *La scambio dei doni*, 1973 and Oppenheim, "Trade", 14. Liverani, *Three Amarna Essays* discussed the "irrational" element of Amarna trade – e.g. in *EA* 40 ivory is sent from Cyprus to Egypt in exchange for ivory from Egypt. Economically spoken this was "irrational". Gifts were sent for reasons of prestige and status and not for commercial reasons (Egypt was a source of ivory and Cyprus not), but in the field of diplomacy this was quite acceptable. The custom of the exchange of gifts is well known in anthropology and under primitive peoples and in early societies, see M.J. Herskovits, *The Economic Life of Primitive Peoples*, 1940, 133 ff. and M. Sahlins, *Stone Age Economics*, 1974, 147 ff., 219 ff. For the exchange of gifts at Mari between kings see *ARM* V 20 (Cornelius, *Aspects*, 70–74).

37 L. Holmes, *JAOS* 95 (1975), 376 ff.

38 J.-R. Kupper, *Les nomades en Mésopotamie au temps des rois de Mari*, 1957, 179 nl; Dossin, *RSO* 32 (1975), 37 f.; A. Pohl, *Or* 19 (1950), 509 and Malamat, "Northern Canaan", 21.

39 J. Sasson, *BASOR* 190 (1968), 53 made the whole group artisans, rejected by Malamat, "Canaan", 165n10.

40 J.D. Muhly, *Copper and Tin,* 1973, 293. On tin in Mari see *ARMT* VII, par. 86.10, 115; XXI, 195; *CAD* A/2, 128; Cornelius, *Aspects,* 153–192.

41 Cornelius, 150–152, with literature: especially Muhly, *Copper and Tin,* 1973, 248–61; *Supplement,* 1976, 97 ff; "New Evidence for Sources of and Trade in Bronze Age Tin", *The Search for Ancient Tin",* 1978, 43–48.

42 Following the new collation of D. Charpin-J.M. Durand, *MARI* 2 (1983), 94.

43 K.R. Veenhof, *Aspects of Old Assyrian Trade and its Terminology,* 1972, 34–35; T.S. Wheeler, *Expedition* 17/4 (1975), 31–39.

44 Muhly, *The Search for Ancient Tin,* 1978, 45–46, fig. 2; R. Maddin *et al., Expedition* 19/2 (1977), 35–47; P. Artzy, *BASOR* 250 (1983), 51–55. Copper was also carried in such ingots, see Muhly, *Iraq* 39 (1977), 81; Wheeler, *et al., Expedition* 17/4 (1975), 31–39; Maddin-Muhly, *Journal of Metals* 26 (1974), 24–30, especially figs. 1–2 for depictions of such ingots. A hoard of such ingots was found off the coast of Turkey (G.F. Bass, *Cape Gelidonya: A Bronze Age Shipwreck,* 1967).

45 Veenhof, *op.cit.,* 3, 13 ff.

46 Leemans, *Foreign Trade,* 105–6.

47 "La route de l'étain en Mesopotamie au temps de Zimri-Lim," *RA* 64 (1970), 97 ff. See the studies of Sasson, *RA* 65 (1971), 172; M. Astour, *RA* 67 (1973), 73–75; Muhly, *Copper,* 293 ff. and especially Malamat, "Syro-Palestinian Destinations in a Mari Tin Inventory", *IEJ* 21 (1971), 31–38 and discussion in Cornelius, *Aspects,* 166–174.

48 Cf. now P. Villard, *ARMT* XXIII, 528–29 (= *ARM* XXIII 556).

49 *Ib-ni-*(d)IM(=*Addu*). W.F. Albright, *The Biblical Period,* 1963, 102n83 compared this name with Jabin of Hazor in the Bible (Judges 4–5). See Malamat, "Canaan", 168.

50 Line 22:30 MA.NA = 1800 sheqels = 14,4 kg.
    Line 26:20 MA.NA = 1200 sheqels = 9,6 kg.
    Line 32:20 MA.NA = 1200 sheqels = 9,6 kg.

Total: 70 MA.NA = 4200 sheqels = 33,6 kg.

51 In the Amarna letters the king of Hazor is also called *šarrum* (*EA* 227:3, cf. 148:41).

52 *op.cit.,* 102.

53 *op.cit.,* 35, which he called "the plum for the Palestinologist in this document".

54 Malamat, *op.cit.,* 35 with references. See *Répertoire* 3, 149. For the archaeological material see A. Biran, *Encyclopaedia of Archaeological Excavations* I, 1975, 313 ff.

55 Malamat, 35.

56 *BibAr* 47 (1984), 249.

57 Astour, *op.cit.,* 73–74; *ARMT* XVI/1, 24 = Syro-Palestine and *Répertoire* 3, 171 = unknown destination on Syro-Palestinian border.

58 Dossin, 102; Malamat, 34–35 and Sasson, *RA* 65 (1971), 172. Qarn Ḥattin in Galilee, the site of a famous battle from the Crusades (G.A. Smith, *The Historical Geography of the Holy Land,* 1935, 441).

59 Dossin, 102, rejected by Malamat, 37. He also rejected a Syrian location at *Ḫa-šá-a-šar(ša/šar ≠za/zar/ṣa/ṣar).* According to Astour between Tunip and Alalaḫ (74), see *ARMT* XVI/1, 15.

60 *ARMT* XIII 29; XVIII 24:14.

61 Compare *A.16*:9 (Dossin, *RA* 64 (1970), 103 ff.).

62 M. Birot, *Syria* 50 (1973), 10 f.; Malamat, *JJS* 33 (1982), 71–79 and *BibAr* 46 (1983), 169–74.

63 He calls him his *mārum* which reflects their dependence and affinity (Malamat, *BibAr* 46 (1983), 171, see A. Marzal, *The Organisation of the Mari State* (Ph.D), 1969, 25; F.C. Fensham, "Father and Son as Terminology for Treaty and Covenant", *Near Eastern Studies in Honor of William Foxwell Albright,* 1971, 121–35 and Munn-Rankin, *Iraq* 18 (1956), 76 ff. On their relations see Cornelius, *Aspects,* 43n71–73.

64 Following Malamat's reading (*JJS* 33 (1982), 73–74).

65 Line 23: *a-na kaspim awīlim šu-u i-ša-mu.*

66 Cf. especially Kupper, "L'usage de l'argent à Mari", G. van Driel, *Zikir Šumim,* 1982, 163–172. Silver also functions in a legal document from this period found at Hazor (W. Hallo-H. Tadmor, *IEJ* 27 (1977), 1 ff.); in an Akkadian letter from Taanach (Albright, *ANET,* 490 and *BASOR* 94 (1944), 12–27) from the 15th century and in an Akkadian letter from Ugarit found at Aphek (Cf. below and note 158 for literature), line 34.

67 P. Einzig, *Primitive Money,* 1966, 203 ff. and M. Müller, "Gold, Silber und Blei als Wertmesser in Mesopotamien", M. Dandamajev, *Societies and Languages of the Ancient Near East,* 1982, 270 ff.

68 *Ancient Mesopotamia,* 1977, 87: "During the Old Babylonian period, payments for real estate, slaves, goods and services seem to have been only rarely made in silver, although prices as a rule are quoted according to that standard . . . the silver did not change hands". Cf. also R.F.G. Sweet, *On Prices, Money and Money uses in the Old Babylonian Period* (Ph.D), 1958, 121 and N. Yoffee, *The Economic Role of the Crown in the old Babylonian Period,* 1977 and D. Pardee, *AfO* 28 (1981–82), 271 on *ksp* in Ugaritic.

69 *ARMT* VII, 330–33; *ARMT* IX, 311–317 and Kupper, *op.cit.,* 164.

70 *op.cit.,* 171.

71 ARM 173: 19–20.

72 Cornelius, 117 ff., *ARMT* VII, 297–98; IX, 113f.; XXI, 194–96 and Leemans, *Reallexikon* III, 509.

73 Cf. J. Bottéro, *ARMT* VII, 297: ". . . servir directement de monnaie"; J.-M. Durand, *ARMT* XXI, 196: ". .c'est l'emploi de l'or comme 'monnaie'" and Leemans, *Foreign Trade,* 121. For tribute: *ARM* II 28; *terhātum*/dowry: *ARM* I 77; taxes: *ARM* VII 217:7 ff.; metals: silver-*ARM XVIII 67,* tin- *ARM* XXI 218; slaves: *ARM* XXI 219; as well as in *ARM* II 28 (on this see Cornelius in *JNWSL* 12 (1984), 54n23).

74 Veenhof, *Aspects,* 350, perhaps also at Ebla, G. Pettinato, *Ebla,* 166.

75 Edzard, *JESHO* 3 (1960), 38ff.; Helck, *Beziehungen,* 400–402, cf. J.A. Knudtzon *et al., Die El-Amarna Tafeln* II, 1417–18 *(hurāṣu).*

76 *ARM* IX 266:1; cf. *ARM* IX 314 and *CAD* L, 159:d.

77 *ARM* VIII 86:1 ff. *(kanākum),* cf. Veenhof, 41.

78 R. Guglielmi, *Lexikon der Ägyptologie* II, cols. 745–47 and W. Hayes in *CAH* II/1, 346–53.

79 *EA* 19:61 and 20:52.

80 G. Dossin, *RA* 64 (1970), 17 ff. On Tema see Dossin, *op.cit.,* 39–40, S. Parpola, *Neo-Assyrian Toponyms,* 1970, 350, *ARMT* XVI/1, 34 and *Répertoire* 3, 235.

81 H. Limet, *Le travail du métal au pays de Sumer au temps de la IIIe dynastie d'Ur,* 1960, 99; H. Neumann, *Altorientalische Forschungen* 6 (1979), 63 and D.S. Attema, *Arabië en de Bijbel,* 1966, 44. Compare *Is* 60:6; *Ps* 72:15.

82 *ARM,* VII 4, IX 84, cf. *ARMT* VII, par. 19; IX, par. 105 and *CAD* M/1, 120.

83 Cf. Cornelius, *Aspects,* 54 ff. for detail.

84 A. Parrot, *Le trésor d'Ur,* 1968; *Syria* 42 (1965), 216 ff., pl. XV.

85 *Iraq* 36 (1974), 155 ff.

86 See interaliar R.D. Biggs-Mc.G. Gibson, *Seals and Sealing in the Ancient Near East*, 1977; H. Kühne, *Das Rollsiegel* in Syrien, 1980; B. Brentjes, *Alte Siegelkunst des Vorderen Asiens*, 1983 and *CAD* K, 543 ff.

87 According to L. Werr, *JCS* 30 (1978), 62–64 a seal found at Tell Harmal originated from Mari, resold by way of trade.

88 Dossin *RA* 36 (1939), 47.

89 Kupper, "argent", 166.

90 *ARM* X 82 and A. Malamat, "Doorbells at Mari" in K.R. Veenhof, *Cuneiform Archives and Libraries*, 1986.

91 "La fonction des sceaux apposés à contrats vieux-babyloniens", *Zikir Šumim*, 1982, 219–44.

92 *BibAr* 46 (1983), 170.

93 *Cuneiform Texts in the British Museum* II 20:8 (= R. Frankena, *Briefe aus dem British Museum-Altbabylonische Briefe* II, 1966, no. 84): *tuppi šarrim* = "tablet of the king". Cf. Leemans, *Foreign Trade*, 105 and H. Klengel, *Handel*, 83 f. *ARM* XIV 52:14 refers to a *tuppi bēlija* = "tablet of my lord" and in the *Wen Amun* tale (= *ANET*, 27; H. Goedicke, *The Report of Wenamun*, 1975, 62 ff., 152), the official who went to Byblos to purchase timber is refused because he was without the necessary documents.

94 Line 10.

95 Cornelius, 257n188 and n192 and M.A. Littauer-J.H. Crouwell, *Wheeled Vehicles and Ridden Animals in the Ancient Near East*, 1979 and J. Wiesner, *Fahren und Reiten in Alteuropa und Alten Orient*, 1971 and now also R.H. Meadow-H.P. Uerpmann, *Equids in the Ancient World*, 1986.

96 Veenhof, *Aspects*, part one; M.T. Larsen, *Old Assyrians Caravan Procedures*, 1967 and P. Garelli, *Les assyriens en Cappadoce*, 1963, 299ff.

97 *ARMT* VII, par 63; IX, par. 89ff. and Cornelius, 265 ff.

98 C. Kühne, *Die Chronologie der internationale Korrespondenz von El-Amarna*, 1973, 62, 119, 105–24 and Edzard, *Reallexikon* V, 416.

99 H. Lewy, "The Assload, the Sack and other Measures of Capacity", *RSO* 39 (1964), 186.

100 The distance between Kaneš and Aššur (Garelli, *op.cit.*, 81).

101 Dossin, *RA* 64 (1970), 97 ff.

102 Oppenheim, *The Interpretation of Dreams*, 1956.

103 Tell Meskene, cf. J. Margueron, *Syria* 52 (1975), 53–85; A. Finet, "La port d'Emar sur l'Euphrate, entre le royaume de Mari et le pays de Canaan", in E. Lipiński, *The Land of Israel: Cross Roads of Civilizations*, 1985, 27–38 and M. Heltzer, *Reallexikon* V, 65–66. On relations with Mari see Tocci, *La Syria*, 1960, 43, 56, 57; Klengel, *Geschichte Syriens* I, 1969, 275–79: *Répertoire* 3, 109 and *ARMT XVI/1, 17*.

104 G. Dossin, in A. Parrot, *Studia Mariana*, 1950, 52 (*N.AN* 4).

105 H. Klengel, *op.cit.*, 115 ff. and Tocci, *op.cit.*, ch. III.

106 *ARM* VII 86: 12; 87:2; 233:4; *A.1270:* 12; *A.3412:* 15–16 and *A.1153*.

107 Read *šaqûm* for (awīl) DÉ. A with Malamat, *JSS* 33 (1982), 72–73.

108 A. Malamat, *op.cit.*, 73 translated: "the persons who came up for trade".

109 The *abstractum* of *tamkārum* = "merchant", cf. G. Steiner, *Iraq* 39 (1977), 11 ff. and E. Lipiński, H. Klengel, *Gesellschaft und Kultur im alten Vorderasien*, 1982, 173 ff.

110 On this at Mari see E. Munn-Rankin, "Diplomacy in Western Asia", *Iraq* 18 (1956), 68–110 and S. Dalley, *Mari and Karana*, 1984, 172.

111 Their legal position was studied by G. Kestemont, *Iraq* 39 (1977), 191–201 and R. Haase, *WO* 9 (1977–78), 213–219.

112 Line 11.

113 *ARM* VI 18:13', 16'; 19:9 f.; 23:25, 32; 31:29; X 18:10 *(ka-le-e-et)*.

114 On trade in Ugarit see I. Cornelius, "A Bird's Eye View of Trade in Ancient Ugarit", *JNWSL* 9 (1981), 13 ff. with literature. Add to this now Liverani, *SDB* 53, 1979, cols. 1329ff.; M. Heltzer, *The Internal Organization of the Kingdom of Ugarit,* 1982; E. Linder, "Ugarit: A Canaanite Thalassocracy", G.D. Young, *Ugarit in Retrospect,* 1981, 31–42.

115 *RS* = Ras Shamra tablet.

116 *Ugaritica* V, 111 ff., no. 36.

117 Rainey, *IEJ* 13 (1963), 43–45; 14 (1964), 101; *BibAr* 28 (1965), 105–6 and *IOS* 5 (1975), 26; *The Social Stratification of Ugarit* (Ph.D.), 1962, 246 and De Vaux, *History* I, 127. This is not to disregard the fact that Ugarit formed part of the greater entity of Syria-Palestine (cf. M. Noth, *The History of Israel,* 1976, 20 and M.S. Drower, *CAH* II/2, 1975, 130n4).

118 M. Dietrich-O.Loretz, *Die keilalphabetische Texte aus Ugarit,* 1976 [= *KTU*] 4.96:3.

119 J.P.J. Olivier, *Akko: Spieëlbeeld van Beskawings,* 1983. On the archaeology see Z. Goldmann, *Encyclopaedia of Archaeological Excavations* I, 14 ff. The references to the toponym Acco in the Ugaritic texts are listed by M. Astour, L.R. Fisher, *Ras Shamra Parallels* II, 1975, VIII, 308 and 339.

120 *KTU* 2.38. See translation of J. Hoftijzer in K.R. Veenhof, *Schrijvend Verleden,* 1983, 95 and discussion of E. Lipiński, *Syria* 44 (1967), 282–84 and Sasson, *JAOS* 86 (1966), 137.

121 On shipping and other maritime matters in Ugarit see Linder, *op.cit.; The Maritime Texts of Ugarit* (Ph.D.), 1970; Sasson, "Canaanite Maritime Involvement", *JAOS* 86 (1966), 126–38; Cornelius, *op.cit.,* 23–25; Heltzer, *Goods, Prices and the Organization of Trade in Ugarit,* 1978, 150ff.

122 On shipwreck in Ugarit see F.C. Fensham, *BO* 6 (1967), 221–224.

123 W. Culican called Ugarit "the first international port in world history" ("The First Merchant Venturers", S. Piggot, *The Dawn of Civilization,* 1961, 153).

124 M. Astour, *JESHO* 13 (1970), 113–27.

125 *RS* 19.42:18 (= J. Nougayrol, *Le palais royal d'Ugarit* [=*PRU*] VI, 1970 79), and perhaps also in *RS* 19.182:6' (= *PRU* VI 81).

126 Astour, *Ras Shamra Parallels* II, 255ff., 342. See also in *JESHO* 13 (1970), 123–26 (126).

127 *RS* 19.96:8ff. (= *KTU* 4.635).

128 *RS* 16. 128:iv:7 (= *KTU* 4.214).

129 *RS* 12.01:8 (= *KTU* 4. 106).

130 *RS* 11.840:3 (= *KTU* 4.96).

131 *RS* 18.42:9 (= *KTU* 4.352).

132 *JESHO* 13 (1970), 123–26.

133 *RS* 23.28:3 (= *KTU* 4.721) and *RS* 19.20:3 (= *PRU* VI 156).

134 On this matter see "Meluḫḫa wood" which I. Gelb (*RA* 64 (1970), 4) interpreted as referring to a product manufactured locally "à la mode of Meluḫḫa" and not necessarily imported from Meluḫḫa. To use a modern analogy, "Parisian fashions" may refer to fashions from Paris (origin) or fashions in the style or type of Paris.

135 *RS* 1957.701:obv.2 (= M. Dahood in L.R. Fisher, *The Claremont Ras Shamra Tablets,* 1971, 31–32). On *krr* see M. Liverani, "Il talento di Ashdod", *BO* 11 (1972), 193–99.

136 See discussion of Astour, *Ras Shamra Parallels* II, 256–58.

137 *RS* 19.42 (= *PRU* VI 79). And perhaps also Jerusalem (line 2) depending on the reading of šal-me-ya.

138 Astour, *op.cit.,* 342.

139 *RS* 19.42:9.

140 *RS* 11.717 + :III:1 (= *KTU* 4.69).

141 *RS* 18.24:15 (= *KTU* 4.337).

142 *RS* 19.42:2.

143 According to R. Stieglitz's interpretation of *ma-ḫa-di-ya* in *RS* 19.42:10 (*JAOS* 94 (1974), 137–38).

144 M. Heltzer, "The Metal Trade of Ugarit and the Transport of Commercial Goods", *Iraq* 39 (1977), *Goods,* 148ff. and Cornelius, *op.cit.,* 21–25.

145 Material on the social position of the merchant can be found in Heltzer, *Goods,* 121–47; Cornelius, *op.cit.,* 15ff.; Astour, "The Merchant Class of Ugarit", D.O. Edzard, *Gesellschafts-klassen im alten Zweistromland,* 1972, 11–26; Rainey, "The Business Agent at Ugarit", *IEJ* 13 (1963), 313–21 and H. Klengel, *Handel und Händler im alten Orient,* 1979, 140–42.

146 *Studi G. Levi della Vida* I, 1956, 409–419. See also I. Gelb, *A Study of Writing,* 1965, 221 and Leemans, "The Importance of Trade", *Iraq* 39 (1977), 2–3.

147 See the studies of P. Garelli, *Les assyriens en Cappadoce,* 1963; M.T. Larsen, *The Old Assyrian State and its Colonies,* 1976; *Old Assyrian Caravan Procedures,* 1967 and K.R. Veenhof, *Aspects of Old Assyrian Trade and its Terminology,* 1972.

148 Edzard, *Encyclopaedia Brittanica* 11, 1974, 977.

149 M.T. Larsen, *JAOS* 94 (1974), 468–475.

150 See the list in K. Galling, *Textbuch zur Geschichte Israels,* 1979, 13–14 with literature.

151 On the use of Ugaritic in Syro-Palestine see F.M. Cross, *ErIs* 8 (1967), 9*; D.J. Wiseman, *JNWSL* 5 (1977), 78–79; A. Herdner, "A-ti-il existé une varieté palestinienne de l'écriture cuneiforme alphabétique?", *Syria* 25 (1946), 164 ff. and Albright, *The Archaeology of Palestine,* 1960, 101–103, figs. 24–25 and *CAH* II/1, 1975, 99.

152 A. Goetze-L. Levy, *Atiqot* 2 (1959), 121 ff.; Lamon-Shipton, *Megiddo* I, 1939, pl. 72:18; K. Katz *et al., From the Beginning,* 1968, 69:55.

153 B. Landsberger-H. Tadmor, *IEJ* 14 (1964), 201 ff; Yadin, *Hazor* III–IV, pl. CCCXV.

154 Yadin, *Hazor,* 1975, 261.

155 Hallo-Tadmor, *IEJ* 27 (1977), 1 ff.

156 M.T. de L. Böhl, *ZDPV* 49 (1926), 321–27; *Baghdader Mitteilungen* 7 (1974), 21–30; Albright, *Archaeology of Palestine,* 102, fig. 25; *BASOR* 86 (1942), 28–31; *ANET,* 490b; C. Campbell, G.E. Wright, *Schechem,* 1965, 208–213 (212).

157 Albright, *BASOR* 94 (1944), 16 ff.; *ANET,* 490b and A.E. Glock, *BASOR* 204 (1971), 17–30.

158 M. Kochavi, *Aphek-Antipratis,* 1977, 6 (Hebrew), 8 (English); D. Owen, G.D. Young, *Ugarit in Retrospect,* 1979, 49 ff; *Tel Aviv* 8 (1981), 1 ff; A. Singer, *Qadmoniot* 16 (1983), 42–46.

159 K. Kenyon, *Jericho* II, 656ff. and Katz, *op.cit.,* 62:48:1, 2.

160 A. Shaffer, and W.G. Dever, *Gezer* I, 1970, 111–113, pl. 24.

161 S. Smith, in J. Garstang, "Jericho: City and Necropolis Fourth Report VI", *Annals of Archaeology and Anthropology* 21 (1934), 116–117.

162 P. Artzy-A. Malamat in Y. Yadin, *Hazor* II, 115–117, pls. CXII:9: CLXXX, cf. Yadin, *Hazor,* and Malamat, "Northern Canaan", 168, 174n20; *JBL* 79 (1960), 18.

163 *UT* 2053; C.H. Gordon, *Ugaritic Textbook,* 1960, 468; K. Jaroš, *Hundert Inschriften aus Kanaan und Israel,* 1982, 32 and Herdner, *op.cit.*

164 D. Hillers, *BASOR* 173 (1964), 45ff.; Albright, *BASOR* (1964), 51–53; M. Weippert, *ZDPV* 82 (1966), 311 ff.; *ZDPV* 83 (1967), 82–83.

165 Albright, *BASOR* 173 (1964), 51 ff.; *Archaeology,* 102, fig. 114.

166 M. Mallowan, *Iran* 3 (1965), 1. Cf. I Kings 10:1 ff., the queen of Sheba may have received news of the splendour of Solomon from foreign merchants.

167 At Amarna in Egypt copies of the Mesopotamian literary epics of *Ereškigal and Nergal* and *Adapa and the South Wind* (*EA* 357 and 356) were found. The last epic reflects ideas that are foreign to Egyptian religion (as shown by M. Dietrich at the Amarna congress).

168 *The Levant at the Beginning of the Middle Bronze Age,* 1983.

169 E. Anati, "Prehistoric Trade and the Puzzle of Jericho", *BASOR* 167 (1962), 25–31.

4 The administration and the army in Judaea in the early Roman period (From Pompey to Vespasian, 63 BC–AD 79)

Denis Saddington

At the end of the fourth century BC the Macedonian king Alexander the Great conquered all the countries of the eastern Mediterranean and initiated what is called the Hellenistic period of Greek history, dominated by his successors, the Antigonids in Macedonia, the Ptolemies in Egypt and the Seleucids in Syria. In what is now modern Israel the Jews eventually succeeded in becoming independent in the second century BC when the Maccabees raised a successful revolt against the Seleucids. Traditionally authority in ancient Israel had centred around a high priest and a king, with the priestly class and land-owning aristocrats forming the leading classes in society. The Maccabee family supplied kings, also exercising the high priesthood, during the second and first centuries BC. These kings belonged to what was called the Hasmonean family. In 63 BC when the Roman general Pompey invaded Judaea two brothers of the Hasmonean dynasty, Hyrcanus, the elder, and Aristobulus, the younger, were disputing the monarchy.

From this time onwards the Jews came under increasing Roman control.[1] The Roman concept of power and authority is contained in the word *imperium*, from which the English words *empire* and *imperialism* are derived. To the Romans *imperium* meant the unquestioning acceptance of authority and obedience to the commands of their executive officials, either in Rome or abroad. The Romans organised the greater part of their empire into administrative districts called provinces. These were large areas, often corresponding to modern countries today, as ancient Africa to modern Tunisia, or Gaul to France. Governors were appointed to administer the provinces and were in office for a year. They had little time for matters other than defence and the administration of high-level justice. Only Roman citizens resident in a province could appeal to Rome against the decision of a governor. The governor was assisted by a quaestor or financial official of high status and a small staff of petty officials.[2]

By its very nature Roman administration could only affect the highest levels of provincial affairs. Accordingly, day-to-day administration had to be left to the local population and their own administrative organs.

When it was absorbed by Pompey into the Roman sphere of influence, Judaea did not become a province. All great powers exert their influence beyond the formal boundaries of their actual empires. The Roman writ ran to areas outside the actual provinces, often where geographical conditions would have made them expensive to conquer and police, sometimes where it seemed politically advisable to allow the existing authorities to remain in power. The commonest form of this in the Roman world was the client kingdom.[3] A king could be formally recognised as a "friend and ally of the Roman people". He would be left to rule his kingdom much as before, but with the diplomatic, if not the actual military, support of Rome, his internal position was greatly strengthened. In return he would be required to support Rome fully: generally this meant aligning his foreign policy with hers, supplying troops and giving other forms of support if required. Pompey chose to turn Judaea into a type of client kingdom. He decided to make Hyrcanus, the older but weaker of the two Hasmoneans disputing the monarchy, high priest. His secular title is not specified, but as he appears later as "ethnarch", he was probably so called then.[4] The term literally means "ruler of a people or tribe" and is less imposing than that of king. It seems clear that Judaea was to be downgraded and that Pompey was hoping that the unambitious Hyrcanus would not cause difficulties. Samaria, Galilee, Idumaea (the Edom of the Old Testament) and Peraea (in Transjordan) were also assigned him. Some form of taxation was imposed. This was to be paid in a lump sum to the quaestor of Syria in Sidon each year.

The Roman world underwent a series of crises in the thirty or so years following the Pompeian settlement of Judaea, and the country often suffered in them. Two features of the period may be noticed: the enactments of Julius Caesar in 47 BC and the rise of Herod.

In 49 BC Caesar had given Hyrcanus' brother Aristobulus two legions comprising some 10 to 12 000 men, all Roman citizens, to attack Hyrcanus.[5] But by 47 BC he had switched his support to Hyrcanus, largely because his right-hand man, the Idumaean Antipater, had rendered him signal service in Egypt.[6] Hyrcanus was now definitely ethnarch, but also "friend and ally of the Roman people", a title usually applied to full kings. Caesar guaranteed the Jews the right to freedom of worship and exemption from the need to supply troops to the Romans. Antipater[7] was granted Roman citizenship and the position of "epitropos", which probably means superintendent of the collection of the tribute paid by Judaea to Rome, but may imply administrative functions as well.

Antipater used his son Herod,[8] also of course a Roman citizen, in administrative functions, as did the Roman governor of Syria. The assassin of Caesar, Cassius, who took control of Syria soon after Caesar's death, appointed Herod *strategos* of Coele Syria (South Syria).[9] The Greek term is imprecise, but implies administrative control over that difficult area. In Herod's struggles to assert his position in Judaea at this time Cassius lent him Roman military support. In 41 BC he became "tetrarch", a term meaning a minor ruler, inferior to an ethnarch. Herod was probably tetrarch of Galilee.

A Parthian invasion of Judaea from beyond the Euphrates led to the fall of Hyrcanus. Herod supported the Romans and when he was in Rome in 39 BC he succeeded in persuading the Roman senate to appoint him king of Judaea. The reality, however, was that Herod had to fight for his country. In 38 he was given two Roman legions[10] and

1 000 cavalry, who were auxiliaries or non-Roman troops. The governor of Syria in 37 again gave him two legions[11] and then came to his further support in person with two additional legions. When Caesar's adopted son became the emperor Augustus, he confirmed Herod in his position and extended his domains to the north to include the Decapolis, a group of 10 Greek-speaking cities south-east of the Sea of Galilee, Batanaea (Bashan), Auranitis and Ituraea (Hauran and south Lebanon), Gaulonitis and Trachonitis (the Golan Heights).

From 37 to 4 BC the Jews had to endure the rule of a Roman citizen who was a converted Edomite and who pursued a vigorous policy of Hellenisation in the many Greek-speaking pagan cities that were within his kingdom. On his death his kingdom was split among his sons. Archelaus was appointed ethnarch only of Judaea, Samaria and Idumaea, Herod Antipas tetrarch of Galilee and Peraea, and Philip tetrarch of Batanaea and Gaulanitis and other northern areas. Some of the "Greek" cities were added to the province of Syria.

Archelaus' position was so insecure that the governor of Syria temporarily left a Roman legion in Jerusalem to help maintain him in power.[12] He remained unpopular.

In AD 6 the Jews and Samaritans succeeded in a joint petition to Augustus in having him (but not his brothers the tetrarchs) deposed. They asked for *autonomia*,[13] a word which suggests independence to the modern ear, but probably meant in practice a return to theocracy under Roman supervision. One could hardly wish Augustus or the governor of Syria away.

Under Augustus there was a new type of province, called the imperial, besides the old republican type described above, which was now called senatorial. Technically the emperor himself was the proconsul of all the imperial provinces (of which Syria was the most important in the East). The emperor sent governors, called imperial legates, to deputise for him in such provinces. However, there were also provinces of lesser importance or smaller area which were entrusted to governors drawn from the second order of the Roman nobility, the equestrian rather than the senatorial nobility. These governors were called prefects, later procurators.[14] Given the nature of the Roman imperial bureaucracy and the slowness of communications in the ancient world, such men had wide authority and used their own initiative. In the case of Judaea the imperial legate of Syria could and did interfere, as when Sulpicius Quirinius[15] (the Cyrenius of the Gospel of Luke in the Authorised Version of the Bible) conducted the first census of Judaea or Vitellius[16] deposed the prefect Pontius Pilate after receiving complaints from the Samaritans.

When Judaea became a province, the Romans imposed new taxes: a poll tax, which was a rudimentary form of income tax, and customs dues. These were, however, collected by Jews themselves. Two tax farmers are known from the New Testament – Matthew and Zacchaeus.[17] The prefect of Judaea (his title changed to procurator in the second half of the first century AD) was stationed in Caesarea (Kaisariye near Tel Aviv), a mainly Greek city unlikely to be disturbed by signs of Roman religion. He only came to Jerusalem on specific occasions.

It was at this juncture that Roman troops were stationed in Judaea on a permanent basis for the first time. The core of the Roman army consisted of legions.[18] These were divisions or brigades some five to six thousand strong recruited from Roman citizens and operating as heavy-armed infantry. They were assisted by non-citizen units of auxiliaries[19] drawn from local populations throughout the empire and retaining their own methods of fighting. They supplemented the legions especially as cavalry and archers or other types of light-armed troops. A unit of cavalry was usually 500 strong. It was called an *ala* and commanded by an officer of equestrian status called a prefect. The rare 1 000-strong *alae* were commanded by tribunes. Infantry units were similarly 500 or 1 000 strong under prefects and tribunes. They were called *cohortes*: some were part-mounted. Junior officers in the *alae* were called decurions, and in the cohorts centurions.

When Judaea became a province, no legions were stationed in it (they were in Syria to the north). The Roman forces there consisted entirely of auxiliaries. Some can be named. In AD 44 we hear of an *ala* of Sebastenians and 5 cohorts of Samaritans.[20] (Sebaste was the name of the city of Samaria itself.) Each was 500 strong, hence a total of 3 000 men. In the troubles that followed the death of Herod in 4 BC, 3 000 Samaritans from his army fought on the Roman side. It is clear that they became regiments in the Roman army. Accordingly it should be noted that a large proportion of the army in Judaea was of local origin, and only "Roman" in the sense that it was organised and commanded by Rome. In the book of Acts[21] we hear of a Cohors Italica and a Cohors Augusta in Judaea. The first in particular was a special unit formed originally of Roman citizens, not provincials like the majority of the auxiliary units. Presumably units of the type were stationed in Judaea as part compensation for the absence of legions. Cohortes Italicae and Augustae are known from first century inscriptions as well as the literary record. An inscription at Carnuntum (some 50 km east of Vienna) on the Danube records a soldier called Proculus, the son of Rabilus, from Philadelphia in the Cohors II Italica.[22] His name is Roman, but that of his father is common in Nabataean Arabia, and Philadelphia (Amman) is in the Decapolis. The inscription records further that the cohort was part of a detachment of archers from the Syrian army (to which the Judaean auxiliary regiments would form an adjunct). (It is probable that the detachment was sent to the Danube in AD 69 when Vespasian, the commander of the Roman army fighting the Jewish War of AD 69–70, made his attempt to become emperor and sent forces ahead to Europe.) A Cohors Augusta[23] is recorded on an inscription found in Batanaea under the Herodian Agrippa II, who was king of the area at the end of the first century. A Cohors Augusta I is known from the famous inscription recording the census of Sulpicius Quirinius in AD 6.[24] It is from such epigraphical evidence that much detail about the Roman army can be recovered.

Most of the army was stationed with the governor in Caesarea. Some units occupied the old Herodian fortresses. There was only one regiment in Jerusalem, whose commander had the high title of tribune.[25] The role of the cohort involved at the crucifixion of Jesus Christ and of the Cohors Augusta at the arrest of Paul show how intimately the army was involved in what we would call not only police but also juridical functions.

With Judaea becoming a province the Jews had exchanged a king, a royal court and a royal army for a Roman governor of secondary status, a few auxiliary regiments, their commanders and their centurions (whose role in the province can again be seen in the New Testament).

Of necessity much had to devolve upon Jewish organs of authority. The High Priest gained in dignity and prestige after Herod's blatant manipulation of his post. He presided over the Sanhedrin, an aristocratic body of some 70 members, to which was assigned wide legislative, administrative and judicial powers, although it appears that capital decisions, or capital decisions involving imperial security, were referred to the governor. The influence of the priestly aristocracy was felt everywhere, as the ubiquity of the scribes and elders shows. There were also local councils with criminal and legislative functions. The theocracy was not fully restored, but much of the "autonomia" desired by the Jews was realised.

The unhappy history of Judaea under the Roman governors of the first century cannot be traced here. Eventually discontent erupted in the Jewish War of AD 66–70. The rebellion was finally crushed by the future emperor Vespasian and his son Titus. The consequences for Judaea were serious. Large legionary forces, supplemented by their auxiliary troops,[26] had been sent into the province, mainly from Syria and Egypt. Some auxiliary regiments were stationed permanently in the province after the war, but there was a major change in that a full legion, the Tenth Fretensis, was stationed in Jerusalem itself. This was commanded by an imperial legate of senatorial status, superior therefore to the equestrian procurator who was in Caesarea.

Much of Judaea became imperial domain, with the Jews regarded as conquered enemies. Yet Vespasian did not introduce the usual city-state type of local administration common elsewhere in the Roman world.

The Temple was not allowed to be rebuilt, and the Sanhedrin and the High Priesthood were abolished. It was the religion of the Pharisees that triumphed, with synagogues grouped round rabbis.

It may seem strange that direct Roman control proved unsuccessful in Judaea in the first century. The Romans did not administer their empire with the heavy bureaucracy familiar from modern imperialisms. Roman control was essentially directed at security: there was no such thing as cultural imperialism. The local populace was drawn in as far as possible. Samaritans and other auxiliaries formed the bulk of the army. Not only an Antipater but an obscure rabbi Saul, the later Paul, could be a Roman citizen.[27] And the Romans made every concession to Jewish religious sensibilities — keeping the offensive standards of the Roman regiments with their image of the emperor out of sight as much as possible, exempting Jews from military service, allowing them freedom of worship and even excusing them the worship of the emperor, provided that they sacrificed to Jehovah on his behalf. The Romans made serious errors, as when the emperor Gaius suspended the privilege of freedom from the imperial cult and the procurators who succeeded Herod Agrippa failed to respond to genuine grievances.

The complex reasons for the Jewish Revolt cannot be discussed here. Basically it seems to have been due to the incompatibility of the Jewish concept of theocracy or independence under a high priest and a Roman imperialism that regarded political and religious loyalty as inseparable. But in spite of the troubles that led to the Revolt, what stands out is the lightness of Roman control. It might even be exercised through a local king, a Herod or a Herod Agrippa, who might at times have to be supported by Roman legions.

Even when the kings were replaced by the prefects or the procurators, much was still left to local control.

---

1 For the Jews under Roman rule, see the comprehensive treatments by E. Schürer, *The History of the Jewish People in the Age of Jesus Christ* (175 BC – AD 135) (1874–1924), revised and edited by G. Vermes and F. Millar, Edinburgh, 1973; E.M. Smallwood, *The Jews under Roman Rule from Pompey to Diocletian,* Leyden, 1976.

2 On Roman provincial administration, see G.H. Stevenson, *Roman Provincial Administration,* Oxford, 1939.

3 On client kings, see P.C. Sands, *The Client Princes of the Roman Empire,* Cambridge, 1908; D.C. Braund, *Rome and the Friendly King,* London, 1984.

4 Josephus, *Antiquitates Judaeorum,* hereafter: *A.J.* XIV, 4, 4, 73; 10, 2, 191.

5 Jos. *A.J.* XIV, 7, 4, 123.

6 Josephus, *Bellum Judaicum,* hereafter: *B.J.* I, 9, 3, 187; *A.J.* XIV, 8, 1, 127ff.

7 Jos. *B.J.* I, 9, 5, 194; 10, 3, 199ff; *A.J.* XIV, 8, 3, 137; 5, 143f.

8 For the Herods in Judaea, see A.H.M. Jones, *The Herods of Judaea,* Oxford, 1938; R.D. Sullivan, "The Dynasty of Judaea in the First Century," in *Aufstieg und Niedergang der römischen Welt,* II, 8, 1977, 296ff.

9 Jos. *B.J.* I, 11, 4, 225; 6, 230; *A.J.* XIV, 11, 4, 280ff.; 15, 11, 452. I. Hahn, "Herodes als Prokurator," in *Neue Beiträge zur Geschichte der alten Welt,* (ed. E.C. Welskopf, Berlin, 1964–5) II, 26, usefully traces the term *strategos* here to its use in the Hellenistic period in the Seleucid area for the commander of a specific district with full military, administrative and financial control. As such it is analogous to the Roman term *praefectus,* on which cf. further below, n. 14 and, for a later example, D.B. Saddington, *C.Q.* XXVIII, 1978, 331f. Naturally too much precision cannot be expected of such terms, especially in periods of turmoil, as after the death of Caesar.

10 Jos. *A.J.* XIV, 15, 7, 434; *B.J.* I, 16, 6, 317. The legions were, however, newly recruited and inexperienced, having been raised mainly in Syria (*A.J.* XIV, 15, 10, 449) under the command of a certain Machaeras.

11 Jos. *A.J.* XIV, 16, 1, 468; *B.J.* I, 17, 2, 327; 9, 346.

12 Jos. *A.J.* XVII, 11, 1, 299; *B.J.* II, 5, 3, 79.

13 Jos. *A.J.* XVII, 11, 1, 300f; 2, 304–6; *B.J.* II, 6, 1, 80f; 2, 84–91.

14 In origin a prefect was a person appointed by a governor to a specific task in his provincial area, usually involving the command of troops. Prefects ranged from comparatively humble officials to the prestigious prefect or governor of Egypt. It is difficult to know the social standing of the early prefects of Judaea, since their previous careers are unknown. They were probably comparable to such figures as Sex. Pedius Lusianus Hirrutus who, after holding the most senior centurionate in a legion, became "prefect of Raetia, Vindelicia and the Vallis Poenina with command over the auxiliary soldiers there", i.e. in a newly conquered area of Switzerland and South Germany which was part of the great Rhine command under Augustus and Tiberius (*Inscriptiones Latinae Selectae,* ed. H. Dessau, no. 2689). On the term prefect, cf. n. 9 above; A.H.M. Jones, *Studies in Roman Government and Law,* Oxford, 1960, 117ff.; M. Ghiretti, "Lo *status* della Giudea dall'età Augustea all'età Claudia", *Latomus* XLIV, 1985, 759ff. The term *prefect* is attested epigraphically of Pontius Pilate on the inscription from Caesarea which names him. It reads [. . .]s Tiberieum/[. . .]ntius Pilatus/[. . .]ectus Iudeae/[. . .]

(where [Po] should be supplied before ntius in the second line, and [praef] before ectus in the third) and was published in *l'Année Epigraphique* 1963, no. 104. The inscription is too fragmentary to be fully understood, but appears to refer to action taken by Pilate in connection with a Tiberieum, a structure in honour of the emperor Tiberius.

15 Luke 2:1–3; Jos. *A.J.* XVII, 13, 5, 355; XVIII, 1, 1, 1ff.

16 Jos. *A.J.* XVIII, 4, 2, 88f. For Pilate's title of prefect, cf. above, n. 14.

17 Matthew 10:3; Luke 19:2.

18 For the legions, see H.M.D. Parker, *The Roman Legions,* 1928, repr. Cambridge, 1961.

19 For the auxiliary forces of the Roman army, see G.L. Cheesman, *The Auxilia of the Roman Imperial Army,* 1914, r. Hildersheim, 1971; D.B. Saddington, *The Development of the Roman Auxiliary Forces from Caesar to Vespasian,* Harare, 1982.

20 For the Samaritans under Herod, cf. Jos. *B.J.* II, 3, 4, 52; 4, 2, 58; for those in 44, *A.J.* XX, 6, 1, 122; cf. XIX, 9, 2, 365.

21 Acts 10:1; 27:1.

22 *Inscriptiones Latinae Selectae* no. 9168, which reads as follows: Proculus Rabili f. Col. Philadelphia mil. optio coh. II Italic. C. R. 7 Faustini ex vexil. sagit. exer. Syriaci stip. VII vixit ann. XXVI Apuleius frater f. c. The letters Col. after Proculus' name almost certainly represent Collina, one of the tribus or voting divisions of the Roman people. Only Roman citizens belonged to a tribus. This makes Proculus a Roman citizen. At the end of the inscription he is said to have served for seven years, having lived for 26 years. His tomb was erected by his brother Apuleius – also a Roman name.

J.-P. Lémonon, *Pilate et le gouvernement de la Judée,* Paris, 1981, 102, is wrong to state that Luke is committing an anachronism by mentioning the Cohors Italica in the 40s. Lémonon assumes that the Coh. II Italica C. R. did not exist before 69, the ostensible year of the inscription of Proculus. In fact, regiments were in existence for many years before being attested epigraphically (if so attested at all). And it should be noted that Proculus died after seven years of service, which implies his recruitment, and the existence of his regiment, by 62 or 63.

23 Published in *l'Année Epigraphique* 1925, no. 121. It records a Lucius Obulnius hecatontarches tes spires Augustes, i.e. L. Obulnius – another Roman name – centurion of the Cohors Augusta.

The name of another regiment in Judaea may be recorded on an inscription of AD 18 under the emperor Tiberius (*Corpus Inscriptionum Latinarum* IX, 3664). Unfortunately, because it is fragmentary, it cannot be fully interpreted. It refers to a prefect of sagittarii or archers who appear to be called Ascalonitanae. If so, we have a cohort from Ascalon (Ashkelon, now 'Askalan) – cohorts were often initially stationed near their area of original recruitment. (Lémonon, o.c.n. 22, 102, does not quote this inscription and so dates the Cohortes Ascalonitanorum too late.)

24 *Inscriptiones Latinae Selectae,* no. 2683, recording Q. Aemilius Q.f. Pal. Secundus in castris diui Aug. sub P. Sulpicio Quirinio legato Caesaris Syriae honoribus decoratus praefect. cohort. Aug. I praefect. cohort. II classicae; idem iussu Quirini censum egi Apamenae ciuitatis millium homin. ciuium $\overline{\text{CXVII}}$. "Q. Aemilius Secundus, the son of Quintus, of the Palatine *tribus* (for which, cf. above, n. 22) in the camp of the deified Augustus under P. Sulpicius Quirinius, Caesar's (i.e., the emperor's) legate (i.e. imperial governor) of Syria, who received decorations. I was prefect (i.e. commander) of the Cohors Augusta I and prefect of the Cohors II Italica; by order of Quirinius I conducted the census of 117 000 male inhabitants of Apamea

(now Famieh, a city in Syria). " It should be noted that Quirinius was using an army officer for the census. The distinction between military and civilian administration was not as clear-cut in antiquity as it is today.

25   For the significance of the title of tribune, cf. Saddington, o.c.n. 19, 210, n. 113.

26   For the Roman forces in Judaea during the Jewish War and under the emperor Vespasian, cf. Saddington, o.c.n. 19, 130 ff. The name of only one auxiliary unit is known, the Ala Gaetulorum (the Gaetuli were a North African people). It is recorded in *Inscriptiones Latinae Selectae,* no. 2544, but it is not known if it remained in Judaea after the Jewish War.

27   For Roman citizenship in Judaea, see A.N. Sherwin-White, *Roman Society and Roman Law in the New Testament,* Oxford, 1963, esp. 172 ff.

Part II
Christian Theology

5 *The Holy Land's contribution to a theology of Church and State*

Godfrey Ashby

As James Michener has pointed out at length in his novel *The Source*, The Holy Land has undergone a great number of political changes in the course of its history and has seen the birth in some sense of three major world religions in addition to the Canaanite religions that preceded Hebraism. For the purpose of this chapter we shall stop short at the conquest of Palestine by the Turks, since the policy of Islam is too large a subject to investigate here. Similarly those peculiar hybrids of European feudalism, the Latin Crusader states, together with the relatively short period of British rule, will be ignored.

There is currently in our Western world, and particularly in South Africa, an understanding of the role of Church and State that can be caricatured as follows. The State is understood in a variety of ways. It can mean the whole "secular" world and how it is organised so that "state" means all institutions of the world of men and will presumably continue in some form or other indefinitely unless and until some form of disaster, chaos or aridity overtakes the planet. It can mean the civil authorities who, in a modern Western country, control or influence almost every aspect of life by means of laws, civil servants, or merely climate of opinion. It can mean a political ideology erected into a system of government, so that any criticism of that ideology is immediately identified as opposition to the State. I would suggest that we have come very close to this third view in South Africa and that any comparisons to Nazi Germany lie in this area, not necessarily in other areas. In other words a totalitarian state, whether of the Right or of the Left, has glorified an ideology, if not deified it, under the name of "the State". In contrast to this, the further we progress along this line towards the deification of the State, the more religion ("Church" for Christians) becomes relegated to an organisation within society responsible for liturgical services in buildings set apart for the purpose, for the encouraging of personal faith in individuals, and for the influencing of the mores of society, provided that these mores are restricted to certain areas of morality. The end of this process is the "Church of State" as described by George Orwell and, beyond that, oblivion.

None of this has any origin in the thought or practice of the Holy Land at any time; it is not an export of Canaan or Palestine or Israel.

In Ancient Israel, and indeed in the Canaan reflected in the Ras Shamra/Ugarit tablets (if that be a true reflection) there is no State and no Church in the modern sense. A city state in the Ancient Near East was ruled by its gods, through the medium of its kings or priests, or both. Its laws were those of its gods and theocracy the only political ideology, however expressed. Hence the Torah is not the ancestor of any modern Western legal system except in the sense that certain of its precepts have been borrowed by and coincide with certain basic modern legal precepts. The Torah is based on theocracy, that the Lord rules His people who are expected to behave accordingly. Anyone who leads, rules or judges does so by divine appointment — and his or her actions are judged accordingly — for no member of the theocratic community, king or commoner, poet or peasant, priest or judge, is above the Torah, above the Divine Lord. The Royal psalms give us a superb illustration of this: if they were composed for royal occasions in the Temple at Jerusalem, they clearly demonstrate the sacral nature of the monarchy. The king was no mere token head of state, taking his oath to a constitution whilst his crown rested on a cushion next to him, nor was he a military dictator, but God's son, His representative before His people, sent to maintain God's justice, to glorify, or at least to bring credit to the name of the Lord. He is, in fact, Church as well as State. (cf. Psalm 72:1–19). Even during the period of the judges, before the monarchy, the judge was raised up and supported by God and could be set aside by God, as indeed happened to Saul. The argument in 1 Samuel 8–10 is not so much a debate about the nature of monarchy, nor indeed is it a transition between a simple, fair, egalitarian, rural tribal life, and a capitalistic élitist oppressive form, on the Canaanite model, as is the view of some liberation theologies. It represents the agonising of Ancient Israel over how the theocracy is to be best expressed in the face of new conditions. The warning of Samuel (1 Sam 8:4–22) is aimed not so much at the aberrations of later monarchs as at the neglect of the real ruler of Israel — the Lord himself.

After 586 BC when priests, and eventually the high-priest, became the leaders of Israel, this was not a takeover, but, in default of the Davidic monarchy, the will of the real ruler being now expressed by those who regulated his worship and expounded his Torah. It was not ecclesiastical domination but a new form of theocracy. Nevertheless, at no time were they above reproach and I would suggest that it was not Jesus's prophetic ministry that caused his death (though it could have done as with many a prophet, since Israel did not expect its leaders, priests or otherwise, to be above reproach), but his Messianic claims. To some he appeared as a claimant to the throne of God, and not only the throne of Israel. To Christians, in truth, this is what he is. I say this not out of provocation but because it is relevant to further sections of this chapter. When Israel was free to be herself

in the Holy Land, there was no State or Church; God — whom nobody thought of denying — ruled through his sacral officers, who were open to judgement by the Torah which applied to all relationships with the Overlord and with the community.

There were, of course, long periods of Israel's history when the Holy Land was a province under the rule of another nation that did not own the Lord and if they were theocracies, were polytheistic or had an inclusive religious set of principles. Assyria, Babylon, Persia, Macedon and Rome ruled Palestine for many a long century. The last of these empires had Christians as their subjects too, who at that time had never had the experience of living as a totally free people in a covenanted land.

What was to be done under foreign domination? First the theological background must be made clear. In the Ancient Near East, if one city or tribe conquered another, then this was a victory for the gods of the conquering power. They had to be worshipped, usually alongside or above the gods of the subject city or tribe. The power of the local (conquered) gods tended to diminish in the presence of those of the conquered. When Isaiah asserted that Cyrus was God's "shepherd", his "anointed" (Messiah) (Isaiah 44:28, 45:1) even though Cyrus does not know the Lord (or owe any allegiance to him) (Isaiah 45:4), this is in fact a theological statement that, far from the God of the Covenant having lost out in permitting other gods to heal Israel or restore her, Cyrus is the unwitting agent of God's plan. So also with the other nations — Assyrians and Babylonians are only allowed to triumph as agents of punishment used by God upon His own people. When Jeremiah advised the Hebrews to accept resettlement in Babylon and work for the good of the whole community there, this was not an abject acceptance of civil authority but a triumphant assertion that God's will was being done. Babylon was to be accepted as part of God's plan, not for her own sake. Similarly, the Jews could only justify the Maccabean Revolt in that they were being forced to give to the emperor what only the Lord had the right to have — worship and sacrifice. This explains why the Maccabean Revolt, as compared to other incidents, was seen as a totally justified act. The Jews were not merely being asked to submit to oppression — they were being asked to sacrifice to an idol —and more than an idol, a mere Greek army officer who had probably usurped the throne of the Seleucids in any case (cf. 1 Macc).

The chapters in Isaiah (40–55) currently ascribed to the Exilic period are of great significance, which has not yet been fully explored. The prophet proclaims to Israel the nature of her future pilgrimage. Israel is to return in triumph to her own land, by God's design and through the divinely appointed agency of Cyrus the Persian.

The "servant" is Israel, as rabbinical scholarship has always identified him. But in Is. 42:1–4 the regal titles of the king are used of him, and his task is outlined as that of the Davidic monarch. Israel, like David and his successors, must bring *justice* to herself and to the nations. This is the first duty of the king, of his people, of the people of God of the State — to bring justice to *all*.

In Is. 49:6 Israel is the perfect disciple, Israel in her true vocation, that of the true Messiah, to be a light to the nations.

In Is. 52–53 the King's calling, the nation's calling, the State's calling, is deepened still further. The servant, the personification of King, people and rule, must be prepared to be disgraced, to suffer to be a sacrifice for sin. This is what leadership means, and only on these terms is there new life and triumph. The key to the servant is the royal psalms. These pave the way for a suffering, disgraced king — for the sake of the people and for the sake of the nations.

This is a new and unexplored political idea — that church and State, leadership and people mean, in God's sight, service to the nations, suffering and disgrace. The State and the leadership is a sacrifice offered to God involving suffering and death — a novel, unacceptable and totally unpopular political theory. Whenever a state or ruler demands such an unquestioning obedience, in its own name or in the name of God, then there could well be a situation analogous to emperor worship. The question then arises — is the answer the sword of Judas Maccabeus, or death unresisting on the Sabbath — Bonhoeffer or Lawum?

Dix describes, in his famous purple passage, "the strange fairy-tale land of the Byzantine Empire". It was no fairy tale to those who lived under it, but a fusion of the theocratic principles of the Hebrew monarchy, the system of the Roman Empire, and the faith in Jesus Christ as Lord — and its language was Greek. Its polity has been much criticised as "Caesaro-Papism", the criticism coming from Western Europe, where Emperor and Pope fought each other for the leadership of Western Christendom. But these principles applied to Byzantium:

- The Basileus was a hieratic figure, dressed as a priest. He was just as much a "religious" figure as the Patriarch of Constantinople, whose authority, in any case, did not extend to Palestine, where the Patriarch of Jerusalem held sway.
- The real ruler was Christ whose empty throne, with the gospel book lying open upon it, dominated the throne-room in the palace at Constantinople.
- No emperor was above reproach. Apart from an alarming series of palace revolutions, mutilations of unsuccessful emperors and intrigues that have rather unfairly been dubbed as "Greek", attacks by prophetic voices upon the emperors and their govern-ments are legion, of which those of St John Chrysostom (who called the reigning empress "Salome" in the course of a sermon preached in the Cathedral of Hagia Sophia) are the best known.
- All Byzantine State officials, even the army, were regarded as office-bearers for Christ. As such their conduct could frequently be judged (and found wanting). As an attempt at a theocracy, the Byzantine Empire remains an attempt. Its interest to us is that it was the last attempt at a theocracy partly based on Hebrew models in the Holy Land.

The Holy Land left no blueprint for a modern political system. Certainly Republicanism and Western democracy — nor, for that matter, a Peoples' democracy — cannot be justified from biblical examples. What has been left to us, however, are some very valid principles to apply to modern states.

- Where rulers claim to be Christian or God-fearing, their laws and actions have to be judged by God's criteria, as primarily set out in the Torah.
- No political system can claim infallibility, whether democratic or otherwise.
- Where rulers do not claim to be Christian or God-fearing, they rule only by divine permission in the eyes of the believing community.
- Subjects owe obedience to their rulers: they also owe them criticism and opposition if that opposition is based on God's will.
- Neither Church-State nor any other such binary opposition (beloved of anthropologists), has any place in God's order, which covers all of life.
- The ban on "idol worship" includes man-made institutions when, by their claim, they usurp God's sovereignty.

Certain areas of the world have left an idealised and unrealistic sense of nostalgia for palmy days — the Habsburg Empire, the British Raj. "Oh to be in Ruritania at Coronation time!" Others have left a sense of deliverance — Nazi Germany, Stalinist Russia, Idi Amin's Uganda, the Generals in Argentina, Caligula's Rome. From the Holy Land there came a vision of hope yet unrealised — that the Kingdom of God will, one day, be expressed in the reign of a King who will rule in justice and peace from Mount Zion, and *all* nations will be blessed.

Out of the Holy Land comes also the vision, never accepted in Judaism and never applied in Christendom, that the rule of justice and peace will only be achieved through leadership that suffers and a state which is consciously offered as a sacrifice for sin.

6 *The significance of the capacity of God as Creator for His relationship to the Land in the Old Testament*

Jacob Helberg

INTRODUCTION

In spite of the important role played by the land in the covenantal promises to Israel (cf., for example, Von Rad 1958:87) the land until recently was not accorded its rightful place in Old Testament theology, and definitely not theology as practised in the West. This is the opinion of Marquardt (1964:13), Davies (1974:24), Rendtorff (1975:23), Brueggemann (1978:xvii; 3 ff., 185 ff.), Santmire (1985:189–99), to mention only a few.

One important reason for this is to be found in the fact that the capacity of God as Creator was not sufficiently brought into account in theology. This can probably be ascribed partially to the fact that Old Testament theology in general works with a scheme in which creational theology is seen as a late development, and is ascribed to the P-source which is regarded as exilic or post-exilic literature. A late dating of a source, however, does not of itself imply that the material is also old.

Although Von Rad pointed out the importance of the promise of the land, he did not work out the implications of this statement fundamentally, but the statement was dominated by the soteriological idea of the history of salvation. Apart from the above scholars, Van der Woude (1969) also points out the strong stress in the Old Testament on God as Creator. In contrast to Von Rad, he points out that the stress in the Old Testament is not on kerygma, the proclamation of the history of salvation, but on instruction in the commandments of the Lord in order that they may be kept in practical life. Schmidt (1984:111) says that "the doctrine of creation . . . is not a peripheral theme of biblical theology but is plainly the fundamental theme".

This chapter will illustrate that just as little as a theology of salvation offers the right perspective on the meaning of land in the Old Testament, is it given by a creational theology. Apart from the elements of creation and history there are also other important elements, such as the Torah, covenant and election. The meaning of these different elements will be looked at briefly. Following that, it will be indicated that the determining factor is the relationship of land to God in his capacity as Creator (and Re-Creator). If one then *has* to talk in terms of a "theology", this could be called a "creator theology". I prefer, however, not to talk in terms of a "theology", especially because we do not here have to do with a vision of just a few authors or theologians, but with a vision of the Scriptures as a whole, as stated by Schmidt above.

For the purposes of this chapter the various books of the Bible are each taken as a unity (cf., for example, Childs 1978:311 ff.), and various possible sources out of them will not be discussed, also not, for example, the point made by Carroll (1981:220) that the motif of the new covenant is a counsel of despair *if* it is to be attributed to Jeremiah.

Each of the various books has its own accent. Isaiah 40ff., for example, uses the word land *(eres)* almost exclusively in a universal sense (cf., for example, Perlitt, 1982:46). The basic approach in the various books concerning this subject is the same, however, so that the books need not be discussed separately.

This chapter focuses on the Major Prophets, with the exception of Isaiah 1–39, and Lamentations.

THE ROLE OF THE GEOGRAPHY IN THE MEANING OF THE LAND

Clements (1965:15, 16) postulates the difference between the religion of Israel and that of the Canaanites as residing in the fact that the patriarchs's gods were "entirely distinct from those of the Canaanite religion with its basis in nature, and its emphasis on fertility, in which the deities had a close and continuing relationship to the soil and to particular places. For the patriarchs their gods were not associated with the soil, nor with the holy places, but were bound together with their worshippers, and were believed to accompany them on their wanderings . . . The importance of such a conception must be particularly seen in the personal relationship which this involved between the god and his worshippers . . . the religion of the partriarchs represents a religious personalism, whereas that of Canaan a religious materialism."

In contrast to the geographical determinacy or the natural determinacy of the religion of the neighbouring nations, the historical aspect played a much more important role in the religion of Israel. Their feasts were not merely natural feasts but also and especially historical ones. One example of this is that at the feast of the first yield of the harvest a confession was made about how God had guided that nation since the time of the patriarchs and brought them into the country (Deuteronomy 26:1–11). In this way the cult, the holy places, etc. could be bound up very closely with God's great deeds in history (cf., amongst others, Ohler 1979:309). Yahweh was not a natural god or a local god or a god of the land, as were the gods of Israel's neighbours. Rather, He guided and determined history (cf. Isaiah 41 ff.; Jeremiah 1:1–3; 2:6 ff.; Ezekiel 1:1 ff.; 6:1 ff.; Lamentations 1:21; 4:22; 5:19). He also introduces Himself as such in the introduction to the Torah, the Ten Commandments (Exodus 20:1; Deuteronomy 5:6).

This does not imply that God is a god of history as against the Canaanite natural gods or geographical gods (cf. the criticism of Brueggemann 1978:185). In contrast, it is Yahweh who rules over creation as the almighty Creator and who brings rain and prosperity, not the Canaanite gods, says Jeremiah (Jeremiah 5:19 ff.; 10:11 ff.; 14:22).

From the fact that Israel's religion was not geographically or naturally determined, it follows that land in the Old Testament is not a "holy land" in the cosmic or the material sense, but only in the derivative sense (cf. Davies 1974: 28, 29). Yahweh did not bind Himself to the land because of an intrinsic value which land would ostensibly have.

For that reason land (or city or sanctuary) does not offer automatic protection. Rather, for the disobedient nation Yahweh commands death there (Ezekiel 8:12; 9:5 ff.; 24:6 ff.; Jeremiah 7; Lamentations 1, 2, 4; Isaiah 66:15 ff.). Yahweh is Himself a sanctuary for the exiles. He maintains and enacts the covenantal bond directly with them, without a sanctuary (Ezekiel 11:15, 16). In the representations of the city and the temple as they will be subsequent to the return to the land, his presence will be dominant (Ezekiel 48:35).

The question does arise now whether the special geographical location of the land is not responsible for its special meaning and that of the nation inhabiting it. The land did in fact hold an important place in antiquity and was a bridge between continents and civilisations (Aharoni 1979:3 ff.) in the sense that it lay between the countries or regions which for many centuries dominated the history of the Middle East, viz. Egypt and Mesopotamia. But the latter were then indeed the dominant forces. The secondary place of the promised land emerges from the description of the borders of the most ideal situation, viz. from the Euphrates to Egypt (1 Kings 4:21). Weinfeld (1983:66) says that the expression has a utopian flavour. The land mostly constituted only a small part of the region, and Israel was continually locked into combat with neighbours to maintain even this modest portion. The land did not have the natural borders of Egypt which must have given the inhabitants a sense of security (cf. below).

Although there was no lack of fertility, a large part of the country was mountainous and even desert-like. The decription of a land "flowing with milk and honey" is not simply geographically based, but has a strong basis in faith and gives expression to the fact that the land is a gift from God (cf. Wildberger 1956:405, 6; Ohler 1979:187; cf. also Caquot 1974:139 for the fact that the expression is not mythological).

It is not the geographical features of the land which gave it its place in history. What is more, its geographical situation, together with the historical course of events, squarely opposed the concept of an own country, as will be indicated in the following section.

THE ROLE OF HISTORY IN THE MEANING OF THE LAND

According to the Old Testament version of Israel's history, Israel was already a nation when the people entered the country, so that the nation was not born in the land (cf. Perlitt, 1983:47, 48; Zimmerli 1983:247). They conquered the land and had not been there since creation. This statement is not essentially affected by Noth (1930), Mendenhall (1973) or Gottwald (1979) and others' approaches in terms of which there was not a large-scale exodus from Egypt and that the land largely landed in the hands of groups of the local population. The fact is that history rather than myth is the determining factor in the possession of land (cf. also Clements 1965:48, 54). Buber (1974:8, 9) remarks in regard to the concept "holy" land and "holy" nation that this holiness is a characteristic imparted to the nation and the land because they were the elect of God. It is rather a political, theo-political, than a cultic category of sanctity, and expresses God's rule over the whole life of the nation and the land. It is wholly and fully a *Geschichtsglaube*. The land of Israel did not have the same sort of situation as Egypt, which was largely bordered by a large and desolate desert, the Nile cataract and the sea, and which gave to them a sense of being naturally enclosed. In Israel there was no such natural border (cf. Ohler 1979:57). The land thus lay, practically as well as historically, in the midst of the nations and countries. It was, whether out of choice or not, closely involved with the events of the nations. Added to that it never really had a homogeneous population. Israel in a certain sense nearly always had to live with other nations in the land, even the name of the country not always being linked with Israel, but Canaan (cf. Ohler 1979:18, 57, 59, 175).

The population of Jerusalem, which since the earliest times of Israel's settlement in the land contained a strong Jebusite element, was in a certain sense typical of the whole of the land.

The gift of the country never became a mere given (Ohler 1979:16, 59). The "rest" promised to Israel (Isaiah 14:3; Jeremiah 31:2) was always linked very securely to expectation. Israel's history, even within the land, was characterised by a struggle to be and to remain himself. Brueggemann (1978:185–189) states that both directions which were opposed and which have for the last few decades dominated theology of the Old Testament, viz. the existentialist, which is especially associated with Bultmànn, and the "mighty deeds of God in history" approach especially stressed by Von Rad and G.E. Wright, did not give adequate emphasis to place, and therefore land. The place is not merely geographical, a vacuum, and history does not take place in a vacuum. Place and events, place and history, are closely linked to each other. For that reason Brueggemann speaks of "storied place".

There are thus more factors involved than geography and history in the sense of a mere spontaneous course of events. In fact, other nations, Israel's neighbours, experienced a totally different course of events in the midst of more or less the same geographical and historical givens. Israel's history was precisely in many instances a history *against* the seeming course of events, against all normal expectations. This history was characterised frequently by progress born of degeneration, or destruction, by wonderful new beginnings (Helberg 1983:7; cf. also Bright 1953:127 ff.).

One of the other factors which determined Israel's history was the Torah.

THE ROLE OF THE TORAH IN THE MEANING OF THE LAND

Israel was, in distinction from other nations, the nation of the Torah. Simon (1982:252) states Buber's viewpoint as follows: "The Old Testament is the Word to the people, the revealed and revealing secret of the people's history, set against national and group purposes. The sacred enters the historical world with law and blessing."

The Torah contracts into the Ten Commandments, which deal with man's relationship to God and his fellow man. Religion and ethics are closely linked to each other in that. For that reason God demands justice from His people (cf. for example Isaiah 1:11–17; Jeremiah 7). Biblical religion is relevant religion in daily life and in relationships. Against the false confidence aimed at the cultic service as such the prophets postulated the demand of right and justice, obedience (cf. Wildberger 1971:192).

The upholding of the Torah is linked to the inhabiting of the land. The purpose of the possession of the land is to uphold the Torah, to direct all of life in accordance with it. The Torah was then also according to the testimony of the Old Testament, given to Israel at Sinai, even before the nation entered the land (cf. e.g. Levenson, 1985:19ff). (It is not necessary for the purpose of this study to answer the question to what extent Deuteronomy or Deuteronomistic literature views the situation from exilic eyes, and therefore wants to give the meaning of the Torah for a return to the land in that period, rather than as a rendering of events in the past; cf. for example, Perlitt, 1983:54.) The loss of the land is also linked to the Torah, and this is not merely hypothetical ("If you do not follow all the words of this law . . . You will be uprooted from the land" (Deuteronomy 28:58, 63)), but factual. Israel's disobedience of the Torah made the nation land in exile (Isaiah 42:24 ff.; Jeremiah 6:11 ff.; Ezekiel 20:24).

The Torah has an ambivalent working, attaining life or death. Of this we find testimony in the nation's reaction following Moses' announcement of the commandments. The very first words are a request to Moses: "Speak to us yourself and we will listen. But do not have God speak to us or we will die" (Exodus 20:19); (cf. also the discussion of Isaiah 40:6–8 below).

Furthermore, it is not merely the loss of the land that is (in the narrow sense of the word) linked to the disobedience of the Torah, but return is linked to the upholding of the Torah (Jeremiah 31:31–38), something which is the fruit of God's new covenant with the nation. There is also the close link between the inner change of the nation and the outward change which will take place in the land to provide food for the people (Ezekiel 36:29–30).

Some scholars, such as Ottosson (1986; cf. also Buber 1950:67) see, on the basis of the geographical description of the Garden of Eden, a link between Eden and the promised land (cf. also Marquardt, 1975:17), as well as a link between the Torah and the tree of knowledge in Paradise (Genesis 2, 3). According to Clines (1974:8), however, Psalm 19b teaches the superiority of the Torah to the tree of knowledge. According to Engnell (1955:116) the tree of knowledge has to do with the possibility of procreation (but not with sexuality as such). (For a discussion of different views, cf. Wallace, 1985:101ff. His own view is that "It is more likely that Genesis 2–3, 6:1–4 and 11:1–9 are intended to convey a broad prohibition against human activity meant to influence or penetrate the divine realm" [p. 132].)

If Ottosson's view should be correct, we have to do, in the tree of knowledge, with a link between the Torah and creation, although not with a direct link. I return to this later. First one has to direct attention to the relationship of the land with the Word, with election and with covenant.

THE ROLE OF THE WORD, ELECTION AND COVENANT IN THE MEANING OF THE LAND

Here "Word" is used in a more general sense than "Torah", if one may be permitted to make such a distinction, and it is dealt with especially as it has to do with election and covenant.

The preamble to the Ten Commandments is as follows: "I am the LORD your God, who brought you out of Egypt, out of the land of slavery" (Exodus 20:2; Deuteronomy 5:6). In this way the Ten Commandments are firmly placed within the framework of the covenant. The fifth of the Commandments links the fact of living inside this land to a covenantal blessing on obedience to parents. Through the calling of Abraham the land is promised to him and his descendants, and together with that a blessing for the nations (Genesis 12:1 ff.). Here one therefore has to do with both election and universalism.

According to Exodus 19:4–6 Israel's existence as the covenantal people is linked to their keeping the covenant: "You yourselves have seen what I did to Egypt, and how I carried you on eagles' wings and brought you to myself. Now if you obey me fully and keep my covenant, then out of all nations you will be my treasured possession. Although (or: because) the whole earth is mine, you will be for me a kingdom of priests and a holy nation." The Creator of the whole earth here stands in a covenantal relationship to a specific nation — on the way to a promised land. He makes Himself and His relationship to His people known through His Word and He upholds this relationship through His Word, as emerges from Genesis 12:1 ff, and Exodus 20:2 (cf. for example Vriezen 1966:238 on the efficacy of the Word with regard to Genesis 12:2 ff.).

But what does this Word do in the history of the nation? Here Jeremiah offers light (1:2–3): "The word of the LORD came to him [Jeremiah] in the thirteenth year of the reign of Josiah ... down to the eleventh year of Zedekiah ... when the people of Jerusalem went into exile". The Word is seemingly ineffectual because in spite of its dissemination, Israel's history culminates in exile. In reality, however, the Word is effective, because the exile that comes is in actual fact a sealing of the dissemination of *this* Word.

Isaiah 40:8 also speaks of the negative effect of the Word. The person who is called there to proclaim the Word hesitates in the face of the command because it is precisely the preaching of the Word which has landed the people in exile. The Word of God, narrowly linked to the breath of God (cf. Psalm 33:6, 9), is like wind which withers the flowers and grass of the fields: "A voice says, 'Cry out'. And I (or: someone) said, 'What shall (or: can) I cry?' 'All men are like grass, and all their glory is like the flowers of the field. The grass withers and the flowers fall, because the breath of the LORD blows on them ...'" At Isaiah's call also something is learnt of the destructive effect of the Word on the people: "Go and tell this people: 'Be ever hearing, but never understanding; be ever seeing, but never perceiving'. Make the heart of this people callous; make their ears dull and close their eyes. Otherwise they might see with their eyes, hear with their ears, understand with their hearts, and turn and be healed" (Isaiah 6:9, 10).

According to the prophet Jeremiah too God's capacity as Creator is closely linked to the covenantal relationship with His nation and the land: "These gods, who did not make the heavens and the earth, will perish from the earth and from under the heavens. But God made the earth by his power, he founded the world by his wisdom and stretched out the heavens by his understanding. When he thunders, the waters in the heavens roar, he makes clouds rise from the ends of the earth ... He who is the Portion of Jacob is not like these, for he is the Maker of all things, including Israel, the tribe of his inheritance — the LORD Almighty is his name" (Jeremiah 10:11-13, 16).

The driving of the nation from the land is also linked to this, as emerges from the following verse: "Gather up your belongings to leave the land, you who live under siege. For this is what the LORD says: 'At this time I will hurl out those who live in this land; I will bring distress on them so that they may be captured'."

In these texts, the formula "covenant" is not used, but they clearly deal with the covenant relation between Israel and Yahweh, a relation which is not based on a natural equivalence between the divine realm and the human but on choice and decision, a relation which implies at once an indicative and an imperative, Yahweh's initiative in the making of the covenant as well as His fellowship with His people, and also the fulfilment of His commandments as an expression of this fellowship (see Nicholson 1986:vii, 210, 5, 6).

God's capacity as Creator is also narrowly linked to the day of Yahweh, the day of eschatological judgement. According to Lamentations (cf. 1:12; 2:21, 22) this day did in fact dawn for the people with the fall of Jerusalem in 586 BC and the carrying off of the people in exile (cf. Helberg 1984:18, 22 ff.; 32 ff.). "Jeremiah and Ezekiel had long since rejected any false hope that anything would remain after the divine judgment on Israel. Israel had to bear divine judgment in full, without any human hope of some starting point for a new future" (Noth 1930:280). The people, from their side, did not have anything left to stand on. Geography and history had been severed, and they had broken the Torah, thus also the covenant; election changed into rejection (Lamentations 2:1 ff.; 3:1 ff.). The death of the nation had come (Ezekiel 37). They did not have anything left to fall back on — except the mercy of God, He who is almighty, the Creator, who can do miracles, who can make the incredible happen, who can create life out of destruction and death (cf. Lamentations 5:21, 22; Ezekiel 37) (cf. also Raitt 1977:233).

LAND AND GOD AS CREATOR (AND THEREFORE RE-CREATOR/ LIFEGIVER)

A study of the Major Prophets indicates that it is precisely the vision on the creational capacity of God with his concomitant capacity as Re-Creator that offers a vision on the restoration of the nation and the return to the land (e.g. Isaiah 40:1-11, cf. verse 12 ff.; 66:1 ff., 22; Jeremiah 31:35-37; 33:19-26; Ezekiel 37:1-14; Lamentations 5:21). Isaiah 40:6-8 stands within the framework of God's creational capacity and power (40:5, 12 ff.). The return is described in terms of cosmic proportions (valleys are filled in and mountains levelled, 40:3, 4), and the Word is linked with eternity (40:8).

As Creator God is incomparable and He does the incomparable (Isaiah 40:12 ff.; Jeremiah 10:6). It is precisely in the most terrible circumstances, the dead condition of exile, that the people's vision is elevated through prophecy above the "reality", to the level of what only the Creator can and will do. This is so different from the seemingly real — that which the kings and the gods of the conqueror do (Jeremiah 10:10-16). It is then with this section of the people in exile that God continues His work (Jeremiah 24, 25). He effects life and progress out of ruin. He surmounts the seemingly impossible: the destructive effect of the preaching of His Word (Isaiah 40:6–8) is surmounted by God's salvational personal presence: "Say to the towns of Judah, 'Here is your God! See, the sovereign LORD comes with power ... He tends his flock like a shepherd" (Isaiah 40:10–11).

Where everything seems to be lost for the people, where there is no vision left, God does what only the Creator can do: He creates life through His Spirit (Ezekiel 37:14). The proclamation of the relevant books, is, therefore, totally different from the emphasis which Naidoff (1978:11) puts on a certain equivalence of man with God as an independent being in Genesis 2–3.

The return to the land is accompanied by an essential change in the people so that they will obey God's Torah and live in the right relationship with Him (Isaiah 51:7; Jeremiah 31:31–34; Ezekiel 36:24–28). The LORD Himself will give His Torah in their hearts. He has all the initiative in terms of the return and of the inner change in their lives. This fact is stressed very strongly throughout the relevant prophetic books. The basis for their change lies not in the people, for they have forfeited all — it does not even lie in their faith or trust in God. Even that is lacking (Isaiah 40:27), and has to be effected by God Himself. All initiative emanates from Him, and everything is also directed at Him. Throughout the book of Ezekiel the refrain is there: "And they/you shall know that I am the LORD" (cf., for example, 6:7, 10, 13, 14). God also states it thus: "I do this not for your sakes, but for My sake" (cf. Ezekiel 36:22–8). The most fundamental ground as well as the purpose for the return is God Himself. The land then does not figure so much as *Lebensraum* for the people, but rather as a medium for revelation, as a way to indicate that He is Yahweh (Martens 1972:351–4; also Martens, 1981:6, 242).

As Creator He is almighty, sovereign and omnipotent. He acts towards Israel, His creation, as a potter would towards the pot that he has created (Isaiah 29:16; Jeremiah 18:4 ff.).

Yet, as firm and fixed as His covenant is with day and night, so firm and fixed is the salvation of His people (Jeremiah 33:19–26; 31:35–7). God's capacity as Creator offers His people grounds for firm trust and at the same time room for the mystery of God's actions.

As Creator He has to do with His own creation; He does not let go the work of His hands. He will show Himself as Yahweh to the people by bringing them back to their land and there to care for them (Ezekiel 37:13, 14; Isaiah 57:13) (cf. also Martens 1972:342–3). The need of the people does not pass Him by as Creator (Isaiah 40:27), especially not that of the poor and the helpless (Isaiah 58:7; Jeremiah 22:16). His Word is effective and this includes redemption (Isaiah 55:6 ff.). His capacity as Creator is closely linked with love and compassion (Isaiah 62:2 ff.; Jeremiah 33:2, 11; Ezekiel 39:25, 29, cf. 37:14; Lamentations 3:22–42).

Nothing in the salvation and the return is automatic. These things pose religious demands, moral-ethical demands included, especially with regard to the poor and helpless (Isaiah 58:6, 7; Jeremiah 5:28; Ezekiel 18:12 ff.). Conversion is a demand, although it is at the same time also a gift (Isaiah 55:6; Jeremiah 31:31–34; Ezekiel 36:16–38).

God is the Creator. To Him belongs creation as a whole, as well as in all its parts. For Him the earth is as important as the land. The universalistic intention of the relevant prophets does not abolish the particularistic intention (cf., for example, Hahnart 1983:133 and his reference to Exodus 19:5 in this respect). The Major Prophets' stress on God's creational capacity, and together with that the universalism, does not have the result that the people in exile should relinquish their country, but precisely that they should return to it. The return is not simply a national event but part of Yahweh's exhibition of His creational power and of His universal government. For that reason it is concerned about the welfare of all nations (cf. Isaiah 42:6; 49:6). The one does not suspend the other. God lives in the land and is simultaneously active elsewhere (Ezekiel 1:1, 3; Isaiah 41:1 ff.).

The Creator stands to man and His people in a living relationship; He is the "living God", in contrast to the lifeless idols (Jeremiah 10:10). The living relationship between God and man implies that man cannot simply *be*, but that he receives his life from God, as described in Genesis 2. By the same token man or nation does not simply "live"; he receives a place, a land, and then as much as he can cope with — such as the Garden of Eden following the creation of man. It is at one and the same time a place which man can nurture and where he can be safe.

The land does not belong to Israel, but to God (Isaiah 57:13; Jeremiah 2:7; 16:18; 50:11; Ezekiel 36:5) (cf. e.g. Von Waldow 1974:495, 496). The ground for ownership of the land is not creation, but the Creator. The people receive the land as a heritage (Jeremiah 12:14; 17:4).

The living relationship between Creator and creature is jeopardised right from the beginning. This contracts in the objectivisation and absolutisation of issues. The tree of knowledge is seen as something which can of itself offer knowledge — God, and the relationship with Him, have been left out of the picture. Whether and how the Torah has to be brought into conjunction with the tree of knowledge is uncertain, as we have already seen. It is clear, however, that Israel, in history, dealt with religion, including the Torah, formalistically. In this regard the prohibition would therefore be valid: Don't touch it! Do not try to dispose of it and to exploit it for personal purposes!

The people were also guilty of the same sort of objectivisation and absolutisation with regard to their place (land and city of Jerusalem), their history, and covenant and election. Thence the disillusionment which Amos prophesied (5:18–20), and about which Lamentations lamented because it did in fact dawn with the fall of Jerusalem and the carrying off of the people into exile.

In contrast to the formalism and the absolutisation of things by the people there are God's actions, which serve in actual fact to bind Him very closely with men, but not with things or places. The following statement of Werblowsky, as quoted by Stegemann (1983:161) can therefore only be true in a relative sense, namely, "that the biblical God does not in the first place have a 'people' to whom he then provides a suitable land, but that he, universally, acts as the owner of a 'land', in which he promised to make small groups of 'clans' into a 'big people'." God is not, in the Old Testament, called the God of the land or of Jerusalem or of another place (except when a heathen speaks, 2 Chronicles 17:26, etc., and in Genesis 31:13, where there is mention of "the God of Bethel", but as *hā'ēl bêt-'ēl* and where one should rather read in conjunction with the Septuagint: "the God who appeared to you"; cf. van Selms (1967:116). The expression "You are my people" also occurs much more frequently than "The land is mine", or something similar (cf. also Martens 1972:319). In contrast to this God *is* called the God of people, e.g. "the God of Abraham, Isaac and Jacob" (Genesis 28:13; Exodus 3:16), and the "God of Israel" (2 Samuel 7:25, 26). Yahweh primarily links Himself to people, and not to places and things. He is a personal God, and for Him the important thing is the relationship with people. It is undoubtedly this fact which created the theological atmosphere for the origination of the synagogue, which Haran (1983:145) regards as one of the greatest innovations in the history of religions.

One has to note that the land in Israel, just like the existence of the people Israel, should not be linked directly to God's creational activity (Genesis 1, 2; cf. 12). Werblowsky (1983:4) maintains that God's relation to the land is analogous to that to His people and is determined by election. Buber (1974:66) goes too far when he maintains that the election of the land is a part of the creational act. The land is linked, however, with the history, with God's special work in history, and in conjunction with God's activity as Creator. This emerges from the link of the universal history (Genesis 2, 3 ff.) with that of Israel (Genesis 12 ff.).

Seeing that God is the Creator and that everything belongs to Him, stands under His domination and is in His service, and to the extent that this is the case, all these things do have a place.

Marquardt (1975:68) justly maintains that just as it is wrong to bind God to a land, so is it also wrong to see God as an alien, *Heimat*-less God who is unfaithful to his own promises. Kaiser (1981:302) states that "there is more to the promise of the land than religious significance, and theological meaning". He links this with the millenium (p. 311), a matter which cannot be discussed in this paper (cf. also Townsend 1985:333, 4).

Diepold (1972:187, 188) also points out that living in the land is constitutive for Israel's existence. To be outside the land means judgement. But a secular existence is also excluded. Land is only possible as theological existence if Israel should realise that it is the people of God and acknowledge Yahweh as the only Lord.

In the light of the foregoing, some remarks can be made about the land, man and divine omnipotence.

LAND, MAN AND DIVINE OMNIPOTENCE

However important the land might be, the central preaching of the Major Prophets and of Lamentations, as is the case in the rest of the Old Testament, is not a land theology, but rather a "creator theology" — if, by way of explication, I may speak in terms of such a terminology. It is, for example, a deficiency in the excellent book of Brueggemann's (1978) that he does state that it is always, in the Old Testament, a question of land *with* God, but that his stress of land in this relationship is dominant. In the development of his approach much less emphasis is laid on the fact that the concern in the first place is with God personally, as in a relationship between a father and a child.

God's being a father and the receipt of the land as an inheritance, are closely linked to each other, as Brueggemann (1974:156 ff.) clearly indicates on the basis of Jeremiah 3:19–25. In this way, too, lordship and return are closely linked and this also indicates why creational traditions are important for II Isaiah, "i.e. Yahweh rules chaos, and lets us see that talk about return is in fact theological affirmation about Yahweh's lordship" (Brueggemann 1972:35).

Brueggemann (idem.) also says that "exile was not simply displacement from land but it was the experience of the end of creation, the exhaustion of salvation history, the demise of king, temple, city, land, and all those supports which gave structure and meaning to life. Put in current terminology it was the experience of the death of God. And when Yahweh's lordship is no longer visible, life returns to the way it was before he ordered it, chaotic (Isaiah 45:18, 19)".

In this regard one has to note that everything had in fact collapsed for Israel. The incredible had happened. Israel, however, did not experience these events as "the death of God", but rather as *the act of God*. It is stated with great emphasis in the relevant prophets and in Lamentations. The chaos which starts for Israel (cf. Genesis 1:2 and Jeremiah 4:23 ff., where there is mention of *tōhû wābōhû;* cf. also Isaiah 34:11 in regard to Edom), is not a chaos confronting God, but the fruit of God's judgement. God does not rule only in a struggle against the chaos, but He also rules the chaos, it is in His service. He is therefore not bound by this consideration to save the nation.

The fact that God as the Creator cares for the people, or for man, does not imply that they have a claim on progress based on merit. The fact that God saved His people from exile is something closely linked to the deliverance from Egypt, and the fact that God cares for the poor and the helpless and takes on their cause gives nobody, neither the nation, the poor, nor the helpless, the right to such salvation and the right before God to a demand that their situation should change.

The history of the calling of Moses — 40 years after he himself had wanted to act, and now at a time when he does not want to do so any longer — as well as the history of the return from exile, stresses God's initiative in this situation, as well as His omnipotence to act as and when He wants to. In both cases Israel was both unable and unwilling to act. Furthermore, after the exodus from Egypt Israel was guided to the desert, where for a whole generation long they suffered great hardship. God is the Creator and therefore acts sovereignly in His dealings with His people. Added to that it is second nature in man (and also of the people) to such an extent to sin that confession of guilt has to be foremost, rather than demands or claims. God wants a relationship in which things turn on Himself, a Father and child relationship, not one in which man is concerned about possible gifts.

Sauter (1978:552 ff.) rightly criticises the theological handling of the exodus motif in political ethics in which the exodus event is seen as the universal victory over each *Fremdbestimmung* realised in most of the various liberation experiences. "Exodus" and "liberation" are understood allegorically here: they encompass the whole problem of the relationship of man and reality which comprehends the whole of mankind. Sauter here refers to J. Moltmann's approach of the church as *Exodus-gemeinde*, which is not a communion of the faithful and which does not derive its strength from the upholding of the transmission of faith, but which attempts to keep up with the dynamic forces of movement of contemporary times (*den Gleichklang mit den dynamischen Bewegungs-kraften der Zeitgeschichte zu erlangen*). More: the *Exulanten* place themselves to the forefront of these forces and through this anticipatory *Vergegenwärtigung* bring into effect the course of a better history. Sauter (1978:554) also refers to Gustavo Gutiérrez, who in his *Theology of Liberation* sees the exploited and the oppressed of the Latin American class society as descendants of Israel under foreign oppression. In the last place Sauter refers (p. 555) to Ernst Bloch, who does not veil the foregoing points of view with biblical reminiscences, but states clearly that with the exodus there is not the beginning of a history, in which the people of God are guided by God, but that it is a moment of the history of God Himself.

In all three cases mentioned, apart from the deficiency noted by Sauter, there is a point of departure in which the creational capacity of God, as outlined in the Major Prophets and Lamentations, does not come into its own. In these scriptural passages the concern is with God as *the* omnipotent and personal God, who has all initiative, and before whom His people should stand actively working in accordance with the demands of the Torah, but also prayerfully and waiting, and in this sense with firm hope — hope vested in God, who is true, and also merciful and full of compassion towards those who know themselves as poor and sinful men, without any claim, but with God's grace and covenantal troth as a basis for their pleas (cf. e.g. Lamentations 3:19 ff.).

The emphasis in the Major Prophets then lies not on the relationship of God to Israel, but God-Israel-exile-land. Exile is part of the harsh reality, and it is not seen as something for which the people can reproach God — rather, the obverse is true. In this regard Brueggemann's (1978:13, 14) statements are true: "The Bible is the story of God's people with God's land ... But Israel's experience is of being in and belonging to a land never fully given, never quite secured ... Israel is always on the move from land to landlessness, from landlessness to land, from life to death, from death to life".

CONCLUSION

The Major Prophets and Lamentations, as the rest of the Old Testament, testify to what we might call an internal line of tension. God is sovereign and omnipotent. He gives the land to man, but He can also take away (from the Garden of Eden), or send away (out of the land). At the same time, however, He offers signs of His grace — clothing, following the débâcle in the garden, His promises following the carrying off of the people in exile. There is a strong eschatological accent, a strong element of expectation: the people do not really possess the land, and yet it is as good as if it were in their possession. They experience alienation, and this is attributed to their sinfulness, as the alienation of man following the expulsion from the garden. This alienation can be suspended through hope and expectation, as in Abraham who received the promise of the land and yet remained a stranger in it. The hope and the expectation are always accompanied by prayer, with a pleading before God. It remains a matter of Creator towards creature, and this is a matter of a living, personal relationship and the active practice of it. We do not have to do with a creational theology in which the creation constitutes the point of departure and the centre, but with the Word about the Creator, which calls us to faith in Him. As Creator of heaven and earth, and as Ruler over the creation and over history, all things belong to Him, and He made man as king of the earth (Genesis 1:26–28; Psalm 8). Yet He did not place man in a place without frontiers, but in a specific place, in a garden. In the same way He placed His people in a specific place, in the land. There man has to serve Him in accordance with the Word, more specifically the Torah, in a living relationship of the covenant, as the people elected by Him, to the blessing of all the nations, to their service.

Geography, history, Torah, Word, election, covenant are all important factors with regard to the important meaning of land in the Old Testament. They obtain their distinctive values but are also relativised, through God as Creator who is the purpose and the basis and the meaning of the land, as the focus of the Major Prophets and Lamentations indicates. He brings His people to their land so that all can know that He is Yahweh, the living, sovereign, omnipotent God, whose presence is salvational (cf. Exodus 3:12–15). He is the God who has compassion for His creation, especially for man, being part of a corrupt, sinful world, more especially even for man in distress. In this His people have a special place in the promised land — and at the same time a special task of service.

BIBLIOGRAPHY

Y. Aharoni, *The Land of the Bible. A Historical Geography,* Tr. by A.F. Rainey. Burns & Oates, London, 1979.

J. Bright, *The Kingdom of God.* Abingdon Press, Nashville, 1953.

W. Brueggemann, "Weariness, Exile and Chaos. A motif in royal theology." *The Catholic Biblical Quarterly,* 34, pp. 19–38, 1972.

W. Brueggemann, "Israel's sense of place in Jeremiah." In J.J. Jackson and M. Kessler, (eds.). *Rhetorical Criticism. Essays in Honor of James Muilenburg,* 1974, pp. 149–165.

W. Brueggemann, *The Land. Place as Gift, Promise and Challenge in Biblical Faith.* SPCK, London, 1978.

M. Buber, *Israel und Palästina. Zur Geschichte einer Idee.* Artemis Verlag, Zürich, 1950.

Caquot, *debaš. ThWAT.* Volume 2, 1974, pp. 135–9.

R.P. Carroll, *From Chaos to Covenant. Uses of Prophecy in the Book of Jeremiah,* SCM Press, 1981.

B.S. Childs, *Introduction to the Old Testament as Scripture.* London, SCM Press, 1979.

R.E. Clements, *God and Temple. The Idea of the Divine Presence in Ancient Israel.* Basil Blackwell, Oxford, 1965.

D.J.A. Clines, "The Tree of Knowledge and the Law of Yahweh", *V.T.* 24, 1974, pp. 8–14.

W.D. Davies, *The Gospel and the Land,* University of California Press, Los Angeles, 1974.

P. Diepold, *Israel's Land.* Verlag W. Kohlhammer, Stuttgart, Berlin, Köln, Mainz, 1972.

I. Engnell, "'Knowledge' and 'Life' in the creation story," *V.T.,* Suppl. 3. E.J. Brill, Leiden, 1955.

N.K. Gottwald, *The Tribes of Yahweh. A Sociology of the Religion of Liberated Israel 1250–1050 BC,* Orbis Books, Maryknoll, 1979.

R. Hahnart, "Das Land in der spätnachexilischen Prophetie." In R. Strecker, (ed.). *Das Land Israel in Biblischer Zeit,* Jerusalem-Symposium 1981, Vandenhoeck und Ruprecht, Göttingen, 1983.

M. Haran, "Priestertum, Tempeldienst und Gebet", In *Das Land Israel in Biblischer Zeit,* Göttingen, Jerusalem-Symposium 1981, Vandenhoeck und Ruprecht, 1983.

J.L. Helberg, *Die Here Regeer. Openbaringslyn deur die Ou Testament,* NG-Kerkboekhandel, Pretoria, 1983.

J.L. Helberg, *Klaagliedere: Ontnugtering en Hoop,* Potchefstroom, 1984.

W.C. Kaiser, Jr., "The promised land: A biblical-historical view", *Bibliotheca Sacra,* 138, 549, January-March 1981, pp. 303-12.

J.D. Levenson, *Sinai and Zion. An Entry into the Jewish Bible,* Winston Press, Minneapolis-Chicago-New York, 1985.

F.W. Marquardt, *Die Bedeutung der Biblischen Landverheissungen für die Christen. Theologische Existenz Heute,* Chr. Kaiser Verlag, 1954.

F.W. Marquardt, *Die Juden und ihr Land,* Siebenstern Taschenbuch Verlag, Hamburg, 1975.

E.A. Martens, *Motivations for the Promise of Israel's Restoration to the Land in Jeremiah and Ezekiel,* University Microfilms International, London, 1972.

E.A. Martens, *God's Design. A Focus on Old Testament Theology,* Baker Book House, Grand Rapids, 1981.

G. Mendenhall, *The Tenth Generation. The Origins of Biblical Tradition,* Johns Hopkins University Press, Baltimore, 1973.

E.D. Naidoff, "A man to work the soil. A new interpretation of Genesis 2-3", *JSOT* 5, 1978, pp. 2-14.

E.W. Nicholson, *God and His Temple. Covenant and Theology in the Old Testament,* Clarendon Press, Oxford, 1986.

M. Noth, "Das System der Zwölf Stämme Israels", *BWANT* IV. I. Stuttgart, 1930.

M. Noth, "The Jerusalem catastrophe of 587 BC and its significance for Israel." *The Laws of the Pentateuch, and Other Studies* (translation of *Gesammelte Studien zum Alten Testament,* München, 1957), 1967, pp. 260-80.

Annemarie Ohler, *Israel, Volk und Land. Zur Geschichte der Wechselseitigen Beziehungen Zwischen Israel und Seinem Land in Alttestamentlicher Zeit,* Verlag Katholisches Bibelwerk CMBH, Stuttgart, 1979.

M. Ottosson, "Eden and the land of promise", Paper read at the 1986 Jerusalem Congress of the International Organisation for the Study of the Old Testament, To be published in *V.T.*

L. Perlitt, "Motive und Schichten der Landtheologie im Deuteronomium", G. Strecker (ed.). *Das Land Israel in Biblischer Zeit,* Jerusalem-Symposium 1981, Vandenhoeck und Ruprecht, Göttingen, 1983.

T.M. Raitt, *A Theology of Exile. Judgment/Deliverance in Jeremiah and Ezekiel,* Fortress Press, Philadelphia, 1977.

R. Rendtorff, *Israel und sein Land,* Chr. Kaiser Verlag, München, 1975.

H.P. Santmire, *The Travail of Nature. The Ambiguous Ecological Promise of Christian Theology,* Fortress Press, Philadelphia, 1985.

G. Sauter, "'Exodus' und 'Befreiung' als theologische Metaphern. Ein Beispiel zur Kritik von Allegorese und missverstandene Analogien in der Ethik", *Evangelische Theologie,* 38(33), Chr. Kaiser Verlag, München, 1978, pp. 538-59.

H.H. Schmidt, "Creation, righteousness and salvation: 'Creation Theology' as the broad horizon of biblical theology", B.W. Anderson, (ed.). *Creation in the Old Testament.* Fortress Press, Philadelphia, London, SPCK, 1984, pp. 102-17. (Translation of *Schöpfung, Gerechtigkeit und Heil.* ZTK 70.1973, 1-19.)

U.E. Simon, "Martin Buber and the interpretation of the prophets". *Israel's Prophetic Tradition. Essays in Honour of Peter Ackroyd.* Cambridge University Press, 1982.

H. Stegemann, "'Das Land' in der Tempelrolle und in anderen Texten aus den Qumranfunden", G. Strecker, (ed.). *Das Land Israel in Biblischer Zeit,* Jerusalem-Symposium 1981, Vandenhoeck und Ruprecht, Göttingen, 1983.

J.L. Townsend, "Fulfilment of the land promise in the Old Testament", *Bibliotheca Sacra* 142(568), 1985, pp. 320–37.

A. Van Selms, *Genesis Deel II,* G.F. Callenbach N.V., POT Nijkerk, 1967.

A.S. Van der Woude, "Genesis en Exodus. Beschouwingen over de plaats van de schepping in de oudtestamentische Theologie", *Kerk en Theologie,* 20, 1969, pp. 1–17.

G. Von Rad, "Verheissenes Land und Jahwes Land im Hexateuch", *Gesammelte Studien zum Alten Testament,* München, 1958.

H.E. Von Waldow, "Israel and her land: some theological considerations", *A Light to my Path. Old Testament Studies in Honour of Jacob M. Myers,* edited by H.N. Bream, R.D. Heim, C.A. Moore, Temple University Press, Philadelphia, 1974.

Th. C. Vriezen, *Hoofdlijnen der Theologie van het Oude Testament,* H. Veenman en Zonen, Wageningen, 1966.

H.N. Wallace, *The Eden Narrative,* Scholars Press, Atlanta, 1985.

M. Weinfeld, "The extent of the promised land — the status of Transjordan", G. Strecker, (ed.). *Das Land Israel in Biblischer Zeit,* Jerusalem-Symposium 1981, Vandenhoeck und Ruprecht, Göttingen, 1983.

R.J.Z. Werblowsky, "Das 'Land' in den Religionen." In G. Strecker (ed.), *Das Land in Biblischer Zeit,* Jerusalem-Symposium 1981, Vandenhoeck und Ruprecht, Göttingen, 1983.

H. Wildberger, "Israel und sein Land", *Evangelische Theologie,* 16, 1956, pp. 404–22.

H. Wildberger, 'mn. THAT. Chr. Kaiser Verlag, München, Theologischer Verlag, 192, Zürich, 1971.

W. Zimmerli, "The 'land' in the pre-exilic and early post exilic prophets", *Understanding the Word. Essays in Honor of B.W. Anderson,* edited by J.T. Butler, E.W. Conrad, B.C. Ollenburger, University, Sheffield, 1985. German equivalent in G. Strecker, (ed.), *Das Land Israel in Biblischer Zeit,* Jerusalem-Symposium 1981, Vandenhoeck und Ruprecht, Göttingen, 1983.

Part III
Aspects of Attraction to the Holy Land

7 Medieval pilgrims, the Holy Land and its image in European civilisation

Aryeh Grabois

Etymologically, the term "pilgrimage" (*peregrinatio* in classical Latin) means the wandering of people across the fields *(per agere),* indicating vagabondage; accordingly, people who left established society in order to practise this vagrancy, whatever the reason, were practically excluded from the legal system of the Roman Empire and their lives were put at the mercy of the ordained society. Adopted by early Christianity, the term changed in sense from pejorative to positive, to mean the journey of those faithful who left their families and the ordained life in order to search for salvation in union with God. The wanderings of these *peregrini* of the early Church were, however, not directed to any concrete point; ideologically, they were supposed to imitate the vagrancy of the Old Testament prophets, as well as the behaviour of the contemporary *anachoretes,* who retired to the desert in search of salvation.[1]

The spread of Christianity in the third and fourth centuries brought about important changes in religious practice, owing to its adaptation to the cultural syncretism of Roman civilisation. One of these changes was the journeying to established places of the cult; interest was aroused in the holy places, such as the graves of saints and martyrs, as well as in the geographical roots of the religion, symbolised by the tomb of Jesus Christ in Jerusalem, the "Holy Sepulchre", as well as other sites related to the tradition of His life and deeds, or to the legacy of the Old Testament. Thus, in the fourth century, the Roman province of Palestine became the Holy Land of Christianity,[2] having imitated already the manifestations of attachment by the Jews to its historical traditions.

These changes also affected pilgrimage. Pilgrims seeking spiritual dialogue with God gradually abandoned the practice of "wandering in the fields" and went instead to sanctuaries and shrines for their devotional exercises. Among these shrines, they particularly visited the tombs of saints and martyrs, such as the basilica of St Peter's on the Vatican hill at Rome, praying there for the intercession of the saint in their favour. Their vows naturally brought them to the Holy Land, where they tried to imitate, in the steps of Jesus Christ, the evangelical style of life.

From the fourth century, pilgrimages to the Holy Land became frequent and the number of pilgrims, arriving even from the remote provinces of the Western Roman Empire, increased. This phenomenon is connected with the settlement in Jerusalem of Helen, the mother of Emperor Constantine, and the building of the basilica of the Holy Sepulchre, which provided the holy city with the shrine that became the destination of pilgrimages and the object of the spiritual devotions of pilgrims.[3]

This revolutionary change in the nature of the pilgrimage did not occur without opposition, however, especially from the Greek fathers of the Church. Gregory of Nyssa, for example, considered such an implementation of pilgrimage as idolatrous, diametrically opposed to its spiritual purposes, and vehemently criticised it in his letter.[4] This conservative attitude lost ground in the same century, however, both because the pilgrims conformed to the new trends and because the Palestinian prelates, supported by the political establishment, favoured the diffusion of the fame of the shrines of the Holy Land. The *Onomasticon,* compiled by Eusibius of Caesarea and translated into Latin by St Jerome, became the first guide for pilgrims visiting the Holy Land and, thereafter, the basis of the "Holy Geography".[5]

The descriptions of their travels and of the Holy Land compiled by the fourth century pilgrims reveal their attitude to this new kind of pilgrimage, which was entirely different to the traditional journeys to the East undertaken by the Roman aristocracy. The Anonymous Pilgrim of Bordeaux (333),[6] the Spanish Abbess Egeria (382–384)[7] and the Roman Lady Paula, whose account had been written by St Jerome at the end of the century,[8] clearly expressed their spiritual concerns in the holy places of Palestine and Sinai. They combined biblical and evangelical traditions in their devotional exercises, but avoided the large Romanised cities, which reminded them of the environment they had left, despite personal relations with some of the provincial magistrates who cared for their lodgings and guides, as emphasised by Egeria in her beautiful relation.[9] Normative behaviour, which became stereotypical, brought pilgrims to omit any reference to their sojourns in cities or palaces, emphasising rather the holiness of the sanctuaries visited and even expressing their disgust at such a manner of life. Writing about Paula's visit to Jerusalem, Jerome states that she declined the offer of one of her relatives, the Roman governor of the Antonia fortress, to be lodged in this aristocratic palace where he had prepared an apartment for her; instead, she preferred a humble cell for the period of her devotions at Jerusalem, before she finally retired to the "wilderness" of Bethlehem.[10]

Thus the spirituality of the pilgrimage became the factor that shaped the "Holy Geography" of pilgrims. Pilgrimages took the form of ritual processions to shrines and other holy sites, avoiding the Romanised cities of Palestine, as well as any reminders of contemporary realities. Moreover, the pilgrimage became the frame of the pilgrims' spiritual perspectives, rooted in the past and informed by the sacred history of the Old and New Testaments. The purpose of their pilgrimage was spiritual union with Divinity and its Revelation since the era of the Patriarchs to the time of Christ, and they identified themselves with this past[11] to such an extent that they actualised it, to become, at least for the period of their pilgrimage, their spiritual present. In so doing, the early medieval pilgrims were oblivious to the fundamental changes that had taken place in the Holy

Land between the Hellenistic and Byzantine periods. They really believed that the sites they visited and worshipped were biblically authentic. For example, the vineyards along the road connecting the small town of Jenin to Naplouse became the famous vineyard where Naboth was murdered by Queen Isabel; and there they would meditate on royal tyranny and the merited punishment inflicted on King Ahab's dynasty.[12] Or, while visiting Nazareth, still a Jewish village until the end of the sixth century, they would worship in the small Byzantine church of the Annunciation, believing that it had been the house of the Virgin Mary. According to the testimony of the Anonymous Pilgrim of Piacenza (580), pilgrims venerated there the "study" where the boy Jesus had learned the Sacred Books, which they saw attached by a chain to the wall "in order to prevent from the Jewish inhabitants to take it away".[13] Of course, they did not object to the fact that the so-called genuine copy of Isaiah's prophecy had been a Greek version of the Sepuagint, adopted by the Byzantine church.

The behavioural norms of the pilgrims brought about a voluntary segregation of Palestinian Christianity from the official establishment. Pilgrims tended to congregate in special hospices, where they lived together during the period of sojourn in the Holy Land. In these *xenodochia,* either at Jerusalem or in the Jordan valley, pilgrims would compare their experiences of holiness and develop a particular image of the country and its sacred history. In Jericho, for example, they lodged in the so-called "House of Rahab", which according to the Pilgrim of Piacenza was converted into a hospice, while her "bed-room" became the chapel. Pilgrims visited the nearby well, which had allegedly been blessed by Prophet Eliseus to be the source of the oasis's fertility, as well as a field blessed by Christ which yielded two crops per year.[14]

The Arab conquest of Palestine brought about fundamental changes, both in the nature of pilgrimage and in pilgrims' attitudes to the Holy Land. The Greek-Byzantine element lost its dominant position in the country, and the new Muslim establishment was obviously not interested in protecting pilgrimage. Moreover, the process of Islamisation created a gap between pilgrims and the Palestinian authorities and population. Many of the shrines that were venerated by pilgrims during the Byzantine period, especially in Transjordan and Sinai, lost their Christian character and became inaccessible to Western pilgrims; some of the Palestinian sanctuaries, such as the Temple area in Jerusalem and the tombs of the Patriarchs at Hebron, which were formerly the destinations of Jewish and Christian pilgrims alike, were converted into Muslim shrines.[15] These changes limited the pilgrimages geographically to the extent that pilgrims were restricted to the main roads connecting the Syrian harbours with Jerusalem and Galilee. Although they were obviously concerned by the activities of the Muslim government, the pilgrims practically ignored them, having been alienated not only by religious but also by linguistic barriers. They regarded the Muslim activities as anti-Christian persecutions, as related for example by the Anglo-Saxon pilgrim Willibald, in the first half of the eighth century.[16]

Fundamental transformations in Western European society also had an impact, both on the nature of pilgrimage and the background of the pilgrims. From the seventh century, most pilgrims were of Germanic origin. As a result they did not inherit the classical cultural legacy and had no affinities with Palestinian Christianity. Moreover, they were more sensible to stories dealing with miracles and supernatural intercession, as manifested by the new trends of the cult of saints and the use of relics as a concretisation of devotion.[17] Accordingly, these pilgrims added another perspective to their wanderings, that of praying for visual manifestations of their faith, such as the miraculous healing of diseases. Part of their pilgrimage was devoted to the acquisition of relics, which they would carry to their home countries in order to perpetuate their contact with the shrine visited and the adored saint. The result was a diffusion of Palestinian relics in Western Europe and, accordingly, the development of trade in these relics. The pilgrims' relations of their travels became an important source for the authority and fame of such relics, and some of these documents, such as the *Vita sancti Genesii,* written at the beginning of the ninth century by an anonymous author, attest to this kind of trade by pilgrims.[18]

Thus under Arab domination (636–1099) political and ethnical factors brought about a total alienation between pilgrims and Palestinian society. This served to strengthen the spiritual attachment of pilgrims to the Holy Land, an attachment which during the Roman and Byzantine periods had caused such a severe lack of interest of pilgrims in the realities of their own age. These pilgrims ignored not only the Muslim régime, but also the Eastern Christians — the Syrians — who spoke Aramaic or Arabic and were total strangers to them.

The pilgrims were able to maintain this segregation through the establishment at Jerusalem in the ninth century of a hospice exclusively for Western pilgrims, where they could sojourn in their own environment and speak their own "romanic" language. Here they were provided with guides, as described by the Frankish monk Bernard in 870,[19] and were able to divorce themselves completely from contemporary life. Their isolation was compounded in the eleventh century when, under the impact of the Millenarian Messianic trends in Western Europe, the number of pilgrims increased and they began to travel in larger groups.[20] As a result, the individual pilgrim had no contact with other travellers or local inhabitants, to the point where his ignorance of real conditions and events was no longer a question of choice.

However, the troubles that affected Palestine in the eleventh century eventually made it impossible for the individual pilgrim to remain unaware of them. Whether these troubles were the consequence of the policy of the Fātimid Caliph Al-Hakam, or the result of the struggle for the domination of Palestine between the Fātimids and the Seljuk Turks, the pilgrims regarded them as anti-Christian persecutions. Their accounts of these "persecutions" intersperse their descriptions of the shrines and sites of the Holy Land, and these rather stereotyped stories were diffused throughout Western Europe. Some of the pilgrims, such as the Cluniac chronicler Ralph Glaber,[21] even attributed the Al-Hakam troubles to an alleged instigation by Jews. Such stories contributed to the rise of anti-Semitic feeling in Western Europe, and to riots and expulsions of Jews from France and Germany, culminating in the violent attacks on the Jewish communities during the First Crusade.

Other stories relating to the struggle between the Fātimids and Seljuks were used as propaganda for the Crusade; pilgrims travelling on the road between Ramleh and Jerusalem unwittingly penetrated battlefields on several occasions. They were convinced that such ambushes were set specifically to prevent pilgrimage and their accounts are fraught with descriptions of the terrible persecutions against Christians and pleas addressed to the Western knights "to rescue the Christian brothers" in the Holy Land.[22]

The Crusader period may be described as the "golden age" of medieval pilgrimage to the Holy Land. With the foundation of the Latin Kingdom in Jerusalem, a political, social and religious structure was established with which Western pilgrims were able to identify in terms of customs, language and cultural similarities. The opening of the Mediterranean for Western navigation improved transportation, especially after the conquest of Acre by the Crusaders in 1104. Regular shipping lines from Italy and Provence to Acre were established and used by pilgrims instead of the difficult roads. Ideologically, the new realm was considered to be the result of a peregrinatory expedition, because of the common terminology of pilgrimage and Crusade.[23]

Despite these affinities, the basic difference between the Crusaders, whose concerns were material and their behaviour profane, and the pilgrims, whose aims were spiritual,[24] created from the very beginning of the Latin Kingdom a chasm between these two groups. The pilgrims did not consider the kingdom to be the heir of the biblical or Utopian realm of Israel, and they deliberately omitted from their accounts descriptions of the Kingdom of Jerusalem. The pilgrims' Holy Land did not include places belonging to the Crusaders' states that had no biblical or evangelical connections. The city of Acre, for example, which was the centre of Crusader society, the harbour of their arrival, and the town where they first met with the people of the Holy Land and stayed several times during their sojourn in the country, is completely absent from the pilgrims' accounts.[25] Their spiritual Holy Land began some miles from Acre, either at Sephorie, on the road to Nazareth, or at Haifa and Mount Carmel. In effect, the geographical boundaries of their Holy Land were the same as those of the pilgrims of the Byzantine period.

The pilgrims of the Crusader period were interested primarily in the shrines, which for them were visual symbols of the sacred history of the Holy Land. This is evident from the writings of the Anglo-Saxon Saewulf in 1102; he dedicated the major part of his account to a description of the Holy places and their condition and of his disembarkment in the stormy port of Jaffa, and contented himself with the remark that King Baldwin, the ruler of the Crusader realm, was "the flower of kingship".[26] His compatriot, Godric of Finchale, emphasised a few years later the exemplary behaviour of ascetic monks and did not find it necessary to even mention the existence of the Crusader kingdom, which did not correspond to his ideal of *contemptus mundi* (the "relinquishing of this world").[27]

The accounts of the Germans John of Würzburg and Theoderic in the second half of the twelfth century represent the same trends.[28] Although they include in their travelogues some information about the Crusader kingdom — John of Würzburg even criticised the Franks for forging the history of the realm by deliberately eliminating any evidence of the Germans' role in the conquest of Jerusalem — they emphasised that their real interest was in the shrines and ritual processions.[29]

It is clear from their accounts that the pilgrims emphatically believed that the monuments they visited were situated on the same sites mentioned in the Bible and, moreover, that they were in fact the original buildings. There is no doubt that they owed this kind of information to their local guides, as well as to the accounts of earlier pilgrims which they had read before embarking on their own pilgrimage. One such monument was the Dome of the Rock at Jerusalem, converted in 1104 by the Crusaders into the Church of *Templum Domini*. The pilgrims firmly believed that this was Herod's Temple, and that they were venerating the very place where Christ and His disciples had been active. Although they were well aware of the destruction of the Temple by Emperor Titus in AD 70, they believed that it had been restored. John of Würzburg wrote that "some pretent it had been restored by St. Helen, the mother of Emperor Constantine; others, by Justinianus; others by Emperor Heraclius, in the honour of the Holy Cross; others, finally, by a certain Emperor of Memphis in Egypt, in the honour of *Allah Kebir,* to wit the Almighty God in order to be venerated there by devoted people of all the languages".[30]

This firm attachment to the biblical legacy even brought pilgrims to believe that new cities occupied the sites mentioned in the Holy Books. Thus, for instance, Ramleh, a city founded by Arab conquerors in the seventh century, became the famous *Ramathayim Tsophim,* the town of the Prophet Samuel.[31] It is important to note that this identification was also accepted by contemporary Jewish travellers, such as Benjamin of Tudela, who among other confusions of biblical sites, took Caesarea for Gath, "the city of the Philistines".[32] This confusion in the Holy Geography extended too to the misinterpretation of biblical verses: Psalm 120:5, translated into Latin as *Habitavi cum habitantibus Cedar,* led Christian pilgrims to believe that, during his wanderings, King David had inhabited "a most excellent city named Cedar" and they duly searched its location in the eastern Galilee, where basaltic rocks were the source of building stones in a "tenebruous" shape, corresponding to their misunderstanding of Kedar as meaning "tenebruous" instead of "nomads".[33]

Compared to Christian pilgrims, Jewish travellers of the same period were far more realistic in their outlook and observations. Their aim was essentially the same as that of the pilgrims — to visit the Holy places mentioned in the Old Testament such as the Mishna and the tombs of the Sages — and they too were ready to accept the leading of guides who misinterpreted locations and identifications of sites, such as the tombs of the Prophet Jonah or of Zipporah, Moses' wife.[34] They were, however, attentive to the condition of the Jewish settlements in the Holy Land. Benjamin of Tudela and Petakhiyah of Regensburg provided some valuable information about the Jewish inhabitants of Eretz Yisrael, including the important community of Acre, with its leaders, as well as the Keraites and Samaritans.[35] Indeed, like the Christian pilgrims, these travellers were not concerned with the Crusaders' kingdom, although their reasons were different to those of the pilgrims; they regarded the Crusader régime as a foreign domination over the land of the Fathers, and rejected its political and social structures as well as its religious practices, which they considered to be "idolatry".[36]

In the thirteenth century, pilgrims' attitudes to the Holy Land changed. While aiming primarily at the same Holy Geography as their predecessors, they began to take a more practical look at the realities of their age. Two main reasons might be attributed to this change. The first is connected with the political conditions prevailing in the country after the Third Crusade. The Crusade had resulted in a division between the Crusader kingdom, which was concentrated in the coastal area and mainly around Acre, its new capital, and the inner areas, which were dominated by the Muslims and which included most of the Holy sites. Accordingly, the pilgrims were compelled to spend the major part of their time in the Crusader area, where they were spiritually unfulfilled, while their travels to the traditional Holy sites were limited to very brief devotional visits to the shrines, when they were at the mercy of their Muslim guards.[37]

The second reason is connected with the changes in the perception of the world which occurred in Western Europe under the impact of the intellectual achievements of the "twelfth century Renaissance" and travels to the East, particularly to the Mongol Empire, which contributed to the creation of a new *imago mundi* or "vision of the world". With the rise of universities[38] "curiosity", which until the beginning of the thirteenth century had been considered a sin by theologians, received a new sense — the desire to acquire knowledge. The pilgrims were swept up in this new wave of thinking, and began not only to perceive these realities, but to include references to some of them in their pilgrimage relations, in addition to the traditional spiritual content of their writings.

The spiritual aims of the thirteenth century pilgrim remained unchanged, still centring around the sacred history of the Holy Land as represented by the shrines and holy sites. In 1217 the German pilgrim Thietmar expressed his disappointment at having to wait for more than a month at Acre, "the city of vice", until a truce had been arranged with the Muslims and he could make the journey to the "genuine land of Christ and the children of Israel".[39] At the same time, James of Vitry, bishop of Acre, who bitterly criticised the Crusader society of his bishopric for its wicked behaviour, wrote to his former colleagues, the masters of the University of Paris, that he still had not been able to visit the real and desired Holy Land, namely Nazareth, representing the New Testament, and Mount Carmel, signifying the legacy of the Old Testament.[40] For the thirteenth century pilgrims, perhaps under the influence of the Jewish Mishnaic traditions, it was evident that Acre, the capital of the Crusader kingdom, did not belong to the Holy Land but, according to the biblical division of the land, to Phoenicia, situated as it was according to Burchard of Mount Sion in 1283 "near the boundaries of the Asserites though it had never been part of the Holy Land".[41]

The brief visits allowed by Ayyubid and Mameluk authorities to the shrines of the Holy Land compelled the pilgrims to spend the major part of their sojourn in the Crusader-dominated areas and especially at Acre. Part of this time was spent visiting and worshipping in the local churches as a substitute for Jerusalem and other holy sites. During the second half of the century, when access to Jerusalem became particularly difficult, processions were organised for pilgrims at Acre, conducting them to 41 churches, where they were granted indulgences.[42]

Thus, some spiritual dimensions were attached to the city of Acre and hagiographical legends were related to it, which was the first step towards its sanctification.[43] At the same time, the intellectual changes that were occurring in Western Europe brought about a new awareness in the pilgrims of their surroundings. They began to pay attention to the landscape, as well as to the fauna and the flora, and in addition to the sacred history of the Holy Land, its natural history also began to feature in their observations.[44] For the first time, too, they became aware of the human element dwelling in the country. Their attention was first drawn to eastern Christians, among them the Armenians, whose piety and exemplary behaviour made a deep impression on them. Their relations include glowing descriptions and accounts of these people,[45] while other oriental Christian sects were described unfavourably.[46] As far as the Jews were concerned, their presence in the country was considered to be worthy of only short mentions;[47] both for the pilgrims and for their audience in Europe, who were accustomed to the Jewish communities in their own countries, the Jews did not represent an unknown element and did not warrant detailed description.

For the pilgrims, however, their major discovery was Islam and the Muslims. Unlike the learned society in Western Europe, who since the twelfth century had already had a fair knowledge of this religion, including translations from the *Qur'ān* and other books,[48] the pilgrims and the laity had a very vague knowledge of the Saracens, and this was limited to political and military aspects. According to them, the "Saracens were pagans and a terrible menace for Christianity".[49] Even though they were based on a superficial knowledge of the Muslim Near East, the pilgrims' descriptions are an important record, and were widely diffused among the masses of European Christians, through both oral and written relations. The first pilgrim to write about the Saracens, Thietmar, wrote that during his six-day visit to Damascus he learned "everything" about the Islam.[50] He sincerely believed that his statement was true; after all, he had learnt more than his contemporaries who did not belong to the university. The result of these "studies" was the dissemination of rather vague notions about Muhammad and the Islamic faith, which they considered to be superstition, and a very favourable impression of the piety of the Muslims, as manifested by their behaviour in prayer, study and the Ramadhan feast. They also learned to distinguish between the sedentary Arabs (villagers and townspeople), the Saracens, the Bedouins and the Shī'ite *Assassins*. Some of the pilgrims even believed that the latter were the descendants of the Essenes, "though they did not anymore practise Judaism".[51] What roused the pilgrims' curiosity most about the Muslims was their practice of polygamy. This exotic system, which they emphasised as being the basic precept of the Islamic religion, caught their imaginations and led them to conjecture how a Muslim might "behave with his seven wives"![52] The stories they would tell on their return to their native countries were intended to ridicule this practice, but they served only to rouse further interest in these people and their strange behaviour. Moreover, their praise of Muslim piety, which according to the testimony of the Dominican Friar Riccoldo da Montecroce (who was well-versed in Arabic and had a sound knowledge of Islam) should have been an example for Christians,[53] and their open admiration of the Bedouins roused the interest of the clerics and laity of Western society, paving the way for a new era of travels to the East, particularly in the fourteenth century.[54]

The pilgrims of the thirteenth century were extremely critical of Crusader society. Despite the religious, social and ethnic affinities between the two groups, the gap between them widened. The emergence of the cosmopolitan *Outremer* society of the thirteenth century, which had none of the religious fervour of the twelfth century Crusaders, brought the pilgrims and Crusaders into open antagonism. The pilgrims were outraged by the profane and "scandalous" conduct of the *Outremer* people, and accused them of both exploiting them and being responsible through their sinful behaviour for the calamities suffered by the Crusading movement. The pilgrims' accounts became an important influence in the discrediting of the Crusade and consequently made the recruitment of knights for the later Crusades more difficult. Burchard of Mount Sion's description of the Holy Land ends with a diatribe against the "Latins", whom he describes as *peiores*, the very worst element in the Holy Land's population. He expressed the view that the Crusaders were criminals who joined the Crusades in order to escape merited punishments in their native lands. According to him, their behaviour had not improved in their adopted country and, moreover, their descendants were even worse. He accused them of "polluting the soil of the Holy Land".[55] Such accounts so influenced public opinion in Western Europe that the fall of the Kingdom of Acre came as no surprise. The Crusaders had come to represent an evil society and had lost all legitimacy. As a result, their rule was no longer considered indispensible, either for the defence of the Holy Land or for the liberty of pilgrimage, a problem which pilgrims had already been compelled to negotiate with the Muslim authorities.

As far as the Jewish travellers of the thirteenth century were concerned, their realistic approach had brought them even before Christian pilgrims to the conclusion that the Crusaders had failed to achieve their mission, a failure which they attributed to the lack of settlement. In the sixteenth century, Nahmanides, in his commentary on the Pentateuch, wondered why this country, which in the past had been so populated and prosperous, was deserted by both Christians and Muslims. His conclusion, based on his belief that both elements had been strangers to the "Land of Israel", brought him to formulate an eschatological vision of the future redemption of Israel and to call for a massive Jewish immigration and settlement.[56] Developing these ideas, the exegete and traveller Nissim of Marseilles, Burchard's contemporary, developed a cyclical view of the Holy Land's history, based on seven periods, after the seven days of Creation. According to his view, three Christian dominations alternated with three Muslim, all of which were characterised by desolation and ruin, while the Sabbath was reserved for the Jewish restoration and settlement.[57] Thus, while Christian pilgrims had sought holiness in the shrines and graves, the Jews advocated that the Holy Land be a country of life and settlement, which was a way of realising the Messianic dream.

The fall of the Crusaders in 1289 signified the end of an era, not only in the history of the Holy Land, but also in the history of pilgrimage. Nevertheless, pilgrims continued to visit the sacred shrines in the late Middle Ages, despite the ruin of the coastal area of Palestine and the desolation of the country which affected the logistics of the pilgrimage and their itineraries. Radical changes had taken place in the nature of pilgrimage as an expression of religious behaviour and the late medieval pilgrims to the Holy Land can be more aptly described as travellers, who combined business travel, exploration of exotic countries and adventure with pilgrimage to the holy places.[58] Under the impact of collective organisation of travel and of the ritual devotions to the sanctuaries, this new kind of pilgrimage neither allowed the individual pilgrim the time for the spiritual exercises that had been at the core of the peregrinatory practice of his predecessors, nor was conducive to religious reflection. The late medieval pilgrimage therefore cannot be dealt with in the framework of this discussion.

As far as the pilgrims of the early Middle Ages and of the Crusader period are concerned, their spiritual perception of the Holy Land was widely diffused in Western Europe. Their accounts of their pilgrimages were related first-hand in vernacular on their return home to audiences who gathered to hear the wonderful sagas of these "travellers of Divinity". These were later transcribed either by the pilgrims themselves, if they were clerics, or by a member of the audience, and roused much interest in European society. Although these accounts were stereotyped, they do reflect the attitude of pilgrims to pilgrimage. With some exceptions in the thirteenth century, these descriptions, which became a *genre littéraire* with its own typology,[59] brought to Europe a spiritual vision of the Holy Land, devoid of any reference to the realities of the age. The Jewish accounts, while they were different in scope to the Christian ones, reinforced this image and, through daily contacts in the markets and fairs, indirectly reached the same audiences.

While the pilgrims' descriptions reveal their deep spiritual attachment to the sanctuaries and other holy sites of the Holy Land, they felt themselves alienated to the lay society of Palestine, both Christian and Muslim. In spite of the chronicles of the Byzantine period or those of the Crusades which provided information on contemporary life and events in the Holy Land, the image of the country as portrayed in the pilgrims' accounts prevailed and became the foundation on which ideas about the Holy Land in Western society were based.

The transmission of this perception, which was corroborated by the study of the Bible in medieval Europe, to the various social entities of Western Europe was facilitated by the foundation of chapels, churches and monasteries dedicated to Palestinian shrines, such as the spread of the "Order of the Holy Sepulchre" in European countries. Moreover, art based on pilgrims' descriptions became an important channel of popularisation of the image of the Holy Land in the West, while the "golden legend" became part of European folklore. In this way, the Holy Land has become an integral part of the cultural heritage of European civilisation.

NOTES

1 Medieval pilgrimages have long been a subject of interest, as reflected by the abundant bibliography dealing with this topic; it is diversified both by the approaches of the authors and by the aspects of the research. A useful synthesis concerning the phenomenon particularly in Europe is that of J. Sumption, *Pilgrimage: an Image of Mediaeval Religion,* London, 1975. For a discussion of the original concept of pilgrimage as adopted by early Christianity, see B. Kötting, *Peregrinatio religiosa: Wallfahrten in der Antike und das Pilgerwesen in der alten Kirche,* Regensburg 1950; see also E.D. Hunt, *Holy Land Pilgrimage in the Later Roman Empire, AD 312–460,* Oxford, 1984. A sociological view of the "religious vagrancy" is the analysis by A. Vexliard, *Introduction à la Sociologie du Vagabondage,* Paris, 1956.

2 See F. Stummer, "Die Bewertung Palästinas bei Hieronymus", *Oriens Christianus,* III, 10 (1935) 60–74 and J. Wilkinson, "Saint Jérôme, sa contribution à la topographie", *Revue Biblique,* 81, 1974, pp. 245—57.

3 On Constantine's buildings see L.H. Vincent and F.M. Abel, *Jérusalem Nouvelle, Recherches de Topographie, d'Archéologie et d'Histoire,* Paris, 1926 and J. Finegan, *The Archaeology of the New Testament,* Princeton, 1969.

4 Gregory of Nyssa, letter II, *Patrologia Graeca,* vol. 46, col. 1013 (see English translation by W. Moore and M.A. Wilson, *Nicene and Post-Nicene Fathers,* 2, 5, Oxford, 1983). On the development of opposition to monastic pilgrimage, see G. Constable, "Opposition to Pilgrimage in the Middle Ages", *Studia Gratiana,* 19, 1976, pp. 125–46.

5 E.Z. Melamed's translation into Hebrew of this crucial work (Jerusalem 1978), together with his introduction and the *apparatus criticus* emphasises the need for a new edition instead of that of E. Klostermann, Leipzig 1904.

6 *Itinerarium Burdigalense,* ed. P. Geyer (*Itinera Hierosolymitana saeculi III–VIII, Corpus Scriptorum Ecclesiasticorum Latinorum,* vol. 39, pp. 1–33), Vienna 1888; see its revised edition with notes by O. Cuntz, in *Itinereria et alia Geographica (Corpus Christianorum, Series Latina,* vol. 175), Turnhout 1965, pp. 1–26.

7 *Itinerarium Egeriae,* ed. P. Maraval, Paris 1982. The English translation by J. Wilkinson (*Egeria's Travels,* London 1972), based on earlier editions, should be consulted because of its notes and bibliography.

8 *Epitaphium Paulae,* letter no. 108 by St Jerome, ed. J. Hilberg, *Sancti Hieroniymi Epistulae (Corpus Scriptorum Ecclesiasticorum Latinorum,* vol. 55), Vienna 1915, pp. 306–51.

9 *Itinerarium Egeriae,* ed. Maraval, pp. 161, 166, 186, 204. During her visit to Haran, in Mesopotamia, the local bishop, according to her testimony, served as her guide while touring monuments concerned with the local origin of the Patriarchs (pp. 212–24).

10 *Epitaphium Paulae,* ed. cit. pp. 315–16. This hieronymian statement, and particularly the final part of the sentence: *elegit humilem cellulam, et cuncta loca tanto ardore ac studie circumivit, ut, nisi ad relique festinaret, a primis non posset abduci,* had an important impact on the behaviour of the medieval pilgrims. It was considered a normative precept of conduct during the pilgrimage because of the author's authority, without any concern for the social status of the pilgrim. It is possible to follow the continuation of this practice until the twelfth century, as reflected by the behaviour of Louis VII, King of France; see A. Grabois, "The Crusade of

Louis VII, King of France: a Reconsideration", in *Crusade and Settlement. Essays presented to R.S. Smail,* ed. P.W. Edbury, Cardiff, 1983, pp. 94–104.

11 The evidence was gathered by J. Wilkinson, *Jerusalem Pilgrims before the Crusades,* London, 1977, with an excellent bibliography. The problem of the "pilgrims' time" imposed however a different interpretation; see, for the Byzantine period, P. Maraval, "Le temps du pèlerin, IV–V siècles", in *Temps Chrétien de la Fin de l'Antiquité au Moyen Age,* Paris 1983, pp. 479–88. The same perspectives were expressed by later medieval pilgrims: see A. Grabois, "Le pèlerin occidental en Terre sainte et ses réalités: Jean de Würzburg", *Mélanges E.R. Labande,* Poitiers, 1974, pp. 367–76 and C. Deluz, "Indifférence au temps dans les récits des pèlerins du XII au XIV siècle", *Annales de Bretagne et des Pays de l'Ouest,* 3 (1976), pp. 303–13.

12 See for example, Peter the Diacon's compilation, *Liber de Locis Sanctis,* ed. P. Geyer, *Itinera Hierosolymitana,* p. 113, blaming Queen Isabel's persecutions.

13 *Itinerarium Antonini Placentini,* ed. C. Milani, Milan 1977, p. 100.

14 Ibid. p. 130. The vocabulary used by the pilgrims of the Roman and Byzantine periods expressed their spiritual concerns, as opposed to the Latin of the Late Empire; see G.F.M. Vermeer, *Observations sur le Vocabulaire de Pèlerinage chez Egérie et chez Antonin de Plaisance,* Nijmeigen, 1965. It became, for the later generations, a normative model.

15 The pilgrim of Piacenza decribed the common gathering of Christian and Jewish visitors to the *spelunca duplex* (the tombs of the Patriarchs) at Hebron in the second half of the sixh century (ed. Milani, p. 187). According to Adomnan's record of the oral relation by the Frankish bishop Arculfus, it seems that towards the end of the seventh century, Christians still had access to this shrine (Arculfus, *De Locis Sanctis,* transcribed by St Adomnan, Abbot of Iona, ed. L. Bieler, in *Itineraria et alia Geographica,* op. cit, p. 209). On the other hand, Mukkadassi, writing in *c.* 975, clearly attests that the sanctuary *(Meshad al-Khalil)* had been a mosque "since the times of Islam" (Guy Le Strange, *Palestine under the Moslems,* London 1898, p. 309). It seems that the conversion process had been accomplished by the beginning of the eighth century.

16 Such had been his captivity in Syria (*Vita seu Hodoeporicon Sancti Willibaldi,* ed. T. Tobler, *Descriptiones Terrae Sanctae,* Munich, 1874, p. 22), and particularly his arrest at Tyre for contraband, having hidden balsam in a casquet filled with *naphte* (ibid. pp. 40–41).

17 See the important methodological remarks by P. Rousset, "Le sens du merveilleux à la période féodale", *Moyen Age* 62 (1956) 25–36, concerning also the period dealt with here.

18 *Vita et Miracula Sancti Genesii, MGH, 55,* XV, 169–172; see J. Mosca, *Carlo Magno ed Harun al Rashid,* Bari 1963, pp. 13–16 and A. Grabois, "Charlemagne, Rome and Jerusalem", *Revue Belge de Philologie et d'Histoire,* 59, 1981, pp. 792–809.

19 *Itinerarium Bernardi monachi franci,* ed. T. Tobler, op. cit. p. 91. On this "foundation of Charlemagne", see S. Runciman, "Charlemagne and Palestine", *English Historical Review,* 50, 1935, pp. 609–20.

20 For example, Hugh of Flavigny, the biographer of Richard, Abbot of St Vanne's of Verdun, states that the abbot had conducted a pilgrimage of 500 pilgrims in 1026 (Hugo de Flavigny, *Chronicon, MGH, SS,* VIII, p. 393). See also E. Joranson, "The Great German Pilgrimage of 1065–1066", *The Crusades and Other Essays Presented to D.C. Munro,* New York, 1928, pp. 3–43, and E.R. Labande, "Eléments d'une enquête sur les conditions de déplacement du pèlerin aux X et XI siècles", *Pellegrinaggi e Culto dei Santi in Europa Fino alla Prima Crociattà,* Todi, 1963, pp. 97–111.

21 Raoul Glaber, *Les Cinq Livres de ses Histoires,* ed. M. Prou, Paris 1886, p. 107. On its impacts

in the development of anti-Jewish attitudes in Western Europe, see R. Chazan, "1007–1012: Initial Crisis for Northern European Jewry", *Proceedings of the American Academy for Jewish Research,* 38–39, 1970, pp. 101–18 and A. Grabois (Hebrew), "From 'theological' to 'racial' antisemitism: the controversy of the Jewish Pope in the twelfth century", *Zion,* 47, 1982, pp. 1–16.

22 See P. Rousset, *Les Origines et le Caractère de la Première Croisade,* Geneva, 1945.

23 For the vocabulary and the use of the peregrinatory terminology by crusaders, see M. Villey, *La Croisade; Essai sur la Formation d'une Théorie Juridique,* Caen 1942, pp. 248–54. For the conceptualisation of pilgrimage-crusade as a result of ideological developments, see P. Alphandéry, — A. Dupront, *La Chrétienté et l'Idée de Croisade,* Vol I, Paris, 1955 and J. Prawer, *The Crusaders' Kingdom,* New York, 1972.

24 E.R. Labande has emphasised the difference in his articles, "Recherches sur les pèlerins dans l'Europe aux XIe et XIIe siècles", *Cahiers de Civilisation Médiévale,* I, 1958, pp. 159–69, 339–347 and "Ad limina, le pèlerin médiéval au terme de sa démarche", *Mélanges René Crozet,* Poitiers, 1966, vol. I, pp. 283–91.

25 John of Würzburg's description (ed. T. Tobler, *Descriptiones Terrae Sanctae,* op. cit., pp. 109–91) is the best evidence in that concern. On the other hand, his pupil, Theoderic, has dedicated a whole paragraph to Acre, in which he expressed his criticism of that city (*Libellus de Locis Sanctis,* ed. M.L. and W. Bulst, Heidelberg, 1976, p. 43).

26 Saewulf, *Peregrinatio,* ed. C. Brownlow, in *Palestine Pilgrim's Text Society,* vol. IV, London, 1892, pp. 31–52; see p. 50.

27 Reginald of Durham, *Libellus de Vita et Miraculis Sancti Godrici,* ed. J. Stevenson, London, 1843, pp. 53–8. See. A. Grabois, "Anglo-Norman England and the Holyland", *Anglo-Norman Studies,* 7, 1985, pp. 132–44.

28 See the respective editions of Tobler and Bulst, already mentioned (note 25).

29 See A. Grabois, "Le pèlerin occidental en Terre sainte et ses réalités: Jean de Würzburg", *Mélanges E.R. Labande,* Poitiers, 1974, pp. 367–76.

30 John of Würzburg, ed. Tobler, p. 118.

31 Theodericus, ed. Bulst, p. 42.

32 Benjamin of Tudela, *Sefer Massaoth,* ed. M.N. Adler, London, 1907, pp. 21–8. See J. Prawer (Hebrew), "The Hebrew Itineraries of the Crusader Period, I: The Twelfth Century", *Cathedra,* 40–41, 1985, pp. 31–90 and A. Grabois (Hebrew), "Travel and Pilgrimages to Eretz-Israel in the Twelfth and Thirteenth Centuries", *Proceedings of the Ninth World Congress of Jewish Studies,* B, 1, Jerusalem, 1986, pp. 63–70.

33 John of Würzburg, ed. Tobler, p. 187. See M. Halbwachs, *La topographie légendaire des Evangiles en Terre Sainte,* Paris, 1941.

34 See Prawer, art. cit.

35 Thus, for example, Benjamin of Tudela provides information about the small Jewish settlement at Jerusalem (p. 26) and on the prestigious Keraite sage Abraham of Constantinople, also resident of the Holy city (pp. 26–9); it resulted that, despite the prohibition of Jewish settlement at Jerusalem since the conquest of the city by the Crusaders, some Jews managed to establish there, protected by the authorities. On the other hand, Benjamin considered the Samaritans as a Jewish sect — "Jewish *Samarantos*"(p. 22).

36 See Grabois, art. cit. (note 32).

37 The German pilgrim Willebrand of Oldenburg (1211) emphasised the restrictions of pilgrimages at Jerusalem (ed. J.C.M. Laurent, *Peregrinatores medi aevi quatuor,* Leipzig, 1864, pp. 185–6).

38 See M. Patch, *The "Other World", according to Descriptions in Medieval Literature,* Cambridge (Mass.), 1950 and C.K. Zacher, *Curiosity and Pilgrimage,* Baltimore, 1976.

39 *Peregrinatio Magistri Thietmari,* ed. J.C.M. Laurent, Hamburg, 1857, p. 1.

40 *Lettres de Jacques de Vitry,* ed. R.B.C. Huygens, Leiden, 1960, pp. 89–90.

41 Burchard of Mount Sion, *Descriptio Terrae Sanctae,* ed. Laurent, *Peregrinatores,* p. 23.

42 *Pèlrinages et Pardouns d'Acre,* ed. H. Michelant and G. Raynaud, *Itinéraires à Jérusalem et Descriptions de la Terre Sainte Rédigés en Français aux XI, XII et XIII Siècles,* Geneva, 1882, pp. 179–99.

43 See A. Grabois, "Les pèlerins occidentaux en Terre Sainte et Acre: d'Accon des croisés à Saint-Jean d'Acre", *Studi Medievali,* III, 24, 1983, pp. 247-64.

44 The first results of this new approach appeared in the account of an anonymous pilgrim, whose visit to the Holy Land is dated at *c.* 1202, and is known as the *Innominatus V–1,* ed. 13.A. Neumann, "Drei mittelalterliche Pilgerschriften Innominatus V", *Oesterreichische Vierteljahrschrift für Katholische Theologie,* 5, 1866, pp. 263–7. See the study of the text by A. Grabois, (Hebrew), "From 'Holy Geography' to 'Palestinography'", *Cathedra,* 31, 1984, pp. 43–66.

45 Already at the beginning of the century, Willebrand of Oldenburg (op. cit., pp. 174–80) had expressed these views; they also appear in Burchard of Mount Sion's description (op. cit., pp. 91–3) towards this end.

46 For example, see *Innominatus V–1* (op. cit., pp. 259–61) and Burchard (ibid. pp. 89–90)., who was particularly critical of the Syrians.

47 Such mentions, made for example by Willebrand of Oldenburg (op. cit., p. 163) or by Thietmar (op. cit., p. 51: "There are here also non-Christians, divided into many sects; first, Jews", attest of this trend of "self-evidence".

48 See N.A. Daniel, *Islam and the West: the Making of an Image,* Edinburgh, 1962 and R.W. Southern, *Western Views of the Islam in the Middle Ages,* Cambridge (Mass.), 1962.

49 Among several works on this topic, see B. White, "Saracens and Crusaders: from Fact to Allegory", in *Medieval Literature and Civilization,* ed. D.A. Pearsall and R.A. Waldron, London, 1979, p. 179 ff.

50 Thietmar, op. cit., p. 11.

51 Thietmar, op. cit., p. 52; Burchard of Mount Sion, op. cit., p. 90.

52 Thietmar, op. cit., p. 9.

53 Ricoldo da Montecroce, *Itinerarium,* ed. J.C.M. Laurent, *Peregrinatores,* p. 135. See U. Monneret de Villard, *Il Libro della Peregrinazione Nelle Parti d'Oriente di Fratre Ricoldo da Montecroce,* Rome, 1948, as well as A. Dondaine, "Ricoldiana. Notes sur les oeuvres de Ricoldo da Montecroce", *Archivum Fratrum Praedicatorum* 37, 1967, pp. 119–79.

54 For example, Fidenzio of Padua, *Liber de Recuperatione Terrae Sanctae,* ed. G. Golubovich, Biblioteca Bio-Bibliographica della Terra Sancta e dell'Oriente Francescano, vol. II, Quaracchi, 1908.

55 Burchard of Mount Sion, op. cit., p. 89; see A. Grabois, "Christian pilgrims in the thirteenth century and the Latin Kingdom of Jerusalem, Burchard of Mount Sion", *Outremer, Studies Presented to Joshua Prawer,* Jerusalem, 1982, pp. 285–96.

56 Nahmanides, *Comm. on Leviticus,* XXVI, 32, ed. Venice 1545:
      "'And your enemies which dwell therein shall be astonished', it is a good new, tiding throughout the Diaspora, for our Land does not accept our ennemies; this is evidence and a promise to us that nowhere in the world was there a land as good and as prosperous and

which is as desolate. For ever since we were exiled from it, it has accepted no nation or tongue, and though all try to dwell in it, none succeeded".

See A. Grabois, "The idea of political Zionism in the thirteenth and fourteenth centuries", *Feistschrift Rëuben R. Hecht,* Jerusalem, 1984, pp. 67–79.

57   Rabbi Nissim bar Moshe of Marseille, *Sefer Nissim* (Ms. Orientaux, No. 720, Biblioteque Nationale, Paris):

"The verse 'and your ennemies which dwell therein shall be astonished' (*Lev.,* XXVI, 32), is indeed very wonderful, for one of three reasons or all of them together, namely, the fame of the beauty of the Land, its holiness in the eyes of all nations, both near and far, and their desire for it. They covet it, envying those that dwell within it, quarreling and making war against them, so that the Land is never quiet and free of its ennemies. For that reason there are not in the whole Land of Israel large, thickly populated cities, but most of it is desolate and laid waste. And when the Jews dwelt there it was 'the joy of the whole world', but when the Jews did not dwell there and it was taken by our ennemies, they could not cultivate it, from the destruction of the Temple and until today. How many countries and cities have been destroyed and rebuilt and resettled by large multitudes after their destruction, even though they are thousand times the size of the Land of Israel? And war is always being waged on the inhabitants of the Land. The Romans, who drove us into exile, held it for some time, but did not endure. They were driven out by the Ishmaelites, who have remained here until today. Since the destruction of the Second Temple the Christians and the Ishmaelites have each usurped one another three times, and neither of them has dwelt in safety, the Ishmaelites always living in fear of attack from the Christians, and the Christians always living in fear of attack from the Ishmaelites. For the Ishmaelites always envied the Christians for living in the Chosen Land, and *vice versa* and therefore until this day they have not settled it properly . . ."

58   Among the numerous works on the later medieval pilgrimage to the Holy Land and its characteristic features, see J.W. Bennett, *The Rediscovery of Sir John Mandeville,* New York, 1954: F. Cardini, "I viaggi di religione, d'ambasceria e di mercatura", in *Le Crisi del Sistemo Communale,* vol. 6 of the *Storia della Società Italiana,* Milan 1982, pp. 157–210; E. Ashtor, "Venezia e il pellegrinaggio in Terrasanta nel basso medievo", *Archivio Storico Italiano,* 143, 1985, pp. 197–223. For the fifteenth century, see H.F.M. Prescott, *The Jerusalem Journey in the Fifteenth Century,* London, 1954.

59   See J. Richard, *Les Récits de Voyage et de Pèlerinage* (Typologie des sources du Moyen Age), Turnhout, 1981.

8 Nineteenth-century travelogues and the land of Moab

Hannes Olivier*

Napoleon's defeat at Akko signalled the beginning of an unprecedented interest in the Holy Land.[1] The vast Ottoman Empire was crumbling, but conflicting interests among the imperial powers of Europe delayed its complete disintegration for yet another century.[2] The Sublime Porte under Sultan Selim III (1789) was barely in control of the different territories and of the events that took place there.[3] One such area was Palestine — immensely important to European nations because of religious sentiments, historical sagas, political expediency, trade and strategic considerations.[4]

Moreover, on both sides of the Atlantic some religious groups deemed it their sacred duty to defend the literal accuracy of the Bible in view of the deplorable historical-critical approach that undermined its authority. The newly founded science of archaeology offered dramatic new means of uncovering the biblical past, hence underscoring the claims of fundamentalists.

Millenarian groups saw in Palestine an opportunity to evangelise the "fanatical Muslims", "stiff-necked Jews" and local Christians bound to dogmatic teachings which needed to be rectified before Christ's Second Coming to Jerusalem, where, according to all accounts of earlier travellers, poverty, crime, oppression and ignorance reigned.

On the other hand the spirit of the free pursuit of science was especially intense in Europe where the ideal of a science of history and of nature without presuppositions was already firmly established.[5] This very spirit, epitomised by the great Alexander von Humboldt, implied among other things travelling to far off places and scientifically exploring all imaginable aspects of the universe.[6] Travel became part of education. According to Karl Barth "atlases and travel books became an indispensable part of the more serious literature, even in bourgeois houses".[7] Consequently, an unrivalled invasion

* The author is indebted to the Alexander von Humboldt Foundation for a bursary which made this study possible. It must be stated that the views expressed in this chapter are those of the author and do not necessarily reflect the views of the foundation.

of Palestine took place: explorers, clerics, adventurers, scientists, military and civil representatives, and some fortune hunters, all searching for a new type of relic to be displayed in the museums of Imperial Europe. During all these hectic activities Transjordania remained relatively untouched because most of the area was outside the effective control of the Ottoman Empire.

THE LAND OF MOAB

Access to the Moabite plateau was always difficult. From both the north and south early travellers were compelled to cross respectively the formidable Wady Mujib canyon and the equally impressive Wady Hesa canyon. Situated between the rugged slopes of the Dead Sea escarpment and the great Syrian desert, only the Wady el-Kerak provided relatively easy access to the plateau from the Lisan.[8]

The plateau at an average elevation of 1 100 m, is gently rolling terrain with an average precipitation of 350 mm spread over five or six months during winter.[9] The thin but absorbent soils (Red and Yellow Mediterranean), abundant rainfall and absence of springs are factors conducive to grain crops such as wheat and barley, and to cattle farming, i.e. sheep and goat.[10] The Kerak/Moabite plateau is reasonably good agricultural land, and is literally dotted with unfortified village sites which show evidence of having been occupied off and on throughout the centuries.[11]

As a result of the increasingly heavy tax burden, the absence of effective control over the Kerak plateau and the numerous raids of the Bedouin tribes, villages gradually began to disappear during the Ottoman period. Only four permanent settlements along the edge of the Dead Sea escarpment were observed by the early nineteenth century travellers, namely Kerak, Khanzira, Iraq and Kathrabba. The whole of the Kerak plateau was dominated by Bedouin tribes such as the Bany Sakhr, Bany Hamideh, the 'Amr, Majaly and Wahabi.

The continual intertribal feuds, the mutual distrust between pastoralists and villagers, and their methods of dealing with the "Franks", did not always whet the appetite for exploring Transjordania.[12] Most travellers found themselves at the mercy of the local sheiks, especially the Majaly tribe which held Kerak. They usually had to hand over a substantial part of their belongings as well as a handsome ransom for permission to leave the area or for so-called "protection".[13] Such circumstances hardly allow for a thorough investigation of the archaeological remains. And yet those travellers who succeeded in penetrating the Moabite plateau left behind an immeasurable treasure of information.

A SHORT OVERVIEW OF THE HISTORY OF THE EXPLORATION OF THE LAND OF MOAB IN THE NINETEENTH CENTURY

Three successive stages in the history of the exploration of the Moabite plateau are discernible:

The early period of exploration (1806–1848)

In sharp contrast with the favourable reaction to the travel reports originating elsewhere in the Holy Land, the initial reports pertaining to Ancient Moab caused hardly any interest in Europe. The extremely valuable account by Seetzen, the first European to cross the Wady Mujib into Moab on 23–4 March 1806 was not published before 1854, although some of his notes and maps were published by Baron von Zach in the "monatlichen Korrespondenz zur Beförderung der Erd-und Himmelskunde" (vols. 17, 18, 26, 27).[14]

Fortunately, Swiss-born Johann Ludwig Burckhardt succeeded in discovering Petra in July–August 1812 when visiting the territory on behalf of the British Society for the Exploration of the Interior of Africa. He wrote:

> After proceeding for twenty-five minutes between the rocks, we came to a place where the passage opens, and where the bed of another stream coming from the south joins the Syk. On the side of the perpendicular rock directly opposite to the issue of the main valley, an excavated mausoleum came in view, the situation and beauty of which are calculated to make an extraordinary impression upon the traveller, after having traversed for nearly half an hour such a gloomy and subterraneous passage as I have described. It is one of the most elegant remains of antiquity existing in Syria; its state of preservation resembles that of a building recently finished, and on a closer examination I found it to be a work of immense labour.[15]

Though not located within the territory of Ancient Moab, the discovery of Petra initiated immense interest in that area in general. Attention was gradually focused on Kerak where many a visitor *en route* to Petra experienced the "sly and enterprising thieves" (Burckhardt: 371) of the "Devil's nest".[16]

In May 1818 a party of several people led by two British naval officers, Charles Irby and James Mangles, crossed the Moabite plateau from south to north. While Seetzen and Burckhardt had travelled in the disguise of Arab sheiks, they did not conceal the fact that they were Europeans, and that they were well-armed! Published for private distribution[17] their experiences and observations about the land of Moab attracted little attention because of all the excitement among Europe's academics about the decipherment of Egyptian hieroglyphs by Champollion, and about the discoveries in Mesopotamia by Rich and Porter.[18] Also, their descriptions did not conceal their contempt for the people of this area, thereby suggesting the unprofitability of exploring it for the British Empire:

> It is surprising that in so monotonous a life they have no amusements, no games, no athletic employments to make a little change in their custom of squatting down and smoke all day. All their carpets, cushions, sacks and in short, every thing they have are covered with vermin, so that it is impossible to avoid them . . .[19]

The same attitude also characterised Layard's account of his visit to this territory in late January 1840.[20] Unlike the detailed observations of travellers such as Seetzen and Burckhardt about natural phenomena and historical remains, Layard's report concentrated on his own resourcefulness in the face of danger:

> I pointed my gun at him and threatened to shoot him. In abject fear, as my gun was levelled at his head and not far from it, he begged for mercy . . .[21]

These "savages", "notorious robbers" and "cutthroats", "who bore a very evil reputation", held him in custody at Kerak and demanded a substantial ransom!

In the same year the British Navy arrived off Acre (together with a few Austrian and Turkish ships) and succeeded in overthrowing Ibrahim Pasha's Egyptian rule in the Holy Land and adjacent territories, which had also included the Moabite plateau for some time.[22]

In May 1848 the competent US naval officer, Lynch, conducted an expedition from the Lisan to Kerak. He made careful observations on weather conditions, fauna and flora, the people he had encountered *en route*, among others some Negroes, and of conditions that prevailed in Kerak among the Christians:

> It was a strange sight to see these wild Arab Christians uniting themselves to us with such heartfelt cordiality . . . They had indeed, our warmest sympathies, and our blood boiled as we listened to a recital of their wrongs".[23]

While the reports of Seetzen and Burckhardt reflect the "scientific" approach of the early nineteenth century, those of Irby and Mangles, Layard and Lynch are characterised by the spirit of Romanticism, stressing adventure, their bravery in view of the dangerous "wild savages", the beauty of the scenery, exotic birds and plants including sketches of Bible-like figures and suffering Christians — all intended for the home market yearning for "scientific" knowledge of far away countries, peoples and for the civilisations of yesteryear.

The period of discovery (1851–1893)

The second phase in the history of the exploration of the Moabite plateau commenced on 17 January 1851, when Louis-Fèlicien de Saulcy discovered at Redjom el-Aabed the stele of the so-called Shihan-warrior. In his words:

> I look and find myself in front of a magnificent Stélon, in black compact lava, representing a basrelief of antiquity . . . To a certainty, we have before us a Moabite sculpture.[24]

In his eagerness to acquire this piece of sculpture De Saulcy unintentionally awakened expectations of immense wealth which led to exorbitant demands among the Bedouin. It would take thirteen years before Duc de Luynes finally succeeded in acquiring it for the Louvre.[25]

After the Crimean War, France exerted considerable political influence on the Middle East. The large-scale excavations under Renan flooded the exhibition halls of the Louvre, contributing to the prestige of Emperor Napoleon III. For almost two decades the French dominated the exploration of the Moabite territory.[26] Except for Roth's brief excursion to Kerak in March/April 1858,[27] the only other two travelogues before 1868 were those of Duc de Luynes (1864) and of Mauss and Sauvaire (1866), both of which contain important topographical information.[28]

On the evening of 19 August 1868 Frederick August Klein of the Anglican Church

Missionary Society in Jerusalem was shown a mysterious black basalt stone in the vicinity of Dhiban.[29] The well-known unfortunate events and unsuccessful attempts to acquire the Moabite Stone from the Bany-Hamideh tribe led to intense international political involvement in this territory, caused by an awareness that even more such treasures might be hidden there. The publication of the translation of the Mesa Stele in Paris on 16 January 1870 and in *The Times* in London the following day, had effectuated an unsurpassed excitement over and interest in biblical archaeology. In the words of Silberman, "The dramatic proof of the historical accuracy of the Bible soon became a popular subject of conversation in drawing rooms, dinner parties, and garden receptions throughout England".[30] On the other hand, it evoked strong feelings in the tense political scene in Europe on the eve of the Franco-Prussian War of 1870.

Unquestionably the most important discovery in the Holy Land, the Moabite Stone, as it was called, injected new interest in the land of Moab. Already in March 1870 the Palestine Exploration Fund sent to Moab Charles Tyrwhitt-Drake and Edward Palmer, who after a thorough investigation concluded:

> Our sojourn in Moab was expensive and unsatisfactory. The Arabs were affected with a mania for written stones, and we were in this way induced to take long and tedious journeys about the country to see stones . . . We visited camp after camp, staying with various sheikhs, passing from tribe to tribe . . . Above ground at least there does not exist 'another Mesa stone' . . . I am convinced that a mere visit even of scientific men to the country will be attended with nothing but disappointment and annoyance.[31]

A second excursion to the Moabite plateau was arranged by the Palestine Exploration Fund. It was conducted in January 1872 by Tristram, who was accompanied by Klein. Tristram encountered some major difficulties in Kerak, for he had to pay an exorbitant sum in "protection money". A dramatic and romantic figure, Tristram seemed always to be keeping in mind his "audience" back home, for he liked to compare such things as "the delicious air like one of the first days of summer in England".[32] For him "every knoll is covered with shapeless ruins, while not a tree is to be seen through the whole country, except here and there a terebinth, always among the débris of some ancient site" (115). His travelogue, nevertheless, contains some excellent descriptions of the topography, flora and fauna of the region. Some 20 years later Bliss still regarded Tristram's travelogue as the best guide book for visiting the Moabite plateau.[33]

Two other events partly related to the discovery of the Mesa Stele need to be mentioned here. On account of the strategic importance of the Suez Canal, inaugurated in October 1869, the British Government launched a full-scale mapping and surveying operation in the Sinai and neighbouring Palestine.[34] The discovery of the Mesa Stele had also attracted great public attention in the United States, in consequence of which the American Palestine Exploration Society decided to conduct a survey of Transjordan.[35] Compared to the highly competent and efficient British team under Wilson, Conder and Kitchener the American undertaking was a huge failure.[36] Conder was later appointed to survey those regions abandoned by the Americans but was stopped in 1882 by the increasingly suspicious Ottoman authorities.[37]

The second event was the Shapira affair. Moses Shapira was an antique dealer in Jerusalem who maintained a network of peasant contacts to obtain a steady supply of ancient artefacts for selling to wealthy tourists. In 1873 he acquired pottery pieces inscribed with ancient letters almost identical to those found on the Moabite Stone.[38] Shapira's "Moabite potteries" were purchased by the Imperial Museum in Berlin. When some doubts were raised as to the authenticity of these documents, Shapira personally conducted the German Consul and Pastor Weser to see for themselves the site of the find.[39] However, Clermont-Ganneau succeeded in raising enough suspicion about the Shapira collection for angry questions to be asked in the Prussian parliament. In 1878 Shapira again acquired a number of scrolls which he believed to be a ninth century BC copy of the Book of Deuteronomy,[40] written in the same "Moabite script". The "Moabite Deuteronomy" caused quite a stir in Europe when Shapira announced its existence. All over Europe people were fascinated by the "World's Oldest Bible" as the "Moabite Deuteronomy" was called. In August 1883 Queen Victoria herself agreed to guarantee the purchase price of one million pounds for these scrolls, but unfortunately for Shapira, Clermont-Ganneau again stepped in and pointed out that they were forgeries. A few months later Shapira committed suicide and the scrolls disappeared.

In the following decades few people visited the Moabite plateau: Hamilton (March 1873),[41] Doughty (December 1876),[42] Bartlett (1876)[43] and Graham Hill (April 1890).[44] Because none of these visits yielded any spectacular new findings beyond the usual descriptions of antiquities and of personal experiences, the earlier excitement about "Moab" was soon replaced by new issues such as the true locality of Golgotha, and the Babylonian version of the Flood, discovered by George Smith in December 1872.

For the sake of completion it is necessary to take into account the large number of travelogues pertaining to the Belqa and adjacent region immediately to the north of the Wady Mujib. People seemed to be obsessed with the idea of viewing the Promised Land from the summit of Mount Nebo like Moses did. Among these visitors were well-known scholars such as Tristram (April 1864),[45] Warren (1867),[46] Northey (April 1871),[47] Kersten (April 1874),[48] who epitomised the positivistic scientific approach of recording every single fact and detail, Thomson, whose monograph became a best-seller in the United States,[49] Schick (1877),[50] Post, whose excellent report includes a list of 843 different plants arranged into 84 categories,[51] Schumacher (September 1891)[52] and Lagrange (April 1893).[53] April was generally considered the most appropriate time for a visit.

The period of scientific investigation (1894–1905)

Following Abdul Hamid's disastrous defeat by the Russians in 1877, the German Kaiser (Wilhelm II) dispatched a number of military and economic missions to Constantinople in order to strengthen the hands of the sultan and to gain some influence in the Middle East, an indirect result of which was better control in the peripheral territories of the Empire, including the Kerak district where the enmity between the Beny Sakhr and Majaly tribes had flared up into open confrontation. In December 1893 a Turkish governor took up office in Kerak and for the first time since Suleiman the Magnificent a garrison of 2 000 troops patrolled the whole area, making it safe for the first time to travel on the Moabite plateau. New government facilities and services such as a post office, telegraph station, military hospital, school, etc. contributed to the thorough investigations carried out there until 1905 when the first revolt against the Turkish authority broke out.[54]

In comparing Hill's travelogues of 1888 and 1895 the dramatic improvement in the security situation is immediately noticeable. Always the incurable romantic (and accompanied by his wife!) Hill traversed the Moabite plateau with new zest and zeal. His report in the *Quarterly Statement* of the Palestine Exploration Fund sounds more like an advertisement for a tourist organisation.

> Another great bonfire was made to scare the flies, and this night I took my bed outside the tent, and slept most happily under the glorious sky, thus enjoying to the full, in the watches of the night, the sight not only of the host of heaven, and the flickering of the flames and shadows, and the refreshing night breeze, but the splendid light of dawn, and the invigorating sip of the fresh-boiled coffee which always accompanies dawn in Palestine. What a happy life this of gipsy wandering. Why return to foggy England and squabbling politicians?[55]

But times were changing; archaeology was coming of age[56] — even in far-off Transjordan. This is effectively illustrated by Bliss's report of his expedition to Moab and Gilead also in March 1895. Photographs, sketches, precise measurements of ruins and architectural plans, copying of inscriptions and some excellent descriptions of archaeological remains and even suggestions of possible sites for excavation, set the example for many reports to come,[57] such as those of Hornstein (1895),[58] Brünnow (1895, 1897, 1898),[59] Lagrange (1896),[60] Vailhè (1896),[61] Musil (1896–1902),[62] Gautier (1899),[63] Wilson (1899),[64] Libbey and Hoskins (1902),[65] Smith (1904)[66] and others.[67] The excellent research work done by Brünnow and Domaszewski together with that of Alois Musil finally put the scientific exploration of the Moabite plateau on a firm footing.[68] Once and for all scholars became aware of the importance of this region for biblical studies. Thus Wilson said in 1899:

> Moab and Edom, though not strictly forming part of the Holy Land, are so closely connected with it that they should be surveyed and examined with the same accuracy as Western Palestine, and excavations should be made before ruins and inscriptions have been destroyed by squatters. The topographical features are interesting; there is much of importance to the geologist; and the discovery of inscriptions like that of King Mesha on the "Moabite Stone", is not only possible but probable. The occupation of the country by the Turks has facilitated exploration, and the sooner it is undertaken the greater will be the results.[69]

Wilson knew quite well what he was talking about, because a few years earlier a substantial portion of the fifth century mosaic map of Madeba was completely destroyed when a new Greek church was built on that site. "Even in its fragmentary state it is one of the most valuable geographical discoveries of recent years in Palestine".[70]

According to Libbey and Hoskins, as early as 1884 a Greek monk had informed the

Patriarch in Jerusalem about the mosaic pavement at Madeba, but had received no reply. The new Patriarch Gerasimos found the letter in 1890 and sent a master mason with orders that if the mosaic was a fine one, to include it in the church which was to be built at Madeba. "The mosaic was at the time almost complete, and, by the testimony of those who saw it, contained the names of Smyrna, and other towns as far away. But the stupid builder, in his great desire to build on the ancient foundations, destroyed the greater part of it, and drove a pilaster right through the priceless piece that he did not completely destroy. After the mischief was done, he went back to Jerusalem, and reported that the mosaic did not possess the importance which had been attributed to it".[71] In January 1897 father Cleopas, the Librarian of the Greek Patriarchate, surprised the archaeological world with his notes and sketches of the Madeba map; indeed, it was one of the most important discoveries in the Holy Land. Like the survey of the area, the restoration of the Madeba map had to wait for many years before Max Miller[72] and Herbert Donner[73] respectively would take the initiative to comply with Wilson's request.

Although the Moabite plateau had come into much sharper focus since 1894, no full systematic survey or any archaeological excavations were carried out there. The politically unstable situation following the rebellion of 1905 and onwards, as well as the almost complete absence of outstanding tells in the time of the large-scale excavations by archaeologists such as Schumacher, Macalister and Reisner, contributed to the subsequent lack of interest in this territory. Albright's excursion to Kerak in 1924[74] received hardly any notice before the discovery of the Balu'ah stele in 1932.[75] Except for a two-week campaign during which Albright made soundings at Balu'ah and Ader,[76] Glueck's[77] surveys between 1936 and 1938 became the final word on the antiquity of Moab for almost the next four decades.[78]

GENERAL CHARACTERISTICS OF THE TRAVELOGUES

Reading the travelogues some general characteristics reflecting the *geistesgeschichtliche* spirit of nineteenth century Europe are to be derived.

Comprehensive scientific approach

> If you would really understand the Bible — which we circulate every year by the millions — you must understand also the country in which the Bible was first written.[79]

These words of the archbishop of York reflect to a great extent the motivation and objectives behind many a travelogue, namely, to provide nothing less than a complete inventory of every natural and historical feature of Palestine. Most of the travellers carried out a series of meteorological observations, compiled notes on the geological, topographical, botanical and zoological features of the Moabite territory, provided exact information regarding distances, weather conditions, temperature and barometric readings, and even examined archaeological ruins as well as prospects for future agricultural development. In addition to camping gear and provisions, surveying instruments, barometers, brass theodolites, prismatic compasses[80] and later the camera, were the indispensable "tools" for assembling such a large body of scientific information. Many of these travellers were well-educated men: Seetzen obtained a doctorate in botany at the University of Göttingen, Burckhardt spoke Arabic fluently, Conder was an excellent royal engineer, Roth an ophthalmologist, and Tristram obtained a masters in Classics at Oxford but was also an eminent zoologist with an enormous bird collection. These travellers knew only too well the "scientific" desires of European academics (in the grip of Darwin's theory of evolution) for facts of nature and of "primitive" people. They would therefore elaborate on strange phenomena like the oshar and oleander trees, the different species of deer, birds and wild beasts like the tiger and hyena (Tristram, 524). Burckhardt's classification of Syrian Bedouins, Tristram's appendix on flora (cf. also that of Post), and De Saulcy's comparative list of place names (456) are typical of this general comprehensive scientific approach so characteristic of the age.

Romantic character

A wondrous moonlight night succeeded, and we had much leisure to observe it (for notwithstanding a great fire of brushwood which George had made to drive away mosquitoes and flies they were too abundant, and the weather was too hot for sleep), until fatigue overcame us and sweet oblivion came. Oh, those glorious Syrian nights! Who that has once seen can ever forget them?" (Hill, *PEFQS,* 1896, 42).

Such and numerous other examples reflect the romantic spirit of those European travellers who deemed it their duty to undertake a new type of Crusade, namely to bring civilisation to the world. While new facts about the people of Palestine and their languages, customs, folklore, food, crafts and modes of existence were diligently investigated,[82] one cannot help noticing the typically European attitude of superiority over these Bedouin people who were occasionally called "sly and enterprising thieves" (Burckhardt, 371) and "treacherous" "cutthroats" (De Saulcy, 397). In their writings they accentuated the differences not only in natural phenomena but especially those in regard to standards of civilisation, modes of existence, manners and customs. On one occasion Irby and Mangles, two British officers, threw some money to a group of women: "We could not refrain from laughing most heartily at so odd a scene, and left them fighting and beating each other most furiously."[83] In an era of exploration and colonisation remarks such as these served to provide a rationale for politicians. Clerics, too, used similar arguments to support their ideology. Lynch (357), Tristram (57) and Post (190) wrote respectively:

The Muslim inhabitants are wild-looking savages, but the Christians have a milder expression ... Christian females did not conceal their faces, which were tattooed like the South Sea Islanders.

If the Gospel had done nothing more — if, in measuring its blessings, we were to reduce it to the standard of a mere humanizing agency — the position of woman under the lowest and the most corrupt form of Christianity, as compared with her treatment under the most refined development of Mahammedan monotheism, would be sufficient to decide the question.

We visited the Latin Church, a dismal enough sanctuary as compared with those of civilized countries, and yet an elevating and educating force in such a desolate land as Moab.

The travelogues often describe the dangers (like venomous serpents and cutthroat savages) and hardships[84] experienced by these travellers suffering for the cause of God and country in such extreme terms that one is inclined to suspect their authors of exaggeration. And yet they were obviously very conscious of the unique opportunity to travel in such far off places: "Here we halted and gazed on a prospect on which it has been permitted to few European eyes to feast" (Tristram, 536).

The Fundamentalist undertone

A considerable number of nineteenth century travellers were involved in some way or other in a search for facts which would substantiate the biblical truth, or at least illuminate its contents.[85] Thus Doughty (22) remarks: "Isaiah speaks of a great Moabitish multitude, and surely, the ancient people were many in these fresh highlands".

The travelogues contain numerous biblical quotations pertaining to the historical geography, fauna and flora of the Holy Land. In some cases the arguments of the classical authors such as Pliny, Josephus and Eusebius were considered with regard to the location of a specific place. Seetzen once remarked that Josephus was "ein gänzlicher Idiot in der Kunde der Natur". Old ruins and roads were carefully studied in order to relate them to biblical toponyms, in particular Isaiah 15 and 16 and Jeremiah 48. It is clear that some were not too familiar with the Bible! Lynch (353) describes the *retem*-tree under which the prophet Isaiah was supposed to have sat! Some doubts regarding the biblical narrative were also occasionally expressed:

> To transport a vast multitude down and up this (Mujib) gorge would have been a serious affair in times of peace, but think how impossible while they were passing through a hostile country! (Bliss, 216)

Archaeological interest

To many of the early travellers the large number of village ruins on the Moabite plateau suggested that it had been densely populated in antiquity, and hence also in biblical times, thus verifying the biblical account of Numbers xxi:

> ... in short, the whole of the fine plains in this quarter, are covered with sites of towns on every eminence or spot convenient for the construction of one; and as all the land is capable of rich cultivation, there can be little doubt that this country, now so deserted, once presented a continued picture of plenty and fertility ... (Irby and Mangles, 370f).[86]

The travelogues mention many ruins that have since vanished, describing their Arabic name, precise locality, relative position to other places, possible inscriptions, and noting features such as Roman milestones, traces of ancient water cisterns and walls.[87] Bliss even suggested excavating Kerak because "only about half the area of the ancient town is now covered by houses."

It is also clear that many mistakes were made. Hornstein (102) wrote: "On the PEF map it [Lejûne] is marked as being at least 30 miles from Kerak, but it is not more than 12 miles."[88] The way in which three of the most important findings of the Holy Land — the Shihan-stele, the Mesa stele and the Madeba map — were handled evoked severe indignation and resentment, but it should be borne in mind that only a very few people were at that time really capable of conducting proper archaeological work. In spite of their errors these nineteenth century travellers succeeded in drawing attention to a much neglected part of the Holy Land.

CONCLUSION

Characterised by the comprehensive scientific approach and the romantic spirit of the age and underscored by fundamentalist interest in the historical truth of the Bible, the nineteenth century travelogues served to inform, excite and to stimulate scholars and adventurers to become involved in rediscovering the Holy Land. Among the most spectacular discoveries were the Mesa stele and the Madeba map, and these attracted enormous public interest and support for further archaeological exploration of Palestine, including the Moabite plateau. Thanks to the courage and endeavour of these nineteenth century travellers and explorers, places such as Petra, Kerak, Madeba, Dhiban and others became well-known entries on every map of the Holy Land.

Even today these travelogues remain an important source of information about the plateau's plants and animals, soil types, water sources and weather conditions, the social structure of and power balance between the different tribes, the interaction between the desert and the sown, the location and identification of ancient places and biblical toponyms, because the face of the Moabite plateau — which remained virtually intact since Roman and Byzantine times — has changed dramatically during the past 50 years or so. For instance, while only four towns were occupied in the early nineteenth century, and about 30 a hundred years later, more than a hundred rapidly expanding villages are presently situated in the territory.[89] Modern housing development schemes, agricultural techniques, water conservation methods and transport systems have obliterated many of these ancient ruins and, therefore, important archaeological evidence for reconstructing the history of the Holy Land.[90]

The so-called New Archaeology, with its interest in settlement patterns, interaction between village-culture and pastoral "nomadism", food-procuring systems, dry-farming and transhumance,[91] can clearly utilise the type of information contained in these travelogues. In so doing it would contribute still more to ethno-archaeological and social anthropological research about the Holy Land.[92]

BIBLIOGRAPHY

1   H. Olivier, *Akko Spieëlbeeld van Beskawings,* Stellenbosse Teologiese Studies no 10, Kaapstad, 1983, p. 54.

2   Y. Ben Arieh, *The Rediscovery of the Holy Land in the Nineteenth Century,* Israel Exploration
    Society, Jerusalem, 1979, 21f.
3   R.K. Hitti, *History of the Arabs,* Macmillan, London, 1970, 745f.
4   The sagas of the Crusaders helped to form the Christian conception of the Holy Land. The
    heroic struggles of Godfrey de Bouillon and Richard the Lion Heart became national epics in
    France and England. This religious yearning to take possession of the Holy Land was
    reawakened in the nineteenth century, according to N.A. Silberman, *Digging for God and
    Country,* "Exploration, archaeology, and the secret struggle for the Holy Land, 1799-1917."
    Alfred Knopf, New York, 1982.
5   K. Barth, "Man in the eighteenth century", *From Rousseau to Ritschl,* SCM, London, 1959,
    pp. 11-57.
6   D. Botting, *Alexander von Humboldt,* Biographie eines grossen Forschungsreisenden,
    München, 1974.
7   Barth, op. cit. p. 16.
8   C.W. Wilson, "Address delivered at the Annual Meeting of the Fund", *PEFQS,* 1899, p. 307.
9   G. Mattingly, "The natural environment of Central Moab", *ADAJ* 27, 1983, pp. 597-605;
    A.H. van Zyl, *The Moabites.* Pretoria Oriental Series, Leiden, 1960, p. 48.
10 P. Gubser, *Politics and Change in Al-Karak, Jordan.* A study of a small Arab town and its
    district", Oxford University Press, London, 1973, pp. 8-40; E.B. Banning, "Peasants, pas-
    toralists and Pax Romana: mutualism in the southern highlands of Jordan", *BASOR* 261,
    1986, pp. 25-56.
11 Cf. J.M. Miller, "Recent archaeological developments relevant to Ancient Moab", in A.
    Hadidi, *Studies in the History and Archaeology of Jordan,* Amman, Department of Anti-
    quities, 1982, pp. 169-73", idem., "Archaeological survey of Central Moab, 1978", *BASOR*
    234, 1979, pp. 43-52.
12 Gubser, op. cit. 53f.
13 J.M. Miller, Palestine Exploration Fund Lecture, 1982 (unpublished).
14 Ulrich Jasper Seetzen, *Reisen durch Syrien, Palästina, Phönicien, die Transjordan-Länder,
    Arabia Petraea und Unter-Aegypten,* ed. F. Kruse, G. Reimer, Berlin, 1854.
15 J.L. Burckhardt, *Travels in Syria and the Holy Land,* ed. W.M. Leake, John Murray,
    London, 1822, p. 424.
16 De Saulcy, p. 378 cf. note 24.
17 C.L. Irby and J. Mangles, *Travels in Egypt and Nubia, Syria and Asia Minor; During the
    Years 1817 and 1818.* T White & Co, London, 1823. It was subsequently published by John
    Murray in 1844 under the title: *Travels in Egypt and Nubia, Syria and the Holy Land;
    Including a Journey Round the Dead Sea, and through the Country East of the Jordan.* For
    the sake of completion the report of William Macmichael, *Journey from Moscow to Con-
    stantinople in the Year 1817, 1818,* John Murray, London, 1819; repr. Arno Press, New York,
    and *New York Times,* 1971) needs to be mentioned though the section (pp. 195-249) re the
    Moabite plateau is by Thomas Leigh, who accompanied Irby and Mangles. It contains some
    quite interesting but generalised observations on the area.
18 W.F. Albright, *From the Stone Age to Christianity,* Doubleday, New York, 1957, 27f.
19 Irby and Mangles, op. cit. p. 485.
20 Sir Henry Layard, *Early Adventures in Persia, Susiana and Babylonia,* John Murray,
    London, 1887, p. 85.
21 Ibid. p. 73.

22   Ibid. p. 88f. In 1834 Qasim al-'Ahmad of Nablus rebelled against Ibrahim Pasha and fled to Kerak where he was accepted by the Majaly sheik. Kerak was subsequently captured by Ibrahim Pasha.

23   W.F. Lynch, *Narrative of the United States' Expedition to the River Jordan and the Dead Sea*. Lea and Blanchard, Philadelphia, 1849, p. 342.

24   F. de Saulcy, *Narrative of a Journey Round the Dead Sea and in the Bible Lands in 1850 and 1851,* edited with notes by Count Edward de Warren. 2 Vols. Richard Bentley, London, 1853, 347 f. the Original French edition, *Voyage autour De La Mer Morte et dans les Terres Bibliques exécute de Decembre 1850 à Avril 1851* (Paris: Gide et J Baudry) was also published in 1853. Parry and M'Millan of Philadelphia published in 1854 another edition called *Narrative of a Journey Round the Dead Sea and in the Bible Lands in 1850 and 1851, Including an Account of the Discovery of the Sites of Sodom and Gomorrah.* Cf. the discussion of the stele by O. Tufnell, "The Shihan Warrior", *IRAQ* 15, 1953, p. 161–6 and E. Warmenbol, "La Stèle de Rugm El-'Abd (Louvre AO5055), "Une Image de Divinité Moabite du IXème-VIIIème Siècle av. N.E.", *LEVANT* 15, 1983, pp. 63–75.

25   (H T P J d'A) Duc de Luynes, *Voyage d'Exploration á la Mer Morte, á Pètra et sur la rive gauche du Jourdain.* 3 vols. Arthus Bertrand, Paris, 1874, pp. 170–73.

26   Silberman, op. cit. p. 68.

27   "Prof Dr J.B. Roth's Reisen in Palästina. IV. Abschnitt: Erste Ausflüge in die Ost-Jordan-Länder, 17. März bis 4 April 1858", *Petermann's Mittheilungen IV,* 1858, pp. 267–72.

28   C. Mauss, and H. Sauvaire, "De Karak a Chaubak", *Bulletin de la Socièta de Gèographie,* XIV, 1867, pp. 449–522.

29   For the details see S. Horn, "The discovery of the Moabite Stone" in C.L. Meyers and M. O'Connor (eds.). *The Word of the Lord Shall Go Forth.* Essays in Honor of David Noel Freedman in Celebration of his Sixtieth Birthday, ASOR, Philadelphia, 1983, pp. 497–505, and S. Horn, "Why the Moabite Stone was blown to pieces", *BAR* 12, 1986, pp. 50–61. Cf. also E.A. Klein, "Peraea. Missionary tour into a portion of the Trans-Jordanic countries", *The Church Missionary Intelligencer,* 1869, pp. 60–64, 92–6, 123–8. This travelogue does not however, mention the discovery of the Mesa Stele, but another by F.A. Klein, "The original discovery of the Moabite Stone", *PEFQS,* 1870, pp. 218–38. Cf. also E.H. Palmer, *The Desert of the Exodus. Journeys on Foot in the Wilderness of the Forty Years Wanderings.* Deighton, Bell & Co. Cambridge, 1871, p. 493, also translated into German *Der Schauplatz der vierzig-jährigen Wüstenwanderung Israels,* Gotha, 1876.

30   Silberman, op. cit. p. 109.

31   E.H. Palmer, "The Desert of Tih and the Country of Moab", *PEFQS,* 1871, p. 72. Strangely enough, Klein's report on a visit to Moab in 1872 does not contain any further reference to the Mesa Stele. Cf. F.A. Klein, "Notizen über eine Reise nach Moab im Jahre 1872", ZDPV 2, 1879, pp. 124–34.

32   H.B. Tristram, *The Land of Moab. Travels and Discoveries on the East Side of the Dead Sea and the Jordan,* John Murray, London, 1874, p. 271.

33   E.J. Bliss, "Narrative of an expedition to Moab and Gilead in March, 1895", *PEFQS,* 1895, p. 217.

34   Compare the minutes of the Annual Meetings of the *Palestine Exploration Fund Quarterly Statements* in 1870, 1891.

35   Silberman, op. cit. p. 115; Cf. Ben-Arieh, p. 195.

36   S. Merrill, "The American Expedition", *PEFQS,* 1976, pp. 47–55. Cf. his popular, highly

romanticised account in: *East of the Jordan. A Record of Travel and Observation in the Countries of Moab, Gilead, and Bashan.* New York, 1881. Merrill states: "The geological, botanical, geographical, and archaeological features of this east-Jordan land are of the highest interest. The fertility of this region, which we commonly call a desert cannot be exaggerated. Its populousness and prosperity in ancient times will always remain one of the wonders of history" (p. 51). It would take, however, another century before the Americans under the leadership of Maxwell Miller started to survey the Moabite plateau! Cf. J.M. Miller, "Archaeological Survey of Central Moab, 1978", *BASOR* 234, 1979, pp. 42–52, the final report of which is still underway.

37 C.R. Conder, *The Survey of Eastern Palestine. Memoires of the Topography Orography, Hydrography, Archaeology,* etc. Vol. 1. PEF, London, 1889. Conder also wrote a voluminous popular account of his experiences in Transjordan, and especially Moab, called *Heth and Moab. Explorations in Syria in 1881 and 1882*, Richard Bentley & Son, London, 1883.

38 Silberman, op. cit. p. 132.

39 H. Kiepert, "Lic Wesers und Shapiras Reise nach Moab", *Zeitschrift der Gesellschaft für Erdkunde zu Berlin,* 8, 1873, pp. 210–17.

40 M. Mansoor, *The Case of Shapira's Dead Sea (Deuteronomy) Scroll of 1883,* New York, 1956. Cf. Silberman, op. cit. p. 213.

41 C. Hamilton, *Oriental Zigzag, or Wanderings in Syria, Moab, Abyssinia and Egypt,* with Illustrations by Fritz Wallis from Original Sketches by the Author. Chapman and Hall, London, 1875 (Unavailable to me).

42 C. Doughty, *Travels in Arabia Deserta,* Jonathan Cape Ltd., London, 1972.

43 S.C. Bartlett, *From Egypt to Palestine,* Harper & Brothers, New York, 1879, who visited Kerak and Shihan in 1876 (unavailable to me).

44 G. Hill, *With the Beduins. A Narrative of Journeys and Adventures in Unfrequented Parts of Syria,* T. Fisher Unwin, London, 1891.

45 H. Tristram, *The Land of Israel; A Journal of Travels in Palestine, Undertaken with Special Reference to its Physical Character.* Society for Promoting Christian Knowledge, London, 1865.

46 R.E. Warren, "Remarks on a visit to 'Ain Jidy and the Southern Shores of the Dead Sea in Midsummer 1867", *PEFQS,* 1872, pp. 57–72.

47 A.E. Northey, "Expedition to the East of Jordan", *PEFQS,* 1872, pp. 57–72.

48 O. Kersten, "Umwanderung des Todten Meeres in Frühjahr 1874", *ZDPV* 2, 1879, pp. 201–44.

49 W.M. Thomson, *The Land and the Book; or Biblical Illustrations Drawn from the Manners and Customs, the Scenes and Scenery of the Holy Land.* T. Nelson and Sons, London, 1885; Vol 3, 1886. Cf. Ben Arieh, p. 156.

50 C. Schick, "Bericht über eine Reise nach Moab", *ZDPV* 2, 1979, pp. 1–12.

51 G.E. Post, "Narrative of a scientific expedition in the Trans-Jordanic region in the spring of 1886", *PEFQS,* 1888, pp. 175–237.

52 G. Schumacher, "Ergebnisse meiner Reise durch Hauran, Adschlun und Belka", *ZDPV* 16, 1893, pp. 72–83, 153–170.

53 P.M.J. Lagrange, "Jenseits des Jordans", *Das Heilige Land* 38, 1894, pp. 97–106.

54 Gubser, op. cit. p. 18.

55 G. Hill, "A journey east of the Jordan and the Dead Sea", *PEFQS,* 1896, pp. 24–46, esp. 42.

56 Silberman, op. cit. p. 156.

57 E.J. Bliss, "Narrative of an expedition to Moab and Gilead in March, 1895", *PEFQS*, 1895, pp. 203–35.

58 C.A. Hornstein, "A Visit to Kerak and Petra", *PEFQS*, 1898, pp. 94–103.

59 R. Brünnow, "Reisebericht" *MNDPV*, 1898, pp. 33–39, 49–51, 81–87 and *MNDPV*, 1899, pp. 23–29, 40–42, 56–61, 65–91.

60 M.J. Lagrange, "Notre Exploration de Pètra", *RB* 6, 1897, pp. 208–30.

61 S. Vailhè, "Dans les Montagnes Bleues", reworked by L. Triol, "Au pays de Moab", *Echos D'Orient* 4, 1900–1901, pp. 333–9; 5, 1901–1902, pp. 49–54, 97–103; 6, 1903, pp. 320–28.

62 A. Musil, *Arabia Petraea, Vol 1: Moab. Topographischer Reisebericht*, Alfred Hölder, Vienna, 1907.

63 L. Gautier, "Am Toten Meere und im Lande Moab", *ZDPV* 24, 1901, pp. 113–26 from the original "Autour de la Mer Morte", *Le Globe*, Journal geographique, organe de la Sociète de géographie de Genève, 39, 1900.

64 C.W. Wilson, "Address Delivered at the Annual Meeting of the Fund", *PEFQS*, 1899, pp. 304–16.

65 W. Libbey and F.E. Hoskins, *The Jordan Valley and Petra*, G.P. Putnam's Sons, New York and London, 1905.

66 G.A. Smith, "The Roman Road between Kerak and Madeba", *PEFQS*, 1904, pp. 367–77 and *PEFQS*, 1905, pp. 39–48.

67 Cf., e.g., A. Sargenton-Galichon, *Sinaï Ma͑ân Pétra. Sur les Traces D'Israel et Chez les Nabatèens*. Lecoffre, Paris, 1904, pp. 113–26.

68 R.E. Brünnow and A. v Domaszewski, *De Provincia Arabia. Auf Grund Zweier in den Jahren 1897 and 1898 unternommenen Reisen und der Berichte Früherer Reisender*, Karl J. Trübner, Strassburg, 1904.

69 Wilson, op. cit. p. 316.

70 Wilson, op. cit. p. 305.

71 Libbey and Hoskins, op. cit. p. 267.

72 J.R. Kautz, "Tracking the Ancient Moabites", *BA* 44, 1981, pp. 27–35.

73 H. Donner and H. Cüppers, "Die Restauration und Konservierung der Mosaikkarte von Madeba", *ZDPV* 83, 1967, pp. 1–33.

74 W.F. Albright, "The archaeological results of an expedition to Moab and the Dead Sea", *BASOR* 14, 1924, pp. 1–12.

75 G. Horsfield and L.H. Vincent, "Chronique: Une Stèle Egypto-Moabite au Belou'a", *RB* 41, 1932, 417–444; E. Drioton, "Propos de la Stèle du Balou'a", *RB* 42, 1933, pp. 353–65. J.W. Crowfoot, "An Expedition to Balu'ah" *PEFQS*, 1934, pp. 16–18.

76 W.F. Albright, "Soundings at Ader, A Bronze Age City of Moab", *BASOR* 53, 1934, pp. 13–18.

77 N. Glueck, "Explorations in Eastern Palestine", I *AASOR* 14, 1933–34, II *AASOR* 25–28, 1945–49; It needs to be mentioned that scholars such as Alt and Noth, have also contributed considerably to our understanding of the historical geography of this region. Cf. A. Alt, "Emiter und Moabiter", *PJ* 36, 1940, pp. 29–43; idem. "Unter Beduinen Moabs", ZDMG 58, 1932, 26f; M. Noth, "Beiträge zur Geschichte des Ostjordanlandes", ZDPV 68, 1946–51, pp. 1–50.

78 J.M. Miller, "Archaeological survey south of Wadi Mujib; Glueck's sites revisited", *ADAJ* 23, 1979, pp. 79–92.

79 Silberman, op. cit. p. 115.

80 Hill, op. cit. p. 1895, p. 31.

81 Layard, De Saulcy and Conder wrote literally hundreds of pages of such material.

82 Lynch, op. cit. p. 345 even set to music the Arab war cry!

83 Irby and Mangles, op. cit. p. 294.

84 Cf. Burckhardt, op. cit, p. 349. The Beny Sakhr were "reduced to such misery that they could not afford to give us a little sour milk which we begged of them" and Layard speaks of his want of water and food one bitter cold night in the desert (67).

85 "The general aspect of the limestone plateau is not unlike that of the Sussex Downs or the Yorkshire Wolds. The plateau affords excellent pasture and where cultivated, yields good crops of barley. There are few scattered trees, and at one spot between Shobek and Petra, there is an oak wood of some size. In the Bible these downs are called the Mishor of Edom and Moab". (Wilson, op. cit. 307f).

86 Cf. Wilson, op. cit. p. 310; Merrill, op. cit. p. 51; Tristram, op. cit. 1872, p. 114.

87 Typical of a description of a ruin, is that by Tristram (1872, p. 114). "The town seems to have been a system of concentric circles built round a central fort; and outside the buildings the rings continue as terrace walls, the gardens of the old city".

88 According to Miller (PEF-lecture, 1982) almost all the nineteenth-century maps are based primarily on Burckhardt's account. Though he was a very accurate observer, some statements are worded in such a way that they were bound to be misleading.

89 M. Miller, "Between the Desert and the Sown": Unpublished paper on the settlement pattern in Ancient Moab.

90 Cf. H. Margalit, "Some aspects of the cultural landscape of Palestine during the first half of the nineteenth century", *IEJ* 13, 1966, pp. 208–23.

91 O. LaBianca, "Objectives, Procedures and findings of Ethnoarchaeological Research in the Vicinity of Hesban in Jordan", *ADAJ* 28, 1984, pp. 269-87. L. Geraty and O. LaBianca, "The Local Environment and Human Food-Procuring Strategies in Jordan: The Case of Tell Hesban and its Surrounding Region", in: A. Hadidi (ed.), *Studies in the History and Archaeology of Jordan* II, 1985, pp. 323–330 Cf. E.B. Banning, "Peasants, pastoralists and *Pax Romana*: Mutualism in the southern highlands of Jordan", *BASOR* 261, 1986, pp. 25–50.

92 Cf. the excellent studies of Gubser and of Robin M. Brown, *Late Islamic Settlement Patterns on the Kerak Plateau, Trans Jordan*. MA (Anthropology) Graduate School of the State University of New York at Binghamton 1984 and U. Worschech et al., *Northwest Ard El Kerak 1983-1984*. A Preliminary Report. München: *Biblische Notizen,* Beiheft, 2, 1985.

9 Mark Twain in the Holy Land

Reingard Nethersole

On 8 June 1867, the one-time pilot on the Mississippi, printer and confederate soldier Samual Longhorne Clemens (1835–1910) left New York harbour on board the *Quaker City* on what promised "to be a picnic on a gigantic scale.

> The participants in it, instead of freighting an ungainly steam ferryboat with youth and beauty and pies and doughnuts, and prodding up some obscure creek to disembark upon a grassy lawn and wear themselves out with a long summer day's laborious frolicking under the impression that it was fun, were to sail away in a great steamship with flags flying and cannon pealing, and take a royal holiday beyond the broad ocean, in many a strange clime and in many a land renowned in history!" (Vol. I, p. 1)[1]

Shortly before this excursion to Europe and the Holy Land, Samuel Clemens had travelled to Hawaii. From there he had sent dispatches which were later gathered in a book entitled *Roughing It* to the *Daily Alta California* in San Francisco. But it was only after the voyage undertaken in 1867 and the subsequent publication of *The Innocents Abroad* in 1869 that the correspondent for the *Daily Alta* and the *New York Tribune* and *New York Herald* became one of the best-paid authors of his day. Samuel Longhorne Clemens, alias Mark Twain, became a household name in North America and later in Europe and his famous *The Innocents Abroad or The New Pilgrim's Progress. Being Some Account of the Steamship Quaker City's Pleasure Excursion to Europe and the Holy Land* made the bestseller list second only to Harriet Beecher Stowe's *Uncle Tom's Cabin*. Mark Twain's first successful book was succeeded by the equally enduring *Tom Sawyer* (mistakenly regarded as a children's book) in 1876, *Life on the Mississippi* in 1883 and *Huckleberry Finn* in 1884. Together with *A Connecticut Yankee in King Arthur's Court* of 1889, *The Innocents Abroad* is one of the first in a series of encounters with Europe by Americans which was to bear ample fruit for American as well as European literature in the twentieth century. Thus, Mark Twain can, arguably, be seen as a precursor to Washington Irving, Hemingway, Stein and a host of other expatriates whose fascination with the "old world" paved the way for literary exchanges between the "old" and the "new" worlds.

Least of all, these innocents abroad, walking the well-trodden path described for them by popular guide-books and Sunday School teachers, are the precursors also of the steady stream of tourists who emigrate across the Atlantic every summer as the "lost tribe of America" (Vol. II, p. 363) to this day. Neither purpose nor attitudes seem to have changed much. There is the excitement of adventure, of new and novel things. "A strange, new sensation is a rare thing in this humdrum life, . . ." says Twain, "and I had it here" (when he met the Czar of Russia) (Vol. II, p. 109). When things and people are, however, "like a message from our own dear native land", they do not warrant description but rather lead to the "shedding of a few grateful tears and execrations in the old timehonored American way." (Vol. II, p. 101). The travellers are proud of their home country, America, for it "has a flag", a constitution and consular representatives along the arduous route. Pride and prowess also seem to overcome language difficulties which occur particularly in connection with guides and place names. Thus, "All guides are Ferguson to us. We cannot master their dreadful foreign names" (Vol. II, p. 93). And "for the sake of convenience in spelling", place names in the Middle East, such as Temnin-el-Foka for instance, simply become "Jacksonville". "It sounds a little strangely, here in the Valley of Lebanon, but it has the merit of being easier to remember than the Arabic name", says Twain (Vol. II, p. 158).

The author, though, is not uncritical of his fellow passengers, who "came ashore and infested the hotels and took possession of all the donkeys and other open barouches that offered" (Vol. II, p. 363). Twain's satire is directed particularly at those travellers who have to carve their names upon important mementoes from the past or worse, break off pieces from buildings and well-known sights to take home with them. Like the travelling companion Blucher, who "has already turned his stateroom into a museum of worthless trumpery, which he has gathered up in his travels" it seems as if tourists gather "mementoes with a perfect recklessness, nowadays; . . ." — nowadays, of course, being 1867. But what is worse, according to Twain, is Blucher's habit of labelling these mementoes "without any regard to truth, propriety, or plausibility" (Vol. II, p. 98).

Ever since we three or four fortunate ones made the midnight trip to Athens, it has afforded him genuine satisfaction to give everybody in the ship a pebble from the Mars Hill where St. Paul preached. He got all those pebbles on the seashore, abreast the ship, but professes to have gathered them from our party. However, it is not of any use for me to expose the deception — it affords him pleasure, and does no harm to anybody. He says he never expects to run out of mementoes of St. Paul as long as he is in reach of a sand-bank. Well, he is no worse than others. I notice that all travelers supply deficiences in their collections in the same way. I shall never have any confidence in such things again while I live. (Vol. II, p. 99)

I have quoted from the text at length in order to afford those who have as yet not read Twain's amusing and enjoyable account of early-day modern tourist travel to the "old world" a glimpse of his style of writing. In spite of frequent comparisons with the land in which everything is bigger, newer, cleaner, tidier and technically more advanced; in short, in spite of very typical American prejudices held by the innocent travellers from the "new world", Mark Twain's keenly observing eye, his sense of humour, his journalistic awareness of catering for "human interest" and suspense and his mixing of narrative with description, interspersed with brief summarising journal entries, retold legends and distancing judgements, make his two-volumed travelogue an important document of modernism.

To be sure, there have been earlier travelogues and reports on semi-scientific and archaeological explorations, but what turns Mark Twain's observations into literature is the way in which he combines a number of different discourses for the explicit purpose to entertain and not only to instruct. Thus he continuously sets off one type of text against another, the "romantic" travelogues inspired by early nineteenth century orientalism against the empirical reality, biblical narrative against the Sunday School stories, the narrated past against the experienced presence.

The sub-title of the book, *The New Pilgrim's Progress,* serves as a conscious reminder of John Bunyan's *The Pilgrim's Progress* of 1678 which, showing influences of late medieval genre systems although written in popular prose, is often regarded as a precursor of the realistic moralising English latter-day novel. Rescued from relative obscurity by early nineteenth century writers and historians, Bunyan's story of a pilgrimage from a Puritan perspective enjoyed widespread popularity during Mark Twain's time.[2] Although *The Pilgrim's Progress* is chiefly concerned with a spiritual, inner-wordly evolution of the idea of progress rather than with an expansion of the realm of worldly experiences, its intertextual relation to *The Innocents Abroad* is illuminating. At first hand, a certain irony regarding the fact that the Puritans left England in order to find a new home first in Pennsylvania and later in Boston, Rhode Island and Connecticutt cannot be overlooked. While the *Mayflower* brought the pilgrim-fathers to the New World, the *Quaker City* takes its WASPish passengers back to the Old World in the opposite direction nearly 250 years later. Secondly, the traditional topic of pilgrimage which so often shaped the French and German epics as much as it did the *Canterbury Tales* has, at the hands of Mark Twain, undergone a further transformation. Had the old, Christian image of the road as a passage through space and time towards greater spiritual fulfilment already changed during the post-Renaissance more secular era when well-to-do young European males sought a completion of their classical education in the hands of antiquity during the seventeenth and eighteenth centuries, the later nineteenth century with its rapidly growing technology afforded cheaper and more convenient ways of transportation. Thus mass-tourism is born and Twain's account may be regarded as one of the earliest documents of this phenomenon. To be sure, Twain did not seek out the beaches and leisure spots, but neither is the purpose of his journey spiritual fulfilment. "One must travel to learn", he says. "Everyday, now, old Scriptural phrases that never possessed any significance for me before take to themselves a meaning" (Vol. II, p. 281). It is this "eye-witness" account, this thoroughly nineteenth-century empirical attitude which believes experience within a logical space-time frame to be the only source for truth which makes Twain's "record of a picnic" into a modernist piece of literature.

Its objective is unashamedly didactic, and in that sense moralising, for

it has a purpose, which is, to suggest to the reader how *he* would be likely to see Europe and the East if he looked at them with his own eyes instead of the eyes of those who have traveled in those countries before him. [. . .] I have seen with impartial eyes, and I am sure I have written at least honestly, whether wisely or not (Preface, Vol. I).

The book, arranged in two volumes of some 720 pages, of which some 230 pages are devoted to what we call today the Middle East, demarcates a journey in space which increasingly turns into an encounter with times past. This shift from spatiality — indicated constantly by comparisons between the vast expanses of America and the smaller but historically more dense localities in Europe, Syria and Palestine — to temporality not only constitutes an expression of nineteenth-century historicism at the hands of the author, but in turn produces an encounter with a number of constitutive forces of historiography. On the surface level of the text constant references to the measurement of time brought about by different and differing ways of transportation (e.g. ships-time counted as "bells")[3] including the need to reset watches in tune with the longitudinal crossings from west to east, mark the importance of time. At first this is simply travelling time, until it becomes the time along whose linearity historical events are fixed as the rise and fall of civilisations. In the Holy Land, however, time appears as both, historically fixed through the evolution of institutionalised Christianity, and recurring because the localities of the Old and New Testament as empirical experiences of a landscape appear unchanging. Historical time leads Twain to the realisation of what he calls "the unsubstantial, unlasting character of fame" (Vol. II, p. 43)[4] whereas narrated time, especially the stories of the New Testament, create for him an eternal presence not dependent upon historical relics.

The past, for Mark Twain, or rather life in the past — for he is only interested in a living past — is always seen through the eyes of the present, and the strange and foreign modes of life become intelligible when compared to the known. That which, particularly in the Middle East, appears at first as odd behaviour, turns into reasonable conduct, because "We do that way in our cities" (Vol. II, p. 37). Nevertheless, the past accumulation of historical places, ruins, art works, and other remnants becomes too much in the end: ". . . I have felt all the time like a boy in a candy-shop — there was everything to choose from, and yet no choice", says Twain when thinking of Rome (Vol. II, p. 12); and Jerusalem offers too many sights as well.

They swarm about you at every step; no single foot of ground in all Jerusalem or within its neighborhood seems to be without a stirring and important history of its own. It is a very relief to steal a walk of a hundred yards without a guide along to talk unceasingly about every stone you step upon, and drag you back ages and ages to the day when it achieved celebrity.

It seems hardly real when I find myself leaning for a moment on a ruined wall and looking *listlessly* down into the historical pool of Bethesda. I did not think such things *could* be so crowded together as to diminish their interest. But, in serious truth, we have been drifting about, for several days, using our eyes and our ears more from a sense of duty than any higher and worthier reason . . .

Our pilgrims compress too much into one day. One can gorge sights to repletion as well as sweetmeats. (Vol. II, p. 326)

Yet, "the grand goal of the expedition" (Vol. II, p. 150), the Holy Land, seemed to have been so eagerly anticipated by the travellers. Twain, the narrator, makes sure throughout the whole book that not only the Holy Land, by which he implies in part the Old Testament regions of present-day Syria, Lebanon, and Israel as well as in particular those areas where "Jesus used to walk", but especially "the goal of our crusade, renowned Jerusalem" (Vol. II, p. 294), remains for ever in the reader's mind. Already in the beginning of the first volume attention is drawn to the Middle East, for apart from the "Plymouth Collection of Hymns to be used on board the ship", special travelling paraphernalia is required only "to use in rough pilgrimizing in the Holy Land". (Vol. I, p. 8) This "chief feature" (Vol. II, p. 150) of the *Quaker City*'s "pleasure trip" is further emphasised by a change in the syntactical structure used for the description of the preparations made by the passengers prior to disembarkation:

Such a burrowing into the hold for the trunks that had lain buried for weeks, yes, for months; such a hurrying to and fro above decks and below; . . . , such a making up of bundles, and setting apart of umbrellas, green spectacles, and thick veils; such a critical inspection of saddles and bridles that had never yet touched horses; such a cleaning and loading of revolvers and examining of bowie-knives; such a half-soling of the seats of pantaloons with serviceable buckskin; the such a poring over ancient maps; such a reading up of Bibles and Palestine travels; such a marking out of routes; . . . (Vol. II, p. 150).

The route, "a tedious, and also a [. . .] risky journey, at this hot season of the year" (ibid.) was to lead the "pilgrims" into "Syria, by Baalbec to Damascus, and thence down through the full length of Palestine." (ibid.) Transportation problems, feared at first, were sorted out, because "As might have been expected, a notion got abroad in Syria and Egypt that the whole population of the Province of America (the Turks consider it a trifling little province in some unvisited corner of the world) were coming to the Holy Land — and so when we got to Beirout yesterday, we found the place full of dragomans and their outfits." (Vol. II, p. 152)

Accommodation throughout the trip in what was to Twain a wild, backward, inhospitable terrain,[5] was provided either in comfortable tents or in monasteries.

Yet, the "glorious privilege to be a pilgrim to the Holy Land" (Vol. II, p. 157) and the "enchanted memory a year hence — a memory which money could not buy from us" (Vol. II, p. 331) barely hide the disappointment expressed by Twain when he notices that "the Sunday-school books exaggerated" (Vol. II, p. 162) the reality which presents itself to his gaze. Everything in the land of the two Testaments, including distances between places, is much smaller than expected. "The state of Missouri could be split into three Palestines, . . ." (Vol. II, p. 206). Twain finds that he has to "studiously and faithfully unlearn a great many things I have somehow absorbed concerning Palestine" (Vol. II, p. 214).

Apart from having everything "on too large a scale" (ibid.) because he "could not conceive of a small country having so large a history" (ibid.), Twain feels cheated by the guide books, which he takes to task for drawing a wrong picture of the countryside, the beauty of Middle Eastern women and the bravery of the Bedouins[6] ". . . rags, dirt, sunken cheeks, pallor of sickness, sores, projecting bones, dull, aching misery in their eyes . . ." (Vol. II, p. 176) make the Syrians appear unlikeable. In the face of the "God-forsaken barrenness and desolation of Syria" (Vol. II, p. 177), Damascus, "the fossile" (Vol. II, p. 182) "in the midst of that howling desert" (Vol. II, p. 179), "this blistering, naked, treeless land" (Vol. II, p. 210), the "desolate country, whose soil is rich enough, but is given over wholly to weeds . . ." (Vol. II, p. 216), Twain says: "If all the poetry and nonsense that have been discharged upon the fountains and the bland scenery of this region [and he includes the landscape of present-day Israel] were collected in a book, it would make a most valuable volume to burn" (Vol. II, p. 224). "Oriental scenes look best in steel engravings", Twain remarks at one point. "I cannot be imposed upon any more by that picture of the Queen of Sheba visiting Solomon. I shall say to myself, You look fine, madam, but your feet are not clean, and you smell like a camel" (Vol. II, p. 281).

Similarly, the land of the Saviour is desolate and in ruins, "— which is gratifying to the pilgrims, for as usual, they fit the eternal words of gods to the evanescent things of this earth; Christ, it is more probable, referred to the *people*, not their shabby villages of wig-wams" (Vol. II, p. 230). Anyway, "the pilgrims will tell of Palestine, when they get home, not as it appeared to *them*, but as it appeared to Thompson and Robinson and Grimes — with the tints varied to suit each pilgrim's creed" (Vol. II, p. 244).

The authors of travelogues and commentators of the Bible who "write pictures and frame rhapsodies, and lesser men follow and see with the author's eyes instead of their own, and speak with his tongue" (Vol. II, p. 243) are as much at fault by constructing a poetical image of the Holy Land as are the various institutionalised forms of Christianity such as the Presbyterian, Baptist, Methodist, Episcopalian and Catholic creeds which in Twain's eyes have falsified the "real" picture as it presents itself to his gaze. Twain's criticism is particularly harsh in connection with the Catholic Church's habit of collecting relics, something which he had already observed in Europe and which he sees in a similar light to Blucher's need of collecting irrelevant and false memorabilia. The Catholics are also to blame, according to our author who prefers his gods to be unseen,[7] for the "claptrap side-shows" (Vol. II, p. 315) and the non-genuine ornamentations of the holiest of Christian places, the Church of the Sepulchre in Jerusalem. In the following passage, which shows Twain's distant, cool and sometimes satirical perspective, his critical attitude towards historical structures, erected as a verification of past events, becomes palatable:

It seems curious that personages intimately connected with the Holy Family always lived in grottos — in Nazareth, in Bethlehem, in imperial Ephesus — and yet nobody else in their day and generation thought of doing anything of the kind. . . . It is exceedingly strange that these tremendous events all happened in grottos [namely the birth of Christ, the slaughter of the innocents in Bethlehem, etc.] and exceedingly fortunate, likewise, because the strongest houses must crumble to ruin in time, but a grotto in the living rock will last forever. It is an imposture — this grotto stuff — but it is one that all men ought to thank the Catholics for. (Vol. II, p. 263)

Twain, who keeps a clear distance also from his fellow pilgrims, whom he criticises occasionally for not practising the teachings of the New Testament,[8] is particularly concerned about the fact that each sect must keep to itself in the Church of the Holy Sepulchre, for "it has been proven conclusively that they cannot worship together around the grave of the Saviour of the world in peace" (Vol. II, p. 300).[9]

Jerusalem, the long-awaited goal of the "pleasure trip" and the crowning glory of the journey through the Holy Land, that picture "familiar to all men from their school-days till their death" (Vol. II, p. 295), is through Twain's eyes "mournful, and dreary, and lifeless" (Vol. II, p. 299). The presence of Muslim rule is acutely felt, but this is not the reason for Twain's depressing depiction. Rather, the image created by the New Testament and the view shaped by others do not fit the presence of Jerusalem and the Middle East as seen by the matter-of-fact gaze of an American correspondent in 1867. He writes:

Of all the lands there are for dismal scenery, I think Palestine must be the prince. The hills are barren, they are dull of color, they are unpicturesque in shape. The valleys are unsightly deserts fringed with a feeble vegetation that has an expression about it of being sorrowful and despondent. The Dead Sea and the Sea of Galilee sleep in the midst of a vast stretch of hill and plain wherein the eye rests upon no pleasant tint, no striking object, no soft picture dreaming in a purple haze or mottled with the shadows of the clouds. Every outline is harsh, every feature is distinct, there is no perspective — distance works no enchantment here. It is a hopeless, dreary, heartbroken land. (Vol. II, p. 357)

Small shreds and patches of it must be very beautiful in the full flush of spring, however, and all the more beautiful by contrast with the far-reaching desolation that surrounds them on every side. I would like much to see the fringes of the Jordan in springtime, and Shechem, Esdraelon, Ajalon, and the borders of Galilee — but even then these spots would seem mere toy gardens set at wide intervals in the waste of a limitless desolation. [. . .]

[. . .] Palestine sits in sackcloth and ashes. Over it broods the spell of a curse that has withered its fields and fettered its energies. Where Sodom and Gomorrah reared their domes and towers, that solemn sea now floods the plain, in whose bitter waters no living thing exists — over whose waveless surface the blistering air hangs motionless and dead — about whose borders nothing grows but weeds, and scattering tufts of cane, and that treacherous fruit that promises refreshment to parching lips, but turns to ashes at the touch. Nazareth is forlorn; about that ford of Jordan where the hosts of Israel entered the Promised Land with songs of rejoicing, one finds only a squalid camp of fantastic Bedouins of the desert; Jericho the accursed lies a moldering ruin today, even as Joshua's miracle left it more than three thousand years ago; Bethlehem and Bethany, in their poverty and their humiliation, have nothing about them now to remind one that they once knew the high honor of the Saviour's presence; the hallowed spot where the shepherds watched their flocks by night, and where the angels sang Peace on earth, good will to men, is untenanted by any living creature, and unblessed by any feature that is pleasant to the eye. Renowned Jerusalem itself, the stateliest name in history, has lost all its ancient grandeur, and is become a pauper village; the riches of Solomon are no longer there to compel the admiration of visiting Oriental queens; the wonderful temple which was the pride and the glory of Israel is gone, and the Ottoman crescent is lifted above the spot where, on that most memorable day in the annals of the world, they reared the Holy Cross. The noted Sea of Galilee, where Roman fleets once rode at anchor and the disciples of the Saviour sailed in their ships, was long ago deserted by the devotees of war and commerce, and its borders are a silent wilderness; Capernaum is a shapeless ruin; Magdala is the home of beggared Arabs; Bethsaida and Chorazin have vanished from the earth, and the "desert places" round about them where thousands of men once listened to the Saviour's voice and ate the miraculous bread sleep in the hush of a solitude that is inhabited only by birds of prey and skulking foxes. [. . .]

Palestine is desolate and unlovely. And why should it be otherwise? Can the *curse* of the Deity beautify a land? [. . .]

Palestine is no more of this work-day world. It is sacred to poetry and tradition — it is dream-land. (Vol. II, p. 358)

Palestine, or to be exact the area of the present state of Israel, no longer sits "in sackcloth and ashes" today. The fact that the Holy Land is very much of this "work-day world" does not render Twain's account superfluous or irrelevant. Instead, Twain's humorous and sometimes shrewd exposure of the deception created by other writers about the Holy Land remains a valuable document to the way in which the "impartial eyes" of a nineteenth-century American saw that Land which today is both a modern socio-political reality and a metaphor of hope and peace, kept alive in the thousands of narratives which created its past as well as its present.

NOTES

1   All quotes used in the text of this Paper refer to *The Innocents Abroad or The New Pilgrim's Progress* in two volumes, Harper and Brothers Publishers, New York and London, 1911.

2   John Bunyan's *The Pilgrim's Progress from this world, to that which is to come . . .* (1678/ 1684) was reprinted in *The Allegorical Works,* Vol. 1 in Philadelphia in 1853. In as much as Bunyan's text stresses the return to the "Biblical Word", based upon the *Authorized Version* of 1611, the important "struggle" of the "pilgrim fathers" and an uncompromising belief in God's prophecies, it bears — in addition to its popularity — a number of sometimes ironic relationships to Twain's secular text. Although this is not the right place, a close textual comparison between Bunyan and Twain would yield remarkable insights into the ways in which a later text "rewrites" an earlier one.

3   See, for instance, Vol. I, p. 32ff and especially Vol. II, p. 100: "We have got so far East now — a hundred and fifty five degrees of longitude from San Francisco — that my watch cannot 'keep the hang' of time any more. It has grown discouraged, and stopped [. . .] These

distractions and distresses about the time have worried me so much that I was afraid my mind was so much affected that I never would have any appreciation of time again: [. . .]".

Apart from his own concern with continuous, unbroken, logical time, Twain notes with amusement as well as bewilderment the different conception of time in the East, particularly when this is related to space (i.e. the time it takes for traversing space). Keeping in mind that the nineteenth century perceives time in a fixed relation to space, emphasising time as the linear regulative within spatio-temporal relations, Twain's observations mark a rapture in the accepted pattern of "before and after". See also Vol. II, p. 259.

4   " [. . .], one thing strikes me with a force it never had before: the unsubstantial, unlasting character of fame. Men lived long lives, in the olden time, and struggled feverishly through them, toiling like slaves, in oratory, in generalship, or in literature, and then laid them down and died, happy in the possession of an enduring history and a deathless name. Well, twenty little centuries flutter away, and what is left of these things? A crazy inscription on a block of stone, which snuffy antiquaries bother over and tangle up and make nothing out of but a bare name (which they spell wrong), no history, no tradition, no poetry — nothing that can give it even a passing interest. What may be left of General Grant's great name forty centuries hence? [. . .] These thoughts sadden me." Vol. II, p. 43.

5   References to "roasting heat, such oppressive solitude, and such dismal desolation" (Vol. II, p. 352), squalor, poverty, and generally, disappointment about the Holy Land are frequent in Twain's account. This is already hinted at in the relevant chapter headings such as "The Melancholy Holy Land", "Where the Crusaders Perished", "Where the Horses Cried", etc.

Granted, Twain undertook the journey during the summer, a time of most unfavourable weather conditions with regard to heat and dryness, but his dismal picture is more the result of a clash between his romantically conceived expectations and the harsh socio-economic realities of the Middle East under Ottoman rule.

6   See especially Vol. II, p. 338. It turns out the Bedouins are an "invention" by the Arab guides in order to extract protection money from the "pilgrims". In addition, it seems as if earlier travelogues set up stories of fierce and dangerous Bedouins for the sake of adventure and suspense. Twain says: "But I believe the Bedouins to be a fraud, now." (Vol. II, p. 211).

7   See especially: "The gods of my understanding have been always hidden in clouds and very far away." (Vol. II, p. 198).

8   See for instance Vol. II, p. 125; p. 172f; p. 265; p. 221; p. 228f, etc.

9   Twain's pertinent comments with regard to the division between Christians into Catholics, Greek Orthodox, Methodists, Episcopalians and others gain particular importance when viewed in connection with American attempts to unite various Christian denominations in Unitarianism after the Civil War. Twain's own belief (see also note 7), including his scathing comments on Catholicism, seems to be similar to that held by those rationalistically inclined Christians who oppose the dogma of the Trinity.

10 The connection between the Falashas and the Land of Israel

Tudor Parfitt

Until recent times the Falashas* were the most isolated section of Jewry with the possible exception of the Bene Israel of the Konkan coast in western India. Their isolation from Jewry was a reflection of the isolation of Ethiopia from the outside world. Two hundred years ago Gibbon described the almost total isolation of Ethiopia in what has become a famous quotation: "Encompassed by the enemies of their religion, the Ethiopians slept for near a thousand years, forgetful of the world by whom they were forgotten . . . they were awakened by the Portuguese, who, turning the southern promontory of Africa, appeared in India and the Red Sea, as if they had descended through the air from a distant planet".

The Falashas were doubly isolated insofar that most of them lived right in the heart of Ethiopia in the mountainous country north of Lake Tana. Thus considerable distances, fiercely inhospitable country and more or less hostile Christian and Muslim populations were between them and the outside world. Even had they managed to get to neighbouring Sudan or to the Red Sea coast, they would have learned little of the wider world. And had they wished to travel on to Egypt or to Palestine many difficulties would have had to be overcome, particularly the lack of transport by land and sea and the dangers from bandits, pirates and slave-traders. Even within their traditional communities the Falashas maintained a physically isolated position *vis-à-vis* their usually Christian neighbours. As Wolf Leslau described their situation even as late as 1947: "Where the Falashas live there is little social contact and they are considered a people apart. It is the self-imposed social and religious isolation of the Falashas which dictates the feelings of the Ethiopians towards them. In fact I have heard some Ethiopians call the Falashas the *attenkun*, meaning 'do not touch me'."[1] If a Falasha inadvertently touched a non-Falasha he would

---

* The derivation of the word Falasha is unclear. It is perhaps from the Ethiopic *fallasa* — to emigrate. They usually call themselves *Beta Israel, Israel* or the Cushitic *Kayla*. The Ethiopian Jews in Israel dislike the term Falasha, claiming that it is pejorative.

be required to spend a number of days in solitary confinement away from the rest of the community. In time past when Falashas received money from their neighbours they would insist upon receiving it "in a vessel full of water, so as to cleanse it from impurity before handling it".[2]

The common assumption, then, is that the Falashas had no contact with the outside world and therefore had no contact with world Jewry or with the Land of Israel until very recent times.[3] Joseph Halévy, who was commissioned by the *Alliance Israelite Universelle* to visit the Falashas in 1868, reported on his return that they had no idea that there were other Jews in the world: when he told them that he, too, was a Jew, a "white Falasha", "these words . . . had a striking effect on the Falashas . . . at last several voices exclaimed: 'What! You are a Falasha! A white Falasha! You are laughing at us! Are there any white Falasha?'"[4]

According to Leslau the Falashas were almost as cut off from the Jewish world when he visited them almost a century later:

> Recently a few European travelers have visited them for one reason or another. The Falashas remember vividly the names of all their visitors; but this cannot make up for the lack of any relationship with Jewry itself. Their only avenue of contact with the external world is through the city of Gondar, if they live near it. Many Falashas living as far as three or four days' distance away have probably never had occasion to visit the city. But even in Gondar there is no news of Jewish life in other countries. No Jewish newspaper ever reaches there, and if it did only a few learned Falashas would be able to read it. The fact that there is no religious persecution at present in Ethiopia, taken in conjunction with this complete isolation in which the Falashas live, will help us to understand why they have no interest in a Jewish national state. It is true that they feel themselves a part of the Jewish religious community, and that in their prayers the memory of Jerusalem lives on, but this memory has a religious character, not a national one.[5]

But even though the Falashas were isolated to a very considerable extent it would be a mistake to think that traditionally they had no connections at all with the Land of Israel. From the works of Elijah of Ferrara, Ovadiah ben Avraham of Bertinoro and Avraham ben Ya'akov Bali the Karaite it can be seen that in the fifteenth and sixteenth centuries there were occasionally Falasha pilgrims and travellers who managed to get to the Land of Israel. Avraham ben Ya'akov Bali gave one account of Falashas who had been taken prisoner and sold as slaves in Egypt where they were bought and manumitted by sympathetic Egyptian Jews: "and then they wished to go to the Holy Land and they went there: some died and some remained [including] R. Shmuel and his son-in-law R. Avraham who became *shamashim* in the Karaite synagogue in Jerusalem".[6] We know little of these Falasha travellers other than that they made their way to the Land of Israel and may have returned to Ethiopia afterwards. It is sufficient however to confirm that the Falashas' conception of Zion was not merely one of *Yerushalayim shel ma'alah* and when the opportunity arose they visited Eretz Yisrael, as did Jews from other parts of the diaspora.

From the beginning of the seventeenth century the internal position of the Falashas in Ethiopia deteriorated sharply. During the reign of the *negus* Susenyos (1607–1623), the military might of the Falashas which had enabled them to maintain an independent kingdom for centuries, was finally crushed. As Bruce put it in his *Travels to Discover the Source of the Nile* (1790):

> The constant success of the king, and the bloody manner in which he pursued his victory, began to alarm Gideon [the Falashas' leader], lest the end should be the extirpation of his whole nation . . . the king gave orders to extirpate all the Falashas that were in Foggora, Janfakara, and Bagenarwe, to the borders of Samen: also all that were in Bagla, and in all the districts that were under their command, wherever they could find them.

The remaining Falasha strongholds and fortresses were destroyed and much of the population was killed. Others were given the choice of being killed or converting to Christianity. As Bruce wrote: "Many of them were baptized accordingly and they were all ordered to plow and harrow on the Sabbath day." Subsequently the Falashas became a poor, persecuted and ever-dwindling minority. Leading uneventful agrarian lives in the Semien Mountains, they had no chance to hear anything of the Holy Land and even less chance to go there. Increasingly uninvolved in the turbulent internal politics of Ethiopia, they were much less liable than hitherto to be captured and sold as slaves — and thus one avenue which in the past had taken some of them to Egypt and on to Palestine was lost.

But in the nineteenth century we know of at least one Falasha who somehow travelled to Palestine. Halévy wrote of him: "The only Falasha who made a pilgrimage to Jerusalem some years previously, not receiving any assistance from the Jews, who thought him a Christian, did not stay there long and died on his return to Abyssinia".[7] This suggests that a tenuous link with the Holy Land had been maintained and in addition, the questions put to Halévy by the Falashas surely indicated that they had a live curiosity about the Holy Land and that Leslau may not be correct in arguing that their "memory of Jerusalem" had merely "a religious character".[8]

> The name of Jerusalem which I had accidentally mentioned, changed as if by magic the attitude of the most incredulous [Falashas]. A burning curiosity seemed all at once to have seized the whole company. 'Oh, do you come from Jerusalem, the blessed city? Have you beheld with your own eyes, Mount Zion, and the House of the Lord of Israel, the holy Temple? And are you also acquainted with the burying-place of our mother Rachel? With glorious Bethlehem, and the town of (Kiebron) Hebron, where our holy patriarchs are buried?' They were never weary of asking me questions of this nature; and they eagerly listened to my replies. I must confess I was deeply moved on seeing those black faces light up at the memory of our glorious history. I informed them that before coming to Abyssinia I had visited Jerusalem and that the city had sadly fallen from its ancient splendour. I told them that the Jewish inhabitants of the Holy City were plunged into misery; and that a mosque stands on the site of the ancient temple. They were grieved at these news, as they had no correct idea of the

107

actual state of the Holy Land; most of them believed that it belonged to Roman Christians.[9]

It should be stressed that the Falashas' ignorance of the "actual state of the Holy Land" was one shared by the overwhelming majority of European Jews during the nineteenth century as well. Halévy was sufficiently impressed by the Falashas' interest in Palestine to suggest to the *Alliance* that the Falashas should be settled in the Holy Land on the grounds that they were "farmers and good workers who love Eretz Yisrael with a passionate devotion and their greatest desire is to leave the land of their exile and go to the land of their fathers and it would be easy to bring Falashas in their thousands to the Land of Israel".[10]

Naturally the Falashas' interest in the Holy Land derived ultimately from the Falasha sacred writings and especially from the Ge'ez Pentateuch and in this they have much in common with the *imitatio veteris testamenti* of the whole of Ethiopian Christian civilisation. Both Falasha ritual and prayers stressed the centrality of the Holy Land in a remarkable way. When a Falasha entered his synagogue he would first turn toward Jerusalem and prostrate himself. The Falasha priests, similarly, pray with their faces turned towards Jerusalem. The prayers of the Falashas are culled to a very large extent from biblical sources. Despite the lack of contact between the Falashas and other Jewish groups for two millenia, the themes celebrated in the liturgy are remarkably similar to those of the mainstream Jewish liturgy: the return to Zion and the re-establishment of priestly worship in a rebuilt Temple are predominant features. A couple of examples might serve to give a flavour of the religious and messianic attachment of the Falashas to the Holy Land:

Do not separate me, O Lord, from the chosen, from the joy, from the light and the splendour. Let me see, O Lord, the light of Israel, and let me listen to the words of the just, while they speak about the law to teach fear of Thee, O Lord, King forever.

Put me with Thy saints and just ones. Thou, Adonai, Thy name is merciful, Adonai, King forever. When all the holy angels rejoice in Thy kingdom, while Thou deliverest Thy people Israel and art gracious unto Jerusalem, Thy city, make me rejoice in Thy kingdom together with Thy chosen Israel. Deliver me, Thy servant . . .

Put me with Thy just because Thou art just, Adonai. Thy name is merciful, Adonai, eternal King. When all the lights of Heaven rejoice in Thy kingdom while Thou deliverest Thy people Israel and art gracious unto Jerusalem, Thy city, make me rejoice in Thy kingdom together with Thy chosen Israel. Deliver me, Thy servant . . .

Put me with Thy monks because Thou art just, O Lord, Adonai. Thy name is merciful, Adonai, eternal King. When the whole earth rejoices in Thy kingdom, while Thou deliverest Thy people Israel and art gracious unto Jerusalem, Thy city, make me rejoice in Thy kingdom together with Thy chosen Israel. Deliver me, Thy servant . . .

Put me with Thy anchorites, for Thou art just, Adonai. Thy name is merciful, Adonai, eternal King. When the mountains and hills and all the trees of the plain rejoice in Thy kingdom, while Thou deliverest Thy people Israel and art gracious unto

Jerusalem, Thy city, make me rejoice in Thy kingdom together with Thy chosen Israel. Deliver me, Thy servant . . .

Put me with Thy just, for Thou art just, Adonai. Thy name is merciful, Adonai, eternal King. When the seas and the roaring waves with their servants rejoice in Thy kingdom, while Thou deliverest Thy people Israel and art gracious unto Jerusalem, Thy city, make me rejoice in Thy kingdom together with Thy chosen Israel. Deliver me, Thy servant . . .

Put me with Thy chosen, for Thou art just, Adonai. Thy name is merciful, Adonai, eternal King. When they [?] rejoice in Thy kingdom, while Thou deliverest Thy people Israel and art gracious unto Jerusalem, Thy city, make me rejoice in Thy kingdom together with Thy chosen Israel. Deliver me, Thy servant . . .

Deliver me and put me with Thy people Israel, for Thou art just, Adonai. Thy name is merciful, Adonai, eternal King. When Thy city, the city of Zion, rejoices, and the mountain of Thy sanctuary, the place of Thy glory, is joyful in Thy kingdom, while Thou deliverest Thy people Israel and art gracious toward Thy servants, make me rejoice in Thy kingdom together with Thy chosen Israel. Deliver me, Thy servant . . .[11]

From these passages it can be seen that the ultimate redemption of the Falashas was viewed as a secondary stage to the redemption of the rest of Israel.

One of the factors underlying the Falashas' interest in Eretz Yisrael was their belief in the imminent coming of the Messiah and the ingathering of the exiles. J.M. Flad, who participated in an evangelical mission to the Falashas in the 1860s, wrote: "I once became acquainted with a monk, Aba Mahari, [a Falasha] who had a firm persuasion that the time was near when God would gather the Jews out of all nations into the land of their fathers. He believed that they would then rebuild their temple at Jerusalem."[12] While Henry Stern, the German Jew who converted to Christianity and worked on behalf of the Church Mission to the Jews, observed that at the same period: "'We believe that Jerusalem will again be rebuilt' is the answer on the lips of every Falasha, when questioned as to the future destiny of his nation. This event they regard as the consummation of their brighter hopes, the realization of their fondest mundane vision."[13]

In the middle of the nineteenth century a number of events combined to sharpen the messianic expectations of the Falashas. The period until 1855 is traditionally called the time of the *masafent* (judges), for as Ullendorff has pointed out "it resembled very closely the era of the Old Testament judges when 'there was no king in Israel: every man did that which was right in his own eyes'."[14] This period of turbulence was brought to an end by the accession to the throne of the Emperor Theodore in 1855. In any event, the time of the disorders was taken to presage the "end of days". For both Ethiopian Christians and Jews, Theodore is the name given to the Messiah and some of the Falashas confusedly came to the belief that the Emperor was indeed the long-awaited redeemer of Israel. At the same time the missionaries who were active among the Falashas tried to impress upon them that Jews elsewhere in the world had accepted that the Messiah had already arrived in Jerusalem. Some of the Falashas came to the conclusion that messianic days were upon them and one, a certain Abba Sägga, in 1862 wrote a letter to the chief priest of the Jews in Jerusalem. The letter was published in the *Journal Asiatique* in 1867 but was apparently never answered.[15]

> God be praised, Lord of Israel, Lord of all spirit and of all that is flesh; this letter is sent by Abba Sägga; may it reach the priest of Jerusalem, Kaka Yusef, the chief priest of all the Hebrews; Kaka Yusef, may it reach you by the hand of Buronkosä. Peace to you, our brother Hebrews! The first letter which you sent by the hand of Daniel son of Ananya, father of Muse. . . . Has the time arrived that we should return to you, [to] our city, the holy city of Jerusalem? For we are a poor people and have neither prince nor prophet and if the time has arrived send us a letter which will reach us, because you are in a better position than us. Tell us and inform us of all that will happen to us. But as for us, a great agitation has disturbed our hearts, for they say that the time has arrived; the men of our country say, 'Separate yourselves from the Christians and go to your country, Jerusalem, and reunite yourselves with your brothers and offer up sacrifices to God, Lord of Israel, in the Holy Land. As for you, Bironkos, man of God, as we love you, so go take for us that letter to our brother Hebrews. Peace to you, peace to you, with much peace, our brother Hebrews, you who are in the Law of the Torah which God gave to Moses his servant on Mount Sinai! I who have sent this letter, Abba Sägga, . . . I sent it to you in seven thousand, three hundred and fifty-four, year of the world [i.e. 1862], in the second month. The letter is finished.[16]

Some of the Falashas were taken in by the missionaries' stratagems and converted to Christianity; but others were not, and stubbornly asked the Emperor to grant permission for a controversy to be held between the Christians and the Falashas in his presence. This dramatic event duly took place at the court in Gondar. Quoting his Falasha sources Halévy wrote:

> . . . five of our priests presented themselves before the king, accompanied by a great number of us, being all resolved to die for our faith if we should not obtain mercy . . . the controversy lasted several days, and our priests had to refute the evidence deduced by the missionaries from certain passages of the Bible . . . when the king saw that our faith was firm as a rock, he became wroth and threatened us all with instant execution . . . Abba Simeon [a Falasha priest] arose, and said resolutely to the king 'In matters of death, O Theodore, thou art master on earth, but there is another master in heaven. . . . At the same time we all got up from the ground and cried out 'Kill us, we are willing to die for the faith of our fathers'. The king, seeing that we were resolute, softened down, and said 'Bravo, Falashas, fear nothing, you shall not die . . .'[17]

The king then offered them a breathing space during which he hoped "they would learn the truths of my religion". The controversy and the false messianic expectations which preceded led some of the Falashas to react in a remarkable way. According to Halévy:

> Some of the priests who had been ordered to appear at Gondar to assist at the controversy, and who had feared a fatal termination, fell subsequently into a singular state of religious exaltation. According to Jewish traditions, a great calamity must

precede the advent of the Messiah; they believed that the behests of Theodore were the harbingers of deliverance, and that the time had arrived for a return to Jerusalem, and for a recovery of the inheritance of their ancestors. All shared in this hope of speedy redemption, and a crowd of poor, simple-minded individuals resolved to start for Jerusalem, which they knew to be situated beyond the Red Sea. Travelling preparations do not take long in Abyssinia; people walk barefooted, and each person bears on his shoulders a small bag of peas, which is the ordinary food of the Falashas on their travels. The children and some gourds of water are placed on donkeys, or carried by young men. In less time than is requisite in Europe to get ready for a short excursion, a numerous troop of Falashas had started to go to Jerusalem.

At the head of his band of pilgrims walked Abbas Mehari, Bitya, Bethebeboo, Wedady, Zeynoo, and Thefeth, all renowned for their piety. Their task was to regulate the order of march, to encourage the timid, and to attend to the sick; to elude enemies on the journey, and to render fatigue bearable. Psalms were recited and hymns chanted. The unhappy pilgrims believed firmly in the intercession of Providence in their favour; they persuaded themselves that the miracles of old would be repeated, and the Red Sea would once more open a path for them within its depth, and that as soon as the Red Sea was crossed they would find manna and birds to feed them, as their ancestors found after their departure from Egypt.[18]

Having crossed the towering Semien range, the pilgrims arrived at the old imperial capital of Axum where the caravan was forced to halt. They waited there for two years, hoping to earn sufficient money through their traditional crafts to proceed to Jerusalem, but they were unsuccessful. Many of them, particularly children and the elderly, died, and finally the remnant were forced to give up their *aliyyah* and return to their native villages.

Had this attempt to reach Eretz Yisrael been successful the Falashas, the descendants of the last independent Jewish state before the establishment of the State of Israel, might have been remembered among the pioneers of the modern return to the land. But disheartened by their failure the Falashas were not to attempt a mass migration again for the next 120 years.

Individuals and small groups of Falashas maintained a desire to go to the Holy Land. The Jewish apostate missionary Stern was approached by a group of Falasha priests who had been involved in the abortive march to Jerusalem just before he left Ethiopia on the way to Palestine. "Several young priests," he wrote, "whose handsome features bore sad and cruel traces of a severe desert pilgrimage, volunteered to accompany me to Jerusalem; but as the mountains of Ethiopia are far better adapted to implant the seed of peace into the troubled heart of an untutored African, than either Syria or any other foreign country, I declined, on the present as on all former occasions, to accede to such proposals."[19]

Throughout the twentieth century, the march of progress has been slower in Ethiopia than elsewhere. There are certainly many Falashas whose way of life today is not markedly different from that of their nineteenth-century forebears. But in one sense the Falashas of today are different. Since the time of Halévy's mission the Falasha religion has been influenced by a major world religion in the form of modern rabbinic Judaism. Thus between the time of Halévy's visit and Leslau's visit in 1947, many features of Falasha observance had disappeared while new ones in line more or less with contemporary "normative" Jewish practice had emerged.[20]

Nonetheless, modern manifestations of Falasha messianism can be seen as being firmly in the tradition of what can be reconstructed of the Falashas' historical relationship with the Promised Land. In 1948 the creation of the State of Israel brought a sense of messianic expectation to the Falashas as it did to many other Jewish groups throughout the world. Assuming that the Temple would soon be rebuilt, a number of Falasha priests encouraged their villagers to sell off their cattle and move to Addis Ababa, from where, it was hoped, they would be able to go to the new Jewish state.[21] Nothing came of this initiative because Haile Selassie, the Emperor of Ethiopia, was against Falasha emigration because he feared it might lead to other minorities in his diverse empire seeking autonomy or special privileges. The State of Israel was no more enthusiastic. No matter what a variety of rabbis had said about the Jewishness of the Falashas — and particularly Palestine's chief Rabbi, Avraham Kook, who in 1921 had declared that it was incumbent upon world Jewry "to save our Falasha brethren from extinction and to rescue 50,000 souls of the House of Israel from oblivion" — there were many, including a number of well-known *ethiopisants,* who argued that the Falashas were not Jews at all. The State of Israel accepted these arguments and it was not until April 1975 that the Israeli Ministry of the Interior was prepared to accord to Falashas the right enjoyed by all other Jews of automatic Israeli citizenship under the 1950 Law of Return.

Whether they were officially regarded as Jews or not, Falashas trickled into Israel. The sea journey from the Ethiopian port of Massawa to Eilat was just over 48 hours. Some Falashas walked from their mountainous areas to the coast and managed to get jobs on freighters which took them up the Red Sea to Eilat where they jumped ship. A very small number managed to save money for an air ticket from El Al, which in 1970 established a regular service from Addis Ababa to Lod. But Israeli consular and immigration officials put many obstacles in the way of Falasha immigration.

The small band of Falashas who managed to make their way to Israel formed themselves into the Israel Falasha Committee. It was led by Professor Tartakower, a sociologist and demographer, and an Ethiopian-born Jew of Yemenite extraction, Ovadia Hazzi, who had become Israel's senior sergeant major in the Israel Defence force. Headed by this strangely matched pair, the society played a major part in persuading the religious authorities that the Falashas were indeed Jews. Thus, in 1973, the Sephardi Chief Rabbi of Israel, Ovadia Yosef declared that the Falashas were indeed "Jews who must be saved from absorption and assimilation. We are obligated to speed up their immigration into Israel . . . for whoever saves a single soul in Israel, it is as though he had saved the whole world."

If the part played by the Falashas in securing their recognition as Jews was considerable, the part played by them in eventually securing their physical redemption was overwhelming. No Jewish group in the history of Zionism has suffered as much as the Falashas did in their recent struggles to get to Israel. They walked vast distances; were attacked by army units, rebel units and bandits; they walked through war zones; they suffered the privations of the march — starvation and thirst; they went knowingly and without medicines into disease-ridden areas in the full awareness that they had no immunity to those diseases; they risked imprisonment and torture — the punishments meted out to those Falashas found trying to leave Ethiopia; in many cases they left areas where there was food and water to go to areas where they knew there was neither. Ten per cent of the Falashas who left their homes in 1984 for Israel died before they reached the Sudan; about 15 per cent of the remainder died in the refugee camps of the Sudan in the following months. It is not the function of this paper to describe the many factors which led to the exodus of the Falashas and the Israeli initiative, Operation Moses, which rescued them.[22] But one fact is clear. The yearning for Zion was an overwhelmingly important factor in their decision to leave and that same yearning is an indigenous part of the remarkable faith of the Jews of Ethiopia. When they left the mountains of Gondar they were struggling to reach what is called in the Falasha liturgy "a city which is white and shining decorated with gold, hyacinth and pearls filled with fruit and plantations of almonds nuts and pomegranates."

REFERENCES

1 W. Leslau, *Falasha Anthology,* New York, 1969, p. xl.
2 J. Halévy, *Travels in Abyssinia,* London, 1877, p. 41.
3 W. Leslau, ibid.
4 J. Halévy, *Miscellany of Hebrew Literature,* ed. A. Löwy, London, 1877, p. 215.
5 W. Leslau, op. cit., p. xli.
6 A.Z. Eshkoli, *Yehudei Habash be-Sifrut ha-'Ivrit, Zion,* I, 1935, p. 316ff. In the sixteenth century Rabbi David ben Solomon Ibn Avi Zimra, the Radbaz, approved the marriage of an Egyptian Jew to a Falasha woman. See S.B. Freehof, *A Treasury of Responsa,* Philadelphia, 1963, pp. 122ff.
7 J. Halévy, *Miscellany,* p. 216.
8 W. Leslau, op. cit., p. 3 n.
9 J. Halévy, *Miscellany,* p. 215.
10 E. Ben Yehudah, *Selef maskileinu* in *Havatzelet,* 10th year, 1880, 29, p. 12.
11 W. Leslau, op. cit., p. 126.
12 J.M. Flad, *The Falashas of Abyssinia,* London, 1869, p. 33. See also *Notes from the Journal of F. [sic] M. Flad,* ed. W.D. Veitch, London, 1860, p. 84.
13 H.A. Stern, *Wanderings among the Falashas in Abyssinia,* London, 1862, p. 193.
14 E. Ullendorff, *The Ethiopians,* London, 1960, p. 82.
15 *Journal Asiatique,* 1867, vol. 9, Feb.-March. Quoted in D. Kessler, *The Falashas,* New edition, 1985, p. 123.
16 Perhaps Buronkosä was a missionary by the name of Bronkhorst. See Kessler, op. cit., p. 124. It could be that the Daniel mentioned in the letter was the same Falasha mentioned by Halévy who had made the trip to Jerusalem. From Jacob Saphir's book *Even Sappir* we know that Daniel went to Jerusalem in 1855 where the reception accorded him was no more than lukewarm.
17 J. Halévy, *Miscellany,* p. 248.
18 Ibid.

19 H. Stern, op. cit., p. 297.
20 W. Leslau, op. cit., p. xii.
21 S.D. Messing, *The Story of the Falashas,* published by the author, 1982, p. 61.
22 But see T.V. Parfitt, *Operation Moses,* London, 1985 and T.V. Parfitt and D. Kessler, *The Falashas: The Jews of Ethiopia,* Minority Right Group Report no. 67.

Part IV

The Holy Land in Hebrew and Jewish Literature

11 The attitude towards the Land of Israel in Spanish Hebrew poetry

Ezra Spicehandler*

In discussing the Jewish Golden Age in Muslim Spain during the tenth and twelfth centuries, Yitzhak (Fritz) Baer asserts that "we obtain most of our knowledge of this period from contemporary Hebrew poetry, fostered and cultivated under the tutelage of Jewish courtiers."[1] This statement in a sense almost validates our specific quest, namely, to explore the attitudes of the Spanish Jewish community of that era toward the Land of Israel as reflected in the works of its leading Hebrew poets. *Almost,* because in so far as these attitudes are concerned, the student must also study the philosophical–theological legacy left by such thinkers as Judah Halevi, Maimonides and Nachmanides, and the many exegetical, *halakhic* and kabbalistic works of the period.[2] This chapter is confined to a discussion of the poets of the period, more specifically to four who are universally acknowledged to be the major poets of the Golden Age: Samuel Hanagid (d. 1056), Solomon ibn Gabirol (1022?–1054?), Moses ibn Ezra (1055 or 1060–1135) and Judah Halevi (1075?–1141?). For the most part, these poets lived and were educated in Muslim Andalusia. While Ibn Ezra and Halevi spent a good part of their lives in Christian Spain, they belonged culturally to the Arab-Jewish milieu of southern Spain and were nurtured by this most fruitful symbiosis.

Modern scholarship has distinguished between two major types of Spanish Hebrew poetry: *Shirat Haḥol,* secular poetry, and *Shirat Haqodesh,* sacred poetry. This latter type has been more rigorously defined as poetry composed for liturgical purposes. This chapter is limited to an examination of *Shirat Haḥol.* Methodologically speaking the study of this so-called secular literature may yield more accurate results. *Shirat Haqodesh* was, by and large, commissioned by communal authorities to embellish the services of the synagogues. Poets who accepted such commissions served as laureates who perforce

---

* I am particularly indebted to my student Jan Katzew for his discussion of the view of Moses ibn Ezra and Judah Halevi *vis-à-vis Arabiyah* and to my colleague Professor Barry Kogan for his most suggestive analysis of Halevi's motives in undertaking his incompleted pilgrimage to the Holy Land.

expressed conventional communal sentiments rather than their own personal views. On the other hand, *Shirat Hahol* tended to be more subjective and expressed more frequently the individual beliefs of their authors. It included wine songs, love poems, paeans to nature, epistolary and occasional verse which celebrated friendship, and marked life cycle events such as marriage and death. Yet here, too, we must keep in mind that the medieval poet not only did not eschew literary conventions but considered them to be legitimate devices placed at the disposal of the man of letters! Moreover, many of the poems celebrating life cycle events were also commissioned by patrons who often demanded and relished the conventional forms of flattery which were part of the Andalusian tradition. Nevertheless, with all these reservations in mind, *Shirat Hahol* is more apt to reveal the poet's personal proclivities. This is usually true when it comes to our subject, which, with the exception of Judah Halevi's *oeuvre* is only occasionally touched upon in secular poetry.

I

Samual Hanagid, the first of this eminent quartet, was a statesman, general, scholar and poet who served as prime minister of the small kingdom of Granada in the eleventh century. Despite his high estate he writes:

By the life of my living Redeemer, until
My dying day, I hope for the ingathering of the dispersed.
I do not say: "I am mighty and steeped in majesty.
My seat is among the kings of glory."
Nor am I tempted, to say:
"You are a god, honored above men,
What, then, might you gain when Joseph[3] is redeemed?
What might you garner when the dispersed are reassembled?"
Standing in the Temple's precincts is good for my soul,
Better than ruling over all creatures.
Quaffing rich beverages on defiled soil
Is, for me, like drinking dregs.

(*Yarden,* I, XXV: lines 8–13, p. 81)

The sentiments expressed here are quite similar to those attributed to Ḥasdai ibn Shaprut, the Jewish courtier who played so prominent a role in the court of Abd'urraḥman III of Cordoba earlier in the tenth century. In a letter to Joseph, king of the Khazars, he allegedly wrote that he contacted him, in order to ascertain: "whether there exists ... sovereignty in Israel's exile. Where [Jews] are not persecuted nor subjugated. If I knew it were so, I would eschew my glory, abandon my high station, forsake my family and trek over hill and vale, land and sea until I reached the place where your Majesty lives." (*Kuzari,* introduction to the traditional text, Warsaw, 1930.)

In Samuel's scale, the restoration of the Temple cult takes highest precedence. Proud of his Levitical lineage, he conjures up in his mind's eye a scene in which pilgrims stream to Jerusalem to celebrate the festivals:

1 My heart burns and my eye tears
Because I yearn for Ḥamat and Mefaʻat[4]

2 To see Sirion's[5] congregation chanting,
Bearing bundles of nard to Moriah

3 And Lebanon's caravan singing upon Ariel[6]
Spreading myrrh and cassia like a sower of seed

4 As in the days when Zion's youths were like
The sun shining upon its beds of spice,

5 And Jeshurun gazed upon princesses
With darling eyes, painted wide by godly deeds,

6 And no daughters dishonored their fathers,
No sons acted villainously and found wanting.

7 I pine for the princess who nestles her lovely
breasts among the lilies of the nut garden[7]
To garner and to plant.

8 Yet there lions roar, thus preventing her
From crossing into it, from entering and reaching it (the garden),

9 Destroyed by alien hands who tore the open buds,
the stone wreaths and the knops[8] from the lovely city's walls.

10 When I see in my mind's eye, the sanctuary, a fallen ruin
And the foundation stone[9] lost among the stoney rubble,

11 I weep bitterly with trembling eye, moan with anguished heart
As if the enemy's lance has rent my heart.

12 O God, will Edom's daughter be exalted forever, dwell
Among the stars, While Zion's is sunken in the deep sea?

13 Are you not wrath (to see) that Judah's daughter is stripped
Bare while the daughter of Uz[10] is decked in jewels?[11]

14 Rise like a lion from its lair or a leopard
From its hills, raise your outstretched and famed arm

15 And shoot your arrows at Boẓrah,[12] and force
Yemen[13] to drink your full cup of wrath.

(*Yarden*, I, IX: pp. 35–6)

This poem contains key motifs which occur in the earlier *paytanic* literature and recur throughout Spanish poetry. Many symbols and allusions are drawn from the Song of Songs and Lamentations. The image of pilgrims marching to Jerusalem bearing their gift-offerings emphasises the centrality of the Temple cult in the mind of Samuel, the Levite. The reference to Edom as the oppressor is somewhat surprising. Palestine was still under Muslim suzerainty in 1041 when the poem was composed. Is this, then, a convention drawn from the *paytanim* or is it difficult for Samuel to view the Muslims in whose midst he had so greatly prospered as being his enemies? The theme of redemption is repeated in several poems. In another *Qasidah*, he expresses the hope that his song will:

49 Yet be chanted within God's sanctuary
   Under the canopy of the beloved bride.
50 Yet be placed in the mouth of pilgrims
   ascending to Zion along straight paths.

(*Yarden*, I, XXII, p. 70)

A similar longing for the temple cult is expressed in a poem written in 1052:

4 Should I live — when there is no Ark nor curtain,
   No glory of the embossed and flowered Menorah,
5 No sanctuary, while the temple precinct and the Holy
   of Holies
6 Have strange fire, and the sacred flame is removed
   Along with the beauty of the bases, the capital and palm figures
   Beautiful as pomegranates — numbering 96?[14]

(*Yarden*, I, XXXI; p. 104)

Samuel's love for Eretz Yisrael was also expressed through acts of friendship and philanthropy. He contributed annually to *Yeshivat Geon Yaakov* and to various synagogues in Jerusalem.[15] In 1056 he sent an epistolary poem to Daniel ben Azaryah congratulating him on his appointment as head of the Yeshivah[16].

40 Would that I were like a winged bird
   Then I would fly to you,
41 To God's house to see the scion of David,[17]
   A handsome man chosen for a handsome post.

(*Yarden*, I, XL, p. 142)

Besides allusions to Zion and Jerusalem, Samuel refers to Ḥamath and Mefa'ath, the two Levite cities,[18] to Mt Lebanon and Hermon,[19] the Sea of Kinnereth,[20] and Yenoḥah and the Jordan and Amanah rivers.[21]

II

Solomon ibn Gabirol (b. Malaga 1021–2, d. Lucena 1053–8), makes few allusions to Eretz Yisrael in his secular poetry. Few of his poems can be considered to be *Zionades*. However, the theme of exile appears in several. Thus in a poem commemorating the installation of an unnamed *Ḥakham*, he speaks of God,

5 Who wakens and redeems the sleepers
   From their exile and speeds the salvation of the
6 Exiled ewe, bereft of offspring, solitary,
   Most bereaved of the bereft,

120

7 Driven from repose to agony
  Devoured as are her daughters
8 Exiled for a thousand years . . .
9 Enemies devoured her and even
  Plot to consume her remnants,
11 She is driven from hand to hand . . .
18 Those who were exiled and reached Spain
   Were reached by curses . . .
20 Hungry and thirsty for lack of water
   Like helpless mountain deer.

(*Yarden*, I, XLVI, pp. 85–7)

Addressing his own soul as he goes into exile (probably from Andalusia to Saragosa), he pleads:

25 Rise and run after it
   Fleet as an eagle or gazelle.
26 If you encounter pain or agony
   Fear not, nor be tormented
27 If you tread over hill and dale
   Or ride the heights of the sea.
28 Turn your back on Spain.
   Tarry not.
29 Until you tread in Zoar (Egypt)
   In Babylon and the Land of the Hart (Israel).
30 There you will walk proudly
   And be exalted and protected.
31 Why do you pine, O anguished pauper
   Do you long for your home? . . .
41 Woe to you; land of my enemies . . .
42 I have no partimony within you

(*Yarden*, CXII, I, pp. 235–37)

Gabirol's patriotism is more intensely expressed in his hymn to the Hebrew language which he wrote as an introduction to a projected grammar:

4 Says Solomon, the Spaniard who
  Gathered in the scattered nation's holy tongue:
5 My heart surveyed the congregation of the Rock (God)
  And pondered over its remnants.
6 Knowing that the holy tongue was destroyed for them . . .
8 Half speak Edomite [Spanish] and half the black
  language of Kedar [Arabic]

121

The poet pledges to write a grammar of his beloved Hebrew.

24 Because I know that Hebrew alone
   Is the fairest of all the tongues . . .

He stresses the superiority of the Holy Tongue:

38 Therefore know the superiority of Hebrew
   Which is above all languages of men.
39 Heavenly dwellers do daily frame in it
   Glorious praise to Him who wraps himself in a cloud.
40 In days of yore it was the universal language
   Until men of foolish counsel were rent asunder
       [a reference to the Tower of Babel].
41 God confused their tongue, only in Hebrew
   Did it remain whole.
42 The father of multitudes [Abraham] inherited it
   And bequeathed it to his sons.
   It was preserved from generation to generation.
43 Even he who dwelt in foreign lands [Jacob]
   When his leg was caught in the snare
   never left it.
44 In it the Torah was given and by it
   All the prophets were sent to heal.
45 Players of lyres played their songs in it
   When the Land of the Hart was mistress.
46 God will do battle with you, O remnant of Jacob,
   If you forget this choicest of tongues.

(*Yarden*, CCXXIV, pp. 376–80)

For the most part, exile for Gabirol, is a spiritual condition rather than a political reality. Thus in a poem in praise of wisdom he reprimands his soul:

13 But my heart, my soul's anguish recalls its sins . . .
15 And finds neither rest nor sleep for its eyes.
16 It sits each night lamenting in a voice
   which wakens the sleepers
17 And they stir at its wail and wake because
   of its lamentations
18 Saying: Why does this crying frighten its neighbors?,
19 Weeping at the night-watch, for Zion and its sons?
20 I respond: Why should I continue to live
   after [the death of] its faithful minions,
21 Its princes and chiefs, its sages and scholars . . .

24 For she [wisdom] is an illustrious bride —
     they, her suitors.
25 She, the ark, they, her two stone tablets.
26 She, the Menorah, they, her cups and branches

(*Yarden,* I, CLXVII, p. 325)

Zion, for him, becomes a symbol for the lost wisdom of ancient times. Following a tradition which harks back to the *kinot* in Talmudic and Midrashic literature, Gabirol employs metaphors which compare great men to holy vessels or Temple objects. Thus in his famous lament at the murder of his patron Yekutiel in 1039, he writes:

26 The button stricken and the ceilings rumbled,
     Yakhin[22] which collapsed and whose round capitals fell

(*Yarden,* CLVI, p. 292)

46 The day when the crown of the nation fell,
     The day on which the perpetual-altar offerings ceased.

(*Yarden,* I, p. 297)

70 My heart moans like flutes for Zion
     And my passion is aroused by its wailing.
     She cries: The wall in which my people
     Found strength and shelter has fallen.
71 Its rampants are no more, its foundations are bared,
     Its stones spilled into the valley.

(*Yarden,* I, p. 297)

41 Do not send this message to the land of the Hart
     lest the mountains tremble and tumble.
42 My people mourn, for the Cherub has abandoned the sanctuary,
     The weapons and the precious vessels have been scattered.
43 Cry in the city and wail, for the Ark has been
     taken and the Tablets broken . . .
45 Today is like the day in which the lion rose for his lair,[23]
     today lions besieged Ariel,
46 Today the crown of the nation has fallen,
     today the perpetual sacrifices on its altars have ceased.

(*Yarden,* I, pp. 294–5)

In another poem lamenting the death of Rav Hai, the gaon of Pumbeditha, *Zion* becomes a metaphor for the great scholar:

1 Weep O children of the exile, O my masses
    Weep for Zion the city of God
2 Wail and mourn in Ephrath
    Cry out in Bethlehem[24]

3   A shout of anguish stirs
    My agony for Zion's daughter in every city.

(Yarden, LIX, p. 301)

Gabirol mentions the following geographic locations in his secular poems: Zion (CLXVII:19; CLVI:70; CLIX:1,3; CLS:4); Jericho (CXCIV:34; CLXVII:19); Jaffa (LV 11:13); the Sharon (III:55, XIII:1, CLXVII:10); Gilead (XCII:4; CXVI:10); Ramah (IV:13); Mizpah (IV:13); Anatoth (XI:6); Mt. Tabor (CLXIV:26); Bethlehem (CLIX:3); Kinnereth (XVII:19); Ephrath (CIX:2); Sinai (CLIX:14); Jordan (XXXVIII:14); Tigris (XLVI:90); Euphrates (XLVI:12; CXVIII:34); (XLIX:38); Maḥanayim (XLIX:16); Penuel (XLIX:19); Tyre (LXIX:2); Ayalon (CXXII:7); Carmel (XCCI:5; LXXVI:8, 15; CXXXII:3–4; CLVI:26–28, 42–49; CLXIV:46; CLXVII:25ff).

III

In his Kitāb almuḥāḍarāt w'al mudhākarāt, Moses ibn Ezra places Gabirol at the end of the first period of Spanish Hebrew poetry:

> At the close of this school's period, there arose a second school which followed its paths and adhered to its rules but was superior to it in the molding of poetry, the power of diction, the strength of thought and the clarity of style. The elder of the school, its most honorable member, its pillar and leader was Rabbi Isaac, son of Ghiat ... of Lucena, the city of poesy ... I studied with him and acquired learning from him. And my trivial work is a mere drop drawn from his sea and the little I have [accomplished] is a mere spark from his sun.[25]

He, then, considers himself a member of the succeeding (third) generation of poets. He places himself and his younger colleague, Judah Halevi, in the third generation.[26]

Moses ibn Ezra, unlike his two predecessors, was to the manor born. A scion of one of Granada's more aristocratic families, he studied at the famous academy of Lucena and at the same time steeped himself in secular studies. His multifarious citations from philosophical and rhetorical works in the Kitāb attest to his profound knowledge of the best of Arabic culture.[27] Indeed he goes so far as to quote passages from the Qor'an to support several of his views, a rather startling practice for a committed Jew. He is most enthralled with the achievements of Arabic poetry and accepts the truism that Arabs and the Arabic language are most attuned to the poetic arts:

> The Ishmaelite group ... does not belong to the communities that excell in the sciences, nor to those nations who are masters of thought. God only endowed them with a talent for eloquence and formed their nature only to be concerned with the art of rhetoric. They are superior to other nations solely in the precision of diction and the composition of rhymed prose and poetry.[28]

He goes on to lament the fact that Jews have neglected the Hebrew language which is the sacred word of God. While he does not specifically say so, he seems to imply that Arabic is superior to Hebrew in the realm of poetry.[29]

His admiration for *'Arabiyah* (Arabic culture) pervades much of his work. When he deals with poetics, he insists that "Since I have already stated that poetry is the science of the Arabs and that in this field Jews walk in their footsteps, I will therefore ignore the views of him who rejects the use of these devices . . . The Arabs have accepted them and made them tools for their works and equipment for their rhyming to the point that when these are found in their verse, they delight in them and when they are absent they become ugly and second-rate even if they are not proven to be so but are so only by common consent. And we must agree with them in accord with their presence and our ability. Since it would be improper to walk only partially in their footsteps and not entirely."[30]

Another indication of Ibn Ezra's symbiotic view of his culture occurs in a *Qasidah* originally addressed to the readers of the *Kitāb.* Here he clearly asserts:

25 And turn, O you pure of heart, to the vision of the wise
And not to magic and charms
26 To the hill of aloes,[31] the mountain of faith, the page of wisdom for those who remember or forget
27 Like willows to instruct the sweet, the eloquence of the Arabs, intelligent in diction,
28 And the wisdom of the Greeks . . .

(Brody, CCXXIII, p. 127)

Nehemiah Aloni has examined Moses ibn Ezra's commitments to *'Arabiyah*[32] and concludes that (1) He stresses the concept of *Zahuth,* eloquence, more than any other poet; (2) He praises Arabic poetry:

15 And Moses' song was truly for a king like
an Arabic song in sweet words

(Brody, XXIV, p. 29)

and

1 And lovely words in Arabic or Hebrew
and wisdom to be held on every side

(Brody, XXX, p. 33)

132 And Hebrew spoken in proper fashion
And the power of Arabic speech, his topics and his rhetoric

(Brody, CCXXIV, p. 243)

(3) He is enthusiastic about Arabic poetics as manifest in his work on the subject and in *Sefer Anaq.* (4) Compared to his four colleagues, his poetry contains few references to geographic locations in Eretz Yisrael. Aloni lists only the following locations: Mahanayim (XLIII:51) Sinai (XCIII:49) as the only references in Ibn Ezra's secular poetry.[33]

In this last instance he is clearly mistaken. I have counted more than 20 biblical sites mentioned by Ibn Ezra, and many of these occur several times.[34]

Nevertheless Aloni is correct in asserting that nowhere in his secular poetry does Ibn Ezra express any expectation of an impending restoration to Zion. My student Jan Katzew has carefully documented this fact. For Ibn Ezra, his forced exile from Arabic Granada about five years after its conquest by the Morabites in 1090 to Christian Castille was real *exile*; his hope for a restoration in Eretz Yisrael was an eschatological dream.[35]

Thus Ibn Ezra can lament:

(1) How long will my feet be sent into exile *(begaluth)*
    And still find no rest?

(2) Fortune has unsheathed the sword of separation
    To pursue me and wielded the axe of wandering.

(3) It turned its children against me so that I cannot stand in one place and (must) like a shadow flee day after day . . .

(10) Enough, O children of fortune, for my body is too weak to bear suffering; go easy, for my soul has no strength.

(11) Tell me, Am I a sea or a sea monster, a child of the *Anaquim* or like Manoah's son (Samson)? . . .

(14) Would that I could meet my brother, intellect, in my alien state (Geruti), I would willingly forgive Fortune's sins.

(15) I run from city to city and find (only) the tents of folly pitched by Fortune's hands.

(16) Unable (weary) to find the gates of my wisdom which were not shut until Fortune was exhausted;

(17) It fails to see the star of my starry virtues (praises) which rise and shine above the orbit of my words.

(18) Its ear is too heavy to hear my speech even when the ears of the deaf are open.

(19) Say to those who plagiarize (my) song that when they robbed my words and purloined my teaching,

(20) And inlaid rubies with gravel
    and planted thorns among the myrtle . . . ,

(21) They are incapable of joining them, until they are able to cross the flood of my tears on foot.

(22) How can one compare the roar of lions to the howling of dogs?

(23) Can a young ass race a horse or a fledgling give chase to an eagle?

(24) My poems will endure as long as the sun shines while they shall be utterly forgotten.

(25) After the nobles of Araby,[36] how can sleep be sweet or my heart find rest?

(26) Will Fortune, after hardening its heart a while relent, incline toward me and do my will?

(27) Will it (Fortune) yet lead me to join the company of my friends who passed me by (i.e. forgotten me)[37]

(28) Or shall my bones be resurrected after I die and, watered by their tears, blossom forth.

(29) Who knows whether they remember (my) love or have cast it off?

(30) Let my right hand wither if I've forgotten them or if I do not desire to rejoice at their sight.

(31) If God would yet return me to Granada[38] my ways shall indeed prosper.

(32) And I will quench my thirst at the waters of Genil[39] which remain pure even when delicious streams turn turbid —

(33) A land in which my life was lovely and the cheek of fortune was extended to me (for kissing)

(34) I ask so little of God, and there is nothing which prevents him from proclaiming liberty for a prisoner of separation and freeing him.

(Brody, LXVIII, p. 66)

Exile, *galut,* is here clearly exile from Granada. Granada and Genil are given Hebrew names and are longed-for as Snir (a pun on Sierra Nevada). The oath "If I forget thee O Jerusalem" (Psalm 137) is applied to Granada and the poet's company of friends.

Ibn Ezra's poetry is replete with contemptuous remarks about the inferior culture of Jews and gentiles in Christian Spain.[40]

His anguish animates many of his poems. Yet, never in his non-liturgical poetry does he directly connect the bitterness and pain of exile with a yearning for Eretz Yisrael. It must be stressed that these feelings are sometimes expressed in the *Shirey Haqodesh* but they hardly spill over into his personal poetry.

There are a few exceptions. A long poem composed to thank God for bringing an end to a drought, is included in the *Brody* collection. Although it is not a liturgical poem, since it is written for a specific occasion, it nevertheless cannot really be considered to be one of *Shirey Haḥol.* Its theology is conventional. The drought is a punishment for sin. The people repent with prayer and fasting. God, in his grace, forgives them and grants them rain. The concluding lines reiterate the expected phrases of national consolation.

(82) And thus he will redeem them, and bring vengeance upon their enemies and despoilation

(83) And fight their battle and render judgement in their favor and oppress their oppressors

(84) And remember their community in times of trouble even while they dwell in the land of their foes.

(Brody, LVI, p. 57)

Similarly in his cosmological *Qasīdah* which was to serve as an introduction to his book *Alḥādiqat fī maʿānī al maghaz walḥaqīqāt.* ("The Garden dealing with True and Parabolic Matters"), he refers to the restoration but only in the final sentence:

165 And one day he will grant redemption to his people and gather its dispersion as well as the day of the resurrection.

(Brody, CCXXXIV, p. 244)

Again one suspects that this poem was not included in *Shirey Haqodesh* by later editors because it was an occasional prayer not used in the liturgy. For a long time it was also mistakenly attributed to the philosopher poet Abraham ibn Ezra.[41]

Like his predecessors, however, Moses ibn Ezra makes ready use of allusions to Zion and the Temple worship in his paeans of praise or his eulogies. So, for example, he says of the patron Eliezer Abu al fataḥ Ben Azhar:

7   Or (how) shall we yearn to make a pilgrimage to Jerusalem (Bet Hamiqdash)
     When you are our cherub and Temple.
8   Or how shall we recall the tablets of the covenant
     when in the ark of your heart, our Holy Ark is deposited.

(Brody, CCXXV, p. 230)

In a eulogy in memory of Rabbi Baruch ben Isaac,[42] he writes:

(12) The capitol of the pillar of Judah has been destroyed, the crown of Ephraim has
     fallen to the earth.
(13) Write to every city to the women who pound their hearts and the men who beat
     their breasts.
(14) Let them rush to meet in the Land of the Hart (i.e. Jerusalem) to recite dirges, and
     with the daughter of Jerusalem.
(15) May the congregation of Einam, weep tears of blood [Hebrew *dam einam*].

(Brody, XLIII, p. 93)

     And let there be silence [*domi*] at the Gates of Sha'arayim.
(16) With them let the people of Ramah cry aloud and let them remove their jewels in
     Aditayim.

And he repeats the conventional hyperbole:

(32) And the Ark of his heart bore the Ark of Testimony and all its law [Torah] is
     engraved on his [Baruch's] two tablets [his breasts?]

(Brody, XCIII, p. 93)

Similar hyperboles are used to mourn the death of Rabbi Abun:

(4) Saying that the throne of Glory and its canopy have been shattered forever
(5) Abun, the words of whose mouth were like a stream in the desert . . .
(12) The earth reeled and the sky's orbit grew faint as a mortal running a race.
(13) Sinai trembled before him . . .

(Brody, XCVIII, p. 99)

It would be inaccurate to conclude that Ibn Ezra rejected the idea of the restoration or that he viewed Zion and the Land of Israel only as symbols. As a pious Jew, he believed in the end of days and in the ultimate restoration of the exile. But all this was to occur in the remote future and in God's own time. Until then, his real exile was from Andalusia and it was there that he dreamed to return. One might, of course, speculate as to whether the absence of songs referring to the Land of Israel in the *Shirey Haḥol* is simply a matter of *genre*, namely that such songs were considered to be secular. This argument, however, is belied by the fact that all *sacred poems* were liturgical and assigned to specific dates in the Jewish calendar. Hence religious poems not included in the services were classified as secular poems. We must therefore assume that for Gabirol and even more so for Moses ibn Ezra the idea of the return was ethereal, eschatological and not to be fulfilled in their own times.

IV

A radical change in the perception of the role of the Land of Israel in Judaism as well as in his personal life manifests itself in the works of Judah Halevi (1075?–1141?). Like ibn Gabirol, Halevi was not only a brilliant poet but a profound Jewish philosopher. But unlike Gabirol whose *Fons Vitae* is a work in general metaphysics which avoids discussing specifically Jewish dogmas, Halevi's *Kuzari* is a thoroughly Jewish work as its Arabic title attests: *Kitāb al-Ḥujjat wa-al-Dalīlfī Naṣr al-dīn al-dhalīl (The Book of Responses to the Arguments against the Despised Religion and Proofs in Defense of It).*[43]

Scholars have not succeeded in determining the date of its composition[44] but the views expressed in it are in consonance with those found in much of Halevi's poetry.

In the second chapter of the *Kuzari,* the king questions the Ḥaver's (=Sage or Rabbi) assertion that the *Kavod* (God's glory) is the divine spark which animates *(mafʿil)* God's people and God's land (II:8, p. 52). He is particularly disturbed by the statement that the chosen people can only be joined *(lehiddabbeq)* to the *Divine Substance (Inyan ha'elohi)* in His land (II:12, p. 53). He asks: "How so? Did not many prophesy [in the period] between Adam and Moses in other places, Abraham in Ur of the Chaldeans, Ezekiel and Daniel in Babylonia and . . . Jeremiah in Egypt?" (II:13, p. 53).

The Ḥaver replies:

Whosoever prophesied did so either in it [i.e. in the Land of Israel] or concerning it . . . Thus was prophecy retained among Abraham's descendants in the Land of Canaan . . . Many prophesied and numerous conditions aided them in this matter: rites of purification, worship and sacrifices and, above all, the proximity of the *Shekhinah*. For the *Divine Substance (Inyan Ha'elohi)*, one might say awaits him who is worthy of it, such as prophets and pious men." (II:4, pp. 53–5)

He continues:

This land was appointed to guide the world . . . (II:16, p. 56) . . . It was there that the calendar was fixed . . . "for the Land of Israel is like the center of the inhabited earth (II:20, p. 58) . . . The knowledge of the Sabbath and the festivals of God is dependent on the land called "God's inheritance" and so this land is also called: "His holy mountain" and "His foot-stool" and "the gate of heaven".

See how the patriarchs endeavored to dwell in it while it was still in pagan hands, how they longed for it when they were far removed from it, so that they saw to it that their bones were carried to it. Remember how Moses pleaded to see it and how difficult for him was the decree which prevented him from doing so . . . Consider how much . . . Persians, Indians and Greeks and others tried to have sacrifices offered there in their behalf . . . and see how they still revere the Land to this very day even though the *Shekhinah* no longer appears there. For all the religions make pilgrimages to it . . . excepting ourselves because of the state of exile and enslavement in which we are cast . . . It would take too long to relate what our sages have said in praise of the land (II, 20, p. 61).

Yet the *Khazar* king insists that the *Ḥaver* quote the Rabbis, and Halevi has him do so for two pages, drawing upon the Talmud and the Midrashim (II:22, pp. 61–2). The king then retorts:

If this be so, you are guilty of transgressing a commandment laid down in your Torah by not going up to that place (II, 23, p. 63).

Humbly, the *Ḥaver* admits his error:

You have shamed me, O king of the Khazars. It is this sin which has kept us from fulfilling what God has charged us with regard to the second Temple . . . For the Divine Substance was ready to rest upon them as it had at first if all had responded to the call and returned to the Land of Israel willingly. But only a small part responded while the majority, and the more prominent among them, remained in Babylonia, preferring exile and slavery to leaving their homes and affairs (II:24, pp. 64–5).

At this point, Halevi coins a beautiful homily on Song of Songs V:2. "'I am asleep and my heart is awake'. Scripture called *galut* 'sleeping' and 'the heart awake', the persistence of prophecy among them". He insists that God keeps alive the aspiration to return to Zion via the vehicle of prophecy but that the actualisation of the prophetic call depends on the will of the one addressed to respond to that call. "For the *inyan ha 'elohi* does not alight on a person unless he himself is ready to receive it . . . if we were willing to draw near to God . . . with a perfect heart, . . . He, blessed be He, would redeem us as He did redeem our ancestors in Egypt (II:24, p. 64)."

At the close of the book, we are told that the *Ḥaver* decided "to depart from the land of the Khazars in order to go up to Jerusalem, and that the king was incensed and said to him, 'What can you seek, these days, in Jerusalem of the land of Canaan when the *Shekhinah* is absent from it and nearness to God can be achieved everywhere with a pure heart and with great yearning. Why should you expose yourself to the dangers of deserts and seas and the enmity of various peoples?'" (V:22, p. 233)

In his response, the *Ḥaver* states:

The manifest *Shekhina (hanir'et la 'eynayim)* is absent since it rests only on a prophet or a community which God has favored and only in an appointed and special place and this is what we are waiting for . . . But the hidden *Shekhinah,* the spiritual *Shekhinah,* is the possession of every Jew who is pure in deed and heart and whose soul's desire . . . is dedicated to the God of Israel. And the Land of Canaan is specially appointed by the God of Israel and religious deeds can only be completely fulfilled there. Many *mitsvot* granted to Israel are invalid for one who does not dwell in the Land of Israel.

The heart is only pure and one's devotion can only be totally dedicated to God in that place ... which is specially appointed by God ... And even if this faith is only imagined or fancied. How much more so when it is real ... Then the passion for this place will be aroused and one's intention will be dedicated only to God. It is especially so for one who yearns for this place from afar and even more so for one who seeks atonement for sins which he committed before he came there since he cannot nowadays offer the sacrifices which God had commanded for each ... So he can only rely on the saying of the sages: "Exile atones for sin." For now he indeed exiles himself to the desired place. And as far as the danger of sea and land these do not come under the rubric of "Do not test the Lord your God" (Deut. 6:16). If a man endangers himself greatly because of his desire and his hope to atone for his sins, he has every reason since he searched his soul, thanked God for the life that has hitherto been given to him and decided that this was enough and that he would dedicate the rest of his days to fulfilling the will of God. (V:23, p. 234)

Halevi's theory of the primacy of the Land of Israel is diametrically opposed to the view of the *'Arabiyah* that Arabia is the choicest of all lands.[45] We do not know whether Ibn Ezra's *Kitāb,* or, for that matter, the *Kuzari* were completed before or during Halevi's stay in Granada in the late 1080s but undoubtedly the two poets were intimately acquainted with each other's views. Ibn Ezra accepted the contention of the advocates of *'Arabiyah* regarding the superiority of Arab culture: "This superiority [of the Arabs as courageous and particularly talented men] is derived from their star and their climate." Perhaps because he felt somewhat uncomfortable with this assertion, he goes on to suggest rather apologetically that Tiberias and the area around the Sea of Galilee is also conducive to eloquence, although they are close to Syria.[46]

Halevi devotes considerable space to the argument that the climate of Israel is particularly suited for prophecy:

You have seen with your own eyes a place in which a particular plant might best prosper or a particular product or animal and whose inhabitants are more specially suited to it ... than others. All this is by means of the balance of their humors. For the perfection of a soul or its imperfection is according to the proper mix of humors (*Kuzari* I: 10, p. 53).

He also argues that since the Land of Israel is the centre of the universe and the place where Adam was deposited after the Fall, it is the location in which all calendation originates (IV:14–21, pp. 55–61). In a poem written shortly before his departure for the Land of Israel, he describes it as "the land of many gates which face the open gates of heaven" (*Brody,* II, p. 165, lines 31–2).

He rejects the claims of the *'Arabiyah* as to the superiority of the Arabic language. While Ibn Ezra is clearly uncomfortable about this claim and nowhere specifically endorses it, he does repeat the Arabs' doctrine about the superiority of their language. He goes on to praise the eloquence of biblical Hebrew, defending it against its Muslim detractors, but he implies that Arabic is superior to Hebrew in rhetoric and poetry while suggesting that Hebrew is superior as the vehicle for God's word. Not so Halevi: "To Hebrew . . . belongs the first place, both as regards the nature of the language and as to its fullness of meanings" (II. 66, p. 80). To the King's challenge: "Is Hebrew superior to other languages . . . that . . . are more finished and comprehensive?" (II 67) he responds "It shared the fate of its bearers, degenerating and dwindling with them" (II 68, p. 81) — an explanation which Ibn Ezra also proffers.

But to return to Halevi's views about the Land of Israel, both Wolfson and Aloni have pointed out that similar ideas were abroad in the Muslim world.[47] Halevi seems to be refuting al-'Araqi's contention that Iraq is the centre of the world.[48] Halevi adheres to the well-known talmudic view that Jerusalem is the *omphalus* of the world *(Ṭibur Ha'olam).*[49]

It was quite natural that Halevi's views as to the primacy of the Land of Israel ultimately led to his introducing the subject into his so-called secular poetry. Before his day, expressions of longing for Zion tended (as we have noted) to be conventional and usually confined to liturgical works. Yehudah Halevi is the first to compose *Shirey Tsion, Zionades,* in which he expresses his passion for Jerusalem and the Land of Israel. His *Divan* contains 23 poems which are animated by this theme. The first eight were evidently composed before he left Spain. Besides the expected expressions of love for the Holy Land, these are poems in which the poet argues with himself as if to allay his fears of the perils he might encounter on his dangerous odyssey. Thus he introduces a second thematic innovation — the poems of the sea journey (approximately 10):

19 Let not your heart totter in the heart of the seas
20 Although you see mountains topple and stir,
21 Sailors whose hands have turned to salt,
22 Craftsmen who cower in sullen silence.
23 They venture out joyfully
24 But return abashed.
25 The Ocean is your only refuge.
26 Nowhere to flee but the waves.
27 Sails sway and topple,
28 Deck boards move and tremble,
29 The wind's hand plays with the waters
30 Like bearers of wheat at the threshing pit.
31 At times they turn to tall stacks,
32 At times to tiny swaying bundles.
33 When they grow strong, they are lions,
34 When weakened, they turn into snakes
35 Chasing one another like serpents
36 Who have lost their hisses.
37 The mighty ship suddenly falls like a small craft in the deep,

38 Mast and banners enfeebled.
39 The vessel and its decks in disarray —
40 Lower, upper and middle.
41 The rope-haulers hands ache,
42 Men and women fall ill,
43 Sailors lose their wind,
44 And bodies despair of their souls.
45 The might of masts is useless,
46 The wisdom of the elders — sapped.
47 Cedar masts are like straw
48 And cypresses turn into dry reeds,
49 The sand ballast, into light shavings,
50 The iron of the brackets like hay . . .

(*Brody*, II, pp. 161–2)

The vividness of his description is enhanced by the short breathless lines and his playful rhyme patterns; the latter unfortunately are lost in translation.

It would serve little purpose to do a word count of the place names which Halevi employs or their variety. Any quick perusal would demonstrate how greatly he exceeds those of all his predecessors combined.

Judah Halevi's stress on the importance of the Land of Israel in contrast to his predecessors, of course, prompts the question as to the causes for this change. As Eli Schweid correctly avers, "The literature of Jewish thought in the two generations preceding Rabbi Judah Halevi's poetic and philosophical works did not stress the significance of the views of the talmudic sages regarding the Land of Israel. Moreover, the entire net-work of ideas involving the special role of the people of Israel as a chosen people (the historical significance of the idea of choice, the inter-relationship between the Holy Land and the holy tongue) had not enjoyed deep theological discussion . . ."

He suggests that the cause of this shift in emphasis was the Crusades, which began in 1096 and ended with the capture of Jerusalem in 1099.[50] That Halevi was aware of the success of the Crusaders can be easily documented:

Zion is in Edom's domain and I in Araby's chain (*Brody* II, p. 155, line 4).

And sons of evil inherited the place of my tent (*Brody* III, p. 88, line 7).

And you caused Edom to rejoice for his hand is lifted high over my holy place (IV, p. 16, line 15).

Jerusalem, the vineyard of the God of the universe, how do you exist among the worshippers of the cross? (IV, p. 70, lines 1–2).

5 May You in Your mercy console the remnant of the sacked city
6 Which You have given over to despoilation by the hand of Shammah and Mizzah [the grandchildren of Edom, cf. Gen. 36:13].

(*Brody* IV, p. 135, lines 5–6, cf. IV, p. 74, 10–13)

But more immediate were the disasters which occurred in Spain itself. The security of the Jews of Andalusia was disrupted by a series of blows. First came the anti-Jewish pogrom in Granada following the assassination of Joseph the son of Samuel Hanagid in 1066, in which 3 000 Jews were killed. The community soon recovered but in 1090 the invasion of the Morabites was an even greater catastrophe.[51] The *coup de grace* to the remnants of Granada's once affluent Jewish community was administered by the Almohades. In the meantime, the Christian *reconquista* progressed rapidly under Alfonso VI of Castille (1075–1107), culminating with the fall of Toledo in 1085.[52a]

These events close to home must have overshadowed those which were occurring in the distant homeland. Halevi, whose secular culture was more Arabic than Spanish, was compelled to escape to Christian Spain. In several of his poems he gives vent to his despair:

9   Seir [i.e. Christian Spain] and Araby have smitten me — I am in my grave.
10 Will the sword forever consume, I call out bitterly to Him.
11 Whether one side or the other dominates, I am always in distress.
12 Will my loins ever be free of oppression.

(Brody IV, p. 205)

and:

7   Between the armies of Seir and Qedar [Arabia] my army perishes and is lost . . .
9   When they fight their wars, we fall when they fall . . .
11 On every side, traps and snares, no one rises to seek
12 The welfare of Israel
13 Wherever they wage battle, for death and destruction
14 One by one are gathered the sons of Israel[52]

(Brody IV, p. 131)

There were, of course, other factors which contributed to Halevi's decision. Barry Kogan critically examines the explanations proffered by a number of scholars, including Schweid.[53]

David Kaufmann's suggestion that the primary motivation was the poet's desire to atone for the sins of his youth is based on Halevi's own words in both his poetry and the *Kuzari*. This was indeed one of the determining motives. But Kaufmann's list of the "sins of his youth" is hardly impressive. It is difficult to accept his contention that the prime sin in Halevi's eyes was his employment of Arabic poetical techniques in the composition of his verse! More convincing is his suggestion that these secret sins were the religious doubts entertained by Halevi when he was studying philosophy as a young scholar. Kaufmann, however, omits the most obvious of youthful sins to which all medieval poets allude if they live long enough, namely, sexual promiscuity or even deviation.

Baer and Gerson Cohen attribute the decision to make *Aliyah* to Halevi's rejection of Andalusia's sybaritic and skeptical courtier culture as being futile and morally reprehensible. He was sure that the trust which Jewish courtiers had placed in their princes, be they Muslim or Christian, is delusive and will fail them in any crisis.[54] Halevi had indeed grown weary of the sycophancy and luxuriating of the Jewish upper classes, and this was probably a contributing factor in making his decision, but undertaking the terrible risks which a journey to Zion in the eleventh century entailed must have been the result of a more pressing spritual need.

Dinaburg and Schirmann's view that Halevi was prompted by Messianic motives points to a more plausible explanation. However, Dinaburg's speculation that Halevi viewed his *Aliyah* as a demonstrative act to spur on other Jews to follow his example cannot be substantiated.[55] On the contrary, he frequently laments that Jews are indifferent to the Land.[56]

I share Kogan's preference for Aaron Komem's more refined messianic thesis.[57] Following the collapse of Granada's Jewry and the gradual advance of the Christian states, several messianic movements arose in Spain. Halevi himself experienced a messianic dream in 1130 in which he was told the exact year of the expected appearance of the messiah. Of course, the predicted messiah failed to appear. The experience overwhelmed the sensitive poet:

1 You fell asleep and rose trembling
2 What was the dream which you had dreamt?
3 Perhaps your dream showed you your foe
4 Impoverished and lowly while you rose exalted.
5 Tell the son of Hagar, withdraw the arm of pride
6 [Raised] in wrath against your mistress' son.
7 I've seen you in the dream abased and desolate
8 Perhaps in the waking [world] you will be similarly desolate.
9 And in the year 4890 all your pride will be crushed.

(*Brody,* II, p. 302)

The poem concludes with allusions to the book of Daniel, the handbook of all millenarians.

The year 4890 AM (1130 AD) passed with no result. Nevertheless, we might speculate that Halevi viewed the dream as a sign that he had reached a high spiritual level and that only his sins and the fact that he was not in the Land of Israel led to the distortion of the divine message. A journey to the Land of Israel would remove these two impediments. The dangers he would have to face in his "act of exile" *('Arikhat Galut)* would cleanse him of his sins. Living in the Land of Israel he would be able to perform many of the *mitsvot* "tied to the land" *(mitsvot hatluyot ba'arets).* At the close of the *Kuzari* he says:

The land of Canaan is appointed *(meyuhedet)* by the God of Israel and only in it can the *mitsvot* be totally fulfilled. There are many *mitsvot* which have been nullified for him who does not dwell in the land of Israel. Heart and soul are only pure in the place we know is chosen by God. (V:23, p. 200)

Halevi hoped that he would attain the *'inyan ha'elohi* (the divine substance) in the Holy Land and thus merit prophecy.

This thesis affords a reasonable explanation not only for his courageous decision but for the ardent fervour of Halevi's poems of Zion. No Hebrew poet ever penned more ecstatic lines expressing his aching love for Zion.

7 I a jackal am who wails at your agony.
   When I dream
8 Of your restoration, I am a lyre for your songs.
9 My heart is stirred by [memories] of Beth-el, Pniel
10 And Maḥanayim and all the sites touched by your saints.
11 There the Shekhinah is your neighbor. And your Creator.
12 Opened the gates of heaven facing your gates.
13 The Glory of the Lord is your light,
14 Neither sun nor moon nor stars.
15 I elect to have my soul pour forth in the place
16 Over which God's spirit is poured upon your elect . . .
19 Would that I could walk about those sites where
20 God revealed himself to your seers and apostles.
21 Who might make me wings that I might wander afar.
22 Passing the fragments of my heart among your fragments
23 I would then fall upon my face on your soil and
24 Passionately love your stones and adore your dust . . .
31 The air of your earth is the very breath of souls,
32 Your dust is sweeter than the finest myrrh,
   And your rivers have the taste of honey.
33 My soul would delight to walk naked and barefooted upon
34 The desolate ruins of your sanctuaries,
35 Where your Ark was sequestered and
36 The cherubim stood room within room.
37 I would cut my glorious crown of hair
   and cast it to the ground, curse Fortune
38 Who desecrated your nazirites in a defiled land.
39 How can I relish food or drink when I see
40 That dogs drag away your young lions.
41 How could the light of day be sweet to my eyes
42 When I see the corpses of your eagles in the mouth of ravens.
43 O Cup of sorrow go slow — let up for a moment for
44 My soul and innermost parts are filled with gall.
46 O Zion epitome of beauty — how you weave the spell of love and enchantment
47 From of yore. The souls of your companions are bound to you
48 Rejoicing in your peace, aching
49 At your desolation, weeping over your ruins.
50 From the captive's pit, they yearn for you, bowing
51 Each, wherever he is, toward your gates,
52 Grabbing hold of your skirts — straining

136

53 To grasp the fronds of your palm-trees, to climb to their tops.
54 Can Babylon or Egypt match your greatness?
55 Can their nonsense be compared to your Urim and Thumim?
56 Can they equal your annointed ones, your prophets,
57 Your levites or your princes?
58 Kingdoms of idolatry shall pass and perish
59 But your might shall stand forever.
60 Your God chose you as his throne. Fortunate, then, the man
61 Who chooses to dwell near your courtyards,
62 Fortunate, too, is he who aspires, reaches and finally sees the rising
63 Of your light, your dawns breaking over him.
64 Sees the goodness of your elect — and delights
65 At your joyous hour, when you are restored to your early youth

With the ardour of his religious commitment and the holy fire of his poetic genius, Halevi rekindles the coals which had been blanketed by the pious conventions of his literary predecessors into a flaming assertion of Israel's eternal commitment to God and Zion.

NOTES

1   *History of the Jews in Christian Spain,* JPS, Philadelphia, 1961, p. 31.
2   For a recent treatment of some of these aspects see *The Land of Israel* edited by Lawrence A. Hoffman, University of Notre Dame Press, Indiana, 1986. Particularly the article "The Link to the Land of Israel to Jewish Thought," by Shalom Rosenberg, "The Land of Israel in Medieval Kabbalah" by Moshe Idel, "The Land of Israel in Pre-Modern Jewish Thought" by Marc Saperstein and the "Land of Israel in Medieval Jewish Exegetical and Polemical Literature" by Michael Signer.
3   The house of Joseph, i.e. Israel.
4   Two levitical towns cf Joshua 21:32; 1 Chron. 6:64.
5   Sirion is traditionally another name for Mt. Hermon, cf Deut. 3:9.
6   Mt. Zion cf. Isaiah 29:1.
7   Literally: Rests her breasts on the lily of the nut garden. The references are to Song of Songs 4:5 and 6:11. The nut garden is a symbol for Zion.
8   I Kings, 6:18, 7:24.
9   Yoma 5b. "There was a stone there (in the Temple) called the foundation stone."
10 Edom's daughter = Rome — Christendom, cf. Lamentations 4:21.
11 Literally owns rings and earrings.
12 Boẓrah, a city in Edom. Isaiah 63:1.
13 Yemen is listed as a son of Esau, Gen. 36:10–11.
14 Jer. 52:23 cf. *Yarden,* I, XL:40–41, p. 142; XLV: 20–25, p. 52.
15 So Ashtor: *The Jew of Moslem Spain,* Vol. II, J.P.S., Philadelphia, 1979, p. 134.
16 See Jacob Mann: "A second supplement to 'The Jews in Egypt and in Palestine under the Fāṭimid caliphs'", *HUCA,* Vol III (1926), pp. 283–8, particularly pp. 285–8.
17 Daniel claimed Davidic descent.
18 *Yarden* I:IX, lines 1, p. 35, XXXI, line 1, p. 103.
19 IX lines 2 & 3, p. 35.

20 XLIV line 14, p. 150.
21 LXII: line 12, p. 200. For another discussion of Samuel's attitude to the Land of Israel, see Nehemiah Aloni, *Shirei Tsion bshirato shel Rabbi Shmuel Hanagid", Sinai,* XXXV (1971), pp. 210–80.
22 The right pillar in the sanctuary of the Temple.
23 The lion of Babylon cf. Jer. 4:7.
24 Ephrath and Bethlehem, cities connected with King David. Rav Hai claimed Davidic descent.
25 *Kitāb almuḥādharāt walmudhakārat,* p. 73, henceforth *Kitāb.*
26 *Kitāb,* p. 77.
27 Noah Brown identifies 73 citations by 46 Arabic poets "Batey Hashir Ha'araviyim bekitāb almuhādhrat valmudhakharat", *Tarbiz,* Vol. XIV (1943), pp. 126–139; 191–201. Cf. *Halkin,* introduction where these figures are scrambled. For a detailed discussion of the Arabic rhetoricians who influenced Moses ibn Ezra see: Yosef Daneh: *Hapoetiqah shel hashirah ha 'ivrit bisefarad biymey habeinayim,* Tel Aviv, 1982.
28 *Kitāb,* p. 29.
29 *Kitāb,* pp. 43, 49–52, 'Ibn Ezra accepts the climatological theory first propounded by the Greeks, that climate determines national character and talent. Arabic rhetoricians argue that the dry climate of Arabia and Iraq are particularly conducive to rhetoric and fine poetry. Cf. *Halkin,* pp. 29–39. For a detailed discussion of this problem see Alexander Altman: *Torat Ha'qlimim, Melilah,* I (1943), pp. 1, ff.
30 *Kitāb,* p. 223.Cf. Nehemiah Aloni: "The reaction of Moses ibn Ezra to Arabiyya", *Actes du XXIXe Congrès Internationale des Orientalistes,* Paris, 1975, pp. 1–16, and "The Reaction of Moses ibn Ezra to Arabiyya", Bulletin of the Institute of Jewish Studies, III, 1975, pp. 19–40.
31 *Song of Songs,* IV:6. Here a convention for true wisdom, i.e. the *Kitāb* itself.
32 "Teguvath R. Moshe 'ibn Ezra La 'Arabiah besefer *hadiyunim vehasihot", Tarbiz,* Vol. 42 (1973), pp. 97–112 and above, note 30.
33 Aloni cites 10 examples: *Brody,* VII:26, p. 10; XXX:1, p. 33, XXX:24, p. 35; LIII:40, p. 52, LXI:14, p. 60; LXXIX:27, p. 82; CLXVIII:17, p. 146; CXC:8, p. 190; CCXXXIV:132, p. 243.
34 Lebanon X:3, p. 4; Beth Rimon XX:43, p. 26; Shnir XX:43, p. 26; Tabor LIII:34, p. 52; LXXXVIII:13, p. 13; XCV:23, p. 97; CX:11, p. 112; CCXXXIV:31; Sinai LVI:7, p. 53; XCIII:49, p. 14; LXXXIII:13, p. 93; CCVII:36, p. 209; Edom LXVI:5, p. 64; XCIII:19, p. 93; Euphrates LXXXVI:3, p. 87; Horeb LXXXVII:4, p. 88; Zion LXXXVIII:3, p. 89; Ramah XCIII:16, p. 93; Jerusalem XCIII:14, p. 93; Mahanayim XCIII:51, p. 94; Gilead XCIX:28, p. 100; Hermon CX:11, p. 112; Kishon CLXXX:7, p. 178; Jaffa CCXXX:13, p. 179; Gibeon CCLI:6, p. 264; Ein Gedi CCLII:16, p. 265; Einam XCLLL:15, p. 93, Sha'arayim XCIII:15, p. 93; Adithayim XCIII:16, p. 93.
35 *Moses ibn Ezra and Judah Halevi: Two Experiments in Exile,* Ordination thesis, Hebrew Union College, 1983. See especially Chapter II. Cf. "Moses ibn Ezra and Judah Halevi. Their Philosophies in Response to Exile:", *HUCA,* LV(1984), pp. 179–195.
36 The likelihood is that the poet means the Arabs. Brody prefers the nobles of the West, i.e. of Christian Spain. *Brody* II, p. 131.
37 pasah — passed over. Brody suggests that this Arabic root means "visit". i.e. and they shall visit me.
38 *hadar rimon* following the model of *hadad rimon* cf. Brody, ibid.
39 A hill near Granada part of the Sierra Nevada range. It must be noted that ibn Ezra was not the only poet to bestow Hebrew names on Spanish cities. Judah Halevi called Denia on the Mediterranean coast of Andalusia Zor = Tyre, *Brody,* I, XLIX:49, p. 97.

40 "I was cast by him into a land in which the candles of my intelligence were extinguished
   The stars of my mind were clouded over by the darkness of dull witted and stammering
   men . . .
   I've entered the borders of evil to a people whose God reviled in anger and the world cursed,
   Among savages who loved the devil and indeed lay in ambush against righteous men. (Ibid.,
   XX:31–34, p. 26).
41 *Brody* II, pp. 437–8.
42 Sic. this is not Baruch ben Baruch but Baruch ben Isaac al-Baliah born in Seville in 1077. See
   Schirmann: "Ḥayyei Yehudah Halevi", *Letoldot Hashirah vehadramah Ha'ivrit*, I, p. 266.
43 I accept Judah even-Shmuel's (Kaufmann) translation. For a discussion of the various
   translations of the Arabic title see his *Sefer Hakuzari Lerabbi Yehudah Halevi*, Dvir, Tel Aviv,
   1972, p. 243 (Kaufmann). All quotations from the *Kuzari* are my translation of Kaufmann's
   rendition.
44 A reference to the book appears in an undated letter. Goitein suggests that the letter was
   written circa 1125. Schirmann believes it was written shortly before Halevi's departure for
   Egypt in 1140. See Schirmann *Letoldot Ḥashirah vehadramah Ha-'ivrith*, I, p. 322, Goitein
   "Otographim miyado shel R. Yehudah Halevi, *Tarbiz,* XXV (1956), pp. 393–416.
45 See Nehemiah Aloni's "Teguvat R. Moshe ben Ezra La 'arabiyah", *Tarbiz,* XLII (1973–4)
   pp. 97–112 and *Kitāb,* pp. 31–2.
46 *Kitāb,* p. 31. "And the City of Tiberias, although it is in Syria, its air and sea . . . excell in
   fineness of language and eloquence of expression." Why Tiberias? Did Ibn Ezra believe that
   the Palestinian *paytanim* lived in Tiberias and its environs? Did he, perhaps, possess sources or
   traditions which led him to this view?
47 Aloni, Op. cit. Zvi (Harry) Wolfson, *Hamaḥshavah hayehudit biymey habeinayim,* Jerusalem,
   1978, p. 272.
48 Dietrici, *Thiers und Mensch von dem König der Genien,* p. 60, lines 16–14 as quoted by
   Wolfson.
49 B. Sanhedrin 37a, cf. *Tanḥumah* (Buber), Qedoshim X, Vol. II, p. 78, 'Eretz Yisrael tiburah
   shel 'olam.
50 *Moledeth Ve'eretz Yehudah,* Tel Aviv, 1979, p. 53.
51 Schirmann, op. cit. p. 290–295 presents a glum picture of conditions prevailing in Spain from
   the close of the eleventh century until Judah's departure. Cf. p. 290 note 72.
52 Compare Ibn Ezra:
   For God's hand is still raised against it
   His anger at its nobles has not been oppressed
   Their notables and leaders found their end, as well as
   High born men and the remnants were gathered one by one.
52a See Yisrael Levin: "Haserel Bimashber Hareqonqistah Beshirato shel Yehudah Halevi", *Otzar
   Yehudei Sefarad,* VII, (1964), pp. 49–64.
53 Kogan: *The Doctrine of Prophecy in Judah Halevi's Philosophical and Poetic Writings,*
   Rabbinical Thesis, Hebrew Union College–Jewish Institute of Religion, 1978, pp. 172 ff.
54 Isaac (Fritz) Baer, "Hamatsav hapoliti shel Yehudey sefarad bedoro shel Rabbi Yehudah
   Halevi", *Zion,* I (1935), pp. 20 ff. Gerson Cohen: *Sefer Haqabalah,* JPS, 1967, p. 24 cf, note 46.
55 Ben Zion Dinaburg, "'Aliyato shel R. Yehudah Halevi lerets yisra'el vehatesisah hamshiḥit
   beyamav", *Minḥah Ledavid,* Jerusalem, 1935, pp. 157–82. Cf. J.L. Fishman (Maimon):
   Shorshei hale' umiut shel R. Yehudah Halevi, *Sinai* V (1941), p. 74.
   Schirmann, op. cit. p. 293.

56 See *Brody,* II, p. 164.
    1. Your words are perfumed with myrrh
    2. And hewn from the rock of Myrrh's hills . . .
    5. You've met me with sweet speech
    6. In which spear-bearers lie in ambush
    7. Words in which bees are hidden
    8. A honey comb, steeped with thorns etc.
57 Kogan, op. cit. p. 176 ff. Aharon Komem. "Bein shirah Linvu'ah", *Molad* XXV (1969)
    pp. 676–97.

SOURCES QUOTED

Samuel Hanagid, *Divan Shmuel Hanagid,* ed. Dov Yarden, Vol. I, Jerusalem, 1966 *(Yarden)*
Solomon ibn Gabirol, *Shirei Hahol shel Shlomoh ibn Gabirol,* ed. Dov Yarden, Jerusalem *(Yarden)*
Moses ibn Ezra: Moshe 'ibn 'Ezra, *Shirei Hahol,* ed. Hayyim Brody, Vol. 1–2, Berlin, 1938 (*Brody*)
Judah Halevy, Yehudah Halevi, Divan *Shirei Hahol,* Vol. I–II, ed. Brody-Habermann, Berlin-Tel Aviv, 1971 (*Brody*)

SOURCES OF WORK IN PROSE

Moses ibn Ezra: Abu Harun Moshe ben Ya'akov 'ibn 'Ezra, *Kitāb 'almuhadharat w'almudha-kharāt,* ed. A.S. Halkin, Jerusalem, 1975 (Halkin), designated as *Kitāb.*
Judah Halevi, *Sefer Hakuzari Le Rabbi Yehudah Halevi,* ed. Yehudah even Shmuel (Kaufmann, Dvir, Tel Aviv, 1973 *(Kuzari).*

12 "Here" and "there" in modern Hebrew poetry

Glenda Abramson

One of the characteristics of the Haskalah was its didactic emphasis on the development and self-liberation of the Jew as a new Jew, a humanist who is aware of his emotions, who respects reason and intellect, who glories in art and particularly in nature, ideas hitherto alien to the ghetto Jew. Many maskilic authors were drawn to the sentimental Rousseauan view of man and nature, partly for polemical purposes and partly as a replacement for their own vanished orthodoxy, and they adopted at least one literary convention that perfectly expressed their liberated Jew's pursuit of an ideal natural life: the Arcadian fantasy, itself an idealised vision of man and nature. "Leading his flocks in ever green pastures, by ever limpid brooks the dreamed-of Jew in Haskalah poetry devotes himself to little else but the contemplation of the wonders of God revealed through the prolific beauties of nature."[1] This new, fundamentally romantic maskilic attitude which had been stimulated in part by Hasidism, found its consummate instrument in the Arcadian literature of the sixteenth and seventeenth centuries, transposed by Moshe Hayim Luzzatto into Hebrew poetry and drama, and flavoured with the sweet herbs of the pastoral such as "leafy bowers", "eternal mountains", "sheep and shepherd lads", and so on, and by its intimations of a carefree dreamworld beyond the reach of time.

It did not take long before the admission of nature and the landscape into the lives and literature of the East European Jewish communities was exploited by writers for the purpose of promoting the ideal of renewal in the Holy Land. This was not a practical ideal, for they were unable to offer their readers a realistic natural background but only a vaguely historical environment that could fruitfully be developed by their imagination. An English critic has noted that "It is abundantly clear that in the 18th-century sensibility feelings were tied to the general; men were excited by generalisations, not by particulars. Men then felt the imagined norm to be more real, more exciting, more poetical, than any particular example."[2] This applied equally to the Haskalah sensibility, with the result that Haskalah nature poetry was generally little more than a compilation of figurative conventions. The non-specific descriptions of the Holy Land did not therefore offend by

141

their conventional images or by their failure to supply strictly factual details. The writers had never seen their task as one of scientific precision, notwithstanding Wessely's injunction to study geography in order better to appreciate biblical locations, and despite the tremendous influence of Shelomo Levinson's *Mehkerei aretz,* but rather as the summoning of a kind of legendary land based on the Bible which left room for a free play of creative ideas. The Holy Land that they conjured in this way had little to do with the real modern Palestine or current Zionist philosophy or even religious fervour for it was written with the rose-coloured ink of secular romantic messianism in which geographical or topographic reality played little part.

The standardisation of Holy Land description was the result of more than literary convention alone; it was also derived from cultural convention combined with sentimental idealism. Despite their secular perspective the writers were drawn to the Bible for their contextualisation, and their view of the Holy Land was initially fashioned almost exclusively from biblical descriptions. Just as the Hebrew language had existed for so long in prayer and in the canon, so the land had eternally been that of the Bible, especially as celebrated in Psalms and the Song of Songs. Yet the writers found themselves somewhat restricted by the comparative paucity of flora, fauna and variation of landscape in the biblical text, with the result that biblical descriptions alone proved inadequate for little other than the naming of authentic locations in the Land of Israel. Place names and references to landscape in the Bible are in any case incidental and subordinate to its events. Erich Auerbach has demonstrated the contraction even of the *events* in the biblical narrative in order to pinpoint its primarily moral intention. This was certainly of little help to imaginative writers attempting to flesh out the beloved landscape.

A partial solution to the writers' lack of graphic information about Palestine and their equal lack of a convincing methodology of nature description was offered by the genre of the pastoral. Its formal conventions grafted onto biblical place names and the Bible's depictions of nature to a certain extent alleviated the problem of describing a land none of the writers had ever seen. The intertextuality of sixteenth and seventeenth-century pastoral literature was maintained in Haskalah writing as a *combined* intertextuality, that of the Bible and seventeenth-century Arcadian literature, making the valid recreation of the landscape therefore dependent upon the writers' knowledge of *texts* rather than of the *place*. One of the first of the Hebrew writers to blend these two sources was Shalom Hakohen (1772–1845), an editor of *Hameassef,* the founder of the influential *Bikkurei ha'itim*, and the intermediary between the western and eastern Haskalah. His was to become one of the most characteristic methods of describing the Palestinian landscape in nineteenth-century Haskalah literature:

> Between the mountains of an ancient land, beside restful streams
> There on verdant pastures beneath the domed sky
> Lay* Abraham, son of Terah, among his flocks
> Tranquil serenity enclosed him, peace entered his heart

---

* Lit. "crouched", from Genesis 49,9

No sound of rustling leaves, the wind had fallen
But for the bleating of the flock, the ringing of their bells
Nothing broke the silence, all was quiet and serene
Only a pure stream wound its way before his gaze . . .[3]

He continues with a description of sunset on the meadows and streams. Shalom Hakohen pursued this trend throughout his poetry and allegorical dramas, influenced by Wessely and exerting an equal influence on Y.L. Gordon a generation later.

Idealisation of an unseen almost abstract land, nostalgia for the glories of the national past free of enclosure and oppression in this land — these romantic preoccupations found their echo in much of the Hebrew verse of the period and resulted in works of greater literary quality than the naïve pastoralism of Shalom Hakohen. Avraham Mapu (1808–1868) set new standards with his lyrical novel of 1853, *Ahavat tziyon,* a pastoral idyll sustained for novel length and drawing linguistically and topographically on the Bible. It was a landmark not only in its being the first Hebrew novel but in Mapu's projection of himself through his protagonists into the biblical landscape which he graphically described. He was deeply impressed by eighteenth-century French pastoral romances and by the works of Eugene Sue, which were later translated into Hebrew (by Kalman Shulmann) and which exerted an undeserved influence on Hebrew writing of the time. In his exploitation of earlier texts and in his return to the idealised past, Mapu amalgamates two major trends common in later Haskalah literature: neoclassicism, realised in the use of the Bible and the pastoral, and romanticism. The romanticism itself was bilateral, composed of the idealisation of the national past as depicted in the Bible together with sympathy with the new European liberal Utopian movements celebrated, among others, by Sue.

The tools of neoclassical pastoralism and romantic idealism took the material of the Bible and reformed it to create a suitable entity which the poets saw as *Eretz yisrael* or *Tziyon.* They were aided further by European examples of romantic literature, such as the works of Byron and Schiller, and also by evocations of the Holy Land itself in European literature such as Byron's *Hebrew Melodies* (translated into Hebrew by M.L. Letteris) and the works of Chateaubriand, Lamartine, Heine, Blake and Scott. The romantic mood of Haskalah poetry reached its peak in the work of Michal (M.J. Lebensohn, 1828–1852) who died of consumption at the age of 24. Like his famous father, Adam Hakohen Lebensohn, Michal had learned German, lived and studied in Berlin and had come into direct contact with German romanticism. In his six *Shirei bat tziyon* he employs a mixture of the Bible and the pastoral as descriptive sources but adds elements of personal reflection which by diffusing its typical maskilic rhetoric, raised his poetry above the purely descriptive or ideological. The first section of this series, *Shlomo vekohelet,* opens with the description of spring in the Holy Land, with the young Solomon in love with a shepherdess, Shulamit, in an echo of *Shir hashirim.* Birds sing, perfumes waft from the mountaintops, spring arrives on a dove's wing (recalling Song of Songs 2:11) to delight the shepherds. Place names abound: Lebanon, Gilead, Bashan, Carmel (149–156).* As

---

* Numbers in brackets refer to lines in *Shirei bat tziyon.*

Michal assumes the guise of Kohelet the poetry loses most of its verdant pastoralism to become a personal affirmation of Kohelet's agonisingly non-romantic world view. Yet we are still reminded of the setting by references to sweet fields and meadows, singing brooks, olive trees and pomegranates (136–140). Seen with the eyes of national longing, Michal's Jersualem in *Shirei bat tziyon* is to be found on the banks of the Jordan and it contains every convention associated with the Holy Land on the one hand: cedars, olive trees, figs, vines, milk and honey; and with the pastoral, on the other: trees, soft breezes, flowers, a sparkling river and eternal spring (1–20). Tova Cohen has noted that the idealisation of a city, following *Laudes Romae*, the praise of Rome, was common in eighteenth-century pastoral literature.[4]

Lebensohn alone among the Hebrew poets of the time seemed to be aware of the paradox of describing a place of which he had no firsthand knowledge. He discovered a solution in another Byronic device, that of combining the descriptions taken from the Bible and from literary convention with those of a landscape he did indeed know well, in which he lived. For the first time in Hebrew poetry certain features of the European environment are projected onto the Holy Land, a device that was to be repeated later by Y.L. Gordon. Michal describes the Lebanon in this way:

The sun rises and lights the heavens
The east wind scatters to the earth the glory of its light
Even the field of snow glows from its radiance
And a sweet melody bursts joyfully from the heights. (101–104)

Avraham Shaanan is of the opinion that in similar verses Michal "frees himself from the Haskalah mechanism of description, he sees and lives the landscape of his close surroundings . . ."[5] Whereas "snow" and "mist" do appear in the Bible albeit not frequently, or else figuratively, they are also typical of Michal's own environment, a snowbound Lithuanian landscape which he is known to have admired. Snow-covered fields glowing in the sun's early rays are in any case less usual for Lebanon where snow is more often seen on the mountaintops. Lebensohn's sources for his evocations of *Eretz yisrael* were therefore certainly the Bible, the pastoral, European romantic poetry and possibly his own European environment.

The pogroms of 1881 proved to the shocked maskilim that enlightenment and anti-orthodoxy alone were not solutions to the dilemma of East European Jewry, and that the well-dressed man in the street was as much a victim as the Jew in his home. Yet Zionism as a political ideology had scarcely been mentioned in Haskalah poetry although Zion, the ultimate aspiration, was its creative source. The themes of Jewish longing for the Holy Land, the resurrection of the ancient glories of Israel's past, the descriptions of a beautiful landscape that were central to the works of the maskilic poets did not crystallise into invocations of Zionism even after the cruel reality of pogroms and even in the best of the poetry, that of Gordon, Bialik and Tschernichowski. This task, says Halkin, whose sneer is almost perceptible in his text, was left to none other than the "poetaster M.M. Dolitzski" (1858–1931). Halkin deplores the fact that J.L. Gordon, the "king of the poets" of that period, "literally bequeathed his pen to none other than Dolitzki . . . that helpless versifier of the new mood of the Love of Zion" whose poetry Halkin dismissed as "hopeless drivel":[6] "Lovely land of song/With fruit and flowers vernal/Through all history's ages/Thou art spring eternal." This was not only the *reductio* almost *ad absurdum* of the lofty ideals of Hibbat Tziyon, but a paring down of the pastoral to a mere lexicon of its effects. It was indeed this kind of poetry that characterised the formative years of modern Zionism. Even Joseph Klausner, who is quick to praise, complains that the work of Dolitzki's contemporary, N.H. Imber (whose *hatikvah* was set to music), needs revision . . . "their language is not faultless or sufficiently poetical . . ."[7] Bialik was particularly scathing, mockingly rejecting the versifying and *melitzah* of these poets, claiming that they showed "no talent, no new ideas, no knowledge of the language and no divine spark." Generally he did not think much even of the Haskalah romantics, Michal, Mapu and Gordon, owing to their lack of what he termed "that psychological and aesthetic value which gives meaning to poetry and raises it to the level of an artistic work".[8] Yet he expressed some admiration for M.Z. Mane, a Hibbat Tziyon poet who, like Lebensohn, died very young (1860–1887) of consumption. He produced good nature poetry in which love of Zion later became prominent and combined, as in Lebensohn's work, with personal suffering. The poet sitting on a hill, alone in a gentle spring breeze, imagines the landscape of the Holy Land. The new Judaea is seen, as late as the 1880s, in Arcadian idyllic terms: in the dazzling sunshine a shepherd's pipe is heard from the distance as the flocks go to drink at the brook. A beautiful young woman, daughter of Israel, is not far off. Mane's poem, *masa'at nafshi (My Soul's Desire),* ends with the wish that both he and the Holy Land may be reborn.

From the 1880s the encounter with Palestine, the actual confrontation on the part of the pioneers with the imagined and longed-for land was electrifying. The Palestinian poets were able at last to write about the reality of the Holy Land: at last seen, touched and smelled it was transmitted to the readers in all its sensuous reality — the heat, the blue, cloudless days, the clear night skies, the marshes, the valleys, the newly planted forests, the real Jerusalem, the heavy winter rains, the strange, exotic plants and trees among which the fabled cedars of Lebanon are scarcely mentioned. The phenomenon of idealisation of the land assumes an altered guise: orthodoxy is transferred to the land which is now in partnership with the pioneer in the mission of salvation. The excitement of the pioneer-poet both physical and metaphysical is obvious in the poetry of this period, but from time to time this is tempered by a nostalgia or yearning not entirely unlike that of the maskilic poets for the Holy Land, except that the object of the yearning has changed, become inverted, so to speak, a rather ironic inversion of ninteenth-century maskilic nostalgia. The reason for this phenomenon is obvious: the pioneers' orientation to the real Palestinian landscape was difficult. It was clearly not the Arcadian vision of olive trees, doves and burbling brooks, but a harsh and largely unfriendly reality in which the newly-arrived intellectual still felt himself an exile. One of the poets, Yitzhak Lamdan (1900–1954), who was dismayed by the hardship of his new life, confessed to missing his European home. However, like the other pioneers, he believed that no alternative existed for the Jews. His hymn to pioneering, *Massada,* venerates the Palestinian landscape but also laments the hardship of existing in it, especially in its extremes, for example the fierce heat of the *hamsin*. He describes his exhausted labourer struggling back to his camp,

> On the roads beyond the camp the *hamsin* struck me,
> From the flaming east wind I came to shelter under a bush,
> But there was no shelter in the shade.
> I threw back my weary head without hope, knowing
> Here even shade melts in the heat. (tr. R.F. Mintz)

This is a far cry from the sweet spring days and the shepherd's distant pipe. In his massive poem Lamdan nostalgically recalls the scenes of his diasporan past, the faintest echo in its biblical allusiveness of the yearning Holy Land poetry of a generation earlier:

> The distant rustling of a pine forest caresses my ear.
> The basket of childhood floats on the cold water of the Ikvah
> Among shady bullrushes . . .
> Leave me, visions of yesterday! Why do you assail me? (tr. RFM)

The reference is, of course, to Moses but the river is in the Ukraine, the river of the poet's childhood, the shady bullrushes, or reeds, a contrast to the lone bush that provides no shelter from the Palestinian heat.

The pastoral vision of the Haskalah comes into its own in David Shimonowitz's (Shimoni's) ecstatic idylls which portray the acclimatisation of the pioneer with the new land. Shimoni was born in 1886 (as were Yaakov Steinberg and Yitzhak Katznelson) and he glorified the newly encountered *Eretz yisrael* as few others have done. His short poem, *Leket (Gleaning),* which provides a line of continuity with the poetry of the Haskalah, is a good example of his rustic idealism even to the trees and fruit. *Leket* describes a poet once again observing a rustic setting: an old Yemenite woman gathers dry branches for a bonfire. She works between the green vines and fig trees. The poetic "I", like many observers of the pastoral scene, lies in the vineyard listening to the birds, musing on the quiet, serene summer. Yet with all this Shimoni, like Lamdan, confessed that he had found his orientation to the land fraught with difficulties. In one of his idylls, *Yovel ha'eglonim (The Jubilee of Coachmen)* he writes:

> Thus I first understood that I still was in exile.
> Gazing at the glorious palm I yearned
> For the wistful white birch of the northland;
> A blossoming winter contrived to entice me,
> But I dreamed of the deserts of snow . . . (tr. Simon Halkin)

Once again this is an inversion of the glowing pastoralism of Haskalah verse, like a magic mirror reflecting back in distorted form the dream of the maskilim. The longed-for trees are not cedars or olives but birches, and snow replaces the reality of scorched fields. Shimoni and Lamdan fail to adjust not to the landscape but to the nature of the landscape, to attain what I believe is termed the "body ego", the physical identification with an environment, its climate, the very texture of the air which is achieved only after many years, if at all in a new country. The ability to penetrate the landscape in this sense initially eluded the pioneering poets. Like Lebensohn and Gordon their own body egos related to the snow and mists, the mountains and cool lakes. However, the earlier poets had eased the path of emotional if not physical identification of the *halutzim* with the Holy Land for even if the location they had sung about was not the one the pioneers were experiencing, their literature had directly exploited the theme of longing for the Land. The altered messianism of the pioneers, the mystic unity with the land had been instilled in them by their Haskalah forebears, however unrealistic and romantic their vision and their literary means may have been.

A sense of displacement and exile did not disappear even later, when the Palestinian settlement was firmly established. Writers continued to stress the need for reorientation in the face of the persistent memory of diasporan life and the conflict engendered by it. The great Saul Tschernichowski sounded some notes of uneasy accommodation and Leah Goldberg, who was born in 1911 and reached Palestine in 1935, remembered with surprising nostalgia the vanished shape of her European city. Her *Tel Aviv 1935,* is typical of the poetry in which the renounced past is superimposed on the present, forming a ghostly and relentless image.

> Like pictures darkening in a camera,
> pure winter nights, rainy summer nights across the sea,
> and dull mornings of great cities
> all reversed . . .
>
> The sound of steps behind you
> Drummed marches of a foreign army.
> It seemed that should you but turn your head
> There's your town's church floating on the sea.

Those of the present generation of writers, the poetic grandchildren of the maskilim, who were born in Europe in the twenties and thirties, have not shed this sense of dualism in their lives. None better than Yehuda Amichai has expressed more clearly, or more thoroughly crystallised the two strands in Hebrew verse, the fierce love of the Israeli landscape and Jerusalem on the one hand, and the sense of displacement sharpened by memories of the lost diasporan home, on the other. The speaker in his autobiographical epic, *The Journeys of the Last Benjamin of Tudela* describes his departure from Germany for Palestine at the age of 12 in 1936. Thereafter the city of his birth assumes a fictional, almost mythological import in his life, symbolic of a period which bears its own particularly tantalising character. Through his poetry he becomes engaged in a reconstitutive process which T.S. Eliot has evocatively described:

> There is only the fight to recover what has been lost
> And found and lost again and again.

One poem (by Amichai, unpublished) serves as a summary for all this poetry of inverted nostalgia from the *yishuv* to the present day in its memories of the poet's early home and his regret at leaving it:

I write from right to left, yearn from left
To right, the sharp pain comes from above and below, the sun
Rises for me in the east, the sea sets from the west
In a breath larger than my life's breath. Winds
Come from every wind. When it is day there, here it is night:
My time precedes theirs or follows it
Like the pursuers pursued in a drawing
On a Grecian urn. I write from right to left.
My forehead is burnt. Like chaff in a field my eyes whiten,
But I love like all this the life
Among forests and along brimming rivers.
And in hard, square words of my language
I must say my pain,
And describe the love that despite it all
I inherited from my forefathers who came from far away
Long ago.

The exact object of the poet's love is equivocal, either Israel or Europe, but it seems finally that in spite of his memory of the forests and rivers of his childhood home and the affection he still feels for the European countryside, he is bound also to love the land of his forefathers, a land of heat and dryness, the extreme opposite in climate and time of his former home. Climate, landscape and language are the painful rods that spark memory into action, leaving him unable to resolve the conflict of memory and attachment.

Many of Amichai's European-born contemporaries reiterate this nostalgia without in any way diminishing their powerful affection for Israel's landscape in general and for Jerusalem in particular. In the case of nineteenth-century East European Jewry the yearning for another land was an existential necessity. The spirit of the future infused Haskalah verse with a limpid optimism but the spectre of the past still haunts the poetry of the Haskalah's heirs. They represent the generation that is neither diasporan nor *sabra* but with at least a foot still extended in the diasporan world, too young to have been pioneers but still bearing the legacy of their parents' struggle, temperamentally inclined towards twentieth-century individualism but culturally tied to Israeli collectivism. Their nostalgia for "elsewhere" becomes emblematic of their malaise as a transitional generation. Still, perhaps it is the human condition, if not only a romantic condition, to long to be where one is not or, as Schmidt von Lubeck claimed, "Dort, wo du nicht bist, dort is das Gluck". Perhaps it is the Jewish condition for one generation to settle, the next to wander or, as Amichai says, "one generation is always a tree/ the next, loose soil." But I think that Nathan Zach, Yehuda Amichai's contemporary, and, like him, living in Israel, should have the last word, not a resolution of the conflict but an expression of the Holy Land's greater power:

All this isn't mine. I look at it
with amazement. Whose is it, then?
I don't know. Perhaps an inheritance? No relative or acquaintance

left me anything. And so?
Perhaps I'll leave if all this isn't mine.
Perhaps I'll go. Shall I go soon?
I don't believe that question is sincere
and I look at myself with amazement.[9]

REFERENCES

1 S. Halkin, *Modern Hebrew Literature,* Schocken Books, New York, 1970, p. 41.
2 F.A. Pottle, *The Idiom of Poetry,* quoted by Joseph Haefrati in *"Hateur bashirat hahaskalah",* *Hasifrut,* vol. 2, 1969–1971 p. 37.
3 *Hatzalat avraham meur kasdim*
4 Tova Cohen, *Mehalom lametziut – eretz yisrael basifrut hahaskalah,* Bar Ilan, 1982, p. 185.
5 Avraham Shaanan, *Hasifrut ha'ivrit hehadashah,* vol. 1, Massadah, 1967, p. 213.
6 Halkin, op. cit. p. 80.
7 J. Klausner, *History of Modern Hebrew Literature,* Cailingold, London, 1932, p. 111.
8 Letter to Ravnitzski, *Igrot Bialik* vol. 2, p. 44.
9 *Timahon, Shirah tze'irah,* Eked, 1969, p. 75.

13 Israel as redemption in
S.Y. Agnon's A Guest for the Night

Zilla Goodman

S.Y. Agnon's book *A Guest for the Night* appears at first to be the simple story of a man's return to his native town (Shibush) after a protracted absence. It describes the town and its inhabitants as they unfold to the narrator in his wanderings through its environs over the duration — just under one year — of his return. But the actualities of Shibush, the composition of its hypothetical present moments as perceived by the narrator, extend across the boundaries of limited space and time.

By the blending of waking and dream, imagination and logic, present and past, Agnon introduces a timelessness into the limited world the book explores. This is enhanced by the employment of such technical devices as analogy and parallelism[1] — across characters, stories and situations — which create echoes that reverberate in a tenor more encompassing than any singular representation of the facts would allow. But most effective in the creation of a feeling of ubiquity is the structure of the tale which is not a tale at all (in the sense of plot, central motif and sequential development), but a series of digressions spreading over a multitudinous array of events with an ever-shifting locus of narrative.

While the narrator's pilgrimage to the past with its accompanying motifs of the key and Beit HaMidrash comprise the manifest purpose of the account, they are essentially only the symbolic emodiments of the thematic concerns which are basic to the book.[2] These are centred upon both the separateness and the unity of all things. The notion of unity and separation gives rise to a great number of associated issues revolving upon the question of opposites, complementaries and the ultimate resolution of apparently disparate elements in an all-containing union. *A Guest for the Night* deals with the tension that derives from the paradoxical relationship in which separate-opposite stands to merged-unity, and attempts to reconcile its inherent difficulties so as to attain redemption — to arrive at a standpoint from which action is possible. The answer of course can never be simple or wholly rational.

The apparently jumbled, structureless narrative mode faithfully explicates both its concrete and conceptual intentions. It expresses the "facts" of the story, creating a feeling

150

of immediacy, of an approximate identity between narrative and narrated time, by its implication that the facts of the story are being presented almost as they occur, without the intervention of the time-gap that the ordering of them would demand. Similarly, the frequent transitions between direct and reported speech, the changes in the pronouns used to denote one and the same speaker at one and the same time, the shifts in the use of tenses within one episode, are all apparently reflective of the movements of a receptive consciousness. The implicit statement of the book is also served by its form. Separateness is portrayed in its description of linear journey (the arrival of the Guest, his stay, and his departure — i.e. the beginning, middle and end of the book, and even the progression of the words and sentences themselves) and by the cohesion imposed upon the tale by the existence of a central reference point (the Guest).[3] The unity of all things is expressed in those factors mentioned in the discussion on narrative mode. Gershon Shaked (via T.S. Eliot) appositely describes the function of the structure of the book as objective correlative to its concerns: the form accurately echoes its content.[4]

At the core of the narrator's journey to Shibush is a desire to revive and recapture the past. He left the town as a youth and he returns to it some 20 years later as a 41-year-old man, prompted in his quest by the destruction of his home in Jerusalem, which he has neither the strength nor the motivation to rebuild.

מה טעם אני כאן ואשתי וילדי במקום אחר אחרי שהחריבו האויבים את ביתי ולא הניחו לי כלום נכנסה בי עייפות יתירה ונתרשלו ידי מלהקים את ביתי, שנחרב חורבן שני.

(p. 193)

He looks to the past for sustenance and for regeneration — perceiving it as an ideal in which to immerse himself, hoping it will prove redemptive. To this end he undertakes a pilgrimage to his native town, Shibush, thereby leaving the conventional locus of pilgrimage, the Holy Land. But, despite the central intention underlying this journey, the enterprise is characterised by a lack of definite purpose and plan. Once the initial stages of the pilgrimage — the journey to Shibush and the acquisition of lodgings — are successfully dealt with, the narrator enters a world which lacks definition. The desire to return which inspired him to assertive action is dissipated by its fulfilment which leaves him denuded of clear intention and therefore prey to whatever circumstances chance upon him. This is, however, as it should be; for, in aspiring the world of the past, the narrator is attempting to actualise that which, in accordance with the linearity of the waking-state world, is irretrievable and incapable of repetition. By invoking the past he leaves the realm of the waking-state with its attendant conditions of linearity, logic and intentionality and enters a world over which sequence, initiative and even individuality hold no sway.

Soon after his arrival, however, he is provided with a purpose which is an external expression of the motive of his pilgrimage. On Yom Kippur, or rather at the end of that day, he suddenly finds himself appointed (albeit in a disparaging manner) as Keeper of Beit HaMidrash — as Master of its Key. Both Beit HaMidrash and its key are laden with emotional value for the narrator. They fulfil a double function. They act as symbols — the first as a symbol of Jewish life of the past, and the second as a symbol of the means to its attainment — and also hold a literal value: Beit HaMidrash is the place in which he studied in his youth, while its key was an object he used in his childhood years. And his home, like the temple, is twice destroyed.[5] These objects and events serve to connote the personal history of the narrator as well as the collective history of the nation. By this merging of both worlds — the individual and the communal — Agnon highlights a variation on the theme of unity and separation: the nation is comprised of individuals while the individual is the embodiment of the nation — each contains the other.[6]

THE NATION AND THE INDIVIDUAL

The identity of nation and individual is further explicated by a series of parallels between the narrator's experiences and the similar experiences undergone by the inhabitants of Shibush.[7] The immediate cause of the narrator's return is the violent destruction of his home in Israel, yet the first sight his home town reveals to him bespeaks much the same fate — Shibush in ruins.

Similarly, the narrator's spiritual crisis, which leads him to seek out the past, is echoed by the spiritual poverty that characterises Shibush. Shibush is crippled in both its physical and metaphysical guises. Just as the narrator is incapable of movement, so the town is suspended in a limbo of inaction and degeneration. War has wrought desolation over Shibush — nothing remains of her former glory but the shells of buildings echoing the skeletal remnants of her earlier religious urge. Similarly, the violent effects of politics have brought about the ruin of the narrator's home, which in its turn is both the representative of and the cause of the spiritual desolation within him. Thus the physical objects of the book act as an objective correlative to the inner states of its inhabitants, and by the paralleling of these elements Agnon emphasises the indissolubility of the individual and the nation.

The identity between the individual and the nation is echoed by the identity between the town and the nation. Just as the individual is the embodiment of the collective people, so is Shibush the metaphoric ubiety that exemplifies both its history and its present state of being. Shibush performs the function of surrogate world, both material and spiritual, of the Jewish people. Even the name of the town is suggestive of a sense of upheaval, of irreparable misconstruction, and may be seen as a comment on the physical and the emotional-religious circumstances of the nation.[8]

In Chapter 40 the names of Shibush personalities parallel names of biblical figures akin to them in function. By this device a meaning is placed upon the present which ramifies beyond its domain and reaches to the historical antecedents of the nation, bringing them to bear upon twentieth-century Europe. The family described in this chapter was once the town's leading family. Its male members were, appropriately, named after the fathers of the nation: Rabbi Abraham and Rabbi Ya'akov-Moshe, whose widow is called Sara. The men of the family are dead as the result of either war or starvation and their widows live in considerably straitened circumstances, barely able to survive. The outer form of the home they live in is analogous to the condition in which the family is situated. This reciprocal relationship is emphasised by the concurrence of these two elements within the same paragraph:

הבית חרב וראשו ניטל ממנו. אדם שניתז ראשו אינו חי כיוצא בו בית. אף דיוטא זו שנשתיירה שם, בסיסו של
הגוף, שבה היתה החנות הגדולה שנתפרנסו הימנה כמה משפחות, ספק קיימת ספק חרבה. אף על פי כן צימצמה
שרה עצמה שם, היא וארבע גיסותיה, נשיהם של אחיו של בעלה, שקצתם נהרגו במלחמה וקצתם מתו ברעב.
(p.216)

The identity between the names of Rabbi Abraham and his family with the patriarchs and
the matriarch suggests not only a correspondence between these two sets of people
— contemporary and ancient — but amplifies it into a total identity. The state of Rabbi
Abraham's family thus becomes emblematic for the state of the nation for the original
Abraham and his descendants are, in fact, nothing less than the source and the subsequent
representation of the nation in its entirety. Thus the present condition of the Shibush
family and its home may be seen as a portrayal of the nation itself and the narrator is
therefore justified in the conclusion he reaches when visiting Sara's home:

נפל פסוק לתוך פי, היתה כאלמנה. כשראה ירמיה את החורבן הראשון ישב וכתב ספר קינות, ולא נתקררה דעתו
בכל הקינות שקונן, עד שהמשיל את כנסת ישראל לאלמנה ואמר היתה כאלמנה, ולא אלמנה ממש, אלא כאישה שהלך
בעלה למדינת הים ודעתו לחזור אצלה. כשאנו באים לקונן על חורבן אחרון אין אנו מספיקים אם נאמר היתה
כאלמנה, אלא אלמנה ממש בלא כף הדמיון.
(p.216)

Shaked is correct in asserting, by extension, that Sara's initiation of the transfer of the
book *Yadav Shel Moshe* — whose miraculous properties save mothers and their nascent
offspring during difficult births — from Shibush to Israel, constitutes the nation's implicit
recognition that the future of the Jewish people is incapable of realisation in the Galut.[9]
The Galut as expressed in Shibush is, at least at this stage in the story, barren, both
literally and figuratively: for many years no child has been born within its confines.

ISRAEL

The coincidence of the narrator's return to Shibush with the eve of Yom Kippur displays
another aspect of the synecdochic relationship between individual and nation. By mentioning it at the start of the book, Agnon immediately introduces the analogic tone which
echoes through its pages. The narrator returns to his home town on the festival of Return,
when most of its inhabitants are striving to achieve a Return.[10] He barely succeeds in
arriving before the onset of the Holy Day, as is shown by the hotel inhabitants' reaction to
his appearance:

אנשי המלון קיבלוני כאורח שבא שלא בזמנו, שכבר קמו מסעודה המפסקת ועמדו לילך וחששו שמא יצטרכו להתעכב
על ידי.
(p.10)

His timely arrival is tragically ironic for he is, in fact, an "אורח שבא שלא בזמנו". The time he

153

attempts to reinstate in Shibush is long past and it is doubtful whether his idealised picture of it was ever a reality.

The theme of journey and return is not confined to the adventures of the narrator, but receives further dramatic exposition in the histories — both collective and individual — of the inhabitants of Shibush. The town-collective was forced into exile during the war years when the men joined in the fighting, while their families (e.g. the Bachs and the Zummers) fled to Vienna to escape the violence of advancing armies and the starvation resulting from the prolonged hostilities. Most of the survivors return to Shibush to try to re-establish their lives there. The collective return is not, however, successful: the unyielding atmosphere of Shibush is stagnant and sterile. This is portrayed by the collective barren-ness that overlays the town, of which Daniel and Mrs Bach's lack of employment is an expression: he is a builder, she a midwife. Neither birth nor building are features of contemporary Shibush, whose chief characteristic — collective hunger, physical and spiritual starvation — is condensed in Elimelech Kaiser's bitter observation:

שמא יודע אדם במה ישבור צומו?

(p. 19)

The individual accounts of journey and return, narrated in the stories of people en-countered by the Guest during his stay in Shibush, comply with one another in their overall features. But the specific detail in which they differ is of importance to the book for it serves to introduce and expound upon various thematic strands pertinent to the concerns of the narrator in the process of learning he undergoes over the one-year period of his return. It also contributes to a primary aspect of the technique on which the book is structured: Agnon's exploitation of antithetical correspondences resonates through the work, giving dramatic actuality to the paradoxical tension in which unity and separation are attuned one to the other by accentuating the notion of unity in diversity and its complementary opposite — diversity in unity, with each informing the other by high-lighting the identity and disparity between the items under consideration.

Among the characters whose experience of journey and return corresponds in some way to the narrator's are Yeruham Hofshi, Rabbi Hayim and Reb Shlomo Bach, all of whom reflect different aspects of the dilemmas and revelations he experiences.

Yeruham Hofshi's journey to Israel and his subsequent return to Shibush is both parallel to and distinct from the narrator's. Inasmuch as his departure from the town received its impetus from the example of the Guest's departure some years earlier, which infused the possibility of settling in Israel with a reality it had up till then lacked —

אמר ירוחם, עד שלא עלית לארץ ישראל לא היתה לארץ ישראל בעירנו מציאות של כלום. . . . אבל מיום שעלית לארץ
ישראל נעשתה ארץ ישראל דבר שבמוחש, שהרי אחד מבינינו עלה שם. . . . נמשכתי אחריך,
שאתה וארץ ישראל נעשיתם לי חטיבה אחת. הייתי אומר הריני עולה לארץ ישראל ונכנס אצלך
ואומר לך בן עירך אני ובזכותך עליתי אף אני. . .

(p. 87)

154

— and, in that it is inspired by the Guest's impulse in leaving, the trace of which lingered in a poem "אהבה נאמנה עד שאולה" [11, 12] written by the narrator, it is one and the same journey. But whereas the narrator's return to Shibush is voluntary, Yeruham's is not, and it is in the divergent causes which prompt their return that the essential difference in their attitudes is embodied. The narrator leaves Israel to return to Shibush because of a spiritual crisis which he hopes to resolve by communion with the past. Yeruham is banished from Israel because of political causes — illegal immigration and an adherence to a communist ideology — and returns to Shibush, to the past, because he has no alternative. Yeruham's political ideology is forward-looking and utilitarian at base; the narrator's ideology is rooted in the past and is spiritual in character. Ironically it is Yeruham who establishes his life in Shibush while the narrator realises that Shibush no longer holds anything for him, and moves on to the future. But Yeruham's life in Shibush is not a perpetuation of the past. It is, instead, an assertion of the possibility of the unfolding of the future within the confines of the past. This positive statement is brought to full explication in Yeruham and Rachel's gift to the town in providing it with its first birth since the onset of the war. Thus, by the end of the book the journeys of Yeruham and the narrator are once more merged, for they reach the identical destination: the narrator learns to accept the new, while Yeruham manages to integrate the past. Both face forward to the future.

Rabbi Hayim's journey differs from both the narrator's and Yeruham's, but implicit in his behaviour on his return is the seed of the realisation the narrator arrives at by the close of the book. Rabbi Hayim is forced into exile during the war years by the Russians, who take him as their prisoner. After his release he wanders around Eastern Europe for many years, finally returning to Shibush during the course of the narrator's stay here. Unlike the narrator, he does not return in a bid to reclaim the past because he is not deluded into attributing it a glory it did not possess. In fact, quite the opposite is true: Rabbi Hayim, who was once one of the town's leading scholars, who so gloried in his knowledge as to seek recognition of it at the price of communal harmony, refuses on his return to open a book, claiming — falsely — that he has forgotten all he once knew. Rabbi Hayim renounces the past so entirely as to abnegate his rights as husband and father. Although the reason for his return is never stated, it is evident from the course of his action that his purpose is one of repentance — of true return. He comes to Shibush not in order to benefit or extract profit from it, but with the intention of giving, of compensating for his past misdoings. He has realised that the expression of worship is not confined to the scholarship obtained in Beit HaMidrash, but that it entails a broader, more integrated approach which brings into closer cohesion the word and the deed of which a true religious life is composed. But Rabbi Hayim never grasps the full meaning of his realisation for, in his enthusiasm to correct the past, he immerses himself in "the deed" to the detriment of "the word".

Although the zeal with which Rabbi Hayim applies himself to the task of repentance is somewhat excessive, he does finally achieve a full return. He becomes truly righteous and is transformed into a true Zaddik, whose humility and faith do not fail him even at the final moments of his life. It is thus fitting that Rabbi Hayim's final request —

155

אבל אני מבקש, שילמדו למנוחת נפשי פרק משניות. לשם זה אני מניח צרור כסף שהרווחתי בגופי. ואני מצפה לרחמי שמים ולרחמי הבריות שייטיבו עם נשמתי וילמדו וילמדו משניות עם פירוש, וילמדו מלה במלה, ויאמרו קדיש דרבנן אחרי הלימוד כנהוג וכמנהג. ואחר קדיש דרבנן יאמרו מזמור ק"ב תפילה לעני.

(p. 406)

is instrumental in awakening the narrator to a clear spiritual resolution which releases him from the bonds of the past. For it is while sitting in Beit HaMidrash, in compliance with Rabbi Hayim's wish, that the narrator comes to the full realisation of that which he has always known but has never fully accepted[13]

שאין תורה כתורת ארץ ישראל.

(p. 417)

and becomes resigned to his impending and permanent (at least in terms of the pre-Messianic world) leave-taking of Shibush — of the past. His new-found understanding is portrayed in an imagined dialogue with the walls of Beit HaMidrash:

מסתכל אני בכתלי בית המדרש הישן ואומר להם, רואים אתם כבר הגיע זמני שאעלה לארץ ישראל. מטים עצמם כתלי בית המדרש, כאילו מבקשים לחבק אותי בזכות שאני עולה לארץ ישראל. אומר אני להם, רצונכם ואני טוען אתכם על כתפי ומעלה אתכם עמי. אומרים כתלי בית המדרש, כבדים אנו ואין כוחו של אדם אחד לטעון אותנו על כתפיו. אלא טול את המפתח ועלה, וכשתגיע השעה נבוא אחריך.

(p. 417)

where their response to his leaving is but a projection of his own stance. Thus, at first, Rabbi Hayim and the narrator stand in antithesis to each other, whereas, at the close of the book their positions are synthesised: like Rabbi Hayim the narrator no longer seeks the past — he knows it to be too heavy a burden for any one man to bear. The death of Rabbi Hayim is testimony to that.

Reb Shlomo Bach's successful journey represents the culmination of the position at which Rabbi Hayim arrives. Rabbi Hayim attains virtue, but a reconciliation of the past evades him because he is too fervent in his denial of it, as his refusal to acknowledge both his scholarly ability and his role within his family portray. His past is too laden with guilt and the memory of it is too painful to allow an admission of its reality. Yet it is incapable of being dismissed; it cannot be demolished. The content of Rabbi Hayim's meditations before his death testify to the insistence with which its sibilance has, through the years, resonated in him —

סבור הייתי שהוא ישן וראיתי שהוא מרחש בשפתיו. הטיתי אזני ושמעתי שהוא אומר ואלו כשרות בעוף, ניקבה הגרגרת או שנסדקה. כיון שהרגיש בי לחש לי, באותה הלכה התחילה המחלוקת.

(p. 402)

Though he travels away from Shibush, Reb Shlomo, by contrast, does not attempt to deny the past. When he first arrives in Israel he continues, as before, in his study of the Mishnayot. But he is not so rooted in the past as to be shackled by it. The sanctity of the

156

land soon prompts him to a new spirit. He finds a new form of worship, which consists of the union of spirit and matter. Reb Shlomo abandons the conventional study of the Mishna to work in the fields, for it is there that he finds the essential content of the Mishnayot is revealed. He neither denies nor longs for the walls of Beit HaMidrash. In Reb Shlomo the past and the present are fully integrated. In him the spiritual dilemma of the nation is resolved and he stands as an emblem of its hope, as the augur of a free and glorious future.

It is a small wonder that Reb Shlomo's peer group on the kibbutz look upon his activities with disdain, for, despite their residence in Israel, they still inhabit the world of the past. Their approach to religion is fragmenting in its effects and consists of passionate arguments about the most petty and peripheral aspects of worship (p. 443). This attitude is but an echo of the religious atmosphere which prevailed over the Shibush of old, typified in the controversy started by Rabbi Hayim, the crux of which were the conditions pertaining to the Kashrut/non-Kashrut of birds, and the object of which was not spiritual refinement but personal vainglory (pp. 148-9); in the division between the Hasidim and the Mitnagdim, and in the endless disputes, divisions and sub-divisions between the numerous groups of Hasidim, each declaring its ultimate and absolute claim to sanctity (Chapter 43). It is not surprising that adherents to such a posture are incapable of comprehending life as a unified whole: theirs is a fragmented intellect whose partite mode of functioning divides all that with which it is confronted. Their "spiritual" life consists of mere religiosity — not true religion.

The religious position that Reb Shlomo achieves, which recognises the coherence of spirit and matter, is portrayed in the book as the desirable one, in that the narrator has his most profoundly religious experiences in those moments in which nature, as exemplified in the mountain, and spirit, as exemplified in Beit HaMidrash, are brought into alignment within his consciousness. An example of this may be found right at the start of the book, in Chapter 3, where the reciprocal relationship between these two elements is emphasised:

אור מופלא האיר מבית המדרש על ההר וכן מן ההר על בית המדרש. אור שכמותו לא ראיתם מימיכם. אור אחד היה ומאורות הרבה היו בו. מקום שכזה אי אתה מוצא בעולם. עמדתי לי והרהרתי בלבי, איני זה מכאן עד שיעלה רצונו לפניו ליטול את נשמתי ממני. ואף על פי שנזכרה לי מיתתי לא הייתי עצב. אפשר שפני לא היו שמחות, אבל לבי היה שמח. וקרוב בעיני לומר, שמעין זה לא הרגשתי זה שנים הרבה, שהלב שמח ואין הפנים משתפות עצמן בשמחתו.

(pp. 16-17)

The narrator's attempt to revive the spirit of old Shibush is contrary to nature: it succeeds, or at least appears to, when nature is at her most hostile and dormant — in midwinter — but spring, the time in which nature generates birth and all attains new being, heralds the failure and death of his endeavour. His unease at the first slight signs of warmer weather —

המולד נראה בעליל. האדמה הבהיקה מן השלג והצינה כאילו הפשירה קצת. דומה שהאויר משתנה והולך. השם יודע אם לטוב ואם למוטב.

(p. 171)

157

— proves to be valid: the arrival of the warm spring air renders visits to Beit HaMidrash unnecessary to the citizens of Shibush who congregated there in the colder days so as to enjoy the warmth of its fire.[14]

Thus the nation's return in the literal sense of the word, to its former position, is not a desirable or redemptive proposition, for its harmony and beauty have long since dissipated and its strength is exhausted. Just as Rabbi Hayim's death is rumoured to have been directly caused by his attempt to rectify past mistakes —

אמרתי לה, ומה גרם לו שיחלה? אמרה צפורה, הדעות מחולקות. יש אומרים שהלך אצל הרב ליפטר ממנו והיתה שם גרגרת של עוף מוטלת לפני הפתח בחצר והחליק ונפל. ויש אומרים אצל ביתנו עמד ונתקל שם בפריץ אחד שכור ונפל.

(p. 393)

— so any attempt to correct the past while acting within its boundaries may be presumed to be destructive.

But there is a return which is immensely desirable, for it comprises the ultimate union of the material and spiritual, and that is the return undertaken by both Reb Shlomo and the narrator — the return to Israel, for "אין תורה כתורת ארץ ישראל" (p. 417). This return is so desirable that even nature expresses its striving to partake of it by leaning eastwards —

היום ירד וצללי אילנות ושיחים מתמתחים והולכים לצד מזרח. אין אני מן הרגשנים, אבל אותה שעה אמרתי, אילנות ושיחים שהם מן הדומם פונים כלפי מזרח ואני שהייתי במזרח פניתי לכאן.

(p. 268)

The approbation of this return is counterpointed by Gündel's request for holy earth for her grave and by Lebtche sending a copy of his book to Jerusalem so that it will have perpetuation and remembrance —

מה שביקשה גינדיל לגופה עשה לייבטשי בודינהוריז לנשמתו, העתקה של ספרו שלח לבית הספרים הלאומי שלנו, כדי לעשות לו זכירה בירושלים.

(p. 444)

There is little hope for the continuation — both spiritual and material — of the nation outside Israel, for —

ברית כרותה לארץ ישראל, מי שאינו עולה לארץ נשכח ומשתכח, אבל כל שזכה יהי בה נזכר ונכתב, שנאמר (ישעיהו ד') כל הכתוב לחיים בירושלים.

(p. 445)

The return to Israel does not, however, of itself comprise a total return or redemption. It requires the emphasis of one of its supplementary aspects so as to bring the power of its positive agency to full fruition.

158

BAYIT

The old way is played out — it no longer holds the potential for renascence. It has been impinged upon by too many confounding circumstances of which war was but the final cataclysmic factor in contributing to its destruction. This situation and its logical corollary — the need to find a new way with which the old may be substituted — is reflected in the accounts described above. Of these the stories of Reb Shlomo and Yeruham Hofshi stand out in the message of hope they provide and the viable alternatives they present. Reb Shlomo's transition from the old to the new is a smooth one though it is not entirely devoid of pain, for its antecedent conditions entail the death of one son — Yeruham — and the virtual loss of another — Daniel. His lack of sentimentality towards the past allows him to discover a new essence, a mode of redemption which is embodied in the land of Israel. Yeruham Hofshi, on the other hand, discovers a different means of salvation which is, in the final analysis, but the complementary correlate to Reb Shlomo's solution. While Israel lies at the core of Reb Shlomo's regeneration, the home and the family form the central focus of Yeruham's new-found resolution. However, as these two characters both represent the nation's successful passage into the future it is fitting that the life of each contain, as it does, not only the thrust of its own direction but traces of its complementary correlate as well. Yeruham Hofshi has lived in Israel and silently longs to return there, while Reb Shlomo's journey to Israel is prompted by familial concerns.

The ironic correspondences between the lives of Reb Shlomo and Yeruham reveal the level of sophistication to which Agnon extends his technique of multi-layered analogy. Yeruham, who is orphaned in infancy, becomes the proponent of family life, while Reb Shlomo, whose son loses his life in Israel, develops into an advocate of life there. Furthermore, the complementary nature of their respective earlier losses combines with the correlation and identity between their spiritual attainments to render Reb Shlomo and Yeruham in the symbolic relationship of father and son. This symbolic relationship is lent concrete credibility and emphasis by the following circumstances: when Yeruham is orphaned at birth it is Reb Shlomo's family who adopts him; Reb Shlomo's dead son was also named Yeruham and he and Yeruham Hofshi were close friends; Yeruham Bach dies at Ramat Rachel and, by his burial there, is united with it, his body materially contributing to the land's creative process of providing nourishment to Israel; Yeruham Hofshi marries Rachel Zummer and the result of their union is the creation of a new life which provides spiritual nourishment to Shibush and to the people of Israel, as it heralds the rebirth of the nation.

The symbolic filial relationship in which Yeruham stands to Reb Shlomo, and the interdependence indicated thereby, corresponds to the supplementary position in which the ideal of "Home" stands to the ideal of "Israel" and to the inextricability of these two concepts within the national *Zeitgeist*.

The narrator's pilgrimage likewise portrays the valency of these two ideals, and the vicissitudes in which they are explicated therein serve to bring into cohesion the concomitant issues of nativity, family and religious worship with which both the narrator and the nation grapple. The Guest's return to Shibush indicates that Israel is, in itself, not sufficient to the task of abolishing spiritual stagnation but is in need of the accompanying ideal of "Home", while Shibush's failure to fulfil that function asserts the impotence of mere nativity in this role. The narrator's recognition of Shibush's deficiency in this regard is suggested in his acceptance of the applicability of the epithet "Guest" as an apposite description of his position in the town —

לאחר התפילה בירכו המתפללים זה את זה בשבת שלום ומבורך והלכו לבתיהם בנחת. אף אני הלכתי לביתי זה מלוני, שהרי גר אני בארץ וביתי רחוק מכאן כמה מאות פרסאות ואיני אלא כאורח נטה ללון.

(p. 122)

— and his awareness of the link between "Home" and "Israel" is expressed in Chapter 24 in his exposition of the Weekly Portion —

פתחתי חומש ודרשתי בפרשת השבוע בפסוק וייקץ יעקב משנתו וגו' ויירא ויאמר מה נורא המקום הזה, אין זה כי אם בית אלקים. לא כאברהם שאמר, בהר ה' יראה, ולא כיצחק, שנאמר בו, ויצא יצחק לשוח בשדה, אלא כיעקב, שקרא בית. ודרשתי בשלש בחינות של עבודת השם. בחינה אחת שאדם מבקש לו דברים גבוהים בחינת הר, ומהלך כל ימיו במחשבות גבוהות. בחינה שנייה בחינת שדה, שדרכה של שדה שזורעים בה וקוצרים בה ויש לה ריח טוב, כמו שנאמר ראה ריח בני כריח השדה. בחינה שלישית, שהיא אהובה על הקדוש ברוך הוא ביותר, זו בחינה בית, שכתוב ביעקב אבינו המובחר שבאבות. ואף הוא יתברך משתבח ואומר, כי ביתי בית תפילה. מובא בזוהר, בית לישראל למהוי עמהון כאתתא בבעלה בדיורא חד בחדוא. שהר ושדה הם מקומות דרור, אבל בית הוא מקום משומר ומכובד.

מובא בספרים, שזכות שלושה אבות עומדת להם לישראל בשלוש הגלויות. זכותו של אברהם עמדה לנו בגלות מצרים, כמו שנאמר, כי זכר וקו' את אברהם עבדו ויוצא עמו בששון וגו'. זכותו של יצחק בגלות בבל. וזכותו של יעקב בגלרתינו זאת האחרונה. לפיכך צריכין אנו לתפוס ביותר בחינת יעקב, בחינת בית יעקב לכו ונלכה באור ה'. ועליהם אמר יעקב, ושבתי בשלום אל בית אבי, ועליהם נאמר כל הפסוק כולו, והיה ה' לי לאלקים.

(pp. 128–9)

Thus his journey to Shibush may be seen to be at odds with the knowledge he already possesses. He leaves Israel — the true national home — and travels to Shibush — an arbitrary geographical location which happens to be his birthplace — abandoning his family — the human component and primary aspect of his individual home — in the process. But his voyage is, in fact, a voyage of confirmation, for, in moving in a direction so contrary to his intellectual awareness he arrives at a spiritual affirmation of its precepts, thereby attaining an integrated understanding which may be called revelation. His return to Israel at the close of the book is a threefold return entailing a return to his family — his personal home — a return to Israel — the national home — and an inner return — to his essential home — arriving at his beginning and knowing it for the first time in its fullness. The narrator is finally able to leave Beit HaMidrash the old house of worship — בית ביתי תפילתי" (p. 369) — for he has found his new centre of worship in the synthesis of Israel extension, the disrupted linear mode of the work may be seen, not only as an exposition of his familial home — who initiates and enables his return from the shapeless mazes of the past.[15,16]

WHOLENESS AND REDEMPTION

The relationship between name and form serves to highlight the undeniably tragic elements of the book. Shibush is, as its name implies, misconstrued. And as Shibush is emblematic for the nation, the nation is likewise in a state of misconstruction. Thus, by extension, the disrupted linear mode of the work may be seen, not only as an exposition of a philosophic proposition, but as the portrayal of a ruined society as well. The book is therefore also an historical statement which, by breaking the code of linearity, faithfully serves the essentially linear demands of history, in that it accurately describes a disintegrated civilisation.

The final resolution of the tale is punctuated by an admission to, and a dramatisation of, the dictates of linearity. The narrator is finally able to act upon the world because he concedes to the inevitability of linearity: he accepts the irretrievability of the past, moves into the present and thereby advances to the future. The culmination of this process is reached in his journey away from Shibush to Israel — the redemptive locus, a spatial redemption — on a train, whose progress is nothing if not linear. This climax is echoed in Shibush's release from its static condition by a birth — a redemptive function, a temporal redemption. Shibush's saviours are Yeruham and Rachel Hofshi, who both represent the potential of the future. Yeruham's idealism is forward-looking though it is not devoid of spirituality, as his abstinence from the eating of meat indicates. Shibush's freedom is heralded by the linear passage of a child into life — a passage which is not only linear in itself, but which delivers its passenger to the dictates of linearity.

These two journeys — the child's and the narrator's — are brought into explicit cohesion by a number of circumstances: the narrator performs the role of Sandak at the child's Brith-Milah; the child is named after the narrator; the narrator gives the child the new key to Beit HaMidrash which he no longer needs,[17] only to find the old key in his possession when he arrives back in Israel. Thus the narrator's spiritual rebirth receives dramatic support from the actual birth of the child, and Israel receives affirmation as the binding centre of worship by the reappearance there of the historical key.[18]

But, though the action of the story ends in an affirmation of linearity, of actual journey to an actual place — the land of Israel — its conceptual latitudes anticipate a finer all-encompassing reality of Zion. This is to be attained at some future time with the advent of the Messiah, when all creation will merge in a joyous undivided unity. Thus the original key waits in Israel to be reunited with Beit HaMidrash at the end of the days, the narrator joins with Israel in longing for that time when all will be immersed in the unity of creation, when name and form will be perfectly one and will reveal their inherent perfection —

התורה שלימה, אלא שהארון שנתונה בו שבור. הכיסופין הללו שאנו נכספים יביאו אותנו לקבל את התורה שנייה, זאת התורה הנצחית שאינה נחלפת לעולם לא במסיבות הזמן וחילופי העתים.

(p. 253)

— in Full Redemption: wholly merged and beyond all separation.

NOTES

1 G. Shaked, *Omanut HaSippur shel Agnon,* pp. 47, 50–55, 233–9.

2 For an exposition of the key as a central motif in *A Guest for the Night* see B. Kurzweil, *Masot al Sippurei Shai Agnon,* pp. 54–68. Kurzweil was the first to point to its importance. Also see A. Band, *Nostalgia and Nightmare,* pp. 316–7 and Shaked, op. cit. pp. 242–3.

3 Shaked, op. cit. p. 247. Shaked observes that the main function of the narrator is that of witnessing.

4 Ibid. p. 233.

5 Ibid. pp. 268–9. For Shaked's analysis of the two destructions.

6 Ibid. p. 236. Shaked comments on the commonality of fate of nation and individual.

7 Ibid. p. 265. Shaked refers to these and to the biographical connection between Agnon and the narrator but says this is of little consequence.

8 Band, op. cit. p. 290. Band refers to the meaning of the root š b š and to its being a metathesis of Buczacz, Agnon's home town.

9 Shaked, op. cit. p. 245.

10 Kurzweil, op. cit. p. 235, on a flawed Yom Kippur and pp. 272–3 on Yom Kippur, Return and the future. For same theme see Band, op. cit. pp. 292–3.

11 Shaked, op. cit. pp. 265–6 for the relationship of the poem to Agnon's biography, its significance in the book and Yeruham Hofshi's reactions to it and complaints about it.

12 Kurzweil, op. cit. p. 306. Kurzweil comments on the poem and its implications for an integrated conception of Jerusalem — composed of ideal and reality — within the narrator's consciousness.

13 For the narrator's complex feelings and guilt about having left Israel see Shaked, op. cit. p. 269, and Band, op. cit. p. 310.

14 Ibid. p. 317.

15 Ibid. p. 312. Band points out that it is the narrator's wife who urges him to leave the key in Shibush, and later to send it back to Shibush; that she also prompts him to return to Israel and sends him the return ticket. Furthermore, he observes that it is she who finds the lost key in his baggage while setting in order their home in Israel. These observations support the thesis forwarded in this chapter about the symbiotic function of Home and Israel in the redemptive process.

16 Kurzweil, op. cit. p. 304 on the blurring of the boundaries between Shibush and Jerusalem, the home and the wife.

17 Band, op. cit. pp. 317–18. Band notes that the key is given "in anticipation of the child's eventual settling in Eretz Yisrael".

18 Kurzweil, op. cit. pp. 304–5. Kurzweil sees the doubling of these circumstances as a resolution of the old and new.

BIBLIOGRAPHY

S.Y. Agnon, *A Guest for the Night,* in *The Collected Works of S.Y. Agnon,* Vol 4, Schocken Books, Tel Aviv and Jerusalem, 1960.

Arnold Band, *Nostalgia and Nightmare,* University of California Press, Berkeley and Los Angeles, 1968.

Baruch Kurzweil, *Masot al Sippurei Shai Agnon,* Schocken Books, Jerusalem and Tel Aviv, 1970.

Gershon Shaked, *Omanut HaSippur Shel Agnon,* HaKibbutz Harzi, HaShomer HaZair, Tel Aviv, 1973.

14 The gates of Zion and the dwellings of Jacob: Zion and Zionism in the work of Isaac Bashevis Singer

Joseph Sherman

Like the Psalmist (Psalm 87:2) who differentiated "the gates of Zion" from "the dwellings of Jacob", Singer distinguishes between the Holy Land as spiritual Zion, the eternal hope of Redemption; and the State of Israel as secular Zionism, the contemporary realisation of Restoration. In all his stories set in the vanished world of *shtetl* Poland, dreams of "the Holy Land", as it is always called there, are clearly linked to the coming of the Messiah and the establishment of the Kingdom of God on earth. The obsession which, in "Passions",[1] drives Leib Belkes painstakingly to construct a model of the Temple out of matches, is an expression of an unassuageable yearning for Redemption at which all the worldly folk around him, including his own wife, brazenly scoff. When they destroy his model, the way materialistic people always destroy spiritual visions they cannot share, Leib Belkes leaves his wife and walks all the way to the Holy Land, on a pilgrimage which stills his longings and is sanctified by God who, as the narrator assures us, "preserves the simple".[2] In "The Little Shoemakers",[3] one of Singer's most overtly allegorical tales, the patriarch of the family, whose name — Abba Shuster — denotes his mythic status,[4] imagines that the rise of Hitler is the last battle before the End of Days, and dreams that soon he and his family will sit "sewing golden sandals for the daughters of Zion and lordly boots for the sons".[5] But the "tremendous crash" which the old man takes to be "the blast of the Messiah's trumpet" is in reality the Nazi bombardment of Frampol,[6] and Abba is resurrected, not in the Holy Land, but in America, to a way of life that is entirely alienating.

Individuals throughout Singer's work tend to find that the easy Messiahs they follow invariably turn out to be false, and the Zions in whose restorations they rejoice remain illusions. The reports of Sabbatai Zevi's triumph which so excite the inhabitants of Goray are meant to bear a striking resemblance to the expectations of our own time:

> At first the kings and princes of the earth had dispatched hosts of giants with drawn swords against Sabbatai Zevi, that they might take him prisoner. But a torrent of great

stones rained from heaven as had been promised for the day of Gog and Magog, and all the giants perished. The world was astounded. The people of Judea were now in high repute. Princes and kings came to honor them and prostrated themselves before them.[7]

The glories of this promise shine more brightly by constrast with the bitter sufferings which precede it; the disillusionments of their inevitable failure are concomitantly more crushing. For Singer, "the gates of Zion" open inwards to individual spiritual regeneration; "the dwellings of Jacob", by contrast, since they are founded on worldliness, are all alike.

All his stories set in modern Israel are told in the first person by a narrator who bears a striking similarity to Singer himself.[8] This device is typically ambiguous. On the one hand, it serves as a valuable hedge to protect the author from accusations of anti-Zionism, since personal observations about particular people need not reflect a general condition; on the other hand, it is only from the particular that the general may be understood, since men, especially Jews, do not live in isolation but in community.[9] The locale of action is always Tel Aviv, a city whose outward appearance reflects its origin in, and commitment to, secularity; its shabby air of transience is a physical correlative of its spiritual vacuity:

> Although Tel Aviv was a new city, the houses looked old and dingy. The telephone didn't work properly, the bathtub seldom had hot water, and the electricity often went off at night. The food was bad.[10]

The *khamsin* is always blowing desert sand into the city's faces and places, not only making life uncomfortable, but serving as a subtly constant significator of impermanence.[11] Like the weather, insect and bird life is almost unremittingly hostile.[12] There is always a clinging smell of decay caused by garbage and rotting fish which blends with the stench of asphalt, the surfacing material of the new roads.[13] Though Hebrew is the tongue spoken and written everywhere, the narrator finds it "strange" and artificial: there seems to him to be a profound and destructive tension between the sacred roots of the language and the secular uses to which it is being put:

> I read the signs over the women's clothing stores. The commission for modernizing Hebrew had created a terminology for brassieres, nylons, corsets, ladies' coiffures, and cosmetics. They had found the sources for such worldly terms in the Bible, the Babylonian Talmud, the Jerusalem Talmud, the Midrash, and even the Zohar. It was always late in the evening, but buildings and asphalt still exuded the heat of the day. The humid air smelled of garbage and fish.[14]

All these details develop a picture of a reality rather than a dream, of a country built not by the Messiah but by men. A modern state, it is indistinguishable from all other modern states, sharing their preoccupations and imperfections. Reading the daily account of "thefts, car accidents, border shootings" in a Hebrew newspaper ironically called *Haaretz,*[15] the narrator of one tale muses, "No, the Messiah hadn't come yet. The Resurrection was not in sight . . ."[16] In another tale, on the corner of Ben Yehudah and Allenby Streets in

164

Tel Aviv, he turns abruptly to his companion, who happens also to be his Hebrew translator, with a challenge:

> "In what way is this the land of Israel? If it were not for the Hebrew signs it could just as well be Brooklyn — the same buses, the same noise, the same stench of gasoline, the same movie houses. Modern civilization wipes out all individuality."[17]

This common social and cultural denominator is what for Singer transmogrifies a sacred trust into a secular travesty. The modern political realisation of Zionism has rendered ambiguous the Messianic promise to re-establish Zion, because it has sundered the spiritual from the material, and has substituted the Gentile culture of 200 years of *Haskalah,* Enlightenment, for the Jewish culture of 2 000 years of *Golah,* Exile. Consequently, it has intensified rather than resolved the modern crisis of Jewish identity. Throughout their long exile, the Jewish people dreamed devotedly of the spiritual restoration of the biblical Holy Land; after their emancipation, they worked energetically towards the material reconstruction of a political homeland. What emerged was inevitably founded on principles which, for Singer, appear more profane than sacred. His *chalutzim,* pioneers, all develop attitudes and mouth slogans similar in essential respects to those of all other radicals and revolutionaries; they discard a traditional identity as Jews to assume a modern self-conception indistinguishable from that of Gentiles. Thus Joziek, in *The Estate,* sends his father "photographs of himself working at a wine press, riding horseback, standing near a tent holding a gun";[18] Tobias Stein, in "The Mentor", "wore a blouse with a sash, and a white-and-blue cap embroidered with the Star of David . . . [and] learned to shoot a rifle . . ."[19] The process of becoming "like the nations" is extended by the pursuit of worldly rather than religious learning. Those who enjoy positions of leadership in modern Israel, therefore, are of necessity the descendants of *maskilim* rather than of *tzaddikim.*[20]

A clear instance is Freidl in "The Mentor". The past in which she grew up was entirely cut off from traditional Jewish values; the present in which she works is wholly governed by secular opportunities and material rewards: "Worldliness, energy and resolution emanated from her."[21] The permissiveness of an "enlightened" world enables Freidl to gratify desires which Jewish Law once rigorously restrained. She openly admits that "There are monogamous women and even men, but I don't belong to them".[22] Inevitably, of course, she suffers from all sorts of neuroses;[23] in Singer's work, sexual abandonment leads automatically to emotional instability, which he regards as the characteristic symptom of a world sick with *Haskalah.* It is typically ironical also that Freidl should have neurology as her field of medical specialisation: she can help neither herself nor others.[24] Modern Jews, cut adrift from those religious mores which once regulated human conduct and so gave it meaning, now float in an emotional limbo in which the most profound of human feelings cannot be defined because they are no longer experienced:

> Exactly what love is I don't know and probably never will know. Everyone understands it in his own way. I've heard countless stories from my patients. But there isn't any explanation for human behaviour — there are only patterns.[25]

Rooting herself firmly in the Darwinian doctrine of the survival of the fittest, Freidl vehemently rejects the narrator's belief that "someone takes charge of this world"; she insists not only that life has no ultimate purpose, but that death is a welcome end. Quite appropriately, therefore, she describes herself as "a complete hedonist".[26] It is part of Singer's artistic purpose to test glib theories of this kind against the pain of lived experience. If Freidl is right, then centuries of Jewish tradition must be wrong; licence should consequently reveal itself as more life-enhancing than restriction. Yet Freidl is profoundly disturbed by the fact that her daughter hates her, and that contrary to all her powers of reason, she cannot persuade herself of the truth of what she would like to believe, "that a child is nothing more than an accidentally fertilized egg and that all the love and loyalty one feels towards it are only blind instinct".[27]

The thrust of the tale suggests that she should not be surprised by her daughter's behaviour. The girl's models, after all, have been the mother's promiscuity and the father's radicalism; the Torah she has learnt has been what her mother calls "the Torah of revolution". In describing the degree to which her husband and daughter are alienated from Jewish values, Freidl reveals the extent to which she herself has lost her identity in modern Israel. Though she speaks eight languages, not one of them is capable of transmitting the resonances of her heart in the novel she wants to write — partly, no doubt, because such resonances no longer exist, but also because, for all her wordly and professional success, she no longer has any real roots. Belonging nowhere, she has indeed been "actually left without a language".[28] When she finally discovers that her sixteen-year-old daughter is regularly spending the night with a man who is ironically designated by the girl's father as her "mentor", Freidl's outraged response springs from instinctual depths which can neither be eliminated by modern conditioning nor theorised away. It vindicates the Law even as it demonstrates its necessity:

> Freidl . . . stood openmouthed. This was no longer the doctor who had spoken those clever words this night but a shocked Jewish mother.[29]

The details which the narrator notices about the daughter's kibbutz as he follows Freidl back to her car serve as visual correlatives of the bleak emptiness of that life lived there which has just been so dramatically exposed:

> We passed the empty dining hall. Naked bulbs lighted the room. A girl was spreading paper on narrow tables. A boy washed the stone floor with a rag mop. The air was pungent with disinfectant.[30]

Reflecting on this vision in the car back to Tel Aviv, the narrator, conscious that Freidl's double standards are also his own, recalls the prophet Isaiah's denunciations of wickedness and is forced to a sobering conclusion:

> The powers that rule history had brought us back to the land of our ancestors, but we had already defiled it with abominations.[31]

Earlier in the story, when the narrator had confided to Freidl that "the history in this land doesn't let me sleep", she had assured him that "you get accustomed to it". In time, she promises, he will cease to hear the warnings of the prophets just as she has ceased to be inhibited about going to the toilet in Jerusalem. Modern day-to-day living in Israel, she implies, is a steady process of desensitisation to holiness and its associations.[32] For the author-narrator, however, the past shapes the present. As much as modern secular consciousness might wish to block out the experiences of that past, they lie buried very near the spiritual surface of the collective subconscious. From age to age, as much as from day to day, it is a condition of man's existence that he must choose, and the experiences of the past must inform that choice. The Jews both chose and were chosen; their election transformed their freedom to choose into a categoric imperative. In the land so redolent with their history and their tradition, they are forever torn between their nature and their Covenant:

> Somewhere below lay hidden golden calves, the jewelry of temple harlots, and images of Baal and Astarte. Here prophets foretold disasters. From a nearby harbor, Jonah had fled to Tarshish rather than prophesy the doom of Nineveh. In the daylight these events seemed remote, but at night the dead walked again. I heard the whisperings of phantoms.[33]

The Zionist dream, however, has often misrepresented the nature of these phantoms and dishonestly traded on them. Singer explores some of Zionism's secular distortions in a story ironically entitled "The Captive". In 1940, its chief character, a refugee painter named Tobias Anfang, could demand, "In a world where human beings are burned in gas ovens, what point is there in art?"[34] He settles in the newly-founded State of Israel, however, "first of all to be a Jew, and perhaps to find a way to Jewish art".[35] For him, "being a Jew" simply means living in Israel; his "way to Jewish art" is forging paintings in the style and under the name of his friend, another charlatan called Zorach Kreiter, who died in the camps. In Israel, Tobias becomes the captive of a vision which, since it is utterly cut off from spiritual reality and makes no demands for moral choice, is nothing more than a grandiose mirage:

> I have fallen in love with Israel . . . I stroll along the sea and literally hear the words of the prophets . . . I'm surrounded by the old Israelites and even the Canaanites and the other nations that preceded Joshua, the son of Nun . . . This land teems with saints and heroes. Although I do not believe in God, I hear His voice.[36]

Tobias is also, more literally, "the captive" of Kreiter's widow Sonia, who pays him to paint the forgeries which she then markets. Both Tobias and Sonia feel themselves to be "reincarnations" in Israel of Zorach Kreiter, who embodied the anarchic spirit of *Haskalah* formerly so much praised as the creative antithesis to the supposedly repressive ethos of *halakhah*.[37] Zionist fervour seems to demand this kind of spirit as the artistic counterpart of political independence, as the number of sales of these forgeries appears to testify. Tobias confides to the narrator that Sonia

> . . . has already sold more Kreiters than he could have produced in his lifetime. But neither the art dealers nor the customers seem inclined to investigate.[38]

167

This kind of work is in no way creatively original, artistically independent, or indigenous to the country: it is simply churned out to meet the demand for instant Israeli culture. Ironically, Sonia's own home is decorated with shadows long vanished:

> We entered a large hall, its walls full of pictures — like a museum . . . In the dim light I recognized scenes of Poland, Paris, a Warsaw market, bewigged women, yeshiva boys, musicians playing at a wedding, Hasidim dancing.[39]

The spirit of piety and the unquestioning faith which informed the ritual garments and actions of the subjects of these paintings now appear as cultural curiosities, relics of the past; they are no longer universally in daily existence in the new land of Israel. Sonia's demand that the narrator become the ghost writer of her dead husband's memoirs, as Tobias is the ghost painter of his pictures, suggests that all branches of this new national art are synthetic. The Zionist cause appears to demand of artists that they adapt to the new ethos or die; as Sonia tells it, "The artists who settle here seem to go through a process of resurrection or they become paralysed."[40]

Singleminded and cunning, Sonia Kreiter exploits the Zionist myth even as she builds it up in a manifestation of spiritual deformity amply bespoken by her physical ugliness. Accurately described by Tobias as "a witch . . . possessed by a dybbuk", she embodies in her own person the ruthless combination of driving energy and blatant hypocrisy which, the story suggests, is typical of that kind of secular progressiveness before which all other considerations must give way. Even as she is perpetrating a large-scale fraud, she is busy "hobnobbing with professors, writers, politicians".[41] She urges the narrator to leave America where, in her view, "there are thousands of Jews being discriminated against"[42] to come to an Israel where, as the narrator frequently notices, Arabs and Yemenite Jews are treated as second-class citizens.[43] A momentary recognition of the falseness of all this moves the narrator to flee Sonia's house: outside, in the sweltering heat, he has "the sensation that [he] had just managed to escape from a great danger".[44] But there he is trapped between Tobias, who shuffles helplessly towards him, and Sonia, who stretches out her arms laughingly to call him back. Tobias becomes an image of the shattered remnant of the Jewry of the past, Sonia the image of its triumphant survival in the present; both lay claim to a part of the narrator. If Tobias is a swindler, it is through impotence; in Sonia's black eyes "a mysterious darkness gleamed" which fills the narrator with a "sudden lust for that ugly creature".[45] At the end, while fierce storms rage outside, cutting Tel Aviv off both literally and symbolically from the rest of the country, the narrator "sat down with Sonia before the fireplace, and from the ouija board she dictated to [him] the first chapter of Zorach Kreiter's memoirs".[46] For all its fraudulence, the story finally suggests, the Zionist myth exercises a well-nigh irresistible attraction for all Jews.[47]

If it is to have any moral or social significance, however, this attraction must be rooted in the awareness that over all Creation there is established both a judge and judgement. Tart criticisms of the shortcomings of the Jewish state in Singer's work are all informed by that other teaching of the Psalms: "Except the Lord build the house, they labour in vain that build it" (Psalm 127:1). It is with this very quotation that the rabbi officiating at Simon Bendel's wedding brushes aside the enthusiasm of the bridegroom and his fellow *chalutzim* in *The Family Moskat*,[48] a novel in which passionate and highly emotive Zionists like Abram Shapiro have no doubt about a Jewish future conceived exclusively in terms of secular learning and modern progress:

> Just let us be a nation in our own land and we'll show them what we can do. Ah, the geniuses'll tumble out of their mothers' bellies six at a time — like in Egypt.[49]

For Rabbi Dan Katzenellenbogen, the book's most powerful representative of traditional orthodoxy, however, there can be no Jews without Judaism, no homeland without Holy Land:

> If, he insisted, [Jews] had no further belief in the Bible, then why should they have any longing for the Biblical land of the Jews? Why not some other country? Any country?[50]

Once he throws aside all traditional restraints, man is shown to be as ludicrous as the narrator of "Brother Beetle" who is trapped stark naked on the rooftop outside the Tel Aviv apartment of a former mistress by the sudden return of her current lover. From this helpless and humiliating position, he looks up to "the numberless stars that hovered strangely near" and down to where "[a] huge beetle crawled at [his] feet" and is overwhelmed by a sense of his own insignificance, and the impossibility of ever comprehending the meaning of human history. Inscrutably part of the Divine plan, man can only acquiesce with complete faith and total obedience. Without these, there is neither purpose nor significance:

> I found myself in infinite space, amid myriads of galaxies, between two eternities, one already past and one still to come … I asked God's forgiveness. For instead of returning to His promised land with renewed will to study the Torah and to heed His commandments, I had gone with a wanton who had lost herself in the vanity of art.[51]

As long as human nature remains unredeemed, the places in which people dwell will all be the same. Poland and Israel, Warsaw and Tel Aviv merge before the narrator's eyes. In one story, a café in Dizengoff Street frequented by merchants, where a stone is passed from hand to hand and scrutinised through loupes, becomes indistinguishable from an earlier café on old Krolewska Street;[52] in another story, the *Shook Ha-Carmel* converts a side-alley into the Krochmalna Street of his boyhood.[53] The past is bound to the present by the unchanging nature of human desires which no education or philosophy can eradicate. Having lost his companion in the crush, the narrator of "Two Markets" suddenly sees her at a stall:

> Apparently she had forgotten that she was a modern writer, a disciple of Kafka, a commentator of Joyce, and that she was writing a book about Agnon. She stood at a stand, rummaging through a heap of female underclothing, absorbed in the ancient feminine lust for bargains … She picked up a pair of black velvet panties with golden stars and silver dots, studied them, patted them, and measured them against her thighs. I approached her, put my hand on her shoulder, and said, "Take them, Meirav. These panties were worn by the Queen of Sheba when King Solomon solved all her riddles and she showed him all her treasures."[54]

Since human nature does not change, there can be no possibility of moral progress without an acknowledgement of the transcendent. Indeed, for Singer, modern life may even be said to have regressed morally, since human viciousness is no longer restrained by adherence to the Law. Man left without a prescribed round of duties, replacing ethics with politics, and the fear of God with the fight for independence, loses all sense of identity. In "The Little Shoemakers", only when the patriarch Abba and his seven sons can once again sit down with last and leather at a workbench can they feel that life in America has reassumed its proper significance. He and his sons once again take up that trade which the story makes paradigmatic with service to the Creator:

> No, praise God, they had not become idolaters in Egypt. They had not forgotten their heritage, nor had they lost themselves among the unworthy.[55]

In Singer's work, the Holy Land, like Egypt, is not a geographical locality but a spiritual condition. The true question is not that of Tobias Anfang, "How can a Jew be illegal in Israel?"[56] but that of Abba Shuster, *"Nu,* and the shoes? Who will mend them?"[57] Without a proper sense of spiritual purpose, Singer suggests, the modern Gates of Zion merely open on to yet another dwelling of Jacob.

NOTES

1   Translated by the author and Dorothea Straus, this is the title story of the collection *Passions and Other Stories,* Penguin Books, Harmondsworth, 1979, pp. 257–71.
2   Ibid, p. 260.
3   Translated by Isaac Rosenfeld, this story appears in *Gimpel the Fool and Other Stories,* Farrar, Straus and Giroux, New York, 1979, pp. 89–119.
4   The name means "Father Shoemaker" from *abba,* father, in Hebrew and *shuster,* shoemaker, in Yiddish. Just as the father becomes a paradigm for the patriarch Jacob, and his sons for the generations of Israel, so his trade becomes equated with the service of God.
5   "The Little Shoemakers", op. cit. p. 108.
6   Ibid.
7   I.B. Singer, *Satan in Goray,* Translated by Jacob Sloan, Penguin Books, Harmondsworth, 1981, p. 97.
8   He is a Yiddish writer who was born and grew up in Poland, but who is now an American citizen visiting Israel, generally for the first time. Sometimes he is called by a form of Singer's own name, like "Itche the rabbi's" in "The Mentor", Translated by the author and Evelyn Torton Beck, in *A Friend of Kafka and Other Stories,* Penguin Books, Harmondsworth, 1975, pp. 93–106. The visit is always clearly specified as being made during the 1950s, when the State of Israel was only a few years old, and the author-narrator (like Singer himself) was in his fifties.
9   Singer has been at pains in several interviews to insist that he is not a propagandist for any cause. He has told Richard Burgin that "the moment the writer begins to dabble with masses, with generalizations, he's already out of his profession." ("Isaac Bashevis Singer Talks ... About Everything", *The New York Times Magazine,* November 26, 1978, p. 38, col. 3.) To Diana Cooper-Clark, he has insisted that "Fiction is always about a few people. You cannot

write fiction about the masses." ("Living on the Edge: An Interview with Isaac Bashevis Singer", *London Magazine,* Vol. 23, No. 12, March 1984, p. 75)

10 I.B. Singer, *Shosha,* Translated by Joseph Singer *et al,* Penguin Books, Harmondsworth, 1980, p. 238.

11 Thus in "The Mentor", op. cit. p. 96, the narrator "saw women covering their faces with kerchiefs to keep from breathing in the fine desert sand that the wind carried", while in "Brother Beetle", *Old Love,* Translated by the author and Elizabeth Shub, Jonathan Cape, London, 1980, p. 123, "in the one moment it took me to get out on the balcony, the thin sand carried by the khamsin wind managed to cover the linens of my bed."

12 In "The Captive", *A Crown of Feathers and Other Stories,* Translated by Alma Singer and Ruth Schachner Finkel, Penguin Books, Harmondsworth, 1977, p. 48, "The sun poured dry fire"; in "Brother Beetle", op. cit. p. 124, "the moths beat against the walls with unbelievable strength, as if in preparation for the final war between man and insect"; while in "The Mentor", op. cit. p. 105, at dawn on the road back to Tel Aviv, "In the east, a cloud spread out like a huge bed of fiery coals. A long row of birds flew by screeching".

13 Thus in Hadar Joseph, the Tel Aviv suburb in which Haiml lives, "Outside it stank of garbage, asphalt, and something else sticky and sweetish that was hard to identify" (*Shosha,* op. cit. p. 248), while in the hot night of Tel Aviv summer, "Gasoline fumes mixed with the smell of softening asphalt and with the freshness that drifted in from the fields, the hills, the valleys." ("The Mentor", loc. cit. p. 96)

14 "Brother Beetle", loc. cit. p. 129.

15 Literally "the land" in Hebrew. But the phrase has traditionally come to denote The Promised Land.

16 "The Captive", loc. cit. p. 48.

17 "Two Markets", Translated by the author and Hannah Koevary, *Passions and Other Stories,* op. cit. p. 201.

18 I.B. Singer, *The Estate,* Translated by Joseph Singer, Elaine Gottlieb and Elizabeth Shub, Penguin Books, Harmondsworth, 1975, p. 72. Horses, guns and dogs, as much as the practice of hunting, always denote for Singer — as they did for the orthodox Jews of Eastern Europe amongst whom he was raised — the violence and cruelty of the Gentile world.

19 "The Mentor", loc. cit. p. 94.

20 Of "enlightened ones" rather than "righteous ones". To orthodox Jews, these Hebrew generic terms carry powerful emotive connotations.

21 "The Mentor", loc. cit. p. 95.

22 Ibid. p. 99.

23 Ibid. p. 102.

24 In this, she resembles Ezriel Babad, the chief character of *The Manor* and its sequel, *The Estate.* But where Freidl, educated in modern secularism, is supremely self-confident, Ezriel, trying vainly to escape the values of his traditional upbringing, has an acute and saving sense of his own limitations. He prescribes hydropathy to cure a young husband suffering from impotence, in an ironic modern application of the traditional orthodox prescription of ritual baths to cleanse impurity. *Vide The Manor,* Translated by Joseph Singer and Elaine Gottlieb, Penguin Books, Harmondsworth, 1975, p. 365.

25 "The Mentor", loc. cit. p. 99.

26 These remarks appear in "The Mentor," loc. cit. between pp. 98–100.

27 Ibid. p. 100.

28 Ibid. p. 102.

29 Ibid. p. 105.

30 Ibid.

31 Ibid. p. 106.

32 Ibid. p. 100.

33 "Brother Beetle", op. cit. p. 129.

34 "The Captive", loc. cit. p. 46.

35 Ibid. p. 49.

36 Ibid. p. 53.

37 *Haskalah* is the Hebrew word for the Jewish Enlightenment; *halakhah* the Hebrew word for the Laws of the Torah.

38 "The Captive", loc. cit. p. 50.

39 Ibid. p. 55.

40 Ibid. p. 56.

41 Ibid. p. 52.

42 Ibid. p. 55.

43 Sonia herself has been "given the large house of an Arab who fled" (p. 51); Tobias, by contrast, lives in "a half-ruined hut surrounded by Yemenites and paupers" (p. 51). The narrator notices that the maids in both his hotel and Sonia's house are Yemenites (p. 49/p. 56); Sonia's garden is being tended by "A short, dark-skinned man who might have been an Arab or Yemenite Jew" (p. 55). The street vendor with a donkey outside the narrator's hotel is an Arab (p. 48) while Tobias takes it for granted that "you know the miserable conditions of the Arab workers" (p. 51). Ironically, in Israel, the Arabs now fill the roles which in Eastern Europe were filled by Jews: in becoming nationally independent, the Jews have also become part of the master class. The realisation of the Zionist dream in Israel has by no means produced a classless society.

44 "The Captive", loc. cit. p. 59.

45 Ibid. p. 57.

46 Ibid. p. 59.

47 My reading of this story is in most essential respects supported by that of Julian C. Rice, given in his seminal article, "I.B. Singer's 'The Captive': A False Messiah in the Promised Land", *Studies in American Fiction,* Vol. 5, No. 2, Autumn 1977, pp. 269–75.

48 I.B Singer, *The Family Moskat,* Translated by A.H. Gross, Penguin Books, Harmondsworth, 1980, p. 488.

49 Ibid. p. 53.

50 Ibid. p. 254.

51 "Brother Beetle", loc. cit. p. 131.

52 Ibid. p. 125. The description, identical but in expanded detail, of old Krolewska [Krulevska] Street is given in *The Family Moskat,* op. cit. p. 409.

53 "Two Markets", loc. cit. p. 201.

54 Ibid. p. 204.

55 "The Little Shoemakers", loc. cit. p. 119.

56 "The Captive", loc. cit. p. 48.

57 "The Little Shoemakers", loc. cit. p. 107.

Part V
Realism and Mysticism

15 The fantasy of theology and the reality of power: Zionism in the thought of Richard L. Rubenstein

Jocelyn Hellig

Richard L. Rubenstein's theology has offered the most incisive, and in many ways realistic, modern analysis of the relationship of Israel to the outside world. In his first major work, *After Auschwitz* (1966),[1] he gave a radical theological response to the Holocaust by positing the death of the God who acts in history. The idea that Hitler, like Nebuchadnezzar, could be seen as the rod of God's anger, was simply "too obscene" for him to accept. His pronouncement must be seen in the context of the failure of normative Jewish theology to accommodate an event of the magnitude of the Holocaust, and therefore in terms of the rejection of the theology of reward and punishment.

Despite his declaration of the death of God, he emphasised the need for the maintenance of the most authentic and archaic Jewish ritual, thus displaying a tension between Jewish belief and practice. Having abandoned biblical monotheism, he advocated an "insightful paganism" which he saw most clearly put into practice in Israel with its new appreciation of the earth and its divinities.[2] His declaration of the death of God resulted in his "bureaucratic excommunication" and an increasing estrangement from the American Jewish community. It is a moot point to what extent this estrangement resulted in the fact that during the seventies he moved away from consideration of the Jewish implications of the Holocaust to its more global entailments. As a corollary, he moved away from a concern with Jewish practice, thus eliminating the abovementioned tension.

In the sixties he criticised the irrelevance of much Jewish theology in that theologians failed to take into consideration the two *kairoi,* or decisive moments of Jewish history for the twentieth century, the Holocaust and the re-establishment of the State of Israel. From the seventies, as his theology began to focus increasingly on the problem of power in the affairs of men, his criticism has become more acute.

His current theology cannot be understood in isolation from power allocation. Power, as related to human dignity, is a recurring theme in Rubenstein's writings. He displays a revulsion for powerlessness on any level. Accordingly, his autobiography is entitled *Power Struggle.*[3] In this work he discusses not only his personal struggle for power of various forms, but also the powerlessness of the Jews during the past 2 000 years, a powerlessness which culminated in the Holocaust. He is critical of Jewish responses during the Holocaust as well as of most theological attempts to understand the disaster.

He maintains that rabbinic Judaism, by accepting limited existence, has imbued Jews with a "servile consciousness". He clearly opts for the "lordly consciousness" as displayed by the men and women of Massada. The Pharisees consented to lead a community whose dignity and security rested on the power, interests and whim of strangers. The Holocaust reminds us that "he who lacks the power to defend himself, yet is unprepared to choose death", must be prepared for the possibility that any obscenity can be inflicted on him or his family. The Zealots opted for death rather than the servile submission chosen by the Pharisees. Although there was no other realistic course for the Pharisees to have taken, it must be acknowledged that every single indignity visited upon the Jews of the diaspora during the next 2 000 years, including the horrors of the Holocaust, was an "absolutely predictable consequence of the conditions accepted by their classic religious leaders".[4]

This schema may sound oversimplified and lacking in nuance. It would be a grave mistake, however, to see Rubenstein's views as simplistic. He is a man committed to truth. He understands clearly both the historic circumstances which led to Jewish degradation and the explosive import of his conclusions. Nevertheless, he will not allow such considerations to deter him. He claims that he will pursue his research in whatever directions it may lead him, no matter which individuals may be offended or which institutions threatened.[5] Interestingly, it has been his own career which has been threatened owing to the inhospitable reaction of the Jewish community to this theology.

Rubenstein's views on power raise some of the most fundamental and disturbing questions facing modern Judaism. Has the return to Israel inaugurated a new type of Judaism, and if so, is diaspora Judaism doomed? Is there still a possibility of a genuine "Jewish" theology? Two hallmarks of his theology are his preoccupation with the history of his people and a strong element of subjectivity. Jewish theology can as little be authentic in isolation from the agonising crucibile of the history of the Jewish people as it can in isolation from the life situation of the theologian. Thus, his theology has always exhibited an interplay between his subjective perceptions and the historic realities facing the Jewish people. He is deeply critical of the major Jewish theologians of our century for not taking adequately into account the explosive realities of our history, and elevating the subjective aspects of their theology to a pre-eminent position. They have permitted the powerlessness which has characterised Judaism over the last two millennia to mould their theology in isolation from the reality of the two *kairoi*.[6]

Both the Holocaust and the re-establishment of the State of Israel are rooted in the defeat of the Jews by the Romans in 70 CE. As "the holocaust of ancient times", it transformed the Jews into a group of wanderers, unwanted guests, always uncertain of their tenure in a host country. In order to survive, the leaders of the Jews, the Pharisees under the Yochanan ben Zakkai, formulated a response to the disaster which, on the one hand, gave the catastrophe *meaning*, and on the other hand gave a practical programme for life while fostering hope. This could only be done by interpreting the disaster in terms of God's punishment of a sinful, disobedient people and formulating patterns of religious behaviour which were a direct adaptation to the Jewish experience of powerlessness.

176

"Yochanan's bargain" is the term Rubenstein uses to refer to this religio-political decision. Jews would foreswear all resort to violence against the Roman aggressor. In return, they would be free to practise their religion. The bargain assumed that future Caesars" would be trustworthy and that all future aggressors would give the Jews the right to practise their religion and to survive. The bargain was kept, more or less, until the time of Hitler. Religious autonomy was given by the Romans in return for political power (although, with regard to the latter, one wonders what option the Jews had!). Exile, degradation and powerlessness became normative for Jews from that time onwards as an ingrained strategy for survival. Rabbinic Judaism is a fruit of that strategy.

As part of this process, focus was changed from the earthly and sensuous to the abstract and intellectual. From the point of view of religious expression, in the place of an altar of stone upon which bloody offerings were slain, Jewish religious life focused exclusively on bloodless worship and a bloodless book.[7] Verbal recitation of sacrificial laws took the place of real sacrifice. Verbal memory of life in Zion took the place of the actual life of the people in its own land. A messianic hope became prominent. The inequities of the present would be rectified in some future age.[8] Although this shift from the physical to the verbal and spiritual is often considered to be an "advance", Rubenstein is convinced that this is not the case and that there was as much loss as gain from the enforced shift.

A hallmark of rabbinic Judaism is its emphasis on behavioural restraint. The rabbis imposed an extraordinary measure of religious discipline in every aspect of human behaviour. While most theologians are content to interpret this as having its source in God's will, Rubenstein prefers a more functional perspective. He suggests that one should at least consider the possibility that Jewish religious practice is rooted primarily in biological, psychological and cultural needs rather than in a divine-human encounter.[9] An alternative explanation to the "God-hypothesis" is the *need* for self-imposition of behavioural restraints. Power allocation lies at the root of his explanation.

An important corollary of the rabbinic adaptation was that because Jews lacked power over their own destiny, they were compelled to control their counter-aggressive hostilities. Jews had to contain their rage. They were trained to distrust emotional spontaneity by extremes of behavioural discipline.[10] The "feeling" side of life had to be rigidly controlled. The mind could be developed, "even over developed", but feelings, especially feelings of release, had to be contained. Jews were trained from cradle to grave never to let go.[11]

Naturally, Jews were embittered by their persecutors but they could only counter-aggress in fantasy, such as the demise of Pharaoh at the Passover *seder* ceremony and the defeat of Haman at *Purim*.[12] They were powerless to retaliate or to prevent their degradation. They were forced to resort to prayer, petition and pleading as their primary resources. Lacking the power to save themselves, they had to look for restraint and compassion in others. Surrender, appeasement and withdrawal became the classic modes of Jewish relations with the non-Jewish world. This pattern of behaviour proved to be fatal in the face of the Nazi onslaught and has led Rubenstein to question the ongoing viability of diaspora or rabbinic Judaism. He has stated openly that diaspora Judaism is doomed.

Because Rubenstein defines history as "the record of the ways in which men have used power that have been deemed worthy of memory",[13] historical reflection being a consideration of the nature and use of power, the Jews have only recently re-entered the arena of history. The return to Israel has turned the intervening 2 000 years of Jewish existence into a parenthesis. But, if Jews have re-entered history, have theologians moved along with them? It seems that, on the whole, they have not.

Rubenstein finds most modern Jewish theologies intellectually indefensible. Theology should be "embodied theology" whose legitimacy can be evaluated by whether the theologian actually means what he says. The ultimate import of theology is its relevance to human self-understanding. The test of good theology is pre-eminently practical:

> *Does it deepen and help to clarify the individual's manifold insights about himself, his community, his religious and ethical values, and his place in the time-table of life in such a way that he can realistically function with minimal conflict between his biological, psychological, and cultural needs, his actions towards others, his beliefs, and his ultimate aspirations?* The wise theologian speaks about God the better to understand himself and his fellowmen. If theology does not enhance our capacity to work and love, it is an expression of disturbed fantasy.[14]

The theologians whose work has been of the greatest influence in our times, such as Franz Rosenzweig and Martin Buber, have largely been the expression of such disturbed fantasy, precisely because they operated only within the realm of powerlessness. The life situation of Rosenzweig, whose theology and philosophy have had a formative influence on modern American Jewish thinkers, was characterised by total physical impotence resulting from multiple sclerosis. His life situation enabled him to elevate the impotence of the Jewish community to greater religious significance than any other modern thinker. Rosenzweig, in his attempt to bridge the schism between Judaism and Christianity, asserted that the Synagogue, which is immortal but stands with broken staff and bound eyes, must renounce all work in this world, and must muster all her strength to preserve her life and keep herself "untainted by life".[15] The Jews are members of the Eternal People "already at its goal".[16] They are already with the Father, having reached the point to which the nations of the world aspire. The Jews have paid a price for having become an Eternal People, the price of withdrawal from the concerns of power and the course of world history. Such concerns afflict the other nations, torn between their pagan reality and their Christian aspirations. Thus, Rosenzweig lauds Jewish powerlessness and rootlessness as emblems of a purified redemptive existence. He states:

> ... we have long ago been robbed of all the things in which the peoples of the earth are rooted. For us, land and language, custom and law, have long left the circle of the living and have been raised to the rung of holiness. But we are still living and live in eternity. Our life is no longer meshed with anything outside ourselves. We have struck root in ourselves. We do not root in earth and so we are eternal wanderers, but deeply rooted in our body and blood. And it is this rooting in ourselves, and in nothing but ourselves, that vouchsafes eternity.[17]

According to Rubenstein, no Jewish theology evades and avoids the genuinely human dimensions of man's condition more totally than Rosenzweig's. It is a quest for eternity through a people completely withdrawn from the vicissitudes of earth and temporality which leads, at best, to a disembodied ghost-existence for both the individual and the community. Rosenzweig's theology is a theology of exile and alienation, the disembodied existence of the diaspora Jewish community being prototypical of true blessedness. Instead of seeing the enforced departure of the Jews from their ancient homeland as a tragedy, he interprets it as a *felix culpa* in that it was only when the Jews ceased to have any power over their own destiny that their redemptive existence with God truly began. Accordingly, Rosenzweig was not enthusiastic about the Zionist project of establishing a Jewish homeland in Palestine.[18]

Rosenzweig cannot be faulted for writing before Auschwitz. However, the fact that he formulated his theology in Germany at the time that Hitler was already preparing his plans for the extermination of the Jews reveals a general sense of unreality about his theology. It is now impossible to read his work apart from the prism of Auschwitz. In the wake of the Holocaust and the re-establishment of the State, the majority of his sentiments become irrelevant. Israelis have no option but to be "tainted" by life and concomitant political power decisions.

Buber is criticised by Rubenstein for failing to come to terms with concrete historical issues. In Buber's work from 1945 to 1965 there is little, if any, evidence of a confrontation with the Holocaust as a theological issue. Neither is he realistic about the State of Israel. Buber's divine-human encounter is atemporal, non-spatial, non-causal, and devoid of *any* kind of content that could be shared in normal discourse. Because of its wholly ineffable nature, it must prove indifferent to the vicissitudes of human history. Judaism, like Christianity, has only a mediated relationship between man and God. For Judaism, the mediation is the Torah. Because of Buber's well-known rejection of Judaism's religious law, the centrality of the inexpressible nature of the divine-human encounter in his thought is understandable. However, Buber speaks in abstractions. Rubenstein finds no discussion of the relationship between power and dignity in Buber's presentation of the dynamics of interpersonal encounter in *I and Thou,* "in spite of the fact that no people was ever compelled to endure a more total assault on its very being than the community of which he was so important a figure. Instead, Buber presents us with images of totally unspecified I's and Thou's relating to each other in openness and mutuality, as if mutual acceptance in the real world can ever ignore the claims of class, caste, status and power".[19] It is, furthermore, insufficient to dismiss the abuse of power as yet another instance of the I–It, for the world "is the arena in which men and women of unequal power confront each other".[20] Therefore, openness, mutuality and acceptance are only possible between those who are more or less equal in station, or between those possessing roughly equal power.

Buber is accused of Utopian rhetoric with regard, among other things, to his attitude to Israel and the Eichmann trial. Buber questioned the legitimacy of a Jewish court sitting in judgement over Eichmann in that: (a) he did not believe that the victims could be judges, (b) he asserted that Eichmann's crimes against humanity were no less monstrous than those against the Jews, and (c) he opposed the State of Israel's right to enact capital punishment.

In regarding the State of Israel as a victim of the Nazis, Buber was mistaken. The State was founded largely because of the terrible lessons to be drawn from the victims of the Holocaust, its purpose being to guarantee that the successor Jewish community would no longer be the gathering place of future defenceless victims. This meant that Israel, as a state, had at times to employ instruments of coercion against both internal and external adversaries. Human nature being what it is, this may involve war or capital punishment. To assert, as Buber did, that the state has no right to take human life, "is to betray a fundamental ignorance of the nature of political sovereignty as well as the imperatives confronting a sovereign state".[21] While a sovereign state has no right to take human life capriciously, "to ask that the state unconditionally forego that right is tantamount to asking for its ultimate dissolution".[22] Furthermore, when Buber asserts that Eichmann's crimes were as much crimes against humanity as they were against the Jewish people, he resorts to an abstraction, "humanity", when the primary target of the Nazis was the Jewish people. This places his crimes within the context of such broad generality as to be without any meaningful content and diminishes real violence done to real people.

Buber's failure to take seriously the life and death problems which confronted his own people at a time in their history when their survival was called radically into question both in Europe and the Middle East reflects his inability to deal with the world of concrete reality. When comparing Buber's life and thought with that of Rabbi Yochanan ben Zakkai in ancient times, Rubenstein finds no relevance in Buber's theology. Yochanan's teachings were directly relevant to his times and he contributed in his own way to the work of reconstruction which followed the misfortunes of his era. "We look in vain for such relevance in Buber."[23]

To assert that these theologies do not enable men to work and love is an exaggeration. Buber's I–Thou encounter, however ineffable, calls for the height of human love and acceptance. Perhaps it would be more true to say that such theologies do not assist Jews in working fruitfully, given the explosive realities of twentieth century existence. The inhibition of self-understanding assumes serious import for Jews seeing that they have experienced power mainly as its object. It is precisely the fact that Jews have been the target of so much aggression that makes the lack of consideration of aggression in modern theology lamentable. Theological adjustments are essential.

Rubenstein admits, with a measure of ambivalence, that Yochanan provided the only realistic option for Jews commensurate with the time and circumstance. His adaptation was authentic and valuable and was redeemed *only because it was accompanied by genuine faith.* But dusk has fallen on the venerable faith that guided the Jewish people. "Today it can only be understood; it cannot be rejuvenated".[24] The death of God is a cultural fact which is real and all-embracing. Rubenstein contrasts the fruitless "God-talk" of American Jewish theologians with the concrete actions of the Israelis. The death of God extends "not merely to the relatively inconsequential matter of whether the divine Thou encounters man in prayer and ritual; it reaches to the far more consequential matter of nuclear terror as the last remaining deterrent to acts of national annihilation".[25]

The persistence of God-talk and the idea of a God who acts in history should be abandoned by theology. (Although theology means "God-talk" and one is forced to question whether abandonment of it does not eliminate Rubenstein's status as a *theologian,* if not forcing theology to surrender itself completely!) It makes no sense, he asserts, to ascribe ultimate responsibility for human history to God, for it is as spurious in moments of victory as in moments of defeat. "In defeat, such assertion makes God the punitive author of history. In victory, such sentiments have the grating sound of *Gott mit uns.*"[26]

American theologians have little to say concerning Israel since their life situations are so far removed from the type of situation facing the Israelis. Although American Jews form part of the comfortable middle-class stratum of society, they have barely any experience in the financial, political and military decision-making process in America and, therefore, lack experience with the realities of decision-making power. As part of the "gilded ghetto", they do not share the power of the Gentile majority.[27] The experience of the Israeli Jews approximates the experience of American Gentiles more closely than it does that of American or diaspora Jews.

Rubenstein has attributed the conservatism of Jewish intellectuals to the threatened character of twentieth-century Jewish existence. In addition to the ravages of the Holocaust the Jewish community is threatened by widespread defection, indifference and intermarriage. Hence, committed Jewish thinkers normally see themselves as conservers rather than as path-finders. Judaism has been attacked so heavily from without and eroded so deeply from within that many perceive his radicalism as internal attack.

It is essential to note that Rubenstein still regards genuine Jewish faith as meritworthy in relation to the survival of diaspora Judaism. At root, his current message can be summed up as follows: In the light of modern experience, the decision to remain Jewish involves great risk. One need not give up one's Jewishness, but one should reckon the potential cost. It seems that only the most authentic and traditional Judaism is worth the risk, and, therefore, is likely to survive. However, those who cling to rabbinic tradition accept a dissonance between its ethos, which reflects the aspirations of a beaten and powerless people, and the existence of a Jewish State in which Jews make their own power decisions. Deep down, they may be correct in their perceptions in that "the threat of annihilation will hang over Israel as long as it exists . . . If Israel is defeated even once, the end will be at hand. Those committed to the survival of Judaism may not want to commit themselves without reservation to so imperilled a vehicle".[28] Furthermore, diaspora Judaism may be doomed except in multinational countries such as the USA and the Soviet Union (even though it is an underground phenomenon in the latter), and with the inevitable rise to full technological competence of post-Confucian Asia, there is bound to be a profound destabilising effect on the two superpowers. Should either of these suffer a military defeat, the future of diaspora Jewry would be uncertain. The 2 000-year strategy of survival through powerlessness would no longer be a viable option.[29]

Rubenstein's pessimism about diaspora Judaism and predictions about its lack of viability seem to be justified if one takes into consideration the increasing rate of assimilation and intermarriage in most diaspora countries. South Africa may be somewhat of an exception in this regard, but here also there is a move toward secularisation and increasing intermarriage and assimilation. One should also note the upsurge of traditional orthodoxy, even ultra-orthodoxy. Indeed, this may be the form that diaspora Judaism is destined, ultimately, to take.

This requires total commitment to a particular life-style which the majority of the world's Jews are unlikely to find attractive. Because of Rubenstein's revulsion for power-lessness, he questions whether there is still justification for maintaining Yochanan's bargain or the religio-cultural institutions which affirm it as the normative expression of Jewish life. He certainly questions his *own* need to be bound by Yochanan's political bargain.[30]

In the same way that Yochanan's bargain had cultural consequences in Jewish life, rejection of it would affect the inner life of Jews. With rejection of the bargain there would be a concomitant rejection of its terms. The evidence of this transformation can be most clearly perceived in Israel. The re-establishment of the State of Israel is the most profound response of the Jews to the Holocaust.[31] The Israelis refuse servile submission based on the model of Yavneh. They established in its stead freedom by means of combat, a strategy not used since the time of Bar Kochba, who led an armed rebellion against the Romans when they appeared to renege of their end of the bargain by not allowing the Jews to have religious autonomy. The revulsion of many young Israelis for servility and for the diaspora can be observed in the body of self-hating literature which has emerged from Israel. It can also be observed in the attitudes of some Israeli intellectuals who have thrown diaspora suffering behind them, and even go so far as to delete Holocaust suffering and anti-Semitism from their range of concerns. They refuse to live by the pathetic slogan "We suffer, therefore we are."[32] However, this may also be interpreted as "disturbed fantasy" in that it stultifies interaction with and understanding of the diaspora.

This leads directly to a consideration of what one might call "Israeli Judaism". Dusk might, indeed, have fallen on the venerable tradition of rabbinic Judaism. The majority of Jews in Israel today have abandoned it. This may point to a transformation of Judaism itself. Israel may be witnessing a rebirth of Judaism, a phenomenon so young that it might not yet be easy to perceive what it is and what its ultimate direction will be.[33]

Zionism, for Rubenstein, is a reversal of powerlessness. It is a closure of 2 000 years of a particular type of Jewish existence. It renders messianic hope for the future futile. It demands that Jews exercise power in a sovereign state, unafraid. As long as there is Massada, there can never be another Auschwitz. The existence of Israel assures that Jews need never die a degraded death and this fact affects the quality of their lives. "If one contemplates the worst possible case that might confront Diaspora Judaism, it is a repetition of Auschwitz and Treblinka; if one contemplates the worst possible case that might confront the State of Israel, it is another Massada. And, in a world in which mutual terror is the ultimate guarantor of the fragile bonds of peace, a nation's willingness to risk death may enhance for a time its chances of survival."[34]

It is not surprising that Rubenstein supported Menachem Begin's incursion into Lebanon in 1982. Israel should not be judged on a different basis with regard to the evil necessities of power politics from that of any other sovereign state. It seems that he would be in agreement with sentiments expressed by many that Israel is subjected to unreason-able demands and double standards not applied by the world or the international media to any other state.[35] Rubenstein would, undoubtedly, attribute this focus on Israel to the Jewish doctrine of chosenness and the resultant central role that Christianity has forced the Jews to play in the divine economy.[36] As a corollary, not only Jews but also Israel must be judged by the harshest and most unrealistic of standards. While Israelis need to confront their life situation unafraid, theologians must address themselves to the issues of power and dignity as they arise in the living situation.

Rubenstein's current theology (and it can only be called "theology" in that it examines the godless world in which we live), rocks the very foundation of what we today have come to know as diaspora Judaism, but it speaks realistically of Israeli Judaism. In the sixties he proposed a viable Jewish theology by supporting Jewish practice of the most authentic kind, and by supporting political Zionism. His pronouncement of the death of the God who acts in history caused an unbreachable rift between himself and the Jewish community. It was not so much what he said, but the manner in which he said it which seems to have been so unacceptable to Jewish sensibilities.[37] In his recent development, he has moved away from Judaism, abandoning his earlier passionate insistence on Jewish ritual, and focusing only minimally on Israel. In his examination of the global implications of the Holocaust, he interprets the Holocaust as the most dramatic of a series of mass population riddance programmes in the face of the modern world's most intractable problem, population redundancy.[38]

Rubenstein's attack on powerlessness and his open denunciation of it are sometimes exaggerated. As his theology has always exhibited a confessional quality, and is by his own admission subjective, it is to be wondered to what extent he too projects an element of "disturbed fantasy".[39] His condemnation of the responses of the Jews to the Holocaust are hurtful, if not untrue. He suggests that, as a result of ingrained behavioural responses, there was no *corporate* resistance to the Nazis. Indeed, this may be so. But one has to enquire whether there was any *real* possibility for mass resistance, whether the small acts of resistance on a daily basis were not in themselves acts of ultimate heroism, and whether the option of suicide, such as that enacted at Massada, was an option of any relevance at all. Rubenstein is fully aware that had Yochanan adopted that *modus operandi,* he himself would not have survived, let alone be in a position to offer a theology.

His pronouncements, which originally hardly endeared him to the Jewish establishment, are probably landing on even more inhospitable Jewish ears, inasmuch as Jews are prepared to listen to him at all. As unpalatable as his views are, there is a great deal of truth to them. Diaspora Judaism needs to examine its basis of powerlessness, while many Israelis need a more empathetic attitude to the diaspora. We cannot dodge the questions: What is the fate of diaspora Judaism? What should be the nature of Jewish theology in our current situation? Is there a new Judaism in Israel? How should Israel and the diaspora interact? We need the often jarring predictions and analyses of a thinker like Rubenstein to make us assess the Jewish future more dynamically. Certainly, to silence him is but to turn a blind eye to the fundamental questions and realities of modern Jewish existence.[40]

NOTES

1 R.L. Rubenstein, *After Auschwitz: Radical Theology and Contemporary Judaism,* Bobbs-Merrill Company, Inc. Indianapolis, 1966.

2 Rubenstein advocates an "insightful paganism" for all Jews, which he perceives to be in evidence in Israel. It is not quite clear what he means by this insightful paganism. However, he is deeply critical of biblical monotheism for he sees it as lying at the root of the godless world in which we live. One of the unintended consequences of biblical monotheism was the development of a "calculating rationality" which measures the value of human beings only in terms of their monetary worth. The beginning point of this can be seen in the Bible's demystification of nature. Its end point can be seen in the Holocaust. While he is totally aware that the biblical scheme has a built-in corrective in that God is supreme and man is a co-steward over creation, with the increasing transcendence of God which occurred with Protestantism, God has disappeared from our lives for all intents and purposes, and men and women, given the power, will resort to mass killing programmes as a problem-solving device in the modern world. This is the unintended "night-side" of biblical monotheism. Thus, his call for insightful paganism seems to be simply a call to a greater awe of and respect for the world of nature.

3 R.L. Rubenstein, *Power Struggle: An Autobiographical Confession,* Charles Scribner's Sons, New York, 1974.

4 R.L. Rubenstein, "Buber and the Holocaust: Some Reconsiderations on the 100th Anniversary of his birth", *Michigan Quarterly Review,* Spring 1979, pp. 395f.

5 Personal correspondence, Letter dated 30 April 1980.

6 In "On Death in Life: Reflections on Franz Rosenzweig", *Soundings,* Vol. LV no 2, Summer 1972, pp. 231f, he points out that Emil Fackenheim, for more than two decades after World War II, saw *no connection* between his theology and the history of his time, a view he has since publicly rescinded.

7 Rubenstein, *Power Struggle,* op. cit. p. 174.

8 According to Rubenstein "messianism is a religious expression of impotence". Jewish messianic redemption looks toward a termination of the alienation of exile and powerlessness. The choice of a slave is that life at any cost is preferable to death. While the slave submits, he works for the day when power relationships will be reversed. The "servile consciousness" is tenable only as long as it is sustained by the hopeful vision of the future in which the present state of degradation will be reversed. It is in this sense that Jews are imbued with a servile consciousness and that their messianism is to be understood. This servile consciousness was taken to its extreme conclusion in Nazi Germany when Jews were made into actual slaves and forced to perform slave labour in the camps.

   See R.L. Rubenstein, "The Fall of Jerusalem and the Birth of Holocaust Theology", essay in *Go and Study,* R. Jospe and S.Z. Fishman (eds.), Bnai B'rith Hillel Foundation, Washington DC, 1980, pp. 227f.

9 R.L. Rubenstein, "Homeland and Holocaust" in D.R. Cutler (ed.), *The Religious Situation, 1968,* Beacon Press, Boston, 1969, p. 45f.

10 Ibid. p. 47.

11 Stanley Rothman, in "Group fantasies and Jewish radicalism: a psychodynamic interpretation", *Journal of Psychohistory,* Vol 6 No. 2, Fall 1978, confirms this observation. He asserts that Jewish marginality has had consequences for Jewish males who could only survive by controlling the urge to strike back at their tormentors. Male children were inhibited from displaying direct physical expression of aggression. The stereotype of the emasculating Jewish

mother may have its roots here, p. 224. Jews usually seek occupations which do not require aggression and which usually demand higher levels of intellectual attainment. Interestingly, he suggests that Jews were seldom alcoholics as it was not safe to act in an unseemly or abandoned fashion in a Christian environment, pp. 224f.

12 Moshe Davidowitz, in "The psychohistory of Jewish rage and redemption as seen through its art", *Journal of Psychohistory* op. cit. confirms this view in that he points out that Jews can only deal with rage in a veiled manner. Unable to express it in the larger world, they can only express it in the internal community. The demonic is therefore imploded and dealt with through historic analogies. This is often expressed in art forms in documents such as the *Haggadah* for Passover, pp. 273–84.

13 R.L. Rubenstein, *Reflections on Religion and Public Policy,* The Washington Institute for Values in Public Policy, Washington DC, 1984, p. 6.

14 Rubenstein, "Homeland and Holocaust", op. cit. p. 61.

15 See Nahum N. Glatzer, *Franz Rosenzweig: His Life and Thought,* Schocken Books, New York, 1972, Second revised edition, p. 342. See also Rubenstein, "Homeland and Holocaust", op. cit. p. 52.

16 Franz Rosenzweig, *The Star of Redemption,* Translated by William W. Hallo, Holt, Rinehart and Winston, New York, 1971, pp. 328 f.

17 Ibid. pp. 304 f.

18 Rubenstein, "On Death in Life," op. cit. p. 230.

19 Rubenstein, "Buber and the Holocaust", op. cit. p. 396.

20 Ibid. p. 397.

21 Ibid. p. 399.

22 Ibid.

23 Ibid. p. 402.

24 Rubenstein, *Power Struggle,* op. cit. p. 19.

25 Rubenstein, "Homeland and Holocaust", op. cit. p. 50.

26 Milton Himmelfarb suggests that Rubenstein wants it both ways. "If Jews thank God for victory, theirs is a *Gott mit uns* religion. If in their prayers they lament but justify exile and persecution 'because of our sins', they are being masochistic, self-repressive". See "Commentary on 'Homeland and Holocaust'" in same volume as "Homeland and Holocaust" cited above p. 73.

27 Rubenstein, "Homeland and Holocaust", op. cit. p. 43.

28 R.L. Rubenstein, "Reflections on Power and Jewish Survival", *Jewish Frontier,* May 1980, pp. 16f.

29 Ibid.

30 Personal correspondence, letter dated 30 April, 1980.

31 R.L. Rubenstein, "Jewish Theology and the Current World Situation", *Conservative Judaism,* Summer 1974, Vol 28 No 4, p. 16.

32 My observations were confirmed in a written report by Dr Harvey Alper (Southern University, Texas), on an international Judaica conference held at Vitznau, Switzerland, 31 August to 4 September 1986.

33 Manfred H. Vogel, in "Dilemma of Identity for the Emancipated Jew" in *New Theology No 4,* Macmillan Company, New York, 1967, pp. 162–77, points out that the Jew's mode of witnessing has changed from biblical times, when he was rooted in the power afforded by the concrete world, through the rabbinic period when, bereft of power, the Law became the

normative mode of witnessing, to the modern period. While Jews could be emancipated, Judaism could not. Since 1948, however, "we may perhaps expect a new mode of witnessing to emerge in modern Israel, with some resemblance to that of biblical Israel", p. 177. This indicates the possible evolution of a new Judaism in modern Israel.

34 Rubenstein, "Reflections on Power", op. cit. p. 17.

35 See, for example, Norman Podhoretz, "J'Accuse", *Commentary,* Vol 74 No 3, September 1982, pp. 21–31.

36 Rubenstein rejects the Jewish doctrine of chosenness for a number of reasons. In this particular regard, he rejects it because of the undue expectation focused on the Jew as a result of the doctrine. Forced by the Christian to play a central role in the drama of salvation, the Jew is either praised as Jesus-like or murdered as Judas-like. By being endowed with a supernatural vocation, the Jew is not permitted to have an average spectrum of virtues and vices and is thus stripped of his simple humanity. Philo-Semitism becomes as dangerous as anti-Semitism as a result of the abovementioned expectation.

37 Michael G. Berenbaum in "Elie Wiesel and Contemporary Jewish Theology", *Conservative Judaism,* Vol 30 No 3, Spring 1976, pp. 19–39, shows that Wiesel and Rubenstein have reached similar conclusions in relation to God and the Holocaust, even up to the point of declaring the death of God. However, because Wiesel makes his statements in the *midrashic* mould, mystifies his statements, approaches Judaism as an "insider", and above all, is a survivor, the Jewish community has accorded him the reception of a Chassidic rebbe, while Rubenstein, who demystifies and who approaches Judaism as an "outsider" has been hounded out of Jewish life. See also Michael G. Berenbaum *The Vision of the Void,* Wesleyan University Press, Middletown, Connecticut, 1979.

38 His major publications since the seventies have had this as their central theme. See, for example: R.L. Rubenstein, *The Cunning of History: Mass Death and the American Future,* Harper and Row, New York, 1975, and *The Age of Triage: Fear and Hope in an Overcrowded World,* Beacon Press, Boston, 1983.

39 Klaus Rohmann in *Vollendung im Nichts?,* Benziger Verlag, Köln, 1977, questions whether Rubenstein has managed to transcend his subjectivity in his theology.

40 While he has been "bureaucratically excommunicated" it should be borne in mind by the Jewish community that their anger tends to corroborate the importance of his statements. As Jacob Neusner has pointed out, the torrent of abuse to which Rubenstein has been subjected may constitute "the highest possible tribute on the part of his enemies to the compelling importance of his contribution", Jacob Neusner *Understanding Jewish Theology,* KTAV Publishing House, New York, 1973, p. 184.

16 An iconographical analysis of Duchamp's Bride image in the Large Glass

Rory T. Doepel

Although the Christian Kabbalah of the Western Inner Tradition, based on the Jewish Kabbalah, was an important source for writers and artists in France, particularly at the end of the nineteenth century and in the early twentieth century, there is little scholarly research in this area. I would like to focus on the Christian Kabbalah as a source for one of the most important and influential twentieth-century artists, Marcel Duchamp, the "symbolist *par excellence*".[1]

Duchamp, who stands alongside Picasso as one of the most significant artists in the twentieth century, produced his first major work, *The Bride Stripped Bare by Her Bachelors, Even* (S279)[2] (more popularly known as the *Large Glass*) (Figure 16.1) between 1912 (the date of conception) and 1923, when it was left "incomplete". In 1934, he started producing a limited edition of the notes which accompany the *Large Glass*. This set of notes (popularly referred to as the *Green Box* (S293)) has the same title as the *Large Glass,* and forms an integral part of the work.[3]

Analysis of the notes and the *Large Glass* is a difficult task, for it demands a reconstruction of the model used for the generation of symbolic content, this model seemingly being based on the Christian Kabbalah of the Western Inner Tradition. Although one can establish that Duchamp would have had access to information on the Kabbalah, it has not been possible to link him with a particular sect, and supporting evidence for using the model is based on relationships between his iconographic programme, imagery and symbols, and those encountered in the Christian Kabbalah.[4] This most hermetic and enigmatic work which has continued to puzzle and fascinate art historians, critics and artists is, it will be argued, explicable if analysed within terms of the Kabbalah.

The *Large Glass,* possibly the most complex work of art produced this century, is divided into two zones. The Bride is positioned in the upper section (top left) (Figures 16.1, 16.2). The lower half is the Bachelors' domain. Here we see the Chocolate Grinder (centre). This is connected by an axle to a Watermill within a Glider. The Waterfall that

FIGURE 16.1 Marcel Duchamp: *The Bride Stripped Bare by Her Bachelors, Even* (the *Large Glass)* 1915–1923 (New York) 104$\frac{1}{4}$×69$\frac{1}{4}$ in (227,5×175,8 cm)
Philadelphia Museum of Art, Bequest of Katherine S. Dreier, 1953 (Photograph by A.J. Wyatt. Staff photographer)

was to turn the wheel of the Watermill is not represented. To the left are a series of figures, the Nine Malic Moulds. The series of lines connecting these figures to a point below the Seven Sives (the conical forms above the Chocolate Grinder) are the Capillary Tubes which carry invisible "illuminating gas". On the extreme right, three elliptical forms denote the Oculist Witnesses. The two zones are separated by three strips of glass (not readily legible in reproductions) which denote the Cooler as well as the Garments of the Bride. The Handler of Gravity (or Juggler) (not rendered) was to have been placed balancing on a ball on the extreme right, above the dividing frame. Many other images and ideas are referred to in notes in the *Green Box*, but are not actually represented in the work itself. One thus needs to read the notes, which are essential for an understanding of the iconographic programme.

Duchamp's *Large Glass* and *Green Box* could be analysed within terms of the Kabbalists' model of the Tree of Life (Figure 16.3) as well as a number of different Trees connected with the idea of various "Worlds" and stages in the Creation. However, given the complexity of both Duchamp's work and the Kabbalah, focus will be placed on the Bride image (Figure 16.2), denoting the Shekinah, God's presence in femine aspect. Related images will be referred to, and it should of course be borne in mind that the meaning of a part is determined by the whole. The sub-texts are rich, the images are interrelated, and the complexity is increased by the fact that symbols and images are at times multivalent, standing for more than one thing at a time. It should also be stressed that Duchamp's *oeuvre* should, ideally, be seen as a whole. To further complicate matters, in Duchamp's work, numbers, letters, words, images, material, the location of an image, dimensionality, and even the creative act of the spectator, are symbolic and must be interpreted. This seems possible, but only if the model of the Kabbalah is used. However, it must also be stressed that Duchamp created new symbols which although concordant with Kabbalistic symbols, are not simply taken directly from the Kabbalah. In other words, he did not simply provide illustrations of Kabbalistic diagrams and symbols.

Reference will be made to the Kabbalists' Tree of Life (Figure 16.3), an analogue of the Absolute, the Universe and Man. The symbolism is complex, for the glyph of the Tree of Life defines 10 points connected by 22 paths. Both the paths and the points on the Tree are associated with a great variety of symbols which define the Tree on both the macrocosmic and microcosmic levels, for the Tree is a symbolic glyph denoting God and His Creation. The Tree as a model is used by Kabbalists to denote aspects of being, states of consciousness, as well as an ideal (defined by the mid-point). Indeed, it may be the most complex symbolic glyph devised by man. It even encompasses the "unthinkable". As a model, it generates problems of a highly abstract nature, and would be used by the Kabbalist in promoting personal development and spiritual growth. The higher we progress up the Tree, the more difficult and complex the issues. At the top, we encounter the nature of the God-head itself. The Bride or feminine apsect of God is located at various points on this glyph. We encounter Her as the upper Celestial Bride at the third point (Binah), but also as the lower Bride at the bottom of the Tree, the tenth point (Malkuth). The symbolism becomes even more complex once one takes into account the fact that in the Kabbalah each of the points on the Tree of Life refers us to another Tree

FIGURE 16.2   Detail: The Bride in the *Large Glass*

190

in its entirety. Duchamp's Bride image may present us with not only a generalised reference to one point of the Tree of Life, i.e. Binah, but simultaneously to the Tree associated with this point, the Tree of Binah. This may well provide us with a model for an interpretation of the image of the Bride as described in notes in the *Green Box*, even though the image is not fully realised pictorially in the *Large Glass* itself.

The Tree is defined by the unpronounceable divine name, YHVH, each letter being associated with a point (or sephiroth) on the Tree (Figure 16.4). Fragmentation of the name occured with the Fall, and the lower Bride, symbolised by the second letter Hé (H), was exiled together with Man from the Garden of Eden. As Scholem notes, the exile of the Shekinah is symbolic of the separation of the masculine and feminine principles in God. This exile is "a symbol of our own guilt, and the aim of religious action must be to end this exile, or at least to work in this direction".[5] The concept of the re-unification of the letters of this name is thus of importance to the Kabbalist, and provides a key for an understanding of the iconography of the *Large Glass*.

The Bride has many aspects, and the symbolism is complex and difficult. She is the "Great Sea", and is symbolised by a fountain. As the "Architect of the Universe", She is associated with the three "mother letters" of the alphabet, i.e. Aleph (A), Mem (M) and Shin (Sh), when located at Binah. She and the Literal Torah are one, and because She is also the "Outer Robe of Concealment", She is connected with garment symbolism, of particular importance for Duchamp. She thus has many facets. In essence, She is the parent of faith and the Sanctifying Intelligence, when considered in relation to Binah on the Tree of Life.[6] Yet She and the Tree may also be regarded as one.

On one occasion, a palm tree was exhibited (possibly fortuitously?) next to a copy of the *Large Glass*.[7] This evokes the Kabbalists' Tree of Life, but also the Bride, likened to a palm tree in the Song of Songs (7:7). In the *Green Box*, Duchamp referred to his Bride as an "*arbor*-type" (AS 1), "*arbor*" being the Latin for tree. And when the work was permanently installed in Philadelphia, he arranged for it to be positioned between two columns, presumably a reference to the two columns of the Tree, the Pillar of Severity and the Pillar of Mercy.[8] A balance between mercy and severity is sought by the Kabbalist.

Not surprisingly, we also encounter a connection between a Bride image and a tree later, in *Etant donnés*, 1946–1966 (S392). In this work (which may not be reproduced) there are a set of twigs directly attached to the bottom edge of the moulded reclining nude female figure.[9] Thus, She too is an "arbor-type". In the note in the *Green Box*, Duchamp specifies that the boughs of the Bride in the *Large Glass* will be "frosted in nikel and platinum" (AS 1), this feature finding its counterpart in *Etant donnés*: the twigs actually attached to the reclining nude were, apparently, dipped into silver paint, and were thus "frosted". In the Kabbalah, the complete Tree of Life itself is sometimes understood to refer to the Bride (Shekinah), also known as the "Betrothed", which supports an identification of Duchamp's "Bride-tree" as the Kabbalists' Bride (Shekinah). It is thus congruent that the *Large Glass* in its entirety may also be seen to be the Bride.

In the Kabbalah, the Bride is associated with the letter Hé in the context of the divine name, YHVH, and the Tree of Life (Figure 16.4). This letter has for its image a window,

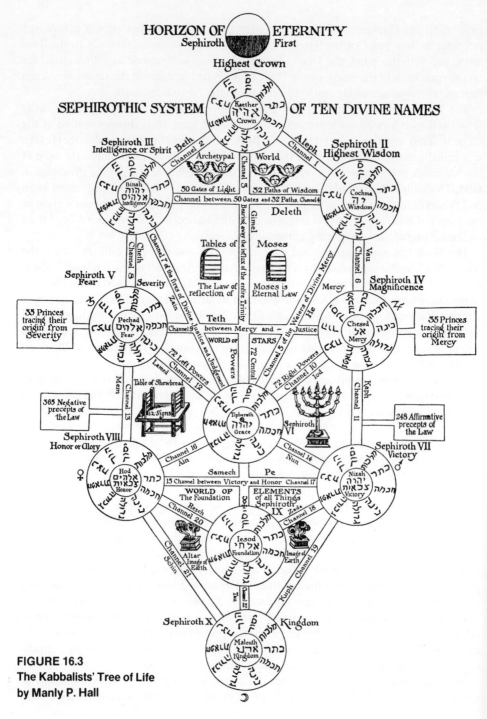

FIGURE 16.3
The Kabbalists' Tree of Life
by Manly P. Hall

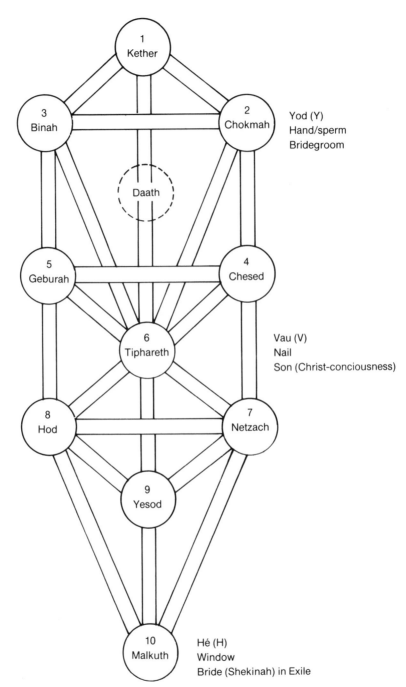

Hé (H)
Window
Upper Bride
Chronos
Saturn

Yod (Y)
Hand/sperm
Bridegroom

Vau (V)
Nail
Son (Christ-conciousness)

Hé (H)
Window
Bride (Shekinah) in Exile

FIGURE 16.4   The Kabbalists' Tree of Life

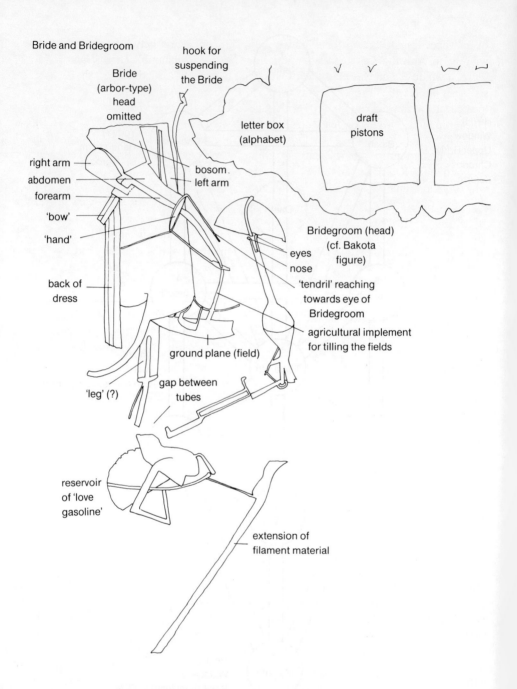

Bride and Bridegroom

Bride
(arbor-type)
head
omitted

hook for
suspending
the Bride

letter box
(alphabet)

draft
pistons

right arm

abdomen

forearm

bosom

left arm

'bow'

'hand'

Bridegroom (head)
(cf. Bakota
figure)

eyes

nose

back of
dress

'tendril' reaching
towards eye of
Bridegroom

agricultural implement
for tilling the fields

ground plane (field)

'leg' (?)

gap between
tubes

reservoir
of 'love
gasoline'

extension of
filament material

FIGURE 16.5   Diagrammatic representation of the Bride

194

of relevance for Duchamp, for there is an implicit connection between the Bride and a window in both the Kabbalah and the *Large Glass* — Duchamp's *Large Glass* is, in a sense, a window, and was permanently installed in front of a window.[10] In shape, it is a synthesis of the letters H and E, equivalents of the Hebrew letter Hé. The Celestial Bride is located at the third point, Binah, on the upper left of the Tree. This may explain why Duchamp positioned his Bride in the upper left of the *Large Glass.*

It will be noted that when one looks through the *Large Glass*, and then through the window behind it, one sees a fountain, perhaps of relevance for the Bride is likened to a fountain in the Kabbalah, and also the Song of Songs (4:15).[11] This too partially explains why Duchamp placed a work called *Fountain*, a small urinal, next to a reproduction of the *Large Glass* in a set of miniature replicas of his work, i.e. *Box in a Valise*, 1941 (S311), which constitutes a small portable museum. Congruently, the watermill at the bottom left of the *Large Glass* was to have been driven by a waterfall. And in the notes, he also refers to the ascension of water, also not rendered.[12] As the Bride is the Great Sea, and as She is symbolised by a fountain, we encounter the notion of a cyclical movement, which suggests the origin from which all was created, to which all will return. She is the "Architect of the Universe", acting in virtue of the Word uttered by God in creation. There are a number of direct parallels between Duchamp's imagery and that encountered in the Kabbalah, these supporting an identification of the Bride in the *Large Glass* as a symbolic reference to the Kabbalists' concept of the Celestial Bride located at Binah on the Tree of Life (Figure 16.4).

Before examining the iconographic implications of the Bride image in the *Large Glass*, one is presented with the problem of reading the image, by no means a simple task. Focusing on the right-hand side of the Bride image in the *Large Glass* leads to the recognition of a separate figure. This has been extracted to facilitate legibility (Figures 16.2, 16.5). This reading of two figures, the Bride on the left and another attached figure on Her right, is not without precedent. N. Coetzee in a sculpture, *Untitled,* 1972 (Figure 16.6), based on the upper part of the *Large Glass*, realized the Bride image as two separate figures. Duchamp's Bride is a matronly figure without a head. She faces towards the right, Her right arm stretched out towards the other figure. Her hand is not detailed. Instead, one sees a tube-like form extending downwards. This meets a horizontal band (slightly curved), which connects the two figures. Two tendril-like growths extend from the region of the hand, one towards the right "eye" of the other figure. Her dress seems to have a bow at the back (on the left). There is no clear definition of the breasts, but one gains the impression that She has a very full figure. Only part of Her left arm is to be seen.

The other figure (on the right) is less easy to read, for this is not naturalistic. The form has very strong visual similarities to a *Bakota Figure* in the Musée de l'Homme in Paris (Figure 16.7). Comparison of the two images facilitates a reading of Duchamp's figure, for we can at once identify the head, the upper section being rendered as a fan-like form divided by a curved vertical strip, this extending downwards to become the nose. On either side of the nose, two small circular forms define the eyes of the figure. The body is reduced to a shaft, terminating in a bulbous double-cone form, this seemingly being derived from the African sculpture. Although Duchamp informed Dr J. Golding that he

FIGURE 16.6   N. Coetzee, *Untitled,* Bronze, 1972. h. 70,9; w. 40,0; d. 18,7 cm (Collection Mr S. Weinberg)

was not influenced by African sculpture, the visual correlation of forms is so strong as to lead one to propose that he must have referred to a sketch (or visual memory) of either the sculpture in the Musée de l'Homme, or a very similar piece in another collection.[13] Further evidence which supports a reading of the right-hand form in the complex of forms denoting the Bride as a separate figure, is provided in Duchamp's preparatory notes for the *Green Box*. In one note, he included a small sketch of a head very similar in form to the head in the *Large Glass* and referred to it as a *tête*.[14] We are, however, obliged to read the form to the right of the Bride not simply as the separated head of the Bride, but as a complete figure in its own right, even though no verbal reference to this figure is to be found in the notes which Duchamp later published in the *Green Box*. This is indeed a curious omission, for Duchamp in a preparatory note for the *Green Box* made reference to this figure.

> The bride stripped bare by her bachelors
> even
> to give a sense of continuity
> to the picture and not incur the objection
> of having only described a fight
> between social dolls.
> The bride
> possesses *her partner* and the bachelors strip
> bare *their bride*.[15]

It is thus quite clear that Duchamp initially conceived of two brides. The Bride has a partner included in the upper complex of images in the *Large Glass*, although his presence seems to have gone unnoticed.[16] It is also pertinent that Duchamp in a discussion of the *Large Glass* with R. and G.H. Hamilton, referred to one stimulus for the work, namely a fairground game in which the players threw balls at the heads of wooden figures of a bride and bridegroom, thus knocking their heads off.[17] The reference to a bridegroom is significant, this possibly being a masked reference to a male figure in the upper part of the *Large Glass*. Equally significant is the reference to knocking the heads off the body, for Duchamp's Bride image has no head.

Before engaging the problem of a detailed reading of other attributes of the Bride, one must examine the iconographic implications of the presence of two figures in this zone. Why is the figure without a head? — a feature that occurs elsewhere in his *oeuvre*, notably the headless dummy which Duchamp produced for the window dresssing of Bretano's Bookstore on the occasion of Breton's publication of *Arcane 17*, 1945. Why did Duchamp specify a separate "partner" for the Bride, noting that he did not want to "incur objection"? Does this statement have a meaning other than "a fight between social dolls"? The dummy in the bookstore window provides one point of entry. In a previous analysis of this work,[18] focus was placed on the absence of the head, and the tap embedded in the thigh, this being seen in relation to Duchamp's later aphorism: "*Parmi nos articles de quincaillerie parasseuse, nous recommandos un robinet qui s'arrête de couler quand on ne l'écoute pas.*" (Among our articles of lazy hardware we recommend a faucet which stops

FIGURE 16.7   Bakota reliquary figure (Gabon), Musée de l'Homme (Photograph: J. Oster)

dripping when nobody is listening to it.) [19] This was understood as a masked reference to a passage in Revelations (22:27):

> And the Spirit and the bride say, Come. And let him that heareth say, Come. And let him that is athirst come. And whosoever will, let him take the water of life freely.

The message is clear: the tap will provide water, but stops when nobody listens to it. The dummy thus comes to be identified with the Bride, which is, from a Kabbalistic viewpoint, the feminine aspect of God. It is thus congruent that She is without a head, for God said to Moses (Exodus 33:23):

> And I will take away mine hand, and thou shalt see my back parts: but my face shall not be seen.

That one may not see the face of the Shekinah or Bride (God's presence in feminine aspect) explains the absence of the head of the Bride in the *Large Glass*. As physical union with the Bride (Shekinah) is an impossibility, Duchamp's Bride is removed from the lower Bachelor's zone. Furthermore, to prevent "objections", Duchamp has provided Her with a "partner", the male Bakota-like figure. The ramifications of the presence of the "bridegroom" ("Partner") in the upper section of the *Large Glass* are considerable if seen within a Kabbalistic context.

To interpret the significance of the Bride and Her groom within terms of the Tree of Life is an onerous task, for it is difficult to establish the full implications of Kabbalistic symbols. As Waite comments:

> I must proceed carefully, not only on account of the difficulties but because the Keys of the Mystery open into a region about which there are grave motives for speaking with considerable reserve, when it is possible to speak at all. [20]

It has been suggested that, given the model of the Tree of Life, it is logical to associate the Bride with the third point on the Tree (upper left). In the Kabbalah, the Bride is said to have a Bridegroom. He would be positioned opposite Her on the right hand side of the Tree, at the second point called Chokmah. Although it is said that "it is forbidden to separate . . . [them], even in thought, it is this which has come to pass".[21] In other words, although the Bride and Bridegroom have become separated, they must be thought of as a connected pair. The problem of the re-unification of the Bride after separation from the Bridegroom is presented. This finds its pictorial realisation in the *Large Glass*, for if we focus our attention on the bottom of the two figures (upper zone of the *Large Glass*), it will be seen that each figure has a "tube" which extends downwards (Figures 16.2, 16.5). These two tubes are not, however, connected. It will be noted that there is a small space between them, as if the broken bond can be re-established by a "spark" between the two ends of the tubes. Congruently, Duchamp suggested that the Bride will "possess" Her "Partner". This mechanical but symbolic sexual image may define the mechanism through which this will occur.

This may also be noted that the image of a tube is associated with the second point on the Tree, Chokmah, the location of the Bridegroom. It is said that the third point, Binah, symbolised by the cup,

> Must be distinguished emphatically from the ... *hollow tube* of Chokmah which transmits the influence in its positive form in an intelligible manner but without understanding its nature. [22]

It is thus appropriate to associate a tube with Chokmah. The relationship of the two tubes refers us to the idea of a potential union of the Bride and Bridegroom, also appropriate if seen within terms of the Kabbalah. It will be recalled that the Bride is not physically accessible to Man. She can, however, be "possessed" by Her "partner", the Bridegroom, for this is a Celestial Union, often referred to in sexual terms, terms which are not applicable when referring to Man's relationship with the Bride.

It is congruent that Duchamp states that the Bachelors in the lower zone of the *Large Glass* "strip bare their Bride". But no sexual union between the Bride and the Bachelors takes place. We thus have the problem of interpreting the symbols in the *Large Glass*, not simply with reference to one Bride, but two, the lower Bride at the bottom of the Tree being the "exiled" Bride who accompanied Adam and Eve after their expulsion from Eden. It may well be this Bride that Duchamp refers to in *Etant donnés*, for in the Kabbalah She is God's *sacrifice* for man after the expulsion: the female figure in Duchamp's assemblage is placed on a pile of twigs, as if on a sacrificial altar. [23] (It may well be that it is the bottom point on the Tree, the tenth point called Malkuth (the location of the lower Bride) that provided Duchamp with ideas and symbols that generated the image of the Chocolate Grinder in the *Large Glass*. Given the complexities of these symbols, this aspect cannot be explored here.) [24]

The Kabbalah places great stress on the importance of the unpronounceable name of God, YHVH (Hebrew), which in itself defines the Secret Doctrine. These letters are symbolic and, when separated, define points on the Tree of Life (Figure 16.4). The first letter Y is associated with the second point on the Tree of Life, Chokmah, the position of the Bridegroom. The first letter H is associated with the third point, Binah, location of the upper Celestial Bride (Duchamp's Bride). The letter V is associated with the mid-point on the Tree, Tiphareth, the sixth point, but also the points numbered four to nine (inclusive). The last H in YHVH is associated with the bottom point on the Tree, Malkuth, location of the lower Bride (Shekinah). When Adam and Eve were expelled, it is said that the Shekinah (Bride) departed with them thus disrupting the Divine Unity. The task of man, redemption, is to partake in the process of re-uniting the Divine name, YHVY. This too, is expressed in complex symbolic terms. Simplistically, it is man's task to transform himself and achieve a state of consciousness defined by the mid-point on the Tree of Life, this sometimes referred to as Christ-consciousness — a state of perfect harmony and equilibrium, comprehensible with the Tree of Life is understood as a microcosmic model denoting Man himself, and not simply the macrocosmic model related to the Creation. At this point, he would integrate and balance all aspects of self, e.g. the intellect (denoted by the eighth point, Hod) and the emotions (denoted by the seventh point, Netzach). It is here that he is no longer at the mercy of the lower earthly stage (the physical aspect,

200

Malkuth, and the animal instinctual level denoted by Yesod). At the mid-point, he is between the "above" and "below", the symbolism of level clearly being operative. The ideal of the Kabbalist would thus be defined by the letter V (Vau) in the context of the name YHVH as related to the Tree of Life. When man transforms himself, the mystic marriage with the Bride takes place, this involving a raising of the lower letter H located at the bottom of the Tree, to the mid-point. This would be symbolised by the bringing together of the letters V and H (the second H in YHVH). When this occurs, a similar enactment (and here sexual symbolism is acceptable) would take place at a higher level, i.e. the letters Y and H (the first H in YHVH), would also be united. In other words, the upper Bride and Bridegroom would be united. In Duchampian terms, the Bride (in the upper section of the *Large Glass*) would "possess" Her "partner". As argued, he is the Bokota-like figure standing to the right of the headless Bride image. A Kabbalistic interpretation of Duchamp's Bride and Bridegroom has led to the suggestion that these figures refer to the upper Celestial Bride and Her Groom, as positioned at the second and third point on the Tree of Life. That Duchamp referred to his Bride as a "married divinity" provides yet additional support for the interpretation. Examination of other details in the *Large Glass* and notes in the *Green Box* substantiates reference to the Kabbalah.

It has already been observed that two tendril-like shapes extend downwards from the mechanical form of the hand of the Bride. One of these stretches towards the right eye of the Bridegroom. On the microcosmic model of the Tree, each point on the Tree is associated with part of a figure. The left eye would be linked to the second point on the Tree (Chokmah), the right eye with the third point Binah (on the upper left of the Tree). That the Bride seems to reach out towards the right eye of the Bridegroom is thus congruent with Kabbalistic symbolism, and further supports a link between the headless Bride in the *Large Glass* and the third point (upper left) on the Tree. She presumably reaches towards this eye, because it is said in the Kabbalah that She is without eyes. One can thus explain the presence of the tendril-like outgrowth.

One also seeks for an explanation for presence of the single tube-like form which extends downwards from Her hand, this meeting with the curved horizontal plane connecting the two figures. Duchamp may have provided a clue to its meaning in a note in the *Green Box* when he referred to the *Large Glass* as an "agricultural machine" (AS 10), probably a reference to the act of ploughing and its significance. If one were to offer a simplistic Freudian interpretation of this image, one might suggest that there is a masked reference to sexual intercourse, the masculine component being denoted by the extended tube piercing the earth. However, for logic to be maintained, one must accept that the act of ploughing is here associated with the female and not the male, as might be expected. In the Kabbalah, it is said that

> when the *Zohar* wishes to apply the idea of a "field which the Lord hath blessed" to the Mystery of Sex, it is not above saying that the King who "tills the field" or is "served by the field" is the Shekinah [Bride], sex-contradiction notwithstanding. [25]

This "sex-contradiction" may well explain why it would seem that it is the Bride in the

Large Glass who "tills" the field, this apparently being denoted by the tube which meets the horizontal plane near the base of the two figures.

It has already been noted that Duchamp called the Bride a "married divinity", argued to be a reference to the upper Celestial Bride. We are thus dealing with a belief and concept of "reality" which refers not to the physical corporeal world, but to the upper regions — the "above" rather than that which is "below". Within terms of the Kabbalah, it is not entirely appropriate that one should have a fully realised finite form to denote the upper Bride. This may well explain why Duchamp in a note in the *Green Box* states that the Bride "does not need to satisfy the laws of weighted balance" (AS 1), and

> In the Bride, the *principal forms*
> are *more or*
> *less large or small*, have no
> longer, in relation to their destination
> a mensurability . . . (AS 89).

Duchamp's Bride does not therefore obey the laws of gravity: She is suspended. She is "*more or less large or small*", which leads us to conclude that the focus is on concept rather than physically finite form, i.e. we are beyond the world of form and matter. Her forms are immensurable, and cannot be fixed in terms of dimension.

Despite the fact that the Bride is intangible, and refers us to the third point Binah (beyond the world of form), She is described in the Kabbalah. It is said:

> And tradition: five sex-organs (*or* parts) are uncovered in her, in the side of the five judgements . . .
>
> And the tradition is as follows: the voice in the wife is exposed;
> the hair in the wife is exposed; the leg in the wife is exposed;
> the hand in the wife is exposed; the foot in the wife is exposed.
>
> However our companions have not studied two of them; and two of them (may have) more exposed (parts). [26]

It will be noted that Her face is not seen, and only one leg, one foot, and one hand are to be seen. Duchamp's Bride (Figure 16.5) has no head. She has only one hand, and it would seem, only one leg is rendered. (The central column emerging from the bottom of her dress next to the curved horizontal plane denoting the "field" may describe the "leg".) Despite the exposure of her "five sex-organs", the Bride in the Kabbalah is a virgin.

Although Duchamp informs us (correctly) that the Bride is the "apotheosis of virginity", he also notes that She has a "touch of malice", and "a shiny metal gallows could stimulate the maiden's attachment to her girl friends" (AS 1). In the Kabbalah, each point on the Tree has both a negative and a positive aspect. The third point, Binah (location of the Bride), is associated with Saturn, who

> has an unpleasant habit of eating his children. In this myth we get again the idea of the bringer into life as the giver of death . . . Saturn with his reaping hook readily becomes Death with his scythe. [27]

One can readily establish a logical connection between a gallows and a scythe. The gallows is associated with punitive action, in the Kabbalah connected with the Pillar of Severity (on the left of the Tree), this being headed by Binah. It is here we encounter Her as the Terrible Mother. She is both the Dark Sterile Mother as well as the Bright Fertile Mother. She is positioned on the left pillar of the Tree, this being the feminine side. She is thus correctly attached to her "girl friends" most immediately the fifth point Geburah (Figure 16.4), the sephiroth or point of the Tree most directly associated with judgement and punitive action.

That Duchamp also characterises his Bride as a flirt, noted by Dr J. Golding,[28] is concordant with other attributes given to Her in the Kabbalah. Although complex, the symbolism is understandable. It is said that the Bride and the literal *Torah* are one, and:

> The *Torah* is like a beautiful and stately woman, hidden in a secreted chamber in her palace with a secret lover. ... This lover constantly passes the gate of her house, searching for her. ... She opens her chamber door and reveals her face to him but for an instant. ... He alone sees it.[29]

In other words, the Bride teases or flirts with Her secret lover, revealing Herself for an instant, this being an act of encouragement to the aspirant who desires union — a union which is however not a sexual or physical union, but a mystical union. The Bride thus "loves" the aspirant who seeks for this union.

Duchamp subtly alludes to the "love" of the Bride through word play. The addition of the word *même* (even) at the end of the full title of the *Large Glass* and *Green Box — La Mariée mise à nu par ses célibataires, même* (The Bride Stripped Bare by Her Bachelors, Even) may be significant as a pointer to Her relationship with the aspirant, for *même* may be a pun on *m'aime*,[30] suggesting that the "Bride loves me" — totally concordant with the Kabbalah. Yet Duchamp also informs us that the Bride "warmly rejects" the advances of the Bachelors, but She is not an "icicle" (AS 1). In other words, She is associated with heat and fire, but this is to be understood symbolically, and not simplistically on the sexual level, for no physical union with the Bride is possible. That Duchamp introduces heat as a symbolic attribute of the Bride is reflected in a note in which he makes reference to a "hot plate" (AS 70), and also a water or air "cooler" as part of the apparatus, this being denoted by three strips of glass in the *Large Glass* (Figure 16.1). The Bride is thus separated from the lower zone by strips of glass which project at a ninety degree angle to the picture plane in the actual work. These isolating plates (the "cooler") simultaneously denote the garments of the Bride. One thus needs to establish the symbolic significance of "stripping bare" and garment symbolism and the isolating plates, the "cooler".

In the Kabbalah, the Shekinah (Bride) is sometimes understood to be an "electrical force or energy",[31] this analogy being concordant with fire and light as symbolic references to the presence of God, readily understood if one thinks of Moses' encounter with the burning bush (Exodus 3:2). Given the power and force of such an energy, one can understand the need for protecting man, also implicit in the idea that man cannot survive a face-to-face encounter with God. This, as noted above, explains why the Bride image in Duchamp's *oeuvre* is usually decapitated, and why, in a note, he suggested the possibility of imitating the appearance of a photograph (a medium dependent on light) in his rendering of the image. [32]

As pointed out above, the Bride may reveal herself in Her aspect as the *Torah*, the outer garment of the Bride.

> Kabbalistic tradition tells us that a student of the *Torah* is well on his way to becoming a "bridegroom of the *Torah*" or of the Shekinah (Bride), for she and the literal *Torah* are one, it is the outer garment of the Shekinah. One who diligently studies the *Torah* clothes the Shekinah, for in her exile she is naked. Every sinner is therefore thought of as one who disrobes the Shekinah (Bride), and in so doing prolongs her exile. [33]

Depending on context, the act of disrobing the Bride may either be a positive or negative action, for one may reveal the true nature of the *Torah* by reading and piercing through the "Outer Robe of Concealment", one of the symbols associated with the Bride. However, if one functions on a lower level, the act of stripping bare is a negative action, for the naked Bride in exile is to be clothed. The aspirant prepares the Bride for mystic marriage by clothing Her. The complexities are further compounded if one keeps in mind the fact that there are two Brides in the Kabbalah, these being positioned at different points on the Tree. The matter is also complicated by the fact that Duchamp, in the final published notes for the *Large Glass*, omitted reference to a second Bride. There is thus a potential symbolic encounter of the Bachelors below and the Bride above, the act of "stripping bare" playing an important role. In a note, he comments:

> The bride accepts this stripping
> by the bachelors, since she supplies
> the love gasoline to the sparks of this
> electrical stripping; moreover, she
> furthers her complete nudity by adding to
> the 1st focus of sparks (electrical stripping)
> and 2nd focus of sparks of the desire-magneto (AS 66).

Given Duchamp's note, one may see the act of stripping as a positive act, for the Bride supplies the "love gasoline" — encouraging the process of revelation. Congruently, this is an "electrical stripping". She, in response, furthers Her nudity by Her own actions — "the 2nd focus of sparks of the desire-magneto" (a part of Her apparatus). In other words, once the Bachelors pierce beneath the surface meaning of religious texts and come to some understanding (and they are aided by the Bride), She further reveals Herself in preparation for Her union with Her partner, the Bakota-like Bridegroom figure on Her left. Thus, paradoxically, on a symbolic level, the aspirant, whilst stripping the Bride, simultaneously clothes Her. This is congruent with a statement in the Kabbalah.

> In the *Sepher Ha Zohar* it is written that there is a garment — the written doctrine — which every man may see. Those with understanding do not look upon the garment but at the body beneath it — the intellectual and philosophical code. [34]

204

And:

> Now, there is no work of the Holy One so recondite but he has recorded it in the *Torah*: and the *Torah* reveals it in an instant and then straightaway clothes it in another garment, so that it is hidden there and does not show itself. But the wise, whose wisdom makes them full of eyes, *pierce* through the garment to the very essence of the word that is hidden thereby. [35]

These passages facilitate an understanding of Duchamp's iconography, for the garment is associated with a body of writing, and not simply the clothes of a person. The Bride is seen to be the *Torah*. One must pierce through and see below the outer garment.

Reference to other imagery in Duchamp's *oeuvre* supports a Kabbalistic interpretation of garment symbolism in the *Large Glass* and *Green Box*. For the parallel to hold, one needs to establish a specific connection between the written word and a garment. This is to be seen in a book-jacket which Duchamp designed. In itself, it is not an important work, but like all Duchamp's productions, fits into a complex programme. The work, *Jacket*, 1956 (S339), simply provides an illustration of a real tail coat seen from the front, and from the back. This image is based on an obvious pun — "book-jacket". The garment of the book is a jacket. One thus associates a book with a garment. This association facilitates an understanding of the significance of the *Green Box*, the text accompanying the *Large Glass*. This too is a garment, an analogue of the Bride, just as the *Torah* is a symbolic manifestation of the Bride. The act of stripping the Bride would be the act of understanding the fuller implications of the notes, the deeper philosophical and intellectual meaning. The Kabbalist would *pierce* through the garment. It is thus pertinent that Duchamp physically pierced through the cover of the actual *Green Box* — the title is rendered by a series of small holes, paralleling his intention of actually piercing the real glass matrix of the *Large Glass*. The act of piercing has an obvious Freudian significance which co-exists with its other symbolic meaning — piercing or penetrating beneath the surface — i.e. understanding the fuller symbolic implications of the notes, and by implication, the Kabbalah.

It has been suggested that the act of penetration is to be understood on two levels. It may signify a deeper level of meaning which needs to be understood, as well as the idea of a sexual union, this in turn denoting a mystical union. One seeks for evidence supporting the interpretation of the piercing of the glass as a sexual reference. Duchamp refers to shop windows in a note, and states:

> ... The penalty
> consists in cutting the pane
> and in feeling regret as soon as
> possession is consummated.
> (AS 136).

He also expressed the idea of firing painted matchsticks from a toy cannon at the *Large Glass*, and drilling holes in the positions determined by the painted heads of the matchsticks (AS 84). Holes were actually drilled through the *Large Glass* in the upper right-hand section, presumably in response to this idea, which like many of Duchamp's conceptions, is multivalent. [36] In a preparatory note for the *Green Box*, he also suggested that the glass could be riddled with holes.

> Make a test riddling with nails of
> different sizes.) — Holes more or less close to each
> other. [37]

Consummation is achieved with the cutting of the glass, echoed in the idea of firing matchsticks at the glass from a toy cannon, and the act of piercing the glass with nails. These implicitly sexual symbols define meaning, rather than simply the physical processes used in the making of the work. For example, it is highly unlikely that a toy cannon would have the power to project matchsticks to the upper region of the *Large Glass*, nor is it likely one could actually make holes in the glass with nails. Again there are complex allusions, for the nail is the image of the Hebrew letter Vau (V) in the Kabbalah, this, as previously noted, defining the mid-point on the Tree and thus a state of being or consciousness, and also the third letter in YHVH, the name which encapsulates the Secret Doctrine in the Kabbalah. Thus to make holes in the glass with nails would seem to refer to the act of union with the lower Bride. This would take place at the mid-point of the Tree. Such an act is symbolic of mystical union.

For the argument to hold, one would expect the glass itself to have symbolic signi-ficance, for one could not interpret the meaning of the nail in isolation. As noted, the window is the image linked to the letter Hé (H), which was shown to refer to the two Brides in the context of the unpronounceable name YHVH (Figure 16.4). (The first letter H defines the Celestial Bride at the third point Binah; the second letter H refers us to the lower Bride at the bottom of the Tree.) This joining together of the second letter H (a window) with the letter V (a nail) has been symbolised by the idea of making a hole in the glass with a nail, a symbolic act which parallels the piercing of the cover of the *Green Box*. Just as the *Torah* is the Bride, so the *Green Box* is the Bride, as is the *Large Glass* itself, for this is a window (H). Not only do we encounter the symbolism of the letter through the material (glass), but also, through shape, for the format of the *Large Glass* itself (as noted), generates the shape of the letter H (Figure 16.1), which suggests that the *Large Glass* itself is also the Bride.

From the above analysis, one can conclude that the piercing of the garment (the *Green Box*) and the glass, operates on several levels. On the lowest physical level, we encounter the idea of a sexual union, in itself symbolic, for such a union with the Bride is an impossibility. A mystical union is implicit unless one chooses to function within terms of the lower physical levels, at which stage one disrobes the Bride. One can choose to penetrate as the act of understanding the Secret Doctrine of the Kabbalah — piercing through the garment of the Bride, Her "Outer Robe of Concealment". In so doing, She is "stripped bare" in an act of revelation, in which She participates, this preceding Her act of possessing Her partner, the Bakota-like figure on Her left.

Focus has been placed on the positive act of "stripping" the Bride, this being associated with the notion of revealing different layers of meaning in the text, these including in a

Kabbalistic context, the literal, the philosophico-allegorical and the theosophical levels of meaning. One approaches the *Green Box* in a similar vein, searching for the outer and inner meanings. One may thus suggest that Duchamp's notes describe mechanical operations, but simultaneously have symbolic significance, explicable within terms of the Kabbalah. It has been noted that the act of stripping the Bride has different meanings in different contexts. Clothing the naked Bride is a positive act, and disrobing Her has negative connotations. That Duchamp may have used both points of reference is suggested by a comment he made on Christ symbolism in a discussion of the *Large Glass*, this referring, it would seem, to the figure of the Handler of Gravity or Juggler, discussed in notes in the *Green Box* (AS 122), but not actually rendered in the *Large Glass*. (This figure is, however, included in a later work, *The Large Glass Completed*, 1965 (S390).) Duchamp stated that the *Large Glass* had something to do with Christ and notes that Christ, like the Bride, was "stripped bare",[38] presumably a reference to Matthew (27:28): "And they stripped him, and put on him a scarlet robe". It thus becomes clear that the act becomes negative or positive, depending on the spectator's reference point. By implication, the spectator who simply approaches the *Large Glass* and *Green Box* as works which define meaning on the sexual level, functions negatively and fails to penetrate the garment. If, however, he reveals different layers of meaning through the process of "stripping", he functions positively, creatively furthering the process of re-uniting the Divine name by an act of self-transformation. It is thus suggested that Duchamp was able to simultaneously generate two antithetical meanings in his references to "stripping bare". This suggestion is totally in accord with Duchamp's view that the spectator brings to a work of art a creative act.[39] Inevitably he must reflect his own personality, values, etc. and thus "completes" the work. Duchamp makes possible, through multivalency, the generation of levels of meaning which encompass the sexual level (so ensuring the "life" of the work of art), but simultaneously allows this level of meaning to point to other levels. We also find that one image can have more than one identity. For example, the three strips of glass attached to the *Large Glass* denote both the "cooler", which separates the two zones, and, simultaneously, the garments of the Bride.

That the Bride-image is connected with upper-level symbolism is also reflected in another aspect of Duchamp's characterisation, for he states that She is responsible for "commands, orders, authorizations, etc." (AS 124). This finds its counterpart in the Kabbalah, for the Shekinah (Bride) came to be identified with the oral law and the Torah.[40] Duchamp implies that it is these "laws and authorizations" which will govern the possibility of achieving an "instantaneous state of Rest". In other words, the aspirant (i.e., the Handler of Gravity and also (implicitly) the spectator) would need to obey and work within terms of the law governed by the Bride. The symbolism becomes even more complex, for in a note, Duchamp also connects the "laws" and "authorizations" with the idea of an "Inscription" in the upper zone of the *Large Glass* (Figure 16.1). Duchamp notes the possibility of "all combinations of letter sent across this said triple form . . ." (AS 77, 81), the latter referring to the cloud-like shape pierced by three distorted square shapes. He also refers to "a sort of *letter box* (alphabet)" which will appear in this section of the *Large Glass*, and notes that in the Inscription each alphabetical unit will be present only once. Although not realised pictorially, the concept relates to another aspect of the Bride in the Kabbalah. We encounter, it would seem, the elements of creation, for in the Kabbalah it is said that the Shekinah (Bride) "is the architect of the world, acting in virtue of the Word uttered by God in creation". [41] Binah, the third point, is conceived of as the "primordial womb"[42] and is associated with the three "mother letters", Aleph, Mem and Shin (A, M, Sh). [43] These give birth, so to speak, to the rest of the alphabet. Duchamp's concept of a "letter box (alphabet)" thus finds its direct counterpart in the Kabbalah, for this generates the notion of the "origin", and the elements of the creation. The three "mother letters" in fact symbolise the three elements, air (Aleph, A) water (Mem, M) and fire (Shin, Sh). We are thus directed to the Kabbalists' notion of the "World of Origins". [44]

The Kabbalist conceived of four (sometimes five) Worlds, which may be associated with the Tree of Life, or each World can be denoted by a separate Tree. Of relevance here is the conception of the World of Origins, also known as the World of Emanation (Atziluth). In a note, Duchamp implicitly connects his Bride with the notion of emanation, for he states:

For the life centre of the bride end up at
a little mathematical spherical
empty emanating ball — (emanating sphere)
always to contrast the married divinity to the celibate
human –. [45]

The Bride is thus connected with the notion of emanation and thus the World of Emanation or Origins (Atziluth). [46] This would be associated with the three upper interconnected points on the Tree of Life. By stressing the emptiness of the ball, Duchamp also draws attention to the interdependence of the two points, Binah and Chokmah (the third and second points), for as has been noted, Binah is likened to an *empty* receptacle which receives its power and energy from the Bridegroom, Chokmah. It is equally congruent that reference is made to the fact that the Bride is a "married divinity", for this draws our attention to the Bridegroom, the Bakota-like figure who supplies the power and force.

That Duchamp finds an analogue for the Kabbalistic conception of the creation by means of the word is significant, for it explains another important conception in the *Green Box*, expressed in the "preface":

Given 1. the waterfall
2. The illuminating gas (AS 124).

It has been pointed out that the three "mother letters" symbolise the three elements, water, air, fire (and also light/spirit). We can readily establish a connection between water and "waterfall". Also, we can understand "gas" as a reference to the element air. But that this is "illuminating" gas may be significant, for there may well be an implicit reference to the element denoted by the letter Shin, i.e. fire (but also light and spirit). Presumably the notion of "illumination" also refers to a process of enlightenment. It is thus pertinent that the "human" (Bachelor), as specified by Duchamp, is "celibate". It is the Bride — a "divinity" — who is married. The "waterfall" (referred to in a note), drives the Watermill, and the "illuminating gas" moulds and is simultaneously moulded by the Nine Malic Moulds (figures) (AS 91–101). Duchamp thus seems to have referred to the elements of the creation which in turn symbolise the three "mother letters" (the origin of the alphabet). His reference to a "letter box" for the alphabet reinforces this contention. The "illuminating gas" undergoes a process of transformation, an "improvement" as it progresses through the Capillary Tubes to emerge at the bottom of the first Sieve. From here it passes through the Seven Sieves ("traps" or "filters") and emerges at the other end, to descend to the bottom (on the right) from which point it splashes and ascends to the top section of the *Large Glass*. Just as the Bride supplies the "love gasoline", so too She is implicitly connected with the idea of the Great Mother of the World, the "architect" who works with the elements of the Creation, which are also symbolised by letters of the alphabet. It would seem that the "illuminating gas" and "waterfall" refer us to the elements and also the three "mother letters", but possibly at a lower level. The aspirant who has reached the mid-point on the Tree would presumably, as the Handler of Gravity or Juggler, be akin to the Magician-Juggler of the Western Inner Tradition, who juggles with the letters and elements. In other words, he would re-enact the process of creation on the microcosmic level.

In the note on the Inscription (AS 76, 81) Duchamp alludes to both the notion of the Bride as the "architect" of the Universe who creates with the alphabet and word, and also Her role as Law-giver, for She gives "commands, authorizations and orders", which suggests not only the laws of the Universe but also the Law. As noted, the Torah is also connected with garment symbolism. It would seem that it is these conceptions which explain why Duchamp, in his portable museum of works, *Box in a Valise*, positioned a small Underwood typewriter-cover on the left hand side of a reproduction of the *Large Glass*. This was positioned in line with the three strips of glass at the junction of the two zones. These denote the "cooler" as well as the "garments" of the Bride. The typewriter-cover is a readymade (factory made article) called *Traveller's Folding Item,* 1916 (S240). A typewriter-cover obviously generates the notion of a garment, even more so since, according to Schwarz, "this item, which Duchamp identifies with a feminine skirt, should be exhibited on a stand high enough to induce the spectator to bend and see what is hidden by the cover".[47] In other words, one is invited to see the "body" beneath the "outer garment". It is thus congruent that a miniature typewriter-cover was placed alongside the garments of the Bride in the small replica of the *Large Glass*.

If one reads this readymade as a commentary on the garments of the Bride, the connotations are rich, for the title, *Traveller's Folding Item*, introduces reference to travelling, this alluding not simply to physical movement, but a symbolic act, one which suggests change and growth, for one "climbs" the Tree of Life. Furthermore, the Juggler or Handler of Gravity, who is positioned on the garments of the Bride, implicitly (on a lower level) has access to a typewriter, this possibly functioning as a symbolic analogue of the "letter box (alphabet)" which was to have been located in the Bride's zone. The alphabet associated with the absent typewriter would allude to the letters (and thus also the elements) which the Handler of Gravity would juggle in his re-enactment of the creation on a microcosmic level. Again one needs to stress the complexity of thematic allusions, these being interconnected, but at various levels. It would not be illogical to associate the three strips of glass denoting the Bride's garments with the typewriter cover, and possibly also with the three "mother letters" of the alphabet, and thus the elements of the creation, air, water and fire (light), these being denoted by the letters Aleph, Mem and Shin.

Congruently, Duchamp in the *Box in a Valise* (as noted) also positioned a miniature version of his *Fountain*, 1917 (S244) next to a reproduction of the *Large Glass*, in a position in line with the point where we would expect to encounter the Waterfall which was to have driven the Watermill (AS 126). The *Fountain* (a readymade urinal placed on its side), is obviously connected with the idea of falling water. Equally congruent is the fact that we encounter a miniature replica of the readymade glass ampoule containing 50 cc of air called *Paris Air*, 1919 (S264) in the *Box in a Valise*, opposite the cloud-like shape in the upper zone of the *Large Glass*, for this is pierced by three shapes referred to as Draft Pistons (AS 80–81), and air is obviously connected with the idea of a "draft". We thus find support for the suggestion that the miniature typewriter cover called *Traveller's Folding Item* was deliberately placed in line with the garments of the Bride, and acts as a kind of commentary or sub-text.

The Juggler or Handler of Gravity (rendered in *The Large Glass Completed*) was to balance on a ball on a glass strip denoting the garments of the Bride. In a preparatory note for the *Green Box*, Duchamp states:

Large insulator
3 planes 5 cm apart.
in transparent material. (sort of
thick glass.) to insulate the "Hanged" from the bachelor
Mach. [48]

There is a connection between the number three (symbolising equilibrium), an insulator ("cooler") and a garment in this note. Perhaps it is not surprising that this particular conjunction of symbols is also encountered in the literature on the Western Inner Tradition. In an analysis of the Tarot card of the Hermit, Sadhu comments:

The *Long cloak* (worn by the hermit) symbolizes separation and insulation in three planes . . . [49]

One of the names he gives to this card is "Initiation", and he associates the three planes with different aspects of man, i.e. the mental, astral and physical planes. The initiations associated with these planes cannot be explored here, but it should be noted that there is a possible connection between Duchamp's imagery and the card. The three strips of glass — the garments — may also refer to the mental, astral and physical planes. It is also feasible that there is a connection between the Hermit and the Handler of Gravity (Juggler) who balances on the Bride's garment. He is the Christ figure in the *Large Glass*, the Magician-Juggler, who has pierced the garment of the Bride. [50] Significantly, it is the task of the spectator to imaginatively position him on the strips of glass in the *Large Glass*.

Having examined the relationship of the two figures in the upper zone, the Bride and Her Bridegroom, and having suggested an interpretation of garment symbolism and the act of "stripping bare", one is left with the task of interpreting other aspects of Duchamp's characterisation. The Bride image is very much more complex than so far suggested, for there are many notes and sketches which provide information on Her attributes, these not actually being realised in pictorial form in the *Large Glass*.

In the Kabbalah, a great many symbols and complex ideas are associated with the various points (sephira) on the Tree. Binah is associated with the Celestial Bride, but also the Greek God Chronos — Father Time. This comes about partly because connotations of Understanding and Age are linked to this sephiroth. We find Duchamp referring fairly directly to time in a note on the Bride. Reference is made to parts of Her mechanism, which are compared to clocks in railway stations, this perhaps also pointing to a proposed major source for the *Large Glass*, a thirteenth-century manuscript by al-Jazari on Arabian technology and water-clocks[51] (Figure 16.8). The meaning may be more complex, for Duchamp in another note in the *Green Box*, writes:

The clock *in profile*
and the *Inspector* of Space (AS 73).

He commented: "When a clock is seen from the side (in profile) it no longer tells the time."[52] But he also notes that the effect of the "electrical stripping" of the Bride should "end in the clockwork movement" (AS 66) and in another note on the *Large Glass*, he comments in a very hermetic reference to the idea of an "instantaneous state of rest = bring in the term extra-rapid" (AS 124), this presumably referring to that instant when the Bride "possesses Her partner". There thus seems to be a reference to both the notion of the instant, time as progression (associated with movement in space), and the timeless, the latter probably being connected to the idea of the Bride as the Shekinah — the female presence of God, who would not (as noted above), be conceived of in terms of a physical finite body in space, nor as an entity existing within terms of a concept of time as chronometric and progressive. The notion of an "instantaneous state of rest" may also be linked with the idea that at that moment when mystical union is achieved, a perfect state of equilibrium is achieved — time ceases to exist as a reference point.

Duchamp, in the *Green Box*, uses mechanical imagery to describe attributes of the Bride. She is a machine with gears and cogs, a steam engine which is then transformed into a combustion-engine. She has a clockwork mechanism, but also a motor which "transmits" timid power and operates on "love gasoline". The "desire-part" is referred to as a "desire magneto". She has cylinders (there is a drawing of Her "sex-cylinder" in the *Green Box* (AS 70)), a "reservoir", and is partly characterised by automobile imagery.

That Duchamp associated an automobile with the Bride may seem strange, but is explicable within terms of the Kabbalah: such imagery is encountered in a Kabbalist text in the twentieth century. D. Fortune writes of the Bride, or more specifically the sephiroth Binah (location of the Celestial Bride) in these terms.[53] This is a most complex issue, for a

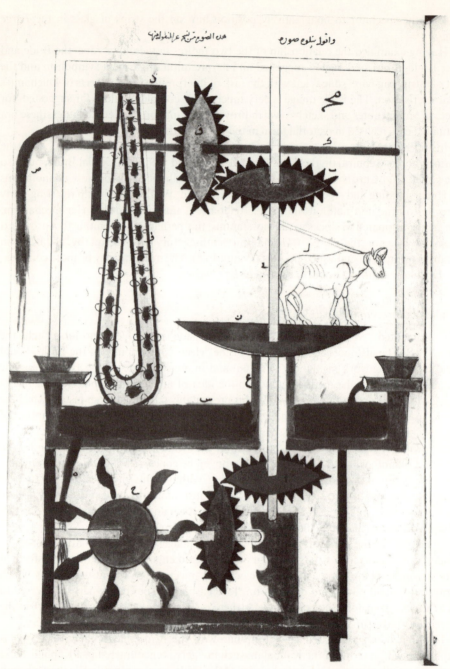

هذه الصورة منزعة عن المغول ١٩   وانفرا بلوغ صورة

FIGURE 16.8   Ibn al-Razzāz al-Jazarī: "Agricultural Machine" from *The Book of Knowledge of Ingenious Mechanical Devices* (Ms Graves 27, fol. 101, Bodleian Library)

212

full understanding of any one point on the Tree necessitates a full understanding of the Tree as a whole, an exercise which cannot be engaged here. It must suffice to briefly elaborate on a few of the ideas associated with the two interconnected sephira, Binah and Chokmah, the second and third points on the Tree, these corresponding, as has been argued, with Duchamp's Bride and Her partner. As Fortune elaborates, Chokmah is male and Binah female, one the mature Father, one the matronly Mother. Chokmah is understood as masculine power and active energy, whilst Binah is female, passive and receptive. The two principles are interconnected. Fortune uses the image of a motorcar to elucidate:

> Chokmah is pure force, even as the expansion of petrol as it explodes in the combustion-engine is pure force. But just as this expansive force would expand and be lost if there were no engine to transmit its power, so the undirected energy of Chokmah would radiate into space and be lost if there were nothing to receive its impulse and utilize it. Chokmah explodes like petrol; Binah is the combustion-chamber; Gedulah [Chesed] and Geburah [the fourth and fifth points on the Tree] are the back and forth strokes of the piston.
>
> Now the expansive force given off by petrol is pure energy, but it will not drive a car. The constrictive organization of Binah is potentially capable of driving a car, but it cannot do so unless set in motion by the expansion of the stored-up energy of petrol-vapour. Binah is all-potential, but inert. Chokmah is pure energy ... Briefly, Chokmah supplies the energy, and Binah supplies the machine. [54]

Thus Fortune characterises Binah (location of the Bride) as a "machine" which is to receive its energy and power from the masculine Chokmah. Duchamp's Bride is similarly characterised, insofar as She is a machine ("The Bride is (basically) a motor"), and is likened to an automobile which has "quite feeble cylinders" (AS 1). It is presumably the Bride's partner who supplies the energy after the first "electrical stripping" by the Bachelors, and the second self-stripping by the Bride, at which point, Duchamp states:

> The car (Bride) wants more and more to reach the top, and while slowly accelerating, as if exhausted by hope, the motor of the car turns over faster and faster, until it roars triumphantly (AS 1).

The "top", in Duchampian terminology as expressed in the notes, is the "3rd Blossoming-crown" (AS 1). It would seem that Duchamp carefully selected the word "crown", for this is the name of the top point on the Tree, i.e. Kether or Crown (Figure 16.4). This point (macrocosmically) defines the point of origin from which all was manifest, and to which all will return. It is the highest state of existence, virtually incomprehensible, beyond words, associated with the God-head itself, and final completion of the "Great Work" on the spiritual level. [55] Interpretation of the *Green Box* notes suggests that this achievement is the consequence of the divine union of the Bride and the Bridegroom.

Analysis of imagery connected with the Bride and Her partner has been confined to the Tree of Life. However, as noted above, each point on the Tree generates another Tree.

213

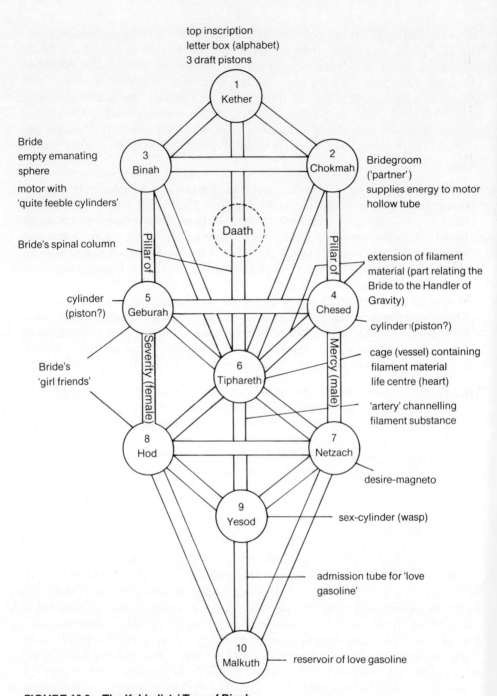

top inscription
letter box (alphabet)
3 draft pistons

Bride
empty emanating
sphere
motor with
'quite feeble cylinders'

Bridegroom
('partner')
supplies energy to motor
hollow tube

Bride's spinal column

extension of filament
material (part relating the
Bride to the Handler of
Gravity)

cylinder
(piston?)

cylinder (piston?)

cage (vessel) containing
filament material
life centre (heart)

Bride's
'girl friends'

'artery' channelling
filament substance

desire-magneto

sex-cylinder (wasp)

admission tube for 'love
gasoline'

reservoir of love gasoline

1
Kether

3
Binah

2
Chokmah

Daath

Pillar of

Pillar of

5
Geburah

4
Chesed

Severity (female)

Mercy (male)

6
Tiphareth

8
Hod

7
Netzach

9
Yesod

10
Malkuth

FIGURE 16.9   The Kabbalists' Tree of Binah

214

One would thus need to establish correlations between the parts of the Bride's apparatus and points on the Tree of Binah (Figure 16.9).

It was noted that Duchamp's Bride has a "sex-cylinder" or "wasp" (S204) not actually rendered in the *Large Glass* (Figure 16.1). In the Kabbalists' rendering of the Tree superimposed on a human figure, the ninth point, Yesod, is specifically associated with the genitals. This point refers to the lower aspects of man. Duchamp, in his drawing of the "sex-cylinder" states: "*Ventilation*: Start from an interior *draft* –". Significantly, in the Kabbalah, the ninth point, Yesod, is also associated with the element air. One can thus explain Duchamp's reference to "ventilation" and a "draft". He informs us that at the base of the conical form of the "sex-cylinder", there are "admission tubes for the love gasoline" (AS 70), which one gleans, is stored in a "reservoir" below the cylinder. One thus needs to locate the "reservoir" of "love gasoline". It will have been noted that there is a point below Yesod at the bottom of the Tree, i.e. Malkuth (Figure 16.4) the tenth point, associated with the four elements, one of which is water. It may be that Duchamp, by referring to a "reservoir", has introduced masked reference to the element water here, for in general, water would be associated with the Bride, for She is known as "Marah, the Great Sea".[56] The organic container-like form at the base of the Bride image may be the "reservoir".

Another part of the apparatus is the "desire magneto" or "desire regulator" (AS 71). Again it seems that the Tree of Life forms the basis for the generation of this image. Desire would be associated with the seventh point on the Tree, Netzach, also connected with fire, this finding its point of correspondence in the idea of magento. Netzach, like Chokmah above, is connected with energy, and on the microcosmic level, with sexual instincts and emotions. This point is associated with Venus.

Bypassing the "desire magneto" is an "artery" channelling what Duchamp calls the "filament substance" from the "sex wasp" ("sex-cylinder"). The image of an artery is associated with the heart, this presumably referring us to the sixth point on the Tree. The "sex-wasp" is operated by a "pulse-needle" which functions in conjunction with a cog-wheel at the base of the cylinder. Duchamp notes that this needle points to the "life centre of the Bride", this comment probably alluding to the fact that the ninth point, Yesod (second from the bottom of the Tree) is linked to the sixth point, Tiphareth, the sephiroth denoted by the heart — the life centre. The heart and "life centre" of the Bride seems to have been denoted by what Duchamp calls the "isolated cage — Containing the filament substance". In one note, this cage is said to be an "open frame" (AS 71).

One should also be able to explain the presence of the tube or rod-like form to the right of the "reservoir" or "container" at the base of the Bride in the *Large Glass* (Figure 16.2). In position, we are orientated at Chesed, the fourth point on the Tree (mid-right), for the image associated with this sephiroth is a rod or wand. It is associated with the number four, and the idea of Love. This point

> is called the Cohesive or Receptive Intelligence because it contains all the Holy Powers, and from it emanates all the spiritual virtues with the most exalted essences.

It is also

> a stage of magnanimity and beneficence. Chesed means not only Mercy and Compas-

sion, but goodwill, loving kindness, and all that is associated with a Divine outpouring of unstinted providence.[57]

It seems possible that the rod-like form suspended from the bottom of the Bride is the extension of the "filament substance" to use Duchamp's phraseology (AS 72), this denoting the influence of the sphere or point, Chesed. Such a reading would be concordant with the reading of the last word of the title of the *Large Glass*, i.e. *même,* as a pun on *m'aime*, implying the "Bride loves me". This love would be transmitted through Chesed. This would explain why Duchamp states that the "Pendu swings in relation to the 4 cardinal points" (AS 70) — its zone of influence is unlimited. The image of the rod reminds us of the Tarot card of the Magician (also called the Juggler) who holds a wand (also a symbol of Chesed) in his left hand.[58] This is pointed downwards towards the earth. It is an instrument of divine influence from above. Such symbolism finds its counterpart in Duchamp characterisation, given that the *Pendu femelle* swings in relation to the four cardinal points — a reference to the earth. However, the symbolism is even more complex.

As noted, one of the main characters in the *Green Box*, not actually realised in the *Large Glass* itself, is the Handler of Gravity (AS 122), also referred to as the Juggler (AS 36). The reciprocal interaction of the Bride and Juggler is of importance, it having already been suggested that when man transforms himself, through the process of "stripping" the Bride, She reveals Herself, assisting the Bachelor (now the Juggler) in his task. This in turn leads to the mystic marriage, and ultimately, to the union of the Bride and Her partner, and the final ascent to the top of the Tree. The Juggler was to have been positioned on the mid-right, balancing on a ball, and is so rendered in sketches, and in a later etching, *The Large Glass Completed*. As suggested, he may well be the Christ figure in the *Large Glass*, the "magician-juggler" associated with the mid-point of the Tree, who is precariously balanced for an "instant". The complexities of this symbolism cannot be entered into here, but what is of relevance for the argument, is the fact that there is an implicit or potential connection between the Bride and the Juggler. Duchamp refers to an extension of the "filament substance", and indicates that it is the "part relating the pendu to the handler", and furthermore, "it resembles a solid flame, i.e. having a solid force. It licks the ball of the handler displacing it as it please" (AS 72). The image of the ball also evokes Chesed, for this like the wand, is one of the symbols associated with this point on the Tree.[59] The potential displacement of the ball would suggest that the balance and equilibrium of the Juggler (Handler of Gravity) is dependent on the Bride, Her influence being exerted through Chesed as defined by the symbol of the wand or rod. This influence may thus be positive and connected with Love, Mercy and Compassion. However, it should be borne in mind that she also has a negative aspect. Thus Duchamp, commenting on the "isolated cage", states that "the storms and fine weathers of the wasp" would take place here (AS 72).

In his discussion of the imagery and mechanics of the Bride, Duchamp introduced verbal references to liquids which undergo a process of transformation. We have already encountered "love gasoline". This is secreted by process of "osmosis" (AS 70), such botanical terminology possibly alluding to the Tree. We have encountered an artery, evoking blood and the image of the heart and thus the life centre. The artery channels the "filament paste" produced by the "sex-cylinder" to the "isolated cage". This filament substance, "extremely sensitive to differences of artificial atmospheric pressure controlled by the wasp" may resemble a "solid flame", and may "lengthen or shorten itself". Duchamp also introduced reference to dew in a note in which he states that the "hot plate" of the "sex-cylinder" will receive dew (AS 70), a substance which has rich connotations in the Western Inner Tradition.

In the Kabbalah, various fluids are associated with different points on the Tree, these in turn being correlated with the human figure.

1 Kether : brain fluid or dew
6 Tiphareth : blood
9 Yesod : semen
10 Malkuth : urine

The word dew or *ros* may have been the basis for the name Rosicrucian, although *rosa* or rose (a word of particular relevance for Duchamp) may have also been a source.[60] In the Kabbalah, dew is referred to as the brain fluid of the Ancient One (correlated with the top point on the Tree), and it is said:

"For the dew is as the dew of lights". "Of lights";
these are the shining of the whiteness of the Ancient One.
And by that dew are supported the holy ones above.
And it is the manna that is ground for just men in the world to come.[61]

For the Rosicrucians, this dew

is more tangible than a gas, and as the manna is said to have fallen from heaven, so this "dew" of thought trickles down between the hemispheres of the cerebrum and finally fills the third ventricle, which is the reservoir, so to speak of this heavenly water.[62]

From here, it passes through a funnel to the rest of the body. Duchamp may well have been inspired by such imagery, for we encounter not only dew, but also a reference to a reservoir, the reservoir of "love gasoline" (a modified form of dew?). Furthermore, the "sex-cylinder" is in the form of a funnel. Dew would thus seem to signify a nourishing substance from the highest source.

The Bride image in the *Large Glass* has been examined with reference to the Kabbalists' image of the Tree of Life and also the Tree associated with the third point, Binah, location of the Celestial Bride. A considerable number of concordances have been established which leads to the conclusion that the model has not been arbitrarily imposed on the *Large Glass* and *Green Box*. The complexity of the model has been stressed, it being noted that each point on the Tree is interconnected. Similarly, Duchamp's symbols are interconnected. The Tree itself can be understood on both the microcosmic as well as macrocosmic levels, defining both Man and the Creation, Man and his relationship to God. We are dealing with dynamic process, with a model for change and transformation, with states of consciousness, but also with the physical world. Interpretation of the *Large Glass* must take into account that meaning is not simply established through analysis of the fixed image of a Bride on a two-dimensional surface. Rather, we are encountering concepts vebally expressed in notes. Complex and very subtle hermetic allusion are contained in the notes, these alluding to processes rather than simply static unchangeable images. The process of interpretation is also a dynamic process, the spectator bringing to bear on the work his own creative act, this concept being in accord with Duchamp's conception of the role of the spectator.

Analysis of the work is complicated by the fact that images are at times multivalent, and also by the fact that we encounter many sub-texts, so to speak. In the analysis of the Bride image in the *Large Glass*, although focus has in part been placed on the machinery and its significance, it should be borne in mind that the Bride in the Kabbalah is virtually an unthinkable concept. In essence, we are dealing with one aspect of the God-head, i.e. the feminine aspect referred to as the Shekinah. She can be considered from many aspects, for She is the Great Mother, but also has a negative side. She is the "Architect of the Universe" but also the Law giver. As the Mother, She is a receptacle but also a machine to be activated by the Bridegroom, Chokmah. The third point, Binah, is "Understanding" and as

> The Third Intelligence is called the Sanctifying
> Intelligence,
> the Foundation of Primordial Wisdom; it is also called
> the Creator of Faith . . . It is the parent of faith
> whence faith emanates. [62]

That one cannot see Her face to face, that She in a sense "flirts" with the aspirant, that She is associated with Chronos but also Saturn, are all pertinent in an analysis of Duchamp's image, as an investigation of his characterisation has shown. That he has provided this "married divinity" with a partner has also been shown to be significant. Equally important, is Her interaction with the Handler of Gravity (Juggler). It has also been noted that other works by Duchamp echo themes associated with the Bride. Focus has been placed on imagery connected with the act of "stripping bare" and the significance of garment symbolism in his *oeuvre*. However, given the complexity of Kabbalistic symbolism, the sub-texts have not been analysed in detail. It must also, of course, be stressed that although the symbolic content is dependent on the Kabbalah, this argued to be a source for the generation of new symbols, Duchamp's *Large Glass* and *Green Box* are not simply illustrations or diagrams of the Tree of Life. Many other aspects could be considered, many other problems posed, including, for example, that of the significance of the readymade in an art-historical context. It has been suggested that Duchamp's work should be seen as a whole, that his works are interrelated. These too can also be analysed within terms of the Kabbalah.

Duchamp's image of the Bride and Bridegroom generates content as complex as the Kabbalah itself, for the moment we encounter Kabbalistic symbolism, we implicitly encounter the Kabbalah as a whole. It must thus be emphasised that focus has been placed on establishing points of congruence which facilitates analysis of one aspect of one image in the *Large Glass*, rather than being an account of the Kabbalah itself, a full understanding of which is undoubtedly a life-time task.

NOTES

1   J. Golding, *Duchamp: The Bride Stripped Bare by Her Bachelors, Even,* London, 1973, p.93. Research on Kabbalistic symbolism in Duchamp's *oeuvre* was initiated by J. Burnham, *Great Western Salt Works (Essays on the Meaning of Post-Formalist Art)*, New York, 1974. This subsequently became the subject of an unpublished Ph.D. thesis, R.T. Doepel, "Arcane Symbolism in Marchel Duchamp's *Large Glass* and Selected Works (1924–1927) by Joan Miró", Johannesburg, University of the Witwatersrand, 1985.

2   The letter S followed by a number refers to the illustrated catalogue in A. Schwarz, *The Complete Works of Marcel Duchamp*, New York, 1970.

3   For reproductions and translations of the notes in the *Green Box*, see M. Duchamp, *The Bride Stripped Bare by Her Bachelors, Even,* translated by G.H., Hamilton and R. Hamilton, projection at the top (also discernible in Duchamp's head of the "Bridegroom"), this being letters AS followed by a number refer to Schwarz's numbering of the notes.
    The original French title was *La Mariée mise à nu par ses célibataires, même.*

4   Texts on Kabbalistic and Christian Kabbalistic symbolism cited, include: G. Scholem, *On the Kabbalah and its Symbolism*, New York, 1965; G. Scholem, "Kabbalah" in *Encyclopaedia Judaica*, Jerusalem, 1972; D. Fortune, *The Mystical Qabalah*, New York, 1979; A.E. Waite, *The Holy Kabbalah*, New York, 1960; C. Poncé, *Kabbalah*, San Francisco, 1978; W. Gray, *The Ladder of Lights*, Cheltenham, 1975.

5   Scholem, *On the Kabbalah and its Symbolism*, op. cit. p. 108.

6   Fortune, *The Mystical Qabalah*, op. cit. p. 139.

7   It is difficult to establish whether or not Duchamp instigated the placing of the palm tree behind the *Large Glass*. However, it seems unlikely that Ulf Linde (who was responsible for the Stockholm replica of the *Large Glass* in 1961) would have allowed an arbitrary intrusion of such a dominant image in the environment. For a reproduction of this replica of the *Large Glass* with palm tree, see A. d'Harnoncourt and K. McShine, (eds), *Marcel Duchamp*, New York, 1973, p. 217.

8   Duchamp was personally involved in the decision to "frame" the *Large Glass* between two metal columns at the request of W. Arensberg. He is remembered as saying to Arensberg that he (Arensberg) would "get his columns". (Personal communication, Mrs E. Wrigley, Director of the Francis Bacon Foundation, Los Angeles, April 1986.) Arensberg, who had a special interest in the occult sciences, Kabbalah and especially the writings of Bacon, was undoubtedly familiar with the symbolic significance of the two columns, a symbol encountered in Bacon's work as well as the Kabbalah, Rosicrucianism and Freemasonry. (The original columns "framing" the work were removed by *c.* 1974.)

9   *Etant donnés* contains a three-dimensional reclining nude partially seen through peepholes in a closed door. One is not allowed to enter the room containing the nude or examine photographs of the actual interior. One is therefore reliant on hearsay evidence. As yet, the notes which constitute an "instruction manual" for assembling the work, have not been published.

10 A. Crowley, "Gematria", p. 25, in *The Qabalah of Aleister Crowley*, introduction I. Regardie, New York, 1973.

Duchamp made the decision to install the *Large Glass* in front of what originally appears to have been a kind of French door (subsequently converted to a window) which opened out onto a fountain.

11   Duchamp chose to place the *Large Glass* in such a position that one could see the fountain through the glass "window". He was not, however, responsible for the positioning of the fountain. In New York in 1915, he did a sketch, and noted: "Framing / the 2 glasses (in) / making a / a window ..." (Duchamp, *Notes*, Paris, 1980, n. 171). This supports the association of the *Large Glass* with a window. He wanted one to be able to "open" this window onto "a landscape of some kind (at will) / garden sea town". Significantly, the Bride is symbolised by the Great Sea which introduces water symbolism. This supports the argument that the conjunction of window and fountain (water) symbolism is pertinent. Even though Duchamp did not construct either the actual window or fountain, his siting of the work was not arbitrary. He did not, however, want the picture to stand out "against the background of natural light" (ibid.). One may glean from this note that fountain, water, window — rather than door symbolism (encountered elsewhere in his work) — is germane.

12   This is implicit rather than explicit. He refers in a note to a splash of liquid at the base (bottom right) of the *Large Glass* which then ascends to the top to form a "sculpture of drops" (AS 119). In another note, he refers to "splashes from upstream and down" (AS 76).

13   Personal communication, Dr J. Golding, London, April 1980. The Reliquary Guardian figure reproduced (Figure 16.7), often referred to as a Bakota figure, may have been produced by the Ossyeba or Mahongwe in Gabon. It was acquired by the Musée de l'Homme (Paris) in 1886. It was used in a variety of rituals, its primary function being a guardian of the ancestral skulls which were once placed in a basket at the bottom of the sculpture, this partially covering the bottom of the sculpted figure. The hollowed out form near the bottom of the central shaft could originally have contained a bag of magical substances considered to embody supernatural powers which it was believed, could be activated through human intervention. Neither the bag nor basket for this particular example have survived. The highly abstracted head has a projection at the top (also discernible in Duchamp's head of the "Bridegroom"), this being based on either a horn-image or hair style. There is no mouth (a feature also seen in Duchamp's characterisation), this finding its counterpart in the absence of the lower mandible of the skulls contained in the baskets of such sculptures. This is possibly because the dead neither eat nor talk. It is perhaps not fortuitous that Duchamp's Bridegroom image has no mouth, not simply because of the argued visual source for his image, but also because it is the Bride who voices the "authorisations and laws". It is also perhaps pertinent that Duchamp appears to have chosen a source with magical and religious connotations for his Bridegroom image, although it is not, of course, possible to evaluate the extent of his knowledge of the iconography of the reliquary figure. One can, however, be certain that it would have been fairly restricted. It should also be noted that the Musée de l'Homme had another similar piece, acquired in 1897 (gift from Charles Roche). (See S. Vogel and F. N'Diaye, *African Masterpieces from the Musée de l'Homme*, New York, 1985, pp. 148–9. Dr A. Nettelton (personal communication) has also assisted with interpretation of the reliquary figures.)

14   Duchamp, op. cit., n. 144.
     The head form referred to in n. 144 was to have functioned as a kind of visual leitmotiv, recalling or echoing the "head" of the Chocolate Grinder. In one sketch in the *Green Box* (S 203), it appears to be attached to the upper part of the Bride. However, in the *Large Glass,* it is clearly part of the Bakota-figure type image. Duchamp thus reverted back to his initial

visualisation of two figures, to be seen in the earlier painting of the *Bride*, August 1912 (S 194), for the sketch (S 203) dates from July 1913. The Bride image in the *Large Glass* was thus established before the sketches in the *Green Box*. (See AS 82, which echoes the form of the two separated figures; AS 71 — echoed in AS 78, and AS 70 — which has no visual correlation with the image in the *Large Glass*.)

15. Duchamp, *Notes*, op. cit. n. 96.

16   Golding, writing on *The Passage from Virgin to Bride*, comments "that we are not intended to 'read' the rest of the picture naturalistically or to identify its component parts in terms of specific body imagery", but notes that in the *Bride*, she regains "a semblance of anatomical legibility". He refers to the "empty armature of the head" of the Bride in the *Large Glass*, and sees the "sex cylinder" as being attached to the "head" (*Duchamp . . .* op. cit. pp. 41–4).

17   M. Duchamp, recorded interview with R. and G.H. Hamilton, BBC, 1959 (*Audio Arts Magazine*, 1978, Vol. 2 No. 4, ed. W. Furlong). Duchamp reiterated this comment to Dr J. Golding (op. cit. p. 43).

18   R.T. Doepel, "Duchamp and Ezechiel", *de Arte*, September 1985 (33), p. 26.

19   M. Sanouillet and E. Peterson (eds), *The Essential Writings of Marcel Duchamp*, New York, 1981, p. 106.

20   Waite, *The Holy Kabbalah*, op. cit. p. 341.

21   Ibid., p. 352.

22   A. Crowley, "Liber 777", in *The Qabalah of Aleister Crowley*, p. 106.

23   This argument is more fully developed in Doepel, "Duchamp and Ezechiel", op. cit. pp. 27–30.

24   For a detailed discussion of the Kabbalah as a model for Duchamp, see Doepel, "Arcane Symbolism . . .", op. cit.. This article is mostly based on research undertaken for this thesis.

25   Waite, *The Holy Kabbalah*, op. cit., p. 374.

26   G. Sassoon and R. Dale, (eds.), *The Kabbalah Decoded*, London, 1978, p. 105.

27   Fortune, *The Mystical Kabbalah*, op. cit. p. 151.

28   Golding, *Duchamp . . .*, op. cit. p. 53.

29   Poncé, *Kabbalah*, op. cit. p. 221.

30   Golding, *Duchamp . . .*, op. cit. p. 60.

31   M.P. Hall, *Man: Grand Symbol of the Mysteries*, Los Angeles, 1977, p. 190.

32   Duchamp, *Notes*, op. cit. n. 147.

33   Poncé, *Kabbalah*, op. cit. p. 220.

34   M.P.G. Hall, *The Secret Teachings of All ages*, Los Angeles, 1977, p. CXXXI.

35   *Zohar*, translated by H. Sperling et al., Introduction J. Abelson, London, 1931–34, Vol. 111, p. 300 (italics added).

36   These nine holes probably also define the concept of the Tree denoting the "World of Points" (see Doepel, "Arcane Symbolism . . .", op. cit. pp. 527–31).

37   Duchamp, *Notes*, op. cit. n. 80.

38   M. Duchamp, recorded interview with R. and G.H. Hamilton, op. cit.

39   M. Duchamp, "The Creative Act" (1957) in L.D. Steefel, *The Position of Duchamp's Large Glass in the Development of His Art*, New York and London, 1977, pp. 266–9.

40   Scholem, *On The Kabbalah . . .*, op. cit. p. 68.

41   Waite, *The Holy Kabbalah . . .*, op. cit. p. 341.

42   Scholem, *On The Kabbalah . . .*, op. cit. p.103.

43   Gray, *The Ladder of Lights*, op. cit. p. 177.

44   Ibid. p. 175.

45 Duchamp, *Notes*, op. cit. n. 153.

46 Duchamp's use of the word "emanation" is considered significant, for it directs us to the Kabbalists' concept of the "World of Emanation". (See Scholem, "Kabbalah", col. 580).

47 Schwarz, *The Complete Works of Marcel Duchamp*, op. cit. p. 463.

48 Duchamp, *Notes*, op. cit. n. 154.

49 M. Sadhu, *The Tarot*, London, 1975, p. 173.

50 For a discussion of Christ symbolism in the *Large Glass*, see R.T. Doepel, "Duchamp's Coding System", Proceedings of the First Conference of the South African Association of Art Historians, Dept. of Fine Arts History, University of Natal, July 1985, pp. 95–106.

51 Doepel, "Arcane Symbolism . . .", op. cit. pp. 206ff., 843–77.
A detailed comparative analysis of the two works reveals astonishing visual parallels, not only with regard to proportional relationships and positioning of forms, but also motifs. For example, the watermill in the *Large Glass*, although seen from a different viewpoint, seems to have been based on the image in the manuscript. If the two works are reduced to the same scale and superimposed, the Bride in the *Large Glass* is neatly positioned in the rectangular frame in the upper-left of the manuscript illustration, and the lines of the two waterwheels are found to coincide. Visual parallels with this, and other illustrations in the manuscript (at present the subject of research for a book) can be established. These are so close as to suggest that Duchamp must have seen the manuscript.

52 Duchamp, *The Bride Stripped Bare by Her Bachelors, Even*, n.p.

53 Fortune, *The Mystical Kabbalah*, op. cit., pp. 150–51.

54 Ibid.

55 The Western Inner Tradition Kabbalist would normally aspire to "locating" himself at Tiphareth, the mid-point on the Tree.

56 Fortune, *The Mystical Kabbalah*, op. cit. p. 139.

57 Ibid. p. 161.

58 For illustrations of Tarot Cards, see B. Butler, *The Definitive Tarot*, London, 1975.

59 Fortune, *The Mystical Kabbalah*, op. cit. p. 161.

60 Hall, *The Secret Teachings . . .*, op. cit. p. CXXXIX.
Duchamp used the name "Rrose" from time to time, which introduces symbolic references to the rose as well as the androgyne, both of which refer us to the mid-point on the Tree of Life.

61 Sassoon and Dale, *The Kabbalah Decoded*, op. cit. p. 7.

62 Hall, *Man . . .*, op. cit. p. 145.

63 Fortune, *The Mystical Kabbalah*, op. cit. p. 139.

ACKNOWLEDGEMENTS

I would like to express my gratitude to the staff of the Philadelphia Museum of Art, the Musée de l'Homme (Paris), the Bodleian Library (Oxford), Mr M.P. Hall (Los Angeles), for assistance in obtaining illustrations and copyright, and to the Central Graphics Department (University of the Witwatersrand) for the production of diagrams.

The Human Sciences Research Council provided financial assistance, which made it possible to study works *in situ*.

I would also like to express my appreciation to Dr J. Golding for his continued support.

Part VI
The Holy Land in Islam

17 The birth of Islam in the Holy Land

Moshe Sharon

I

The formative period of Islam and Islamic civilisation is probably one of the best-documented periods in history. Yet, in spite of the tremendous abundance of traditions relating to every conceivable aspect of the inception and development of early Islam, the questions concerning the nature and circumstances of the appearance of Islam in history are becoming more and more fundamental and difficult to answer.

The fact that Islamic history has had to be reconstructed almost solely on the basis of Islamic tradition, and the fact that this tradition has been shaped and reshaped and contaminated by later political rivalries, theological disputes and social tensions, throws the whole field of Islamic histgraphy open to debate. The attitude of modern historians of Islam oscillates between complete and almost complete rejection of Islamic tradition as an inadequate source for the reconstruction of early Islamic history, as was done by Crone and Cook in *Hagarism*,[1] and full acceptance of the tradition as an authentic reproduction of Islamic history.

II

For more than a century modern orientalism has created the tools needed for the appropriate evaluation of Islamic tradition, taking into consideration that, in most cases, this tradition represents the history not as it was, but rather as it should have been, according to the motives and needs of whoever compiled the tradition.[2]

Already in 1916, Snouck Hurgronje, commenting on Paul Casanova's *Mohammad et la Fin du Mond*, published in 1911, summarised the problems facing modern Islamic historical research:

The generations that worked at the biography of the Prophet were too far removed

225

from his time to have true data or notions; and, moreover, it was not their aim to know the past as it was, but to construct a picture of it as it ought to have been according to their opinion.[3]

Although Snouck Hurgronje's remarks are concerned mainly with the *sīrah*, they are valid for Islamic tradition relating to the inception of Islamic civilisation in general.

The extent of the falsification and invention of tradition was put on record by Goldziher, who described the methods of invention and the historical circumstances in which invention took place, as well as the motives behind such invention.[4]

At the turn of the nineteenth century, Julius Wellhausen laid the foundations for the critical reading of the historical account along the same principles. He made it clear that information can be gathered even from doubtful statements. Such statements, he remarked, do not necessarily lose their significance, "for invention must have its motive, and motive is all that we require."[5]

The abundance of material of this nature naturally allows for many interpretations. Far from wishing to deny the existence of the Prophet or from discarding Islamic tradition altogether, I wish to offer another interpretation of Islamic historical tradition which deviates from the classical, generally accepted, framework for the birth of Islam. At this stage, I shall follow Paul Casanova's example, namely to present the theory and leave the more detailed proofs for other publications.[6]

III

The generally accepted picture of the birth of Islam follows the lines of Islamic tradition, in that it accepts the fact that Islam was created in Arabia as a result of Muḥammad's activity in Mecca and Madīnah. From the Arabian Centre it went out to conquer the remnants of the world of antiquity and create a new Empire and a new civilisation.

The fact that at its inception as a political and religious force Islam experienced tremendous convulsions in the form of civil wars which led to permanent schisms in it, has been explained by the assertion that after the death of Muhammad the authority of his successors in Madīnah was challenged by various groups of Muslims.[7]

In opposition to the theory of the unified beginning, I believe that Islamic tradition tells us a different story. The activity of the Prophet in Arabia, the nature and details of which we can only guess, brought into existence groups or communities of *mu'minūn*, believers first in Arabia and then, after the collapse of both the Sassanians and the Byzantines, also outside Arabia — notably in Iraq, Syria and Mesopotamia, in addition to the community in Madīnah and probably also in North and East Arabia. Each one of these communities had a leader called *amīr al-mu'minīn* — literally, the chief of the faithfuls. This is why it is possible to find few *amīrs* at the same time. The group called *khawārij* had its *amīr al-mu'minīn* as well as the Kufaite community which was led by 'Alī, who came to be called *amīr al-mu'minīn par excellence*,[8] and a group of *mu'minūm* in Yamāmah.[9]

One of the most important groups of *mu'minūn* was led by members of the Umayyad family in Syria, while another, the *mu'minūn* of Madīnah, was led by 'Abdāllah b.

226

Zubayr. At this early stage, namely during the first half of the seventh century, the term *Islam* did not yet denote a common defined faith for these *mu'minūn* communities. They derived their initial monotheistic inspiration from the Prophet (or perhaps from more than one Prophet), but under the influence of the Jewish, Christian and classical environments they developed along separate lines.

IV

The most important development took place in Syria. Following the tradition of the Arab rulers of the Syrian desert, the Ghassānides, the first Umayyad leaders, obtained — most probably from the Byzantine emperor — the title of Phylarch or *malik*, in addition to being the chiefs of the faithfuls, *amīr al-mu'minīn*.[10]

The later, unified Islamic traditions, which on the whole assumed an anti-Umayyad character, stressed the fact that the Umayyads were *mulūk*. The term *malik* in these traditions has a negative connotation: the aim of the enemies of the Umayyad was to show that the Umayyads should not be regarded as legitimate *khulafā'*, or caliphs — substitutes to the Prophet — but rather as temporal "kings". In reality, however, the traditions preserved an accurate historical message. The title *malik* was the traditional title of the Ghassānid Arab kings of Syria, who are known in Arab legend as *mulūk ash-shām*.[11] At least one of these kings, al-Hārith V, obtained from the Byzantine emperor Justinian in 529 the titles of *patricius* and Phylarch.[12] The Umayyads, who had established themselves in Syria long before the date suggested by tradition for the appearance of Islam, emerged eventually as the heirs to the Ghassānid authority as well as to the Ghassānid title. There are also grounds for assuming that the Umayyads forged positive relations with the Byzantine rulers in Syria and probably even with the emperor in Constantinople. The story about the meeting between Abū Sufyān and the Byzantine emperor Heraclius around the year 628, although of a legendary-polemic nature, could not have been invented without some factual basis. It would have been difficult to describe this legendary meeting had Abū Sufyān or any other prominent Umayyad not indeed met high-ranking Byzantine officials. It should not be surprising, therefore, that the Umayyads emerged and were accepted as the *mulūk* of Syria as well as the *amirs,* leaders of the faithfuls, *mu'minūn*.[13] It is the term *khalīfah* which is of no meaning or relevance in this period prior to the creation of the unified and standardised Islamic historical tradition. The first known Umayyad leader of the *mu'minūn* in Syria was Mu'āwiyah, although there are indications that his brother Yazīd must have preceded him.

The appearance of the Umayyads as the leaders of the *mu'minūn* and the "kings" of the Syrian Arabs constitutes an internal contradiction within the standard Islamic history. On the one hand, the majority of the Umayyads have been presented as bad Muslims and usurpers, but on the other hand the first two known Umayyad rulers of Syria were "nominated" by no less than 'Umar, the second Caliph in the standard Islamic *heilige Geschichte*.

It is clear that in the history of the unified beginning of Islam, the existence of

Umayyad rule in Syria could not have been ignored. The only way to incorporate it into the ideal, centrally controlled Islamic state, carefully and conveniently arranged by the later Muslim historians, was by having the Umayyad rulers of Syria "installed" in their positions by the second and third Caliphs of the standard unified beginning. In reality, however, we must treat the Umayyads in Syria as an independent phenomenon in the long process of the creation of Islam.

Mu'āwiyah crowned himself as a *malik* in Jerusalem. An act of this kind, if the tradition is true, would have been meaningful for both the Christian Arabs of Syria and the *mu'minūn* community, without really challenging the supreme Byzantine authority, which, as we have pointed out, bestowed similar titles on some of the great Arab leaders.[10]

It is difficult to ascertain exactly what Mu'āwiyah's *imān* or faith was. Even if one takes into consideration the fact that the later anti-Umayyad traditions made an effort to blemish him and his son, it is clear that his relations with Christianity were very close. He relied in his rule on the Arab tribe of Kalb that was, on the whole, Christian, and consolidated his alliance with this tribe by marrying the Christian daughter of one of its leaders, who bore him a son, Yazīd, whom he chose to be his heir. A prince who had grown up among both Christian and *mu'minūn* communities was the natural choice to lead the Christian Arabs of Syria as well as the *mu'minūn* community there.

The faith of these early Umayyad *amīrs* of the faithfuls far from resembled the Islam which evolved later. Around the core of the *mu'minūn* community was a large contingent of Christian Arabs, Jews and Samaritans with a very sophisticated scriptural tradition based upon the names of biblical prophets, kings and saints. This scriptural tradition, in addition to being recorded and popular, was supported by the holy places of antiquity. These impressive holy places were connected with the Christian dogma of salvation as well as with the concrete message of the Jewish prophets, and the Jewish historical and eschatological tradition.

Accepting the historical seniority of the Jewish and Christian revelations, the *mu'minūn* of Syria shared with the Jews and Christians not only their prophets and saints, but also their places of worship. Whichever way one looks at it, the fact is that *mu'minūn* and Christians shared the Cathedral of St John in Damascus, and in all probability many other Christian houses of worship too.[14]

For Mu'āwiyah and other early Umayyads, including 'Abd al-Malik, Jerusalem was a holy city in the biblical sense of the word. For the populations of Syria, of all religions, she was the stage of ancient prophecy and linked in one way or another with such great names as Abraham, David, Solomon and Jesus of Nazareth.

The earliest existing inscriptions, with which we shall presently deal, attest to the fact that the *mu'minūn* in Syria and the official church were locked in a fundamental debate concerning the nature of Jesus. There was nothing new in such a debate: the church itself had been torn because of it for centuries, and every ecumenical council called to deal with the problem had only led to the birth of yet another Christian "heresy". In this context, one can easily understand the involvement of the *mu'minūn* in this debate.

Jerusalem was important in the context of this debate: the *mu'minūn* stressed its connection with the general prophetic side in which Jesus was also included, while the

Christians emphasised its being the place where the history of salvation began and would be completed. It was Jerusalem of the Crucifixion, the Resurrection and the Second Coming.

This brings us to the enigmatic building of the Dome of the Rock. According to the much-discussed tradition recorded by Ya'qūbī,[15] 'Abd al-Malik is said to have conceived the idea of diverting the Ḥajj from Mecca to Jerusalem, and for this reason he built the Dome over the Rock on the Temple Mount in Jerusalem. Goldziher accepted the tradition completely, while Goitein rejected it as a Shī'ite fabrication.[16]

In fact, Ya'qūbī's tradition tells us a story in the reverse. The Dome of the Rock, a unique monument with apparently no real function, is the key to the re-evaluation of the circumstances surrounding the beginning of Islam. Once we understand the true meaning of the Dome of the Rock we will have a true picture of the birth of Islam as a unified religion out of the diversity of the *mu'minūn* communities.

V

'Abd al-Malik was a ruler with great vision and no less ambition. After a long crisis, he re-established Umayyad rule in Syria with himself at the head of the *mu'minūn* community, and proceeded to bring under his rule the two other major centres of *mu'minūn*: Iraq and Ḥijāz. His problems in Syria were more theological than political, for under the influence of both Christianity and Judaism, the *mu'minūn* community could have easily lost its independent identity, taking into consideration that the great Arab tribes of Syria had long ago been converted to Christianity. There was a great need, therefore, to erect for the Syrian *mu'minūn* a centre of worship that took into account the attachment to past holy history and yet emphasised the uniqueness of the new faith. The inscription, dated 72/691, some 240 metres long in the Dome of the Rock, tells the story.[17] The inscription has three distinct motives: first, the acceptance of all prophets as true prophets and of their revelations as authentic; second, the absolute rejection of the Sonship of Jesus and the insistence on his being a human prophet, though with a divine spirit; and third, for the first time, the presentation of Muhammad as the most important of all prophets and of Islam as the name of the true religion.[18] The Dome of the Rock was thus built as the major sanctuary of Islam and as a symbol of its superiority over the other religions.[19] *Islam* was born as a term which was to unify all the groups of *mu'minūn* under the slogan of *dīn al-ḥaqq*, the "true religion" with which Muhammad was sent in order to rule over all the other religions.[20] Islam was also declared the religion of the state, though the state was not yet unified.

VI

The Dome of the Rock was built mainly for the *mu'minūn* of Syria, with no relation whatsoever to the *ka'bah* in Mecca, for at that time the *ka'bah* was not in 'Abd al-Malik's hands, and was not yet part of his reforms. When they did not use the Christian churches for worship, the *mu'minūn* of Syria and Egypt (who shared the same religious cultural world) built their own mosques, with the *qiblah*, the direction of prayer, turned to the *east*.

The traditions about east-facing *qiblah* in the mosque of 'Amr b. al-'Āṣ in Fustaṭ cannot be accidental. Yāqūt, who wrote early in the thirteenth century, quoting earlier sources, says that "eighty disciples of the Prophet *(ṣaḥābah)"* supervised the building of this mosque. "The *qiblah*," he says, was "very much turned towards the east" (*musharraqah jidan)"*. True, the printed text of Yāqūt's geographical dictionary says that the *qiblah* was only "slightly turned to the east" but, Yāqūt's sources, as we shall presently see, attest to the correct reading. Yāqūt himself or, more probably, one of the copiests of his book erroneously copied the word *qalīlan* (slightly) from the following sentence in his book.

Ibn Duqmāq, on the authority of earlier sources, refers to a similar tradition which also points out the fact that "eighty of the *ṣaḥābah* (the names of few of whom are mentioned) were present when the *qiblah* of the mosque was built, and it is said that it was very much turned to the east, and that Qurrah b. Sharīk, after he had destroyed the mosque at the time of (caliph) Walīd b. 'Abd al-Malik, (he rebuilt it and) turned its *qiblah* slightly to the south *(tayāman bihā qualīlan)"*.

Also Maqrizi, quoting al-Kindi, describes in detail the building of the same *qiblah*. In his tradition not eighty *ṣaḥābah* attended the building but eight and some say that there were only four. 'Amr b. al-'Āṣ instructed the builders saying "turn the *qiblah* to the east and you will be facing the sanctuary" *(sharriqū al-qiblah tuṣību al-Ḥaram)"*. The "sanctuary in this tradition, cannot mean the sanctuary of Mecca. Yazīd b. Ḥabīb who is quoted as the source for this account adds that the *qiblah* was then "built turned very much towards the east *(fa-shurriqat jiddan)* and 'Amr b. al-'Āṣ when he prayed in the Friday mosque *(masjid al-jāmī)* used to turn in prayer almost completely towards the east *(yuṣallī nāḥiyat ash-sharq illā ash-shay' al-yasīr)."*

The end of this tradition is, however, of extreme importance for our discussion. An eyewitness is quoted as saying: "I saw 'Amr b. al-'Āṣ entering a church and he prayed therein and he did not turn away from their (namely, the Christians') *qiblah* but very little *(dakhal kanīsah fa-ṣalla fīhā wa-lam yanṣarif 'an quiblatihim illā qalīlan)."*

The number of the *ṣaḥābah*, mentioned as present at the building of 'Amr's mosque alternates in the various traditions between eighty, eight, four and two. The number, however, is not the important factor, because the *ṣaḥābah* presence was indicated to lend the traditions about the eastern *qiblah* a status of high authority.

The fact that 'Amr b. al-'Āṣ is said to have prayed in a church could not be unusual, for the early *mu'minūn* shared the churches with the Christians. The additional note that 'Amr turned a fraction from the Christian *qiblah* may very well be a later insertion indicating that 'Amr did not want to look completely like a Christian.

These traditions about the mosque of 'Amr b. al-'As in Fustāṭ with its east-facing direction of prayer should not surprise us. For the *mu'minūn* in the Christian-dominated territories mosques could not have been different from the churches that had their apses facing east.[21]

Exciting archaeological proof of the tradition concerning the eastward direction of prayer in the early mosques of Syria exists not far from Be'er Orah in the Negev. There I

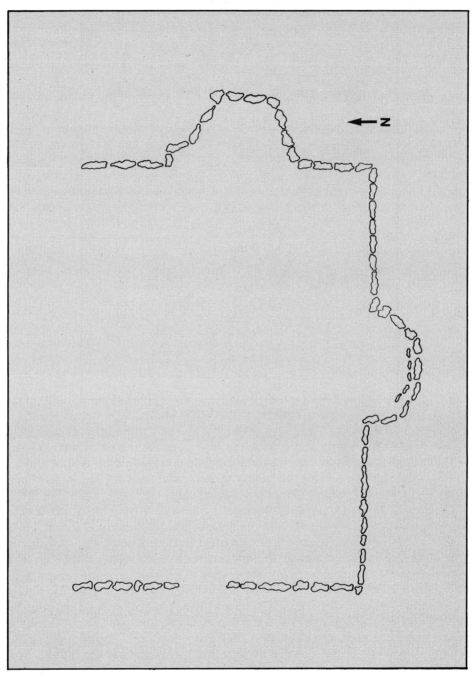

FIGURE 17.1   Schematic plan of the mosque in Be'er Orah

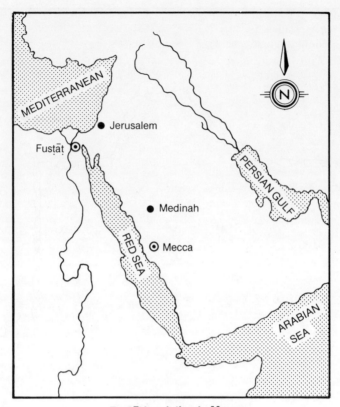

Fusṭāṭ in relation to Mecca

found an open mosque with two miḥrābs, one facing east and one facing south (Figure 17.1). The one facing south was clearly a later addition made after 'Abd al-Malik's reforms came into effect. This little desert mosque symbolises the last stage of our theory.[22]

The building of the Dome of the Rock did not provide 'Abd al-Malik with a fully satisfying answer to the problem of how to emphasise the superiority of Islam and turn it into the religion of the unified state. Jerusalem could well have been an adequate religious place of worship for the Syrians and the Egyptians, but it meant nothing to the Iraqis, the Hijāzies or the Mesopotamians. A place of worship which would represent the centrality of Muḥammad, the Arab nature of the new religion and which would be totally independent of all other religions, yet connected with the biblical genealogy, had yet to be found. The choice fell on Mecca and the *ka'bah*. On the one hand there existed the ancient tradition connecting the *ka'bah*, or Mecca in general, with Abraham, and on the other hand there was no question that the activity of the Prophet had begun there. 'Abd al-Malik decided to make Mecca into the sanctuary *par excellence* of the new state religion that he had begun in Syria, but first he had to conquer it, as it was ruled by another *amīr al-mu'minīn*, 'Abdallah b. Zubayr. Moreover, there was a unique connection between 'Abdallah b. Zubayr, the Prophet and the *ka'bah*. This connection was stressed by traditions originating in the Zubayrid family.

The poet al-'Uqaylī praises 'Abdallah b. Zubayr as a righteous person who had the knowledge to interpret the Prophet's words and as a godly man who dwells in the *ka'bah* like one of its doves.

The Prophet was so fond of 'Abdallah b. Zubayr that he called his beloved wife, 'Ā'ishah, who in reality was 'Abdallah's maternal aunt, *"umm 'abdallah"*, 'Abdallah's mother. The special relation of 'Abdallah to the *ka'bah* is further attested by the fact that he was called *'ā'idh al-bayt*, he who finds refuge in the House (namely, the *ka'bah*).[23]

In 693, two years after the building of the Dome of the Rock, Mecca was conquered. The conquest of Mecca was the final stage in ascertaining the establishment of the unity of Islam. In the Islamic tradition the event is marked as the time in which the various *mu'minūn* communities rallied around 'Abd al-Malik. It is not far-fetched to assume that 'Abd al-Malik's conquest of Mecca, which marks the beginning of Islam's imperial history, was retrospectively introduced into Muḥammad's *sīrah* as the major event in the Prophet's career. In the *sīrah*, it was the Prophet who conquered Mecca and purified the *ka'bah*, with the Umayyad Abū Sufyān playing a major role in the whole affair.

'Abd al Malik ordered the *ka'bah* to be destroyed and rebuilt according to what was officially declared to be the Prophet's *original* plan. Symbolically it meant that Ibn Zubayr's sanctuary was not really the Prophet's sanctuary. In the year 76/695 'Abd al-Malik prepared the pilgrimage to Mecca, demonstratively inaugurating the new *ka'bah* and giving an official public expression to the elevated position of Mecca.[24]

The new *ka'bah* thus represented the culmination of 'Abd al-Malik's reforms: a central independent Arab sanctuary was finally established with the Prophet at its centre, and now the Ḥajj could be diverted, also for the Syrians, from Jerusalem to Mecca. Ya'qūbī, either intentionally or because in his time the true meaning of 'Abd al-Malik's reforms was forgotten, inverted the tradition and reported a story which made sense to him that the Ḥajj was diverted from Mecca to Jerusalem. All the mosques were then ordered to have their former eastward-directed *qiblahs* changed to face Mecca. This is when our little mosque in the Negev had its southern *qiblah* added to it. The traditionalists, who could not envisage the birth of Islam in the Holy Land, could not have known that in the order of the development of early Islam, Jerusalem preceded Mecca. That they had, however, a notion of this development is attested by the fact that a tradition was preserved in the *sīrah* stressing the fact that Jerusalem was the *qiblah* before Mecca. It is probably here that we have to look for the roots of the tradition which assure us that at the End of Days the *ka'bah* will be conducted to Jerusalem "like the bride conducted to her bridegroom".[25]

NOTES

1   P. Crone, and M. Cook, *Hagarism*, Cambridge, 1977.
2   That tradition was invented to suit political, social, religious, economic and other needs was a well-known fact to Muslim scholars. They even classified the motives behind the invention of

ḥadīth, but they used methods of ḥadīth criticism that were almost no use for ascertaining anything about either the information included in the traditions or their origins. See Abū al-Faraj, 'Abd ar-Raḥmān b. 'Alī b. al-Jawzī, Kitāb al-Mawḍū'āt, ed. 'Abd ar-Raḥmān Muḥammad 'Uthmān, Madinah, 1966, I, pp. 37–47; 'Alī b. Muḥammad b. 'Araq al-Kinānī, Tanzīh ash-Sharī'ah al-Marfū'ah 'an al-akhbār ash-Shanī'ah al-Mawḍū'ah, ed. 'Abd al-Laṭīf et al., Beirut, 1979, I, p. 13.

3 C. Snouck Hurgronje, Mohammedanism, New York and London, 1916, p. 23.

4 I. Goldziher, Muslim Studies, ed. S.M. Stern, II, Oxford, 1971, pp. 126f.

5 J. Wellhausen, The Arab Kingdom and its Fall, translated by Wier, 1927, Khayats reprints, Beirut, 1969, p. 505.

6 For another view of Arab conquest of Syria see M. Sharon, "The military reforms of Abū Muslim" in M. Sharon (ed.), Studies in Islamic History and Civilization, Jerusalem, 1986, pp. 105–12, and forthcoming "The Umayyads as ahl al-bayt" in JSAI, 1988.

7 The idea that harmony and unity characterised the beginning of Islam was expressed in a tradition which attributes to one of the Prophet's disciples the following words: "At the time of the Prophet, may Allah save him and give him peace, our faces were all turned in one direction, but after the death of the Prophet ... we turned ourselves hither and thither" Nu'aym b. Ḥammād al-Marwazī, Kitāb al-Fitan, MS BM or 9449 fol 6b.

8 Muḥammad b. Abū al-Qāsim b. 'Alī aṭ-Ṭabarī, Bishārat al-Muṣṭafā li-Shī'at al-Murtaḍā Najaf 1383/1963, p. 186.

9 These were the followers of the prophet Musaylimah, who was called amīr al-Mu'minīn. There can hardly be a question that the term, describing the leadership of a community of monotheists, existed before Muḥammad and during his time, and the usage of this term by him and by his successors was not a novelty. See Mughulṭāy, Az-Zahr al-Bāsim fī Sīrat Abī al-Qāsim, Ms. Leiden, or 370 fols, 213b–214a, (on the title used by Musaylimah). Aḥmad b. Hajar al-Haytamī, aṣ-Ṣawā'iq al-Muḥriqah, ed. 'Abd al-Wahhāb 'Abd al-Laṭīf, Cairo, 1375, p. 88 regarding its usage by the Prophet for 'Abdullah b. Jaḥsh (I wish to thank Professor M.J. Kister for furnishing me with these important sources.)

10 The fact that Mu'āwiyah was called concurrently with the others by the title of amīr al-mu'minīn is attested by the fact that later traditions tried to prove the contrary. See Dhahbī, Siyar A'lām an-Nubalā, ed. Munajjid, Cairo, n.d. I, p. 82; 'Abd ar-Razzāq, Muṣannaf, ed. al-A'ẓamī, Beirut 1392/1972, X, p. 371, where Mu'āwiyah reportedly says: "You are the mu'minūn and I am your amīr".

11 Y a'qūbī, Ta'rīkh, Beirut, 1379/1960, I, pp. 206–7.

12 M. Sharon, "The cities of Palestine under the Islamic rule" Cathedra, 40, Jerusalem, 1986, p. 99 (Hebrew) and note; C. Brockelmann, History of the Islamic Peoples, London, 1956, p. 7.

13 Abū Faraj al-Iṣbahānī, Kitāb al-Aghānī, Būlāq, 1284–1285, rep. Beirut, 1390/1970, VI, pp. 94–5. It is clear that the aim of the tradition is to prove that Muḥammad's Prophethood was foretold by the Christians and recognised by no less than the Emperor Heraclius himself, who symbolises, in this type of tradition, Christendom as well as Christianity.

14 See Balādhurī, Futūḥ al-Buldān, ed. M.J. De Goeje, Leiden, pp. 125–6-. cf. G. Le Strange, Palestine under the Moslems, London, 1890, p. 231.

15 Ya'qūbī, op. cit. II, p. 261.

16 I. Goldziher, op. cit. pp. 44–5 and n.1 in p. 45; S.D. Goitein, "The historical background of the erection of the Dome of the Rock", Journal of the American Oriental Society, LXX, 1950, pp.

104–8; and the extensive study of O. Grabar "The Umayyad Dome of the Rock in Jerusalem", *Ars Orientalis*, III, 1959, pp. 33ff.

17 The long inscription above the arches of the inner arcade (on both sides) is supplemented by two inscriptions on copper plates on the northern and eastern gates of the Dome (removed in 1973 and never returned to their places). Published by M. Van Berchem, *Matériaux pour un Corpus Inscriptionum Arabicarum, Jerusalem, Haram* (II B2), Le Caire, 1927, nos. 215, 216, 217, pp. 228–55; E. Combe, J. Sauvaget and G. Wiet, *Repertoire Chronologique d'Épigraphie arabe*, Cairo 1931 . . . nos. 9–11).

18 The verses Qur'ān, 3: 18–19 were carefully, and entirely, quoted at the end of the inner face of the inscription.

19 Cf. Grabar, op. cit., p. 44a.

20 Qur'ān, 9:33.

21 See Yāqūt, *Mu'jam al-Buldān*, (ed. Wuestenfeld) Leipzig, 1866–1873, *s.v.* "Fustāt"; Ibn Duqmāq, *Kitab al-intisār*, I, pp. 62f.; Maqrizi, *Khitat*, II, pp. 246–7, 249; IBn Taghri Birdi *An-Nujūm az-Zāhirah*, Cairo, 1936, pp. 66–7; S. Basheer, *Muqaddimah fi at-Ta'rikh Al-Akhar*, Jerusalem, 1984, p. 60. See also Kindi, *Wulāt*, p. 13, where it is stated that 'Amr's *qiblah* faced Yaḥmūm, a mountain range to the east of Fustāt. The mosque of 'Amr b. al-'Āṣ in Cairo was not turned directly to the east but towards the winter sun rising point in the northern hemisphere, namely in 117°. See G. Hawkins and D. King, in *J.H.A.*, XIII, (1982), pp. 102–9; D. King, *Muqarnas*, 2, (1984) pp. 73–84. Thanks are due to Dr A. Elad and U. Avner from the Hebrew University for drawing my attention to many of these references.

22 B. Rothenberg, *Timna, Valley of the Biblical Copper Mines*, London, 1972, p. 221 and Figure 71. For Beno Rothenberg who was the first to describe the structure near Be'er Orah, the mosque was an enigma. The archaeologist Uzzi Avner, who drew my attention to the mosque, reported large quantities of Umayyad pottery in the place. The structure is far more complete than what appears in Rothenberg's drawing.

23 See. Muṣ'ab b. 'Abdallah az-Zubayri, *Nasab Quraysh*, ed. E. Levi-Provançal, Cairo, 1953, pp. 237–9, Balādhuri, *Ansāb al-Ashrāf*, IVB, ed. M. Schoessinger, Jerusalem, 1938, pp. 17 (1. 6), 19 (1. 15), 21(1. 21: where 'Abdallah b. Zubayr reportedly says: "I am only a dove among the doves of this sanctuary"), 25 (1. 11), 27 (1. 9), 29 (1. 4), 52 (1. 21), 54 (1. 8); V, ed. S.D. Goitein, Jerusalem, 1936, p. 363 (1. 12). 'Abdallah b. az-Zubayr's supporters were referred to as *ahl al-masjid* (Dinawari, *al-Akhbār aṭ-Tiwāl*, ed. 'Abd al-Mun'im 'Āmir and Jamāl ad-Din ash-Shayyāl, Cairo, 1960, pp. 266 (1. 1), 314 (1. 9).

24 See Balādhuri, *Ansāb al-Ashrāf* XI, = *Anonyme arabische Chronik*, ed. W. Ahlwardt, Griefswald, 1883, p. 177f. *Aghāni*, IV, p. 52. One tradition in the *Aghāni* leaves no doubt as to the importance of the year 73/693. This is not only "the year of unity" but also the year in which the Caliphate of 'Abd al-Malik only begins: "when 'Abd al-Malik assumed his functions as caliph in the Year of the Unity." Ibid. p. 102.

25 See Al-Wāsiti, *Faḍā'il al-Bayt al-Muqaddas*, ed. I. Hasson, Jerusalem, 1979. English translation of some of the most relevant traditions for our discussion in I. Hasson, "Muslim literature in praise of Jerusalem", *The Jerusalem Cathedre*, Jerusalem, 1981, pp. 177–83.

18 Jerusalem and Mecca, the Temple and the Kaaba. An account of their interrelation in Islamic times

Heribert Busse

I

Throughout antiquity, Palestine and the Ḥidjāz have been in mutual contact. Both areas were connected by the famous incense road, which ended at Gaza in the north, extending from the Ḥidjāz to the coast of South Arabia. Besides merchandise, and often together with it, ideas could travel freely on that road. This is reflected in the religious history of Palestine and the Ḥidjāz, particularly in the history of the Kaaba. In pre-Islamic times this sanctuary seems to have undergone influence from the south, which is reflected in traditions which say that the Tubbaʿ, the legendary king of South Arabia, embellished and adorned the Kaaba on coming to Mecca. The Quraish reconstructed the sanctuary when Muhammad was a young man, giving it — as is told in tradition — the shape of a Syrian building. Being a sanctuary of a Semitic religion, the Kaaba has much in common with the Temple of the Jews, as can easily be imagined. This misled scholars like R. Dozy in the middle of the nineteenth century into concluding that the founders of the Kaaba were Israelites who had been expelled from Palestine in biblical times.[1] On the basis of certain features of its architecture, a Christian origin has recently been claimed by G. Lüling.[2] Examining the reports which we have at hand, Uri Rubin has shown in a recent article the energy the Quraish displayed on the eve of Islam, making the Kaaba the cult centre of Mecca.[3] Our theme is the manifold relations between the Temple and the Kaaba in the religious lore of Islam. The main source of information of Jewish lore referring to the Temple is, of course, the Bible, and for the post-biblical literature the monumental work of Louis Ginzberg, *The Legends of the Jews*, (7 vols., Philadelphia 1968 (reprint)). The Islamic sources are abundant; much is to be found in the *Akhbār Makka* of Abu'l-Walīd Muḥammad b. al-Azraqī (ed. F. Wüstenfeld, Leipzig 1858).[4] This chapter aims at giving an outline of the subject; full treatment will require a more comprehensive study of the sources.

Before going into details, it may be useful to sketch the network of relations between the Temple and the Kaaba that came into existence in Islamic times, when the Kaaba had been transformed into a monotheistic sanctuary. The Temple was destroyed by the Romans in the year AD 70, and the site was desecrated by heathen statues when Hadrian founded Aelia Capitolina, which was intended to replace the Jewish Jerusalem. The Temple had two successors, first the Church of the Holy Sepulchre, then the Ḥaram al-sharīf, which was established by the Muslims on the Temple Mount soon after the Arab conquest of Jerusalem. Jewish traditions concerning the Temple were transferred to the Ḥaram al-sharif; part of them came directly from the Temple, part of them via the Church of the Holy Sepulchre which the Christians had learned to look on as the New Jerusalem, i.e. the New Temple. From the Ḥaram al-sharīf of the Muslims, the Temple traditions were transferred to the Kaaba. However, links between the Temple and the Kaaba had already been established by Muhammad, as we shall see when we examine the relevant passages in the Koran. Finally one has to keep in mind that the Temple and the Kaaba have a common ground in Semitic religion. On the basis of these considerations, one may assume that the relations between the four sanctuaries developed in three successive stages: (1) relations based on the common Semitic origin of the Temple and the Kaaba, going far back into pre-Islamic times; (2) relations established by Muhammad when he declared the Kaaba to be a building erected by Abraham (or Adam); (3) the transfer of traditions from the Temple to the Kaaba via Ḥaram al-sharif (or the Church of the Holy Sepulchre) in order to make the Kaaba a sanctuary equal to the Temple or even superior to it.

II

It is a remarkable coincidence that the Kaaba entered history at about the same time that the Temple lost its function. The Meccan sanctuary is mentioned under the name *makouraba*, which means "temple", in the famous Geography of Ptolemaios. The next mention of the Kaaba occurs no earlier than in the Koran. Muhammad calls it *masdjid*, *bait*, or *al-bait al-'atīq* ("the ancient house") (Surah 22:29), and *ka'ba* (Surah 5:95, 97). The name *al-bait al-'atīq* fits in with the assertion in Surah 3:96 according to which the house in "Bakka" (which is more or less identical with Mecca) was the first place of worship designated for its people. This is undoubtedly the Kaaba. It is called "the ancient house" because it came into existence prior to any other sanctuary. Looking for another place of worship in the Koran comparable to the Kaaba, we come across the *masdjid* of the Israelites in Surah 17:7, which was twice invaded by enemy forces and destroyed. This is, of course, the Temple in Jerusalem. Since the house in Bakka is "the ancient house", the Temple must be of a later origin. This is in keeping with Muhammad's assertion that the Kaaba had been founded by Abraham. Although nothing is told in the Koran of David and Solomon as the builders of the Temple,[5] there can hardly be any doubt that the prophet knew at least something of the story. On the other hand, the name *al-bait al-'atīq* may be related to the idea of it as the navel of the world, which was quite common in Semitic religions.[6] Mecca is called *umm al-qurā*, "mother of the cities", in Surah 6:92

and Surah 42:7. This may mean that the Arabs assumed already in the time of the Jahiliyya that Mecca or the Kaaba respectively was the centre of the world. Consequently, the Kaaba would be the oldest sanctuary on earth. This is again a common concept in Semitic religions, here applied to the Temple, and to the sanctuary in Mecca as well.

There are many other elements which the Temple and the Kaaba have in common, as we shall see later. Abraham is connected with the Temple in Jewish tradition in that the Temple is said to have been built on the site of Abraham's sacrifice (2 Chronicles 3:1). It may be assumed that Muhammad had some idea of that story when he told how Abraham built the Kaaba. One can easily imagine how in oral transmission the Temple and the Kaaba were confused to such a degree as to become one and the same thing, and how easy it was to turn Abraham the priest who offered a sacrifice into Abraham the builder who erected an altar or a temple, namely the Kaaba. We know that in Jewish tradition the site of the Temple is said to have been the first thing that God created, and that the site had been Adam's dwelling place. Because of the fact that the Kaaba was believed to be the navel of the world, Muhammad vacillated with regard to Abraham's function in connection with the Kaaba: besides the story already mentioned that he was the builder of the Kaaba (Surah 2:127), Muhammad also put forward the opinion that the patriarch purified the sanctuary (Surah 2:125). The latter assertion would mean that the building already existed when Abraham came to Mecca, and that it had been his function to clean the Kaaba of the impurity of heathendom which had been introduced after Adam. On the basis of this Koranic teaching, Islamic tradition has concluded that the Kaaba was built by Adam, not by Abraham.

Nothing is said in the Koran as to the place of Abraham's sacrifice. The story is told, with many details, in Surah 37:99–111. However, the name of the son to be slaughtered is not mentioned. Because the story of Isaac's birth follows the story of the sacrifice (V. 112–113), Islamic tradition has drawn the conclusion that Ishmael was the son who had been assigned as victim.[7] The word *sa'y* (V. 102), which means the ritual of running between aṣ-Ṣafā and al-Marwa, forming part of the ritual of the pilgrimage, has induced some Koran interpreters to localise the sacrifice near the Kaaba. Most commonly held is the belief that it took place somewhere at Minā, near Mecca. In order to include the Meccan sanctuary in the episode, the story is told that the horns of Abraham's ram were suspended in the Kaaba.[8]

A close connection between the Temple and the Kaaba is to be seen in the Koranic story of Abraham's prayer following the cleaning or the building of the Kaaba. There are three versions of the prayer (Surah 2:126; 2:127–129; 14:35–41). It has a model in the Bible in the prayer of Solomon upon the completion of the building of the Temple (1 Kings 8:22 *et par.*). Following this prayer Solomon offered a sacrifice (1 Kings 8:62–66 *et par.*). An allusion to a sacrifice has been preserved in the Koran in one of the three versions of Abraham's prayer: he prayed, together with Ishmael: "Our Lord! Accept (this) from us" (*rabbanā taqabbal minnā*) (Surah 2:127). The verb which is used here, *taqabbala*, refers to God's acceptance of a sacrifice, as is clear from Surah 5:27, where the story of Cain and Abel is told: "They each presented a sacrifice. It was accepted from one (*fa-tuqubbila min ahadihima*)". Since *taqabbala* requires an object (*qurbān*, "sacrifice", or a similar word), the missing of the object in Surah 2:127 may be interpreted as an attempt to eliminate the suggestion that Abraham offered a sacrifice when he built (or cleaned) the Kaaba. According to the Islamic creed God does not require any sustenance of man, nor does He require that they should feed Him (Surah 51:57). On the other hand, it remains open whether this allusion to a sacrifice found its way into the Koran from the biblical account of Solomon's sacrifice at the inauguration of the Temple or from the biblical story of Abraham ordered by God to slaughter his son.

Ḥadjdj is an element which belongs essentially to the Kaaba. Accordingly, it was introduced by Abraham, the builder of the Kaaba (Surah 3:97; 22:27–33). This is another element which the Kaaba has in common with the Temple. Solomon said at the end of his prayer of inauguration: "And the foreigner too . . . if he comes from a distant country . . . hear from heaven . . . so that all the peoples of the earth may come to know your name and revere you" (1 Kings 8:41–43). Surah 22:27 is in keeping with this: "They will come . . . through deep and distant mountain highways . . and celebrate the name of Allah."

III

It has become evident that Muhammad's sayings about the Kaaba have a number of elements which are somehow related to the Temple. After the conquest of Jerusalem and the occupation of the Temple Mount, Islamic tradition transferred further elements from the Temple to the Kaaba. Examining the numerous examples of characteristics in common between the Temple and the Kaaba in Jewish or Islamic tradition, we have to bear in mind that some of them are based on the common Semitic heritage. This applies, as already mentioned, to the idea of the navel of the earth; it may also apply to the idea of the terrestrial sanctuary which has a counterpart in heaven. In his dream, Jacob saw Jerusalem on earth and Jerusalem in heaven.[9] The Temple in heaven was created 2 000 years before the creation of the world.[10] According to a tradition quoted by al-Azraqī, the site of the terrestrial Kaaba was created 2 000 years before the creation of the world.[11] Upon the return of the Israelites from exile, when the Temple was about to be rebuilt, the prophet Zacharias saw the altar in heaven upon which Archangel Michael offered a sacrifice; the site of Solomon's altar was exactly beneath it.[12] The same is said of the Kaaba; the celestial Kaaba is exactly above the terrestrial sanctuary.[13]

Other elements may have been transferred from the Temple to the Kaaba in Islamic times. A few examples may suffice to stress the point. In the Temple, the Ark of the Covenant was placed upon the Foundation Stone (*even shtiyah*). God's ineffable name is carved in the Stone.[14] Islamic authorities tell of inscriptions on stones which were found in the foundations of the Kaaba when renovation work was undertaken.[15] Adam offered his first sacrifice on the spot on which later Abraham was ready to slaughter his son and where Solomon was to build the Temple.[16] In the same way Adam worshipped God in a tent which was the predecessor of the Kaaba.[17] It is interesting to note that the Temple and the Kaaba both had predecessors in the shape of tents which were in due course replaced by solid structures. Solomon's Temple was inaugurated on Yom Kippur;[18] the Kaaba received in former times a new cover (*kiswa*) on the tenth day of 'Ashūrā, i.e. on the tenth day of the first month of the year, which is the Jewish Yom Kippur.[19] The Temple is a building which is inimitable. For this reason, the masons died upon its completion, which prevented them from building a heathen sanctuary of the same shape.[20] In Mecca, the first house that was built in the shape of a cube like the Kaaba was allegedly pulled down because it was not allowed to imitate the sanctuary.[21]

According to Jewish tradition the priests were barefooted when officiating in the Temple because of the presence of the Shekhinah.[22] After the reconstruction of the Kaaba by the Quraish, al-Walīd b. al-Mughīra is said to have been the first visitor who took off his shoes before entering the sanctuary. This became a custom among the Quraish.[23] It is interesting to note that al-Walīd b. Al-Mughīra was a fierce opponent of Islam. Apparently it was easier to ascribe this custom to a man like him than to admit a possible Jewish origin.

The cloud was the sign of God's presence to the Israelites. Yahweh went before them in the wilderness in the form of a pillar of cloud to show them the way (Exodus 13, 21). When the Ark of the Covenant was brought into Solomon's Temple, the cloud filled the Temple of Yahweh, and because of the cloud the priests could no longer perform their duties: the glory of Yahweh filled Yahweh's Temple (1 Kings 8, 10–11). According to Ezekiel the veil behind which Yahweh concealed himself consisted of a cloud with light around it; a stormy wind blew from the north (Ezekiel 1:3–4). In rabbinical literature the Shekhinah is the bearer and the vehicle of God's presence.[24] In the Koran the cloud of the Israelites is described as having another function: it does not show them the way but gives them shade (Surah 2:27; 7:160). In the story of Saul (Ṭālūt) as told in the Koran, the Shekhinah (*sakīna*) appears closely connected with the Ark of the Covenant (*tābūt*) (Surah 2:248).[25] In post-Koranic tradition the cloud and the Shekhinah are interchangeable. Both play an important part in the story of Abraham building the Kaaba. The cloud or the Shekhinah respectively directed him to the site of the sanctuary.[26] The cloud is described as having a head which talks to Abraham. It is said to be a stormy wind,[27] which reminds one of Ezekiel's previously mentioned vision. An angel appeared to Ezekiel, showing him the shape and measurements of the Temple.[28] Those three elements have been combined in a report which says that Abraham set out from Syria (or Armenia) for Arabia, accompanied by an angel, the Shekhinah and the cloud.[29] The cloud stopped above the site on which the Kaaba was to be built, and Abraham laid the foundations on the outlines of its shadow.[30] According to another legend the cloud formed a ring as though it was a snake and settled down on the foundations of the Kaaba which had been laid by Adam.[31]

Now to the Black Stone. Its veneration was one of the most problematical rites of the pilgrimage. The simplest attempt to put it into the framework of Islamic belief was to refer to the fact that the prophet himself had kissed it when he performed his last pilgrimage (*ḥadjdj al-wadā'*).[32] There were, however, other means to give the Black Stone Islamic attire. For instance, it is told that a Syrian inscription was found on it. A Jew was able to read it: God is the Lord of Bakka and the founder of the Kaaba.[33] According to

240

another tradition the Black Stone is of heavenly origin, a hyacinth of Paradise.[34] As such it radiates a light which illuminates the Ḥaram, or the whole world. It has two eyes, a tongue, and is able to speak,[35] which is a variant of the story that an inscription was found on it. On the Day of Judgement, it will bear witness to the faith of the pilgrims who touched it reverently when visiting the Kaaba.[36] According to other traditions, touching the Black Stone brings about remission of sins.[37] It is a receptacle of documents, as is the Ark of the Covenant of the Jews: it is said to have devoured in its mouth the parchment on which God's covenant with Adam was written.[38]

According to Jewish and Christian tradition, the Temple Mount in Jerusalem will be the scene of the Last Judgement. Consequently, eschatological episodes were transferred from Palestine or the Temple respectively to the Ḥidjāz and the Kaaba. For Muslims and Christians the Last Judgement will be preceded by the return of Jesus, who having defeated his opponent, the Antichrist or the Dadjdjāl respectively will suffer death. According to Muslim belief he will be buried in a grave which has been prepared by the side of the Prophet's Tomb in Medina.[39] The beast of the Book of Revelation (Ch. 13) will emerge from beneath al-Marwa near the Kaaba. The return of Jesus and the coming of the beast are two of the five signs which herald the end of the world and the coming of the Last Judgement.[40]

The Kaaba is, in the same way as the Temple, a sanctuary of universal significance. This is mirrored in the efforts to give the Kaaba a place in the story of the creation of the world and to make it the centre of the universe. The same is intended when the mountains are listed from which the stones to build the sanctuary were taken. A list in which the names of mountains immediately surrounding Mecca are given[41] reflects the older situation, when the Kaaba was a heathen sanctuary of local importance only. Another list shows the claim to universal acknowledgement: the stones to build the Kaaba were brought to Mecca from five mountains: Libanon, the Mount of Olives, Sinai, Djūdī and Ḥirā.[42] These mountains are famous for the part they play in the Judaeo-Christian-Islamic history of salvation.

IV

Whereas the sanctuary of Mecca is mentioned many times in the Koran, as we have seen above, the name of Jerusalem does not occur in the holy book of the Muslims. The Temple (masdjid) is only mentioned expressis verbis in Surah 17:7, in the story of its destruction on two occasions, which is a clear reference to the destruction of Solomon's Temple by the Babylonians and the Herodian Temple by the Romans. The name al-masdjid al-aqṣā in Surah 17 was connected with the Temple Mount at a later stage.[43] We have to start from the assumption that 17:1 and 17:2–8 were originally separate pieces which were put together when the Koran received its final editing (which does not necessarily mean that the masdjid of 17:1 was then identified with the masdjid of 17:7). An indirect mention of Jerusalem occurs in Surah 2:142–150, in the story of the changing of the direction of prayer (qibla). The new qibla is al-masdjid al-ḥarām, i.e. the Kaaba.

We have good reasons to suppose that Jerusalem was the *qibla* which Muhammad observed before he changed it to Mecca.

As long as the Prophet stayed in Mecca it is likely that he prayed in front of the Kaaba, facing its façade, in the area which U. Rubin has recently identified as the *ḥidjr*.[44] It is in consequence of the fact that the façade forms the north-eastern wall of the Kaaba that Muhammad prayed in a south-westerly direction. There are reports in which it is said that he prayed towards the Kaaba on its south-eastern wall, which means that the Temple and the Kaaba lay on one line.[45] However, this is nothing but an attempt to project the Jerusalem *qibla* back into the Meccan period of Muhammad's preaching.

Although the Temple aroused Muhammad's interest for a limited time only, the Temple Mount became an important Islamic sanctuary soon after the Arabic conquest of Jerusalem. The Islamic occupation of the Temple Mount took shape in three successive stages: at first the area was transformed into a mosque for mere pragmatic reasons; then the site was identified as the place of the Jewish Temple, and consequently the Dome of the Rock and the Aqsa-Mosque were designed and built in the reign of 'Abd al-Malik and al-Walīd; the third and final stage was reached when the Holy Rock (*al-ṣakhra*) was identified as the site of Muhammad's Night Journey *(isrā')* and Ascension (*mi'rādj*). This happened probably between al-Walīd's death in 96/715 and the end of Omaiyad rule in the middle of the second/eighth century.[46]

The localisation of *isrā'* and *mi'rādj* on the Temple Mount has become the sole *raison d'être* of the Ḥaram al-sharīf as an Islamic sanctuary. The localisation was possible because the site had been recognised as the location of the Jewish Temple. It was from the Temple that Muhammad's Ascension had to start, i.e. the Ascension to the heavenly sanctuary, the counterpart of the sanctuary on earth. However, there is ample evidence that the localisation of these events in Jerusalem was preceded by their localisation in Mecca. This is attested by traditions on the Ascension in which Jerusalem is not mentioned at all, which means that *isrā'* was at first understood as Muhammad's Ascension to heaven from the Kaaba (or a place in Mecca). This was possible because the Arabs believed already in pre-Islamic times that the Kaaba had a heavenly counterpart. At least Muhammad believed it when he told the story of his Ascension *(isrā')* from the Kaaba on earth (*al-masdjid al-ḥarām*) to the distant sanctuary (*al-masdjid al-aqṣā*) in heaven (Surah 17:1). Later on, when the Ascension was localised in Jerusalem, the term *isrā'* of Surah 17:1 (here rather *asrā*, from which *isrā'* was derived) was interpreted as meaning the Night Journey from Mecca to Jerusalem; the Ascension was now termed *mi'rādj*, which means "ladder", i.e. the instrument of Ascension. It is known in this function from the story of Jacob's dream as told in the Bible: "A ladder was there, standing on the ground with its top reaching to heaven", etc. (Genesis 28, 12).[47]

Islamic tradition ascribes the identification of the Temple Mount as the site of *isrā'*, and *mi'rādj* to 'Omar b. al-Khaṭṭāb, the alleged conqueror of Jerusalem and founder of the Ḥaram al-sharīf. It is not necessary to go into the details of this legend. One element of it is, however, important in our context, that is the role which Ka'b al-Aḥbār, allegedly a converted Jew, played as a transmitter of Jewish Temple traditions to 'Omar and the Arabs when they conquered Jerusalem. There is undoubtedly a historical nucleus to the story. We are allowed to assume that biblical and Talmudic traditions concerning the Temple were transmitted to the Muslims. Ka'b al-Aḥbār may be taken as representing Jewish converts to Islam who passed information to the Arabs when the latter took possession of Jerusalem and the holy places. Part of the traditions concerning the Temple may also have reached the Muslims through Christian converts to Islam. This is explained by the fact that the Church of the Holy Sepulchre was, according to Christian lore, the successor of the Temple, as already mentioned. A striking example is the altar of Abraham opposite Golgotha, which means that Abraham's sacrifice had been transferred from Mount Moriah, the site of the Temple according to Jewish tradition, to the Church of the Holy Sepulchre.[48]

From the Ḥaram al-sharīf traditions of Jewish provenance concerning the Temple were transferred to the Kaaba. A number of examples have been mentioned in the preceding section of this chapter. One has the impression that a competition was taking place between the Ḥaram al-sharīf and the Kaaba, Jerusalem and Mecca, Palestine and the Ḥidjāz. Our question here concerns the ways in which Temple traditions migrated from Jerusalem to Mecca. What happened when these traditions first migrated from the Temple to the Ḥaram al-sharīf seems to be clear. The transmitters were, as previously mentioned, in the first line converted Jews. To a lesser extent converted Christians must have been involved, as some traditions seem to have migrated to the Ḥaram al-sharīf via the Church of the Holy Sepulchre. It may be asked whether converted Jews or converted Christians, or both, were acting as transmitters of Temple traditions from the Ḥaram al-sharīf (or the Church of the Holy Sepulchre) to the Kaaba. This was a secondary migration; Temple traditions migrated first to the Ḥaram al-sharīf, thence to the Kaaba. In the latter case one should expect that the mediation of Jews or Christians was no longer required, since the traditions had already been appropriated by the Arabs, i.e. by the Muslims by birth. However, al-Azraqī mentions a number of cases in which Jews or Christians acted as transmitters. A few examples may be listed: learned men of the people of the book, i.e. Jews or Christians, allegedly advised the Tubba', the legendary king of South Arabia, to honour the Kaaba.[49] An allusion to Bakka is said to be found in Psalms.[50] Ka'b al-Aḥbār allegedly found an allusion to the Well of Zemzem in the Bible.[51] A Jew deciphered, as already mentioned, the inscription on the Black Stone. Besides Ka'b al-Aḥbār, Wahb b. Munabbih is mentioned, a standard authority on Jewish and Christian traditions in the early Islamic period: he found in an old book that God ordered the angels to venerate the Kaaba.[52]

There are, accordingly, good reasons for assuming that Temple traditions were transferred to the Kaaba either by Jewish and Christian converts or by Arab Muslims who had gathered them in the Ḥaram al-sharīf.[53] This is clearly attested in a story told by al-Azraqī in the name of Muhammad b. 'Alī b. al-Husain, a great-great-grandson of the Prophet Muhammad: when he made the ṭawāf — the circumambulation of the Kaaba —with his father, the latter was asked by a pilgrim from Syria about the origin of this ritual. The question is closely connected with the origin of the Kaaba itself. Muhammad's father gave the man the information he had asked for. In the course of their conversation it came to light that the interrogator was an inhabitant of Jerusalem, and that he had read both the

Old and the New Testaments.[54] The purpose of the story is evident. It is threefold: (1) the inhabitants of Jerusalem know everything about the origin of the Temple or of the Ḥaram al-sharīf respectively; however, the knowledge of its history does not contribute anything to the knowledge of the history of the Kaaba, since there is no similarity between the two sanctuaries; (2) the Bible does not contain any information on the origin, function or meaning of the Kaaba. The message conveyed by the story is an assertion that the Kaaba has nothing to do with the Temple; it is a sanctuary in its own right; (3) the story itself is proof of Jewish or Christian mediation, or both, in the process of transfer of Temple traditions to the Kaaba.

V

In conclusion we can say that the Temple and the Kaaba had a common ground in Semitic religion, the result of which was that certain characteristics ascribed to the heathen Kaaba were the same as those ascribed to the Temple. On the basis of these attributions, Muhammad transformed the Kaaba into a monotheistic sanctuary; apparently he also made use of elements from Jewish sources. Taking up the Koranic sayings, Islamic tradition transferred further elements from the Temple to the Kaaba. This perhaps started immediately after Muhammad's death and the beginning of the expansion of Muslim rule into Syria and Palestine. When the Ḥaram al-sharīf on the Temple Mount was founded, a competition started between this sanctuary and the Kaaba. Traditions like *isrā'* and *mi'rādj* migrated from Mecca to Jerusalem, but it was the Kaaba which enjoyed the greater profit, being transformed into a sanctuary which was to become, in the eyes of the believers, the true Temple. From this viewpoint, the Jewish Temple is a plagiarism of the Kaaba, not vice versa. It may be added that the competition between Jerusalem and Mecca developed against the background of the struggle for supremacy between the new political centre in Syria/Palestine and the conservative circles in Arabia who continued to consider the Ḥidjāz as the cradle of Islam and themselves as the legitimate leaders of the new religion.

NOTES

1   R. Dozy, *Die Israeliten zu Mekka von Davids Zeit bis ins 5. Jahrhundert unserer Zeit-rechnung. Ein Beitrag zur alttestamentlichen Kritik und zur Erforschung des Ursprungs des Islams.* Aus dem Holländischen übersetzt, Leipzig, 1864.

2   G. Lüling, *Der Christliche Kult an der Vorislamischen Kaaba als Problem der Islamwissen-schaft und Christlichen Theologie,* Erlangen, 1977.

3   Uri Rubin: "The Ka'ba. Aspects of its ritual, functions and position in pre-Islamic and early Islamic times", in *Jerusalem Studies in Arabic and Islam 8,* 1986, pp. 97–131.

4   Wüstenfeld's edition of the Arabic text is accompanied by a German translation, which is, however, only a summary of the contents. For further reference to the sources see A.J. Wensinck; *A Handbook of Early Muhammadan Tradition,* alphabetically arranged, Leiden 1927, Reprints 1960 and 1971.

5   Solomon built *mahārīb* (Surah 34:12), which means *palaces,* the Temple being one.

6   Maurice Gaudefroy-Demombynes, *Le Pélerinage à la Mekke. Étude d'Histoire Religieuse*, Paris, 1923, p. 30 (with reference to the sources).
7   In fact the story is composed of several pieces: Abraham's emigration (v. 99); his prayer for a son and the annunciation of the birth (of Isaac) (vv. 100–101); the sacrifice (vv. 102–111).
8   Azraqī, p. 106. According to Aḥmad b. Ḥanbal, "a horn or horns were removed from the Kaaba on Muhammad's order", see Wensinck, *Handbook*, p. 120.
9   Ginzberg III 447.
10 Ginzberg I 3.
11 Azraqī, p. 4.
12 Ginzberg IV 354. VI 440,No. 31.
13 Azraqī, p. 15.
14 Ginzberg I 352.
15 Azraqī, pp. 42, 118.
16 Ginzberg I 285.
17 Azraqī, pp. 8, 11.
18 Ginzberg IV 156.
19 Azraqī, pp. 175 seq.
20 Ginzberg IV 155.
21 Azraqī, p. 196 states that the inhabitants of Mecca built round houses out of awe of the See also Toufic Fahd, *Le Panthéon de l'Arabie Centrale à la Veille de l'Hégire*, Paris 1968, p. 205, n. 1, and Barbara Finster, "Zu der Neuauflage von K.A.C. Creswell's 'Early Muslim Architecture'", in: *Kunst des Orients IX* 1/2, p. 96.
22 Ginzberg V 420, No. 122.
23 Azraqī, p. 118.
24 For the Shekhinah, see Arnold M. Goldberg, *Untersuchungen über die Vorstellung von der Shekhinah in der Frühen Rabbinischen Literatur – Talmud und Midrasch*, Berlin, 1969.
25 For the etymology of *sakīna* see Th. Nöldeke, *Neue Beiträge zur Semitischen Sprachwissenschaft*, Strassburg, 1910, pp. 24 *seq.*, and A. Jeffery, *The Foreign Vocabulary of the Qurʾān*, Baroda, 1938, p. 174.
26 Azraqī, pp. 9, 27, 29.
27 Azraqī, pp. 27 *seq.*, 30.
28 Ezekiel, ch. 40.
29 Azraqī, pp. 27 *seq.*, 29. Abraham was staying on the site in Jerusalem on which the Temple was later built when God ordered him to build the Kaaba, Azraqī, p. 200.
30 Azraqī, pp. 9, 27.
31 Azraqī, p. 31.
32 See Wensinck, *Handbook*, p. 220 (s.v. Stone).
33 Azraqī, p. 43. Gaudefroy-Demombynes, p. 30, n. 4.
34 Azraqī, pp. 227, 358.
35 Azraqī, pp. 32, 228, 358.
36 Azraqī, p. 229.
37 Azraqī, pp. 229, 234.
38 Azraqī, p. 229.
39 For a description see Richard F. Burton, *Personal Narrative of a Pilgrimage to Al-Madina and Meccah*, New York, 1964, reprint, I 317 (with a sketch indicating the position of the grave).

40 Azraqī, pp. 386 *seq.*

41 Azraqī, p. 155.

42 Azraqī, pp. 7, 30. See also T. Fahd, *Le Panthéon,* p. 207, and n. 2 (another tradition, quoted from Yāqūt).

43 See my forthcoming article "Jerusalem in the story of Muhammad's Night Journey and Ascension", to be published in *Jerusalem Studies in Arabic and Islam.*

44 Rubin, *The Ka'ba,* pp. 98 *seq.*

45 See Ibn Ishāq, *Sīrat rasūlillāh,* ed. F. Wüstenfeld, 1858-60, pp. 190, 228 (A. Guillaume, *The Life of Muhammad,* 1955, pp. 135, 157 *seq.*)

46 See n. 43.

47 *Mi'rādj* occurs in the Koran in the plural only (Surah 43:33), meaning *stairs.* The verb 'aradja is used of angels and of the logos *(amr)* ascending to heaven (Surah 32:5; 70:4).

48 See Virgilio C. Corbo, *Il Santo Sepolcro di Gerusalemme,* Jerusalem, 1981, I 50 (attested by Adamnan/Arculf in about 675 AD). See also Herbert Donner, *Pilgerfahrt ins Heilige Land,* Stuttgart, 1979, p. 346.

49 Azraqī, pp. 84 *seq.*

50 Azraqī, p. 43.

51 Azraqī, pp. 292 *seq.* See also Rubin , *The Ka'ba,* p. 110, and notes.

52 Azraqī, pp. 9 *seq.*

53 The mediation of converted Jews with reference to the different names of the Kaaba is taken into consideration, albeit hesitantly, by T. Fahd, *Le Panthéon,* p. 226.

54 Azraqī, pp. 4 *seq.*

19 Islam versus Christian Europe: the case of the Holy Land

David Ayalon

The struggle for superiority between Islam and Christianity, and particularly between Islam and Christian Europe (with a greater stress on Western Europe), is one of the major factors (if not the most important) which have shaped the destiny of the human race over many centuries.

It is quite natural that the Holy Land, so sacred to all three monotheistic religions, should figure so prominently in that struggle.

In this chapter I shall try to briefly examine how this struggle was reflected on the soil of that land, attempting, at the same time, to establish the place of developments there within their wider context.

I shall start with the wider context, as I see it. In my view, the steadily growing technological preponderance of Christian Europe which began during the medieval period gave it, among other advantages, a more or less correspondingly increasing military superiority over the lands of Islam.[1] That superiority, however, became evident at sea much earlier than on land. The main reason for this was that the Muslims possessed on land a socio-military body the like of which existed neither in Christendom nor in any other civilisation, before the advent of Islam or after it. This was the Mamlūk military institution, which succeeded in delaying on land, for a good number of centuries, the inevitable outcome of Christian Europe's rising power.

These two major facets of the Muslim-Christian European contest found one of their most telling expressions on the soil of the Holy Land and its extensions during the period of the Crusades (1196–1291). What I would like to emphasise is that the implications and meaning of the final results of those Crusades went far beyond that particular trial of strength and that particular period. I shall explain what I mean by this statement later in this chapter. At this point I shall confine myself to saying that in evaluating the final outcome of the Crusades, not only what happened on land should be considered, but also what happened at sea, which was of greater importance in the long run.

But before discussing the Crusades and the Holy Land, a brief summary of the main characteristics of the Mamlūk socio-military institution should be given. This institution was, on the one hand, part and parcel of the Muslim slave-system (which was characterised, generally speaking, by its moderateness and leniency). On the other hand, it constituted a very special category within that system. In fact, it would be more appropriate to define the Mamlūks as slaves who became masters, and who formed the topmost élite layer in Muslim military society. Most of them were brought over as slaves to the lands of Islam from beyond the Muslim border,which means that they were born infidels. They were purchased only from the countries lying to the north-east and north of the Muslim territories, which means that they were fair-skinned. Blacks could not form part of the Mamlūk military élite. Within Muslim civilian society there also existed a basically negative attitude toward blacks. However, in certain ways they merged much more easily into that society than they did later into Western Christian society.

The Mamlūks imported by the slave-dealers were mainly nearing puberty or were adolescent. They were hand-picked, and only the very best could pass the scrutiny of the experienced selectors.[2] When they reached their Muslim destiny (usually the court of a ruler or important personality), they were converted to Islam. First they were taught its basic tenets, and then they were trained militarily according to the best methods available at the time. Their training was, of course, that of cavalrymen. Having terminated their period of learning and training, they were usually (though by no means always) manumitted. The important thing about this procedure was that loyalty and fidelity between the patron and his slave in Islam became effective only *after* the manumission (*al-walā' li-man a'taq*). The patron and his manumitted Mamlūks formed a kind of "big family" and strong bonds of allegiance tied the Mamlūk to his patron and to his colleagues in servitude and manumission. Those bonds developed on the basis of a very deep-rooted awareness[3] that Islam is far superior to any other religion, monotheistic or otherwise. In addition to this, there was yet another characteristic unique to the Mamlūk institution, without which all the other characteristics would have been of little value: the institution constituted a one-generation nobility. The sons of the Mamlūks were ousted from it. New Mamlūks had to be imported continuously, so that the ranks of the military élite would constantly be filled with fresh recruits from the same source of supply, thereby preserving the inborn military qualities characteristic of the people of their homelands.

One of the main reasons why the slave traffic in general, and the Mamlūk traffic in particular, could be carried out continuously on such a large scale was that the peoples of the slaves' countries of origin (whether Mamlūks or non-Mamlūks; fair skinned or blacks) usually co-operated willingly with the slave dealers. This was true of the rulers of those countries, of the heads of the tribes, and even of the close relatives of the prospective slave, including his father and mother. The scale of values of those people was different, and, consequently, family relations were different from the accepted ones in more civilised countries.

Slave traffic was extremely remunerative to all concerned. In addition, the material lot of the slave was usually better in his new country than in his original one. This was true of many of the black slaves, and particularly so of the Mamlūks who were destined from the very outset to join the military élite, and had excellent chances of rising to the highest

248

ranks. Some of them could even hope to bring over their relatives to the countries which adopted them.

There were, however, important drawbacks to this system, the most important of which were: (a) there was little or no control over the homelands of the Mamlūks, especially to Muslim rulers whose states were distant from those homelands: (b) Muslim rulers nearer to the homelands could interfere with their passage through their territory to further destinations; (c) a Mamlūk was very expensive; (d) it took a number of years to turn a raw boy slave into a fully fledged Muslim adult warrior, and the whole process was very costly. The patron had to invest much and wait some years before reaping the benefit of his investment.

In spite of all these drawbacks and its relatively small numbers, the Mamlūk institution achieved great success,[4] both in expansion and in defence. It lasted for about 1 000 years, from the first half of the ninth century to the first half of the nineteenth. It certainly outlived its purpose for a very long time, but for a much longer time it played a decisive role in Muslim history. Nothing even remotely similar has ever existed on any appreciable scale outside the boundaries of Muslim civilisation.

We now come back to the Holy Land in the time of the Crusades. During that period the immense might of the Mamlūk system and the growing weakness of Muslim naval power were revealed in all their magnitude both in the Holy Land and its neighbouring territories. These two factors were the clearest indicators of future developments in the confrontation between Islam and European Christianity.

The Holy Land, and, above all, Jerusalem, were the obvious targets of the Crusaders. However, both the Muslims and the Franks realised that the pivot of the whole war was Egypt. The side that held Egypt would ultimately hold Palestine and Syria, and be able to drive the enemy out of them. Egypt was the ideal base for military operations against the Syro-Palestinian region or part of it.

But neither Egypt nor any of its neighbouring lands had the proper kind of armies to repel a Crusader invasion,[5] let alone oust the Crusaders from the Muslim territories which they occupied. That task could only be possible with the aid of Mamlūk forces brought over from the distant north and north-east. The great — and, as later events proved, irreversible — shrinkage of the Crusaders' hold on the Holy Land and other parts of the Syrian region began with the coming to power of the Ayyūbids (1169–1250). Contrary to the accepted view, the Mamlūks made up the core of the armies of that Kurdish dynasty, and without them the military achievements of Saladin and his successors could not have taken place. Towards the end of the Ayyūbid reign, the Mamlūk element was considerably strengthened. The Baḥriyya regiment (the Mamlūks of the Ayyūbid sultan al-Ṣāliḥ Najm al-Dīn Ayyūb), which put an end to the Ayyūbid reign and established the Mamlūk reign (1250–1517) in its stead, won, on Egyptian soil, very shortly before that (February 1250), a resounding victory over one of the biggest and strongest armies which the Franks ever sent against the Muslims during the Crusading period. Furthermore, the commander-in-chief of that army, the famous St Louis (Louis IX, king of France) was taken prisoner, together with the greatest part of his surviving army. This was the second and last time in Muslim history that a monarch of a great Christian kingdom was taken prisoner by a

Muslim army. The first was in the famous battle of Manzikert (1071), which left Anatolia wide open to the Seljuks and their Turcomans, thus paving the way to the rise of the Ottoman Empire. The decisive factor in this Muslim victory over the Byzantines was again the Mamlūk regiment of Alp Arslan (the captive king was Romanus Diogenes).

Within less than half a century after coming to power, the Mamlūks had wiped the Crusaders out of Syria and Palestine and brought an end to the Crusades. Their prestige and glory were enhanced by their stopping the advance of the Mongols at 'Ayn Jālūt in the Plain of Esdraelon (1260), and putting an end to all their future attempts to conquer Syria or parts of it. These great victories were acknowledged and celebrated throughout the great centres of Islam.

The backbone of the might of the Ottoman Empire was its janissary corps, a direct offshoot of the Mamlūk system. Without the janissaries the Empire would never have reached its far-flung boundaries, and would never have threatened as it did the heart of Europe for centuries.

In order to complete the picture, just a few remarks about the Mamlūk institution *before* the Ayyūbids, the Mamlūks and the Ottomans. The person who made the Mamlūks the central military element of Islam was Caliph al-Mʿutaṣim (833–842). His unflinching determination to bring about that far-reaching revolution in the structure and composition of the Muslim armies forced him to abandon Baghdad as the capital of the Caliphate (and, for all practical purposes, the centre of the Muslim world) and to build a new Caliphal capital, Sāmarrā, which was situated upstream on the Tigris, thus commanding Baghdad. This new capital was built, first and foremost, in order to serve the Caliph's Mamlūk corps, and perpetuate its existence as the pivot of Muslim power.

The role of Sāmarrā as the capital of Islam was short-lived. But the Mamlūks, as the core and backbone of the armies of Islam, continued to exist, as already mentioned, for about 1 000 years. Particularly worthy of note in the early centuries of Islam are the Mamlūk armies of the Sāmānids (874–999) and the Ghaznawids (962–1186) in the eastern regions of Islam. The Sāmānids penetrated deep into the lands of the Turks in central Asia and beyond, and the Ghaznawids were the major factor in widening the boundaries of Islam in India.

The Seljuks, who began penetrating the Muslim lands at the turn of the eleventh century, soon came to the conclusion that they would have to rely on Mamlūks as their élite troops. The greatest known protagonist of the Mamlūk system, both in theory and in practice, was the famous Vizir Niẓām al-Mulk. As already stated, the victory at Manzikert was won mainly because of the steadfastness of the Mamlūks of Alp Arslān. The Zangids (the Syrian branch: 1146–1181) were one of the main successors of the Seljuks. This was a Mamlūk dynasty. Its élite army consisted of Mamlūks. The Ayyūbid dynasty sprang out of the Zangid state, and the rulers of the Mamlūk sultanate came out of the Ayyūbid empire.

Only against the general and grand background of the Mamlūk institution in Islam can the great military achievements of the Mamlūks on land against the Crusaders and the Mongols, who appeared most unexpectedly from the East, be properly understood and evaluated. It is very noteworthy that both Frankish and Muslim warriors had an extremely high regard for the military ability of their adversaries.

The situation at sea was, from a certain period onwards, completely different from that on land. During the eleventh century the Frankish navy gradually succeeded in reducing Muslim naval power to a minimum in most of the Mediterranean without a major battle. This was a vital prerequisite for the success of the Crusades, without which their efforts would have been nipped almost in the bud.

From the time the Crusaders set foot on Syro-Palestinian land, the Muslims failed to build up a naval power which would be strong enough to cut the Crusaders off from their homelands. The sea routes were almost completely open for the supply of materials and reinforcements to them throughout the Crusading period.

It took the Muslims almost 100 years to gather sufficient power on land to present, for the first time, a real threat to the whole Crusading enterprise. After the battle of Ḥaṭṭin (1187) near Tiberias, the Muslims succeeded in reconquering Jerusalem, the focal point of the whole struggle, and vast Crusader territories, including very substantial parts of the coast, its ports and fortifications. In short, the end of the Crusades was in sight. However, at this very optimistic phase from the Muslim point of view, a growing Frankish force concentrated in Tyre was creating the conditions for the counter-offensive of the Third Crusade.

During this crucial stage in the history of the Muslim-Christian European struggle, a new Muslim military strategy was born, namely the systematic destruction of the towns, ports and fortresses on the Syro-Palestinian Coast, with particular stress on the Palestinian section of the coast, because of its proximity to Jerusalem and its suitability for landing. This was a complete departure from the strategy adopted by the Muslims during the first hundred years or so of the Crusaders' invasion, and had no real parallel in Muslim history since the advent of Islam.

After the arrival of the Crusaders, the Muslims showed no inclination whatsoever to destroy the ports which they still held, including the most important of them, although they had ample time to do so. Tripoli was captured by the Crusaders only in 1109, Tyre in 1124, and Ashkelon — the key point for an attack either on Egypt or Palestine and beyond — only in 1153.

The ease with which the Muslims conquered so much of the Crusader territories as a result of their 1187 victory, and the reverses which they suffered quite soon afterwards, pushed their military leaders, headed by Saladin, to adopt a new policy, which they carried out rapidly, albeit with much sorrow and internal antagonism. They became convinced that the only efficient way to fight the Franks was to destroy the harbours and coastal fortifications which the Muslims still held, in order to prevent their being captured intact by the formidable enemy.

Fortunately the sources, particularly *al-Fatḥ al-Qussī* by ʿImād al-Dīn al-Iṣfahānī, Saladin's close companion, enable us to follow quite systematically the development of that policy. As soon as the Muslims realised that they could not capture Tyre, and became convinced of the imminence of the Crusaders' counter-attack, their attention focused on Acre, which they succeeded in capturing from the Franks. They found its fortifications to be quite inadequate, and they were first inclined to destroy it together with Jaffa. However, they finally abondoned the idea and decided to fortify Acre as best they could in the relatively short time still available to them. The famous eunuch Qarāqū sh, the builder of the Cairo wall and citadel, was charged with this task.[6] Thus the siege of Acre became the focus of the Third Crusade.

The turning point was the fall of Acre after a very protracted siege. Saladin had to retreat southwards and when he reached Ashkelon, Richard the Lion-Heart was advancing in the same direction. He decided against stubborn opposition to raze Ashkelon to the ground, explaining that there was no alternative, and that if there had been he would rather have sacrificed his sons than remove a single stone from that town.

Parts of al-Iṣfahānī's above-cited book are very helpful in explaining the background and causes of the policy of destruction which began in Ashkelon, and which continued up to the end of the Crusading period and for some time beyond it. Here is a selection of excerpts.[7]

The sea reinforces them [i.e. the Crusaders].[8]

As long as the sea reinforces them and the land does not repel them, they will remain a permanent scourge upon the lands [of Islam].[9]

This enemy is not a lone one, against whom a device can be effective, and on whom destruction can be brought. For he [i.e. that enemy] comprises everybody who is beyond the sea, and all those who are in the lands of the infidel [literally: infidelity]. There is not a single town of theirs, or a village, or an island or a province, be it big or small, which did not fit out its ships and did not alert its squadrons . . . reinforcement after reinforcement came from them continuously . . . as for their kings, who arrive by land, their countries were emptied of them, according to a steadily flowing information.[10]

Saladin, in a meeting with his commanders during his army's retreat from Acre, stated:

You should know that this enemy of God and of ours has come with [all] its cavalry and infantry . . . and brought to combat the whole of infidelity against the whole of Islam *(qad baraza bil-kufri kullihi ilā al-Islām kullihi)* . . . and it had exhausted all that it could *(istanfada wus 'ahu)* [in the sense: mobilised all its resources] . . . As for us, there is no succour in our rear which we can expect, or a force which we can summon. Only our people was afflicted by that people. Only our army is facing the army of infidelity. There is none among the Muslims who will come to our succour and there is none in the lands of Islam who will help us.[11]

These excerpts, though written during or near the height of the Crusaders' counter-offensive at that time, reflect a deep perception of the realities of the naval balance of power between Islam and West European Christianity. What the Muslims became convinced of, with full justification, 100 years *before* the expulsion of the last Crusader from Palestine and Syria, was that under the very best circumstances (from the Muslim point of view) the Muslim coastline would remain for the foreseeable future the battle front between Islam and Christianity. This would also apply to the periods of relative peacetime between the two opponents. The fact that all the islands of the eastern

252

Mediterranean, including Cyprus and Rhodes, were in Christian hands, could only strengthen that very realistic conviction. After Saladin's demolition of Ashkelon and up to the end of the Crusades, the Muslims systematically destroyed the coastal fortifications and many of the port towns they captured from the Franks, together with their ports. Generally speaking, they did this with greater thoroughness on the Palestinian section of the coast than on its Syrian section, because of its proximity to Jerusalem, and because of its being more suitable for landing from the sea. To call this kind of demolition "scorched earth policy" would be most misleading, for the usual meaning of this term is an operation of destruction of a temporary character, which is carried out when the enemy attacks, or threatens to attack. As soon, however, as the enemy retreats, or the threat is removed, the act of rebuilding usually starts. In the case of the Muslims it was completely different. The operation of demolition started, habitually, as soon as the enemy had been ousted, and the demolished place was left in ruins for a long time, in most cases for centuries.

It should be emphasised and re-emphasised in this connection that this was the greatest act of destruction for defence purposes ever carried out *in the recorded history of the human race.* The permanent effects of this destruction are also unparalleled. The uniqueness of that operation in human history, or even in a more limited history, have never been pointed out by any scholar other than the present writer; certainly not its import and implications in the wider context of the struggle for supremacy between Islam and European Christianity.

Perhaps the best proof of the Muslims' admission of their naval inferiority and their disbelief in their ability to rectify that situation within a definite period is the following fact. From the middle of the thirteenth century onwards, and up until the total expulsion of the Franks in 1291, the Crusaders' power declined steadily. For no less than 40 years the Muslims were able to play a cat-and-mouse game with them and capture their strongholds one after the other at their convenience. Yet they continued methodically to destroy the coastal strongholds, and in many cases blocked the destroyed ports by the debris which they threw into the water, thus demonstrating their intention to put those ports out of use for a very long time. Even the fact that the same areas which had been the target of the Crusaders' invasion had now been defended by the extremely powerful Mamlūk army, which was far stronger than anything the Muslims had since the beginning of the Crusades, was not sufficient to dissuade them from their consistent policy of destruction.

Finally, the hindsight we possess today was obviously not available to the Muslims at that time. As is well known, the Crusading spirit did not die out in 1291. Plans and schemes to revive the Crusades did exist, and some of them did not look impractical at all. The full scale of the divisions within the Frankish camp was unknown to the Muslims; but even if they had known about them, they would have had no guarantee that those divisions would continue indefinitely.[12]

As a matter of fact the Franks had, on paper, the means of defeating the strongest Muslim military power in the later Middle Ages through a naval blockade, which would have deprived it of vital raw materials like wood and metals, and, no less important, of a very substantial part of its Mamlūks, because many (perhaps most) of them were brought over to Egypt and Syria on board Frankish ships. This was, of course, a theoretical possibility, because the chances of a Frankish united front against Islam were very meagre indeed. What I wish to point out, however, is that even a divided Christian Europe, beset by internal problems and antagonisms, could have reduced, without difficulty, the Muslim naval power in the Mediterranean sea to near insignificance.

Islamic naval inferiority came about at a much earlier date than military inferiority on land. A major cause of this delay, as I have already stated, was the Mamlūk socio-military institution, the like of which neither Europe nor any other civilisation possessed. But it *had* to take place because that institution was bound to become outdated sooner or later, both as a result of the grinding process of the relatively slow-growing European technological superiority, and as a result of technological breakthroughs.

One of these breakthroughs was the invention and introduction of firearms. Although the adoption of that weapon was very slow and painful, it was a breakthrough all the same. Particularly important is the fact that in Europe, generally speaking, it was adopted more efficiently than in the Muslim armies. Even more important: in Europe there existed the proper industrial foundations for its manufacture and development in the future.

One of the main obstacles for the efficient employment of firearms in most of the Muslim armies, above all the Mamlūk armies (with the exception of the janissary offshoot), was that the élite units of those armies consisted of cavalrymen. This was particularly decisive when the handgun, the personal weapon of the soldier, was introduced on a grand scale. It meant, for quite a long period, dismounting from the horse.

There is no doubt that the Ottomans defeated the Mamlūks and wiped out their empire mainly because of their superiority in firearms, and their correct handling of the weapons. The Ottomans were much more open than any other great Muslim state to technological innovations, and to adapting their military machine to them. They had a superb infantry, and developed a very impressive naval power. However, since the production of weapons went hand in hand with industrial development, and since the Ottomans did not have a strongly developed industrial sector, they were faced with two equally bad alternatives: either to produce weapons of their own, which could not be of the highest quality, or to import weapons from European industrial centres, which had their own interests in mind and quite often preferred to sell obsolete or obsolescent types of armament to their less industrially developed clients.

The temporary dominance of the Ottoman navy in the Mediterranean sea, or, more precisely, in parts of it, might create a misleading impression. At that time the naval struggle moved gradually but steadily to the great oceans, and it was a purely Western European struggle in which the Muslims could not take part, in spite of the fact that it changed the face of the globe in a way which proved to be very detrimental to Islam.[13]

As already stated, Muslim military inferiority on land was bound to come, and it did, at a steady pace. After a long and almost uninterrupted series of defeats, Muslim rulers came one after the other, with great reluctance and against a very strong internal antagonism, to the conclusion that they would have to build their armed forces, *from top to bottom,* according to the European model. The first to do so in the vast area which includes the whole of Africa and the whole of Asia, together with the islands of the Pacific Ocean, was Egypt's ruler Muḥammad 'Alī, in the first half of the nineteenth century. In order to achieve that aim, he had to remove the older military elements (mainly cavalrymen), particularly the Mamlūks, whom he wiped out, and the Bedouins, whom he settled. The main element from which he built his new navy was Egypt's *fellahin*. The fruits of his military revolution were reaped quickly. Under his rule Egypt expanded over most of the Arabian peninsula, conquered the Sudan,[14] the whole of the Syro-Palestinian region and penetrated deeply into Anatolia, to be stopped only by the European powers' intervention. *Never in its recorded history had Egypt expanded so far beyond its borders.*

Today all the Muslim armies are based on the European model and have hardly any connection with the older armies of Islam. This is also true of the non-Muslim armies in the vast area mentioned above, which are likewise modelled on the European pattern.

To sum up: the Crusading phase in the struggle between Islam and Christian Europe, which centred on the Holy Land and on Jerusalem, had implications in history which went far beyond that particular period and geographical area. These implications are reflected in the temporary occupation of some Middle Eastern countries — including all the areas which the Crusaders ruled — by European powers in the first half of the twentieth century. These powers had to leave those countries for reasons other than the local military might.

The wrong impression may be created by ending this discussion here. European society was certainly more open to innovations and changes in the military and in other fields than Muslim society, but it was also beset by prejudices and conservatisms which continued well into the twentieth century. In 1925, Field Marshal Earl Haig, the commander of the British Expeditionary Force in the Western Front in the First World War, asserted emphatically that the aeroplane and the tank could only be accessories to man and the horse. Other British personalities in key military positions continued in the mid-thirties to praise the horse as an essential element in modern warfare, and demonstrated great reluctance to accelerate the process of mechanisation of the British army.[15] The Soviet marshal Semion Budenny was still sure in 1967 that in a third world war the horse would play a decisive role.[16] Not less significant was the attitude of the American naval command after the First World War to William Mitchell, who strove to provide air cover to the American naval units.[17]

NOTES

1   This increasing military superiority had, of course, its ups and downs. In this chapter only existing situations and their impact are discussed. In my view, it is too early to pinpoint the whole set of underlying causes which created those situations. Although I put here the stress on the technological and military aspects, it should be remembered that these aspects are only part of a much wider background. Another thing that should be borne in mind is that it is, of course, very important to establish where a certain invention or innovation came into being. But what is far more important is how it merged into the general stream of creativeness and

activity (or the lack of them) and what was the follow up resulting from its appearance and adoption (in those cases where it *was* adopted).

2   These were the ideal stipulations, which were ignored from time to time, but not to a degree that could endanger the system.

3   The word "fanaticism" would be completely misleading within the conceptions of those times.

4   The Mamlūks always constituted a small part of the whole body of armed forces of any state, including the Mamlūk sultanate.

5   Of course, the expression "proper kind of armies" applies to the ideas and conceptions of those times.

6   See especially *al-Fatḥ al-Qussī fī al-Fatḥ al-Qudsī*, Leiden, 1888, pp. 117–19.

7   These excerpts were cited in Arabic transcription, without translation, in my "The Great Yāsa of Chingiz Khān — A Reexamination", part C₂, *Studia Islamica,* Paris, 1973, pp. 153–4. Here only the translations are given.

8   Al-Iṣfahānī, op. cit., p. 233, 1.6.

9   Ibid., p. 204, 11.20–21.

10   Ibid., pp. 222, 1. 14–223, 1. 13.

11   Ibid., p. 109, 11. 4–11.

12   I dealt with the destruction of the Syro-Palestinian coastal fortifications and towns in "The Mamlūks and Naval Power — A Phase in the Struggle between Islam and Christian Europe", *Proceedings of the Israel Academy of Sciences and Humanities,* Vol. I, Jerusalem, 1965, pp. 1–2; in Baḥriyya (the Navy), *EI*², and in other studies. The detailed description of the demolishing of each of those strongholds is contained in a chapter on the naval power of the Mamlūks, which had not yet been published.

13   Besides firearms, the most important technological innovation in the later Middle Ages was the printing press. In Europe it spread very quickly and its tremendous impact was felt in many major fields. In Islam its introduction and spread were incomparably slower, as a result of a deliberate policy of the Muslim authorities, who allowed (in the Ottoman Empire) the Jews, the Greek Orthodox and the Armenians to have printing presses at quite early dates, but forbade them to print anything for the Muslims. Printing in Arabic characters started in Europe long before it started in any Muslim country. This is an important example of the difference in attitude towards change between Islam and European Christianity.

14   In fact, the Arabian Peninsula and the Sudan were conquered at a very early stage of Muḥammad 'Alī's military reformation, and before the recruitment of the Egyptian *fellah* to the new army.

15   B.H. Liddell Hart, "Horse, Foot and Tank", *Spectator*, 28 September 1956, pp. 412–13.

16   Harrison G. Salisbury, "Budenny Recalls Soviet Setbacks", *New York Times,* 10 October 1967.

17   Part of what is said in this chapter is based on a much more detailed examination in other studies of mine.

20 New discoveries in Islamic archaeology in the Holy Land

Myriam Rosen-Ayalon

Since time immemorial the Holy Land has been a privileged area for the converging of various civilisations. This was true in ancient times, which we know through prehistoric discoveries, and as late as the medieval period. Indeed throughout the Middle Ages, which was the Islamic period in the Holy Land, one witnesses the repeated occurrence of cultural and artistic trends borrowed from elsewhere, and in particular from neighbouring countries.

Various recent archaeological discoveries show interesting parallels with relics found elsewhere in the Muslim world, thus creating a fascinating chain of relations within Islamic civilisation.

The four "milestones" that have been selected for this discussion out of the numerous discoveries that have been made should help to illustrate this phenomenon. It is not our task to list the finds, or to survey the various excavations performed in the Holy Land, but rather to investigate these four examples, as test-cases, and to examine their relationship with some contemporaneous sites of similar artistic interest.

In terms of archaeology, Islamic archaeology is usually referred to as "later period", or "lower period", meaning that it concerns periods that are relatively recent. Actually, Islamic archaeology is the newest of studies in this discipline, with a much shorter history to its credit.

The temptation to discuss the most beautiful archaeological finds is always great, and indeed it was difficult to decide which would be the most meaningful examples for this study. However, at the risk of sounding "esoteric", the four examples chosen are believed to serve best the purpose of this discussion. All of them clearly illustrate the recent archaeology in the Holy Land and provide the necessary elements for comparisons on a wider scale, with finds outside the land where they were discovered. Each example bears a very different message and relates to a different period or stage of Islamic history in the Holy Land.

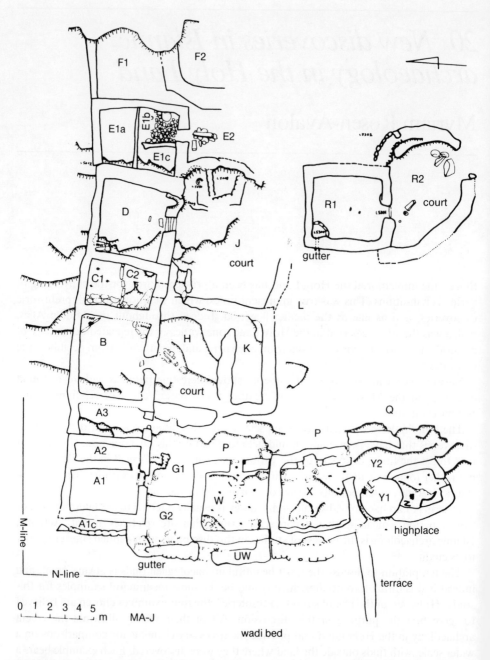

FIGURE 20.1   Seventh to eighth century desert dwellings: early Muslim architecture in the area of Sde-Boker

In order to facilitate this presentation, the respective topics will be introduced in chronological order.

The first subject to be discussed relates to a project which I have been heading for the past five years, commonly known as the *Sde-Boker* project.

Since 1981 a very systematic study has been conducted in the Central Negev, which has yielded some rather unexpected results. So far the work has covered only a relatively small part of a rather large area, where interesting vestiges have been found.

Without going into all the details of this complicated excavation, which was carried out in the field by Y. Nevo, I would like to draw attention to the following features:

A. 1. The site has revealed an unusual type of stone architecture, built as a series of units. Several such units are lined up in a row, each one with a single opening. These units combined create a relatively elongated compound, with series of elements of the same type (Figure 20.1).

   2. Another interesting element is what we would call "platforma" or *bimot*. These are somewhat elevated platforms, which are usually round and are occasionally related with other elements, such as courtyards, or "astellas", as they shall be called here.

   3. Astelae of various kinds were unearthed. Some were found still standing, others inclined, and in some cases they had even been lying down, but it should be clearly stated that they had not fallen down. They were deliberately put in their position, supported by stones. All of them are very much homogeneous and contemporary, standing on the same virgin soil; those astelae are either related to thresholds of the various entrances, or as already referred to earlier, to some of the platforms.

   4. Seventh to eighth century ceramics are incorporated into the abovementioned elements, and provide an extremely valuable clue to the age of these finds.

It should be stressed from the outset that both the architecture and the finds are absolutely homogeneous. They all belong to one single period and were all found in the excavated area, lying on the "virgin rock". The pottery, though scanty, is very typical of well-known and accurately dated ceramic. The lamp fragments (Figure 20.2) are most relevant, for they relate all the pottery to the early Islamic period, which in the Holy Land has been dated as the seventh to eighth centuries. These lamps are identifiable both by their shape and technique of manufacture, as well as by their decoration. They have a somewhat almond shape, and are made of two halves pressed separately into a mould. A knob handle is added at the end of the process of manufacturing. The moulded decorations are varied, ranging from geometrical to floral motifs, and occasionally even small animals. The most meaningful decoration, however, is undoubtedly the epigraphic decoration.

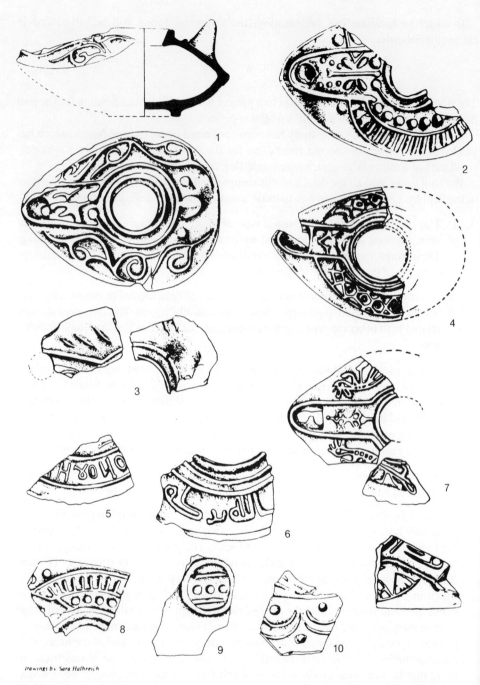

Drawings by Sara Halbreich

FIGURE 20.2   Samples of pottery, mainly lamps, from the excavations at Sde-Boker

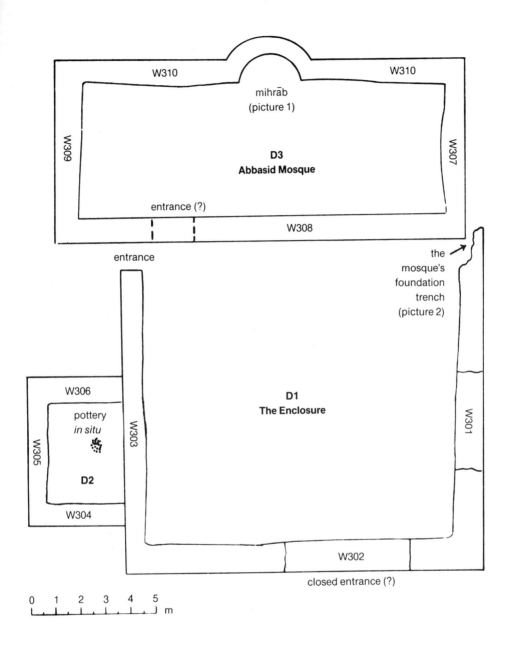

FIGURE 20.3   Plan of an open-air mosque

261

These inscriptions are, indeed, of enormous interest to us. In this very typical group of lamps, which have been fairly accurately dated, the inscriptions are found in either Greek or Arabic. The usage of the Arabic script on lamps does not antedate the Muslim conquest of the Holy Land, but clearly identifies the Islamic era. On the other hand, the continued use of Greek script indicates a custom which is prevalent in other areas as well. The use of Greek coins with Arabic countermarks until 'Abd al-Malik's monetary reform is a case in point.[1] Another example is the case of a recently discovered inscription in Hamat Gader on the shore of the lake of Tiberias, where an inscription from AD 662, in the name of Caliph-Mu'āwiya, is written in Greek.[2]

The lamps and lamp fragments are therefore part of a much wider phenomenon. Similar pieces have also been found in neighbouring countries,[3] an indication of the coexistence of the two civilisations; Greek-Christian and Arab-Muslim, at a turning point in the history of the Holy Land.

B. A very special type of mosque (Figure 20.3) was surveyed in the same area, dating from the eighth to the beginning of the ninth century. Several of its kind are known in the wider area of the Negev, all of them possessing very similar features. This "open-air" mosque probably never comprised more than a few layers of stone, in order to seclude the worship area. It is duly oriented towards Mecca, with a *Miḥrāb* (praying niche) in the middle of its orientation wall (the *qibla*).

C. A spectacular collection of rock inscriptions was unearthed. Nearly 600 inscriptions have been registered and inventoried so far and these records are almost ready for publication. Of course, in a brief survey such as this it is not possible to discuss the complex problems of paleography, onomasticon or the many other facets of this extraordinary discovery in the Negev. Yet three points should be stressed in connection with this subject.

First, some of these inscriptions have been dated from the seventh century up to the late eighth and perhaps early ninth century. Second, the inscriptions contain some very interesting names, including some typical pre-Islamic names, such as Imru' -al Qays (Figure 20.4), and it may even be possible to trace genealogies or families. A third and last point that should be made is that this wide and rich discovery, although it is of paramount interest to the history of the Holy Land, should not be viewed as a unique and isolated case. It belongs, in fact, to a much wider phenomenon that is apparent in various parts of the Near East.[4]

Among these inscriptions are also numerous pictoglyphs, which once again deserve a separate, more detailed study that is beyond the scope of this chapter.

The finds in the Negev probably comprise one of the most exciting chapters in the "Jāhiliyya" of the Holy Land. It is stamped, in all probability, by a specific set of circumstances which makes it even more intriguing, for it is probably a "local Jā-hiliyya", with all its implications on the process of Islamisation, and the many socio-cultural relations which they reflect.[5]

★   ★   ★

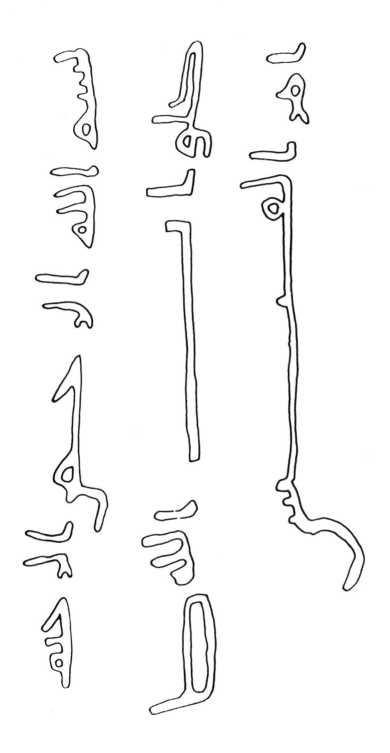

FIGURE 20.4 Early Islamic rock graffiti from the Negev. "In the name of Allah the compassionate the Merciful, may Allah bless Imru' al-Qays"

The second subject for discussion is the famous excavations conducted during the seventies by Professor Mazar in the south and south-western area of the Temple Mount in Jerusalem. These excavations, which carried on for nearly 10 years, once again constituted a revolutionary discovery. The whole area surrounding the Haram al-Sharīf (the Temple Mount) yielded a number of buildings (Figure 20.5). By and large, they all seem to belong to what we may classify as secular architecture as distinct from religious architecture. An amazing fact is that no reference whatsoever relating to any such architecture in Jerusalem can be found in any historical source. Most of the buildings share many features in common, the basic plan being a quadrangular house with a central courtyard onto which rooms open on all four sides.

Among the various buildings unearthed, one stands out in particular, and this is the central one. It is also the largest of all, and the best preserved, with a rich variety of architectural decoration. Columns, carved stone, and fragments of frescoes all contribute to recreate an image of the luxurious building it must once have been. The plan itself is reminiscent of the various "Umayyad Palaces" uncovered in the Syro-Palestinian area from the nineteenth century onwards.[6] The similarity between the two goes even further, for the excavations also yielded a most valuable clue — the beginning of the spring of an arch in what was once the upper part of the wall of the building in a section that faced the Haram al-Sharīf. The existence of such an arch would suggest that it was once part of an arched passage leading from the building to the Al-Aqsa mosque which it faces. Such an architectural device was used in early Islamic architecture to provide the ruler with the shortest connection between his quarters in the palace and the mosque.[7] The building is in all probability, therefore, the *Dār al-Imāra,* the House of the Governor, which fills a gap of major significance in our discovery of the architecture of Jerusalem in the early Islamic period.

The secular Umayyad architecture in Jerusalem is contemporaneous with the well-known religious monuments of the Dome of the Rock and the al-Aqsa Mosque, and concurs with contemporary secular architecture in neighbouring countries.

If one were to plot the architecture of Jerusalem on a chronological table one would probably be surprised to discover that the *Dār al-Imāra* ranks amongst the very earliest examples of these compounds. There is no doubt that the plan of the building is in line with many other palaces known elsewhere in the Muslim world.

There is another important point that should be raised in connection with the discovery of this Umayyad compound. In the southernmost part of the city, the ancient walls that surrounded the old city of Jerusalem lie immediately above the foundations of some of those buildings. The city walls as they are seen today, which completely encircle the old city, were last restored during the first half of the sixteenth century under the initiative of the Ottoman sultan Suleiman the Magnificent.[8] The fact that the sixteenth century walls were built above the foundations of the Umayyad secular architecture clearly indicates that during the early Islamic period the city walls must have been situated beyond these buildings, and the city, at this part at least, must have extended to the south beyond its sixteenth century limits. This provides us with valuable information about the topography of Jerusalem during the early Islamic period.

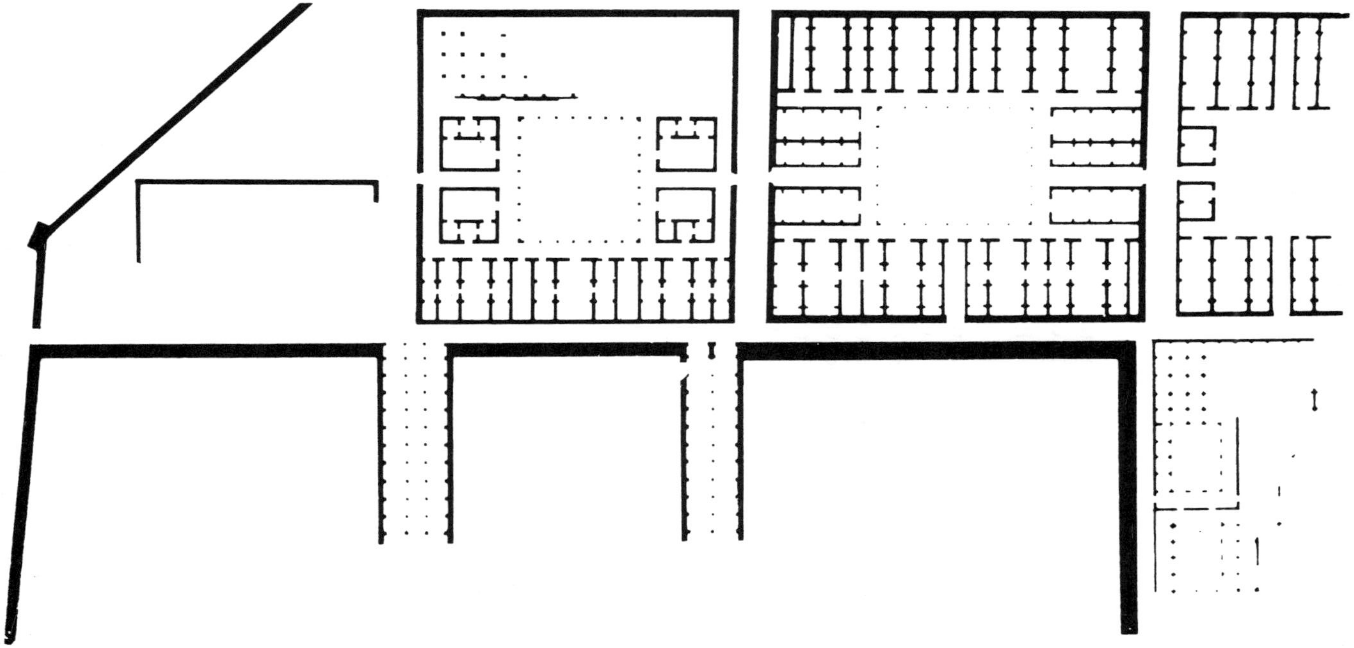

FIGURE 20.5   Umayyād architecture in the excavated area around the Ḥaram al-Sharīf (after M. Ben-Dov)

The third subject chosen for discussion concerns a completely different field.

Owing to some unexpected repairs performed in the courtyard of a private house in the old quarter of Ramla in 1973, a group of three Islamic mosaics was uncovered. Not many floor mosaics from the Islamic period have been discovered, and their scarcity seems strange in the light of the flourishing art of mosaic decoration in pre-Islamic periods. Those that have been discovered date from the early centuries of the Islamic era. The Ramla mosaics are no exception in this respect, but they reveal at the same time some startling differences.

Two of the mosaics are still connected to a plain strip of white stone cubes, which links them together. The third mosaic must have once also been part of this ensemble, though at some later stage a wall built there created a separation between the first two mosaics and the third one.[9]

The two mosaics that remain connected are quite different in their respective patterns, but both their decorations are based on an over-all geometrical entrelac, creating a series of medallions. Most of these medallions contain various motifs, which are mostly floral but occasionally geometrical and sometimes even abstract. There is no doubt, however, that the most fascinating part of the discovery lies in the third mosaic.

This example is unique in every respect, and nothing has been found in any part of the Muslim world that can compare with it. Despite the fact that it is partly damaged in its upper area, the composition is still clear. Two columns, whose bases and capitals can both be identified, support an arch (which was damaged in earlier times). Within this arch is an inscription, also set in cubes of mosaic (Figure 20.6). The arch, supported as it is by a pair of columns, can be clearly identified as a *miḥrāb* (praying niche), and this is the only example where mosaic has been used to illustrate a *miḥrāb*. In addition, this is the only known instance where there is an inscription on a floor mosaic, a discovery which is even more unique for the fact that the inscription is actually part of a coranic verse. The passage of verse refers clearly to a prayer, and stresses the fact that we are in front of a praying niche. This would seem to suggest that the mosaic once belonged to some kind of chapel, within what must have been a private home. Private *miḥrābs* are known to exist in few cases in homes in Samarra[10] dating from the ninth century.

The finds collected at the site together with the group of mosaics would all point to an eighth century dating, which is also in accordance with the stylistic elements of the three mosaics.

The fourth and last example to be discussed brings us back to Jerusalem, to another extraordinary discovery.

As already mentioned, the walls of Jerusalem as they are today date back to a sixteenth century Ottoman restoration. They follow, to a great extent, the medieval layout of the city walls, yet there are several parts where it is clear that the walls once demarcated a somewhat wider boundary to the city.

During the seventies an archaeological excavation directed by Magen Broshi took

FIGURE 20.6   Mosaic from Ramla (Courtesy of the Department of Antiquities and Museums in Israel)

place in the area of the Zion Gate, in the south-western section of the walls. In this dig part of the walls was uncovered, as well as a passage, which Broshi identified as one of the Ayyūbid gates,[11] dating back to the first half of the thirteenth century. This discovery, which in itself is very interesting, was surpassed by the finding of an extraordinary piece of monumental inscription which relates to the foundation of the Ayyūbid sector. (Figure 20.7).

The inscription is rendered in powerful and rhythmic Ayyūbid script, giving clearly the name of the Ayyūbid sultan al-Malik al-Mu'aẓẓam 'Īsā, who ruled in the first half of the thirteenth century.[12]

In order to fully perceive the importance of this discovery, it is important to refer to a most exceptional chapter of Muslim history at that time. Many historical sources refer to the fortifications of Jerusalem, and the rebuilding of the walls by al-Malik al-Mu'aẓẓam 'Īsā. But shortly after having built these walls and gates of the city, as stated on the inscription, a new military strategy was adopted and al-Malik al-Mu'aẓẓam 'Īsa ordered

FIGURE 20.7   Ayyūbid inscription from Jerusalem (Courtesy Magen Broshi)

the destruction of the newly completed walls. This was part of a more general policy, which can be followed in various parts of the coastal area of this part of the Muslim world.[13] In a nutshell, the idea was to prevent the Crusaders from planning a return to Jerusalem, and this manifested itself in a scorched earth policy (discussed in the previous chapter). The broken inscription discovered by Broshi is the evidence confirming this extraordinary policy.

The Ayyūbid period in Jerusalem has not been studied enough, and there is still much to be discovered there related to this period.[14] Broshi's discovery was thus of tremendous archaeological and historical value.

Each of the four archaeological discoveries chosen for discussion in this chapter dates from a different period of Islamic history in the Holy Land and each holds a special position in the history of its civilisations. Each deserves far deeper study than has been possible here and, indeed, if this brief survey arouses curiosity enough to stimulate such study, it will have achieved its purpose.

NOTES

1 K.A.C. Creswell, *Early Muslim Architecture,* Oxford, 1969, Vol. I, Part 1, pp. 130–31.

2 Joshua Blau, "The Transcription of Arabic Words and Names in the inscription of Mu'āwiya from Hammat Gader", *Israel Exploration Journal,* Vol. 32, no. 2–3, 1982.

3 Florence Day, "Early Islamic and Christian Lamps", *Berytus,* III, 1942, pp. 65–79.

4 Adolf Grohman, *Arabic Inscriptions,* Expédition Philby-Rickmans-Lippens en Arabie, Louvain, 1962; Henry Field, *Camel Brands and Graffiti from Iraq, Syria, Jordan, Iran, and Arabia,* Supplement to the Journal of the American Oriental Society, 1952.

5 M. Rosen-Ayalon, and Y. Nevo, *The Early Arab Period in the Negev,* Jerusalem, 1982.

6 Creswell, op. cit., Vol. I, Part 2, *passim.*

7 Creswell, op. cit., Vol. I, Part 1, pp. 54–8.

8 Max van Berchem, *Corpus Inscriptionum Arabicarum,* Le Caire, 1923, Jérusalem "Ville", pp. 431–49.

9 Myriam Rosen-Ayalon, "The First Mosaic Discovered in Ramla", *Israel Exploration Journal,* Vol. 26, 1976, pp. 104–19.

10 Ibid., note 73.

11 Magen Broshi, "New Excavations along the Walls of Jerusalem", *Qadmoniot,* 9, 1976, p. 78 (in Hebrew).

12 M. Sharon, "The Ayyūbid Walls of Jerusalem. A New Inscription from the Time of al-Mu'azzam 'Isa'", in *Studies in Memory of Gaston Wiet,* Myriam Rosen-Ayalon (ed.), Jerusalem, 1977, pp. 179–93.

13 David Ayalon, "The Mamluks and Naval Power — A Phase of the Struggle between Islam and Christian Europe", in *Proceedings of the Israel Academy of Sciences and Humanities,* Jerusalem, 1965, pp. 1–12.

14 M. Rosen-Ayalon, "Art and Architecture in Ayyūbid Jerusalem", *Eretz-Israel,* Vol. 18, 1965, pp. 65–72, in Hebrew. English summary p. 67.

Part VII
Modern History and Politics

21 The United States and the Holy Land in the nineteenth century

Jacob M. Landau

INTRODUCTION

The writing of history nowadays is becoming increasingly difficult. Despite the cumulative availability of primary sources and the marked growth in such technical aids as xerography, microfilm and computers at the service of historians, preconceptions and political passions frequently obscure the issues. In our own case, it is sometimes argued that since all Great Powers were very actively involved in the power politics of the Ottoman Empire in the nineteenth century, the United States must have been involved as well. Alternatively, it is believed that since the United States became politically involved in Middle Eastern affairs in the twentieth century, with particular emphasis on Palestine, this must have been the case in the nineteenth century as well.

This chapter examines the nature of US involvement in Palestine during the nineteenth century. It commences with a brief account of American interests in the Holy Land in preceding years, then proceeds to focus on the growth of these interests and its ramifications during the nineteenth century, pointing out the change which occurred early in the twentieth century.

BACKGROUND

The Holy Land constituted a component of North American spiritual awareness even before the United States achieved independence, continuing its influence subsequently as well. Several manifestations of this phenomenon are evident.[1]

The biblical heritage

In the American tradition of the Colonial era, the Bible was a potent cohesive factor. The individual outlook of puritans and pilgrims, their family life and social gatherings, political organisations and spiritual views were all permeated by biblical influence. The adoption of personal and place names with a biblical origin was very widespread. There are, for instance, 27 towns and countries called Salem, as well as 15 Zions. In one such town, Zion City, Illinois, all streets bear biblical names. Indeed, the Bible was the most widely-read book at that time, an intimately known and prized inheritance. When the US Congress, early in its career, voted to appropriate funds for the import of 20 000 Bibles, it was doubtlessly acting in this tradition.[2]

The Hebrew language

The special role played by the Hebrew language was probably due to this biblical influence. While one may doubt the authenticity of the story that Hebrew, along with Greek, was considered as a substitute official language, Hebrew was revered nonetheless in its religious and later its scholarly contexts. Incorporated into the seals of several major universities, Hebrew was considered *de rigueur* for a well-educated person and consequently declared mandatory for some time in the curricula of several universities, such as Yale. In general, however, Hebrew remained part of curricula at theological faculties and schools alone, thereby becoming of prime concern mostly to religious-minded persons both within and without those schools, as exemplified in the efforts of Joseph Smith, the founder of the Church of Jesus Christ of the Latter-Day Saints (the Mormons), to study Hebrew and promulgate it among his flock.[3] Since the end of the eighteenth century, Hebrew has been studied increasingly in departments of Semitics at American universities as well.

Visiting the Holy Land

Up to the end of the eighteenth century, there was little American travel to Palestine. Such voyages were expensive, time-consuming and even dangerous; most Americans could hardly afford them and were preoccupied with their own concerns, namely the creation of a new polity, society and economy. The nineteenth century, on the other hand, witnessed a visible growth in travel by Americans (and others) to the Holy Land, for religious pilgrimages, commercial transactions, or simple curiosity, as travel became cheaper, safer, quicker and more comfortable (via ocean liner). To borrow a term from Ben-Arieh, this era marked "the rediscovery of the Holy Land."[4] Many of the tourists and pilgrims were saddened by the barren landscape they encountered,[5] although others perceived beauty beyond the desolation. Several recorded and published their impressions, thus stirring up further interest in various circles.[6] Mark Twain's *Innocents Abroad* may be the best-known of these works.

Settling in the Holy Land

Palestine, a small, poor country which was merely a remote backwater of the Ottoman Empire during the nineteenth century, could offer no incentive but the ideological one for any American or other Westerner to settle or even reside there for an extended period of time. Hence religious conviction was the prime mover for missionaries and other Christians to move to Palestine. The former established schools and hospitals, in Jerusalem and elsewhere. Other notable examples are those of agricultural colonies set up by Clarinda Minor (in 1853) and by George Jones Adams and 156 colonists from Maine (in 1866) — both near Jaffa — and by the Spafford Vester family, which established the so-called American Colony in Jerusalem (at the end of the century),[7] essentially a philanthropic institution. Since the 1880s, Jewish agricultural settlement of Palestine began in earnest, in the name of another ideology, Zionism. Small groups of American Jews joined the settlers who wished to reclaim the land and live on it by dint of hard, physical labour.

THE UNITED STATES AND THE HOLY LAND IN THE NINETEENTH CENTURY

The brief background presented here largely explains the trends and interests which conditioned attitudes of individuals and groups of Americans towards the Holy Land. In contrast, the United States' Administration, although not uninfluenced by the above-mentioned factors, appears to have approached Palestine in a manner dictated by its perception of an absence of any vital economic, political or military interest. This remained true throughout the nineteenth century, even though some Soviet and Arab historians have unsuccessfully attempted to extrapolate United States' Middle Eastern interests from the twentieth century into the nineteenth.[8]

Having considered the role of the Holy Land in American awareness, we proceed to focus on American interests and presence in the Holy Land during the nineteenth century.

The economic element

The nineteenth century witnessed a marked increase in US commerce with other countries. Free trade was indeed consistent with individual enterprise and the liberty of commerce, which were perceived as basic rights. The growth of American commerce chiefly meant exporting wheat to the Ottoman Empire and buying Izmir figs and raisins from Turkey and dates from the Arab lands. In time, other products were added to both imports and exports. By 1900, American exports to the Ottoman Empire reached the modest amount of $500 000 per year; imports were evidently higher, but still less than $7 000 000 annually.[9] Little to none of this commerce concerned Palestine. On the one hand, Palestine had little to sell during most of the nineteenth century, except for limited quantities of sesame and oranges, none of which were exported to the United States; on the other hand, Palestine's inhabitants could hardly afford to buy much (those who were able to do so purchased the desired items from local trading centres, especially Damascus). Moreover, the country had no deep-water harbour, nor any sizable seashore town to attract any but the occasional visit of an American ship. It was only during the early twentieth century — more accurately, in 1908-1913 — that so-called "dollar diplomacy" could first be perceived in the Ottoman Empire (although not in the Holy Land). At that time, a group of American investors, headed by Admiral Colby M. Chester (hence the usual appellation of

"The Chester Project") unsuccessfully attempted to obtain railroad concessions.[10] This matter, however, is outside the scope of this chapter.

Political and military elements

These elements appear to have been absent from the range of American interests in the Holy Land throughout the nineteenth century. The very rare visits of US Navy ships hardly signify any sustained military interests. One characteristic example is provided during the Crimean War: in 1853 the US Consul in Beirut asked the American Government to dispatch warships to Syria. During one of those visits, in 1854, carbines were distributed, for defensive purposes, to Americans who had founded an agricultural establishment near Jaffa. Political matters were expressed chiefly in the appointment of United States Consuls and Vice-Consuls, although (as indicated below) such appointments signified little if any political involvement at that time. Evidently, US political activity focused on the moves of American diplomats in Istanbul,[11] among whom Palestine was an infrequently discussed topic. Indeed, American consular agents in Palestine spent much of their time, in the words of Frank Manuel, "protecting travellers, . . . furthering the work of the Protestant missionaries and their schools, and protesting outrages against Christians and Jews."[12]

The first US Consul in Jerusalem was Warder Cresson, nominated in 1844. However, regular appointments began only after the end of the Crimean War, in 1856, beginning with John Warren Gorham. There were 14 consular appointments (Gorham included) between 1856 and 1900, i.e. an average of about three years for each term of office. Actually, several Consuls served for only a year or less. In Jaffa, where Lazarus M. Murad, a convert to Christianity, was nominated Vice-Consul in 1865, there were eight different Vice-Consuls (Murad included) between 1865 and 1900, or an average of just over four years per term of office. These relatively short spans were not conducive to acquisition of expertise, particularly because nearly all these functionaries were unfamiliar with Ottoman affairs or the special conditions of Palestine, which they knew mostly from reading the Old and New Testaments. Despite these circumstances, however, many proceeded to intervene in local affairs, frequently using their own judgement to bridge over the great distance between their post and Washington. A recent unpublished Ph.D. thesis at the Hebrew University of Jerusalem has examined the involvement of US Consuls in nineteenth century Palestine in Jewish affairs,[13] largely reflecting their overall activities as well, which may be broadly divided into general and specific categories.

General activities

While the nature of the activities of US Consuls in Palestine varied according to the immediate circumstances, the term of office and the character of the incumbent, many such activities revolved around the protection of American citizens through both economic assistance and direct intervention on their behalf. Several of the Consuls in Jerusalem considered it their duty to apply this protection to non-American Christians and Jews in

276

the Holy Land, particularly if they were stateless or Ottoman subjects liable to harsh treatment. Here libertarian and humanitarian sentiments combined with a desire to increase the number of the Consulate's protégés (a process then in progress at certain Consulates of other Powers as well). One instance — although by no means exceptional — was the granting of American protégé status in 1870 to several Jews in Palestine by Richard Beardsley (the United States' Consul in Jerusalem from 1870 to 1873), who obviously stretched the interpretation of their right to obtain it.[14] In several cases, such protection was granted without appropriate reference to Washington. In others, US Consuls in Palestine tried hard to obtain funds for the needy and destitute, mostly among the Christians and Jews, even if they were non-Americans. Again, these were largely private initiatives, rarely approved or funded by the United States Government.[15]

Settlers, archaeologists and missionaries

More particularly, however, United States representatives in the Holy Land aided and protected US citizens throughout the nineteenth century, including the rare American tourist who was molested physically or robbed. More frequently, however, US Consuls had to intervene in favour of American settlers, archaeologists and mostly missionaries. Owing to unsafe conditions in parts of the country and the labyrinthine intricacies of Ottoman bureaucracy, the United States representatives in Palestine had much more trouble with the few Americans there than their small number warranted.

American settlers in Palestine were not numerous, but they were undoubtedly dedicated, having exchanged the relative comforts of life in the United States for the hardships awaiting them in the Holy Land. As noted above, religious convictions motivated Clarinda Minor and others to establish an agricultural colony in Jaffa, in 1853. In 1866, a larger Millenarian group, mostly from Maine, came to settle there under the leadership of a mystic named George Jones Adams; a nucleus of the latter group moved to Jerusalem and became part of the above-mentioned American Colony there, which gradually grew to 150 persons, all Christians (mostly Protestants). However, modest numbers of American Jews came to settle in the Holy Land as well, chiefly during the latter part of the nineteenth century. In 1879, American Jews in Jerusalem set up a separate community with its own synagogue.

Religious sentiment was compounded by intellectual curiosity in ancient civilisations among archaeologists who would later define themselves as "Biblical Archaeologists". An important part of the field work of American (and some other) archaeologists in nineteenth-century Palestine consisted of mapping. The best-known of these Americans was Dr Edward Robinson, Professor of Biblical Literature at Union Theological Seminary in New York. In 1838 he toured Palestine together with another American, Eli Smith (an industrious missionary, educator and publisher of Arabic works).[16] The new scientific maps he prepared with painstaking accuracy on various aspects of biblical archaeology constituted a turning point in the cartography of Palestine.[17] Somewhat later, in 1870, a group of Americans set up the American Palestine Exploration Society in New York, emulating the archaeological and cartographical work of the Palestine Exploration Fund which the British had founded several years previously. In 1873, a delegation of the American Palestine Exploration Society mapped Palestine, west of the Jordan River, and produced 12 sheets covering some 500 square miles each, together comprising about 150 formerly unrecorded place names.[18] Finally, in 1900, the American School for Oriental Research was established in Jerusalem; it served as the focus for biblical archaeology studies by Americans.

Even more than settlers and archaeologists-cartographers, Protestant missionaries emphasised the American presence in nineteenth-century Palestine. Missionary activity in Palestine was part of a much larger effort to evangelise the world, co-ordinated in the first half of the century by the American Board of Commissioners for Foreign Missions (incorporated in 1812). In 1819, the Board which represented chiefly Congregationalists and Presbyterians, sent the first two delegates to study conditions for missionary work within the Ottoman Empire.[19] Within a few years, a base was established in Beirut, with stations fanning out into Palestine, where the focus of activity was, not unexpectedly, Jerusalem. The Board's delegate, Levi Parsons, actually resided in Jerusalem for several months in 1821. In 1824 Reverends Pliny Fisk and Isaac Bird were arrested there for selling Bibles to Armenian pilgrims. A year later Fisk's death was followed by suspension of the Protestant missionary effort in Palestine. The station was reopened, in 1834, by William McClure Thomson and his bride Eliza and discontinued again nine years later. The activities of American Protestant missionaries in Palestine continued somewhat sporadically, bolstered by visits from the base in Beirut. They were undoubtedly hampered by their late arrival into the Ottoman Empire and consequent lack of the legal status of a *millet*, or officially approved religious group (a status already held by several other Christian communities, the Muslims and the Jews). The American Protestants confined themselves to circulating Bibles, teaching and tending to the sick and the poor. Most of these efforts were directed at other Christian denominations and not at Muslims (to avoid conflict with the Ottoman Administration) and only slightly towards Jews (a fairly closed religious community at that time).

Ottoman response

Throughout the nineteenth century, the Ottoman Central Government in Istanbul considered the United States as having no direct interests in its Empire — in sharp contradistinction to the major European Powers. However, the Government maintained some reservations about certain American activities in the Holy Land and acted accordingly. This matter has been considered elsewhere in some detail by myself,[20] based on Ottoman sources. Here, we cite only the main points.

For the first three-quarters of the century, the Ottoman Empire still maintained a semblance of political and military power. Several of the sultans who reigned during that period even attempted to institute reforms from above. Nevertheless, they remained suspicious of any externally introduced change which did not have their sanction. Thus an 1824 *firman*, or imperial order, prohibited the import and circulation of Bibles — probably to avoid antagonising the Muslim population. The administrative measure was obviously not directed solely at American missionaries. However, the central authorities largely permitted local officials to circumscribe the activities of foreigners throughout the Empire and even to circumvent promises extracted from Istanbul. Hence American consular agents, settlers, archaeologists and missionaries, in Palestine and elsewhere, conducted an almost uninterrupted battle-of-wits with the Ottoman bureaucracy, which had mastered the fine arts of procrastination and confusing issues.

During the last quarter of the century, the problems of the Ottoman Empire acquired perilous immediacy. During the reign of Abdul Hamid II (1876–1909), the Empire was fighting a rearguard battle for its very survival; its military weakness had become obvious in its serious defeat by Russia in the 1877–1878 war and the Empire's loss of Cyprus and Egypt to Great Britain (1878 and 1882) and Tunisia to France (1881). Economically, its situation appeared hopeless as well. No less serious internal dangers were increasing with the growth of particularist nationalisms in the Balkans and in the Empire's Asiatic provinces. Consequently, the Ottoman authorities kept a watchful eye on movements they suspected of aiming at disintegration of the Empire. The occasional support offered by US consular agents to Jews in Palestine and to the Zionist movement aroused (unfounded) suspicions of "complicity" by the United States administration. Consequently, Ottoman diplomats in the United States were instructed to observe Zionist activities there, the press and the possible involvement of the American administration. Several quarrels ensued between the Ottoman authorities and US Consuls in Palestine, who intervened in favour of their protégés.

The Ottoman authorities were even more concerned about the Armenians in the Empire, as the latter presented demands of a more political nature and occasionally accompanied them with acts of violence. Late in the century, American missionaries interceded warmly in favour of the Armenians and even stirred up public opinion in the United States, increasing Ottoman suspicions and providing recurring cause for conflict.

CONCLUDING REMARKS

During most of the nineteenth century, American interests in the Holy Land remained cultural and religious. However, a new situation began to take shape during the final years of that century. Increasingly frequent interventions by US consular agents, nearly always on humanitarian grounds, nurtured feelings of suspicion traditionally inherent in Ottoman bureaucracy from the top to the lowest echelons. The resulting rejection of American demands, or delays in fulfilling them, incensed the American consuls, whose continued insistence aroused further suspicion of US intentions. The above-mentioned Chester Project, in the early twentieth century, further increased Ottoman misgivings about US involvement resembling that of the other Powers. Consequently, the project was shelved.

The twentieth century saw a marked change in US involvement in the Middle East — and of course in Palestine — which assumed the political, military and economic features characteristic of the strategic interests of a Great Power.

NOTES

1   Among the relevant literature, particularly useful is Moshe Davis, (ed.), *With Eyes Towards Zion*, Arno Press, New York, 1977.

2   Further examples in A.I. Katsh, *The Biblical Heritage of American Democracy*, Ktav Pub. Co., New York, 1977.

3   Details in Davis, op. cit., pp. 10–11.

4   Yehoshua Ben-Arieh, *The Rediscovery of the Holy Land in the Nineteenth Century*, The Magnes Press and Israel Exploration Society, Jerusalem, 1983.

5   For examples, Jacob M. Landau, *Abdul Hamid's Palestine*, André Deutsch and Carta, London and Jerusalem, 1979.

6   For the most famous American travellers in the Holy Land, cf. David H. Finnie, *Pioneers East: The Early American Experience in the Middle East*, Harvard U.P., Cambridge, MA, 1967, esp. ch. 7.

7   Bertha Spafford Vester, *Our Jerusalem: An American Family in the Holy City, 1881–1949*, Doubleday, Garden City, N.Y. 1950.

8   See also W.A. Williams, *America and the Middle East: Open Door Imperialism or Enlightened Leadership?* Rinehart & Company, New York, 1958, esp. pp. 57–8.

9   J.A. De Novo, *American Interests and Policies in the Middle East 1900–1939*, University of Minnesota Press, Minneapolis, Minn., 1968, p. 16.

10 Ibid., pp. 58–87, for details.

11 Cf. Thomas A. Bryson, *American Diplomatic Relations with the Middle East: 1784–1975: A Survey*, Scarecrow Press, Metuchen, N.J. 1977.

12 Frank F. Manuel, *The Realities of American-Palestine Relations*, Public Affairs Press, Washington, D.C., 1949, p. 8.

13 Ron Bartour, "American Consular Aid to Jews in Eretz-Israel in the Later Years of Ottoman Rule, 1856–1914", Unpublished Ph.D. Thesis, The Hebrew University of Jerusalem, 1985 (in Hebrew).

14 Ibid., pp. 55–7.

15 For a general survey of American philanthropic activities in the area, see Robert L. Daniel, *American Philanthropy in the Near East*, Ohio University Press, Athens, Ohio, 1970.

16 Ben-Arieh, op. cit., pp. 85–91.

17 The fruit of this visit was E. Robinson's *Biblical Researches in Palestine, Sinai, Arabia Petraea and Adjacent Regions*, published in 1841 in both English and German, which immediately bestowed on its author deserved renown.

18 A.L. Tibawi, *American Interests in Syria 1800–1901*, Oxford University Press, Oxford, 1966, pp. 230–31.

19 For details, see Joseph L. Grabill, *Protestant Diplomacy and the Near East: Missionary Influence on American Policy, 1810–1927*, University of Minnesota Press, Minneapolis, Minn., 1971. This work, however, pays scant attention to Palestine.

20 Mim Kemal Öke and Jacob M. Landau, "Ottoman Perspectives on American Interests in the Holy Land", in: Moshe Davis, (ed.). *With Eyes Towards Zion*, Vol. II, Praeger, N.Y., 1986, pp. 261–302. For a different interpretation, cf. Ali Ihsan, Bagis, "The Jewish Settlement in Palestine and the Ottomans' Policy", *The Third International Conference on Bilad al-Sham: Palestine, Vol. III. History of Palestine*, University of Jordan — Yarmouk University, 1984, pp. 1–9.

22 The Jews of Baghdad and the Holy Land

Sylvia G. Haim

As is well known, the overwhelming majority of the Jews of Iraq emigrated to Israel in 1950–51. The events relating to this migration have given rise to numerous publications in Israel and elsewhere. Many of these writings, particularly those which came out in Israel, have to be read in the context of the Israeli political scene — a scene marked by lively party-political contentions. In reading the literature one has to keep in mind the efforts of new migrants to make a niche for themselves in an unfamiliar and very competitive society, and therefore to establish their Zionist credentials in a state where Zionist ideology is the basis of political and official action. This chapter does not aim to examine the merits or otherwise of this literature, but to provide a picture of the way in which the community looked upon its relation — as a Jewish community — to the Holy Land before and after the political developments which followed the First World War. These developments in local and international politics, in the spread of various ideologies, and in the increasing sharpness of the Palestine problem, all transformed the conditions the community had for so long taken for granted and in which it had been accustomed to live and prosper.

Baghdad is referred to rather than Iraq because it is the Jewish community of the capital which was by far the most important in the country. It also used to form the largest single community of the capital. From this community originated very important small but thriving centres in Bombay, Calcutta, Shanghai, Manchester — the David Sassoons, the Khedouries, Gubbays, and others. Iraq Kurdistan also had its Jews, Kurdish speaking rural communities, but these small and oppressed communities started immigrating into Baghdad after the First World War. Baghdad moreover was the Rabbinical focus for all the communities of the provinces as well as for Bombay, Shanghai and the other settlements. It was also a source for religious knowledge to the communities of Persia, the Caucasus and perhaps even Central Asia.

A perusal of *A History of the Jews of Baghdad* by David Solomon Sassoon (Letchworth 1949) gives an idea of the traditional character of the community. One point which emerges clearly from the book is the importance of the religious authorities in the last century and the influence and sway they wielded over the faithful. This contrasts sharply with the period after the First World War when the Chief Rabbi, for one, is said to be "a puppet in the hands of the notables of the community". This change is ascribed partly to the introduction of modern education especially by the Alliance Israélite Universelle.

Reviewing the life and role of various *ḥakhamim,* the author calls Ḥakham Yosef Ḥayyim (1833–1909) who succeeded his father as Chief Rabbi at the age of 26 (1859–1909), the "last of the great rabbis" of the community. His reputation still lives within the community. It is interesting to note that Sassoon mentions his "more than ordinary zeal for Palestine and his feelings for the community of Israel in general". What did this "zeal for Palestine" mean in the last century and how did it express itself? We are told that Ḥakham Yosef Ḥayyim's "first journey to Palestine and his acquaintance with Kabbalistic lore made such an impression upon him", that he introduced certain changes in the prayer book. But just in case one is tempted to confuse this impact with Zionism, it is well to remember that during the last years of his life he was invited to be the Chief Rabbi of Jerusalem but declined the honour.

If Rabbi Yosef Ḥayyim did not move to Jerusalem, it is not because such a move was unknown. David Sassoon mentions that "in the year 1856 a new movement impelled by real love for Zion and Palestine, arose among the Jews of Baghdad, which resulted in many of them leaving their native city and immigrating into Palestine". Among them was Rabbi Mani, who eventually (1858) settled in Hebron as a teacher in that city, and whose descendants in today's Israel occupy important positions. Rabbi Eliahu b. Slimān Mani (1818–1899) was somewhat older than Yosef Ḥayyim, but he also studied Kabbalah; this was with Ḥakhām Eliahu b. Moshe Ḥayyim – Yosef Ḥayyim's father.

Others who went to Jerusalem formed a special community and founded their own synagogue called *Shoshannim le-David.* They formed a *Wā'ad 'adath ha-bablim.* In an alley in Jerusalem, not far from Mea Shearim, there is a tablet in a doorway of what must have been the communal centre of the Iraqi community. It lists the names of the benefactors, most of whom bear well-known Baghdadi family names. From a slightly later date, there is also the small synagogue set up for Hakham Ftaya. For a detailed study of yet earlier migrations — as well as the mass immigration — *The Jews of Iraq in the Land of Israel* by Abraham Ben-Yaacob (Jerusalem 1980) may be usefully consulted.

Whether it was interest in Kabbalah or political and economic factors which impelled people to emigrate to the Holy Land during the last century, it was certainly not Zionist ideology. The community was a traditional community organised as an Ottoman *millet.* After the Balfour Declaration, Zionist emissaries were sent to Baghdad and met with two different reactions. A few enthusiastic individuals moved to Palestine, but their response could not be considered representative. The other much more important and representative reaction came from the leaders of the community and was one of cautious objection. Menahem Daniel, the scion of one of the greatest land-owning families in the south of the country, a former member of the Chamber of Deputies in Istanbul, and later the only Jewish Senator in the Iraqi Senate, a position in which his son Ezra followed him, wrote to the Zionist Organization and raised two very strong objections. He feared that there might be an upheaval in the community such as when Shabbetai Zvi claimed to be the Messiah. Such uncontrolled enthusiasm could have undesirable and dire consequences. He also argued that Zionist activity might create among the Muslim population a feeling of antagonism which would be very harmful to the more or less peaceful existence of this ancient community.

In 1929 Sir Alfred Mond, a prominent British industrialist, went to Baghdad at the invitation of the authorities in order to advise on possible investments. There was a demonstration by the pupils of the Central Secondary School (al-madrasa al-i'dādiyya al-markaziyya) in protest against the visit of such a Zionist. These schoolboys later became important political leaders; their teachers were pan-Arab nationalists — Izzat Darwaza, Darwish al-Miqdadi and Akram Zu'aitar, all three of whom were Palestinians.

In the twenties, with the establishment of the Kingdom of Iraq and the desire to bring the country to full independence, there was quite a movement towards broader and higher education in which Jews participated fully. This trend placed them at the spearhead of the educated and professional élite. The Jews were fully committed citizens with a large stake in a country to which their ancestors had come 25 centuries earlier and from which their ancestral roots had emerged with the Patriarch Abraham. They were not used to thinking of themselves as anything but the sons of this country, to which they felt a very strong attachment. This is not surprising, considering that Arabic had for centuries been their mother-tongue and had, from the 1920s, become the first language of instruction in all their schools including the Alliance schools. An article by Ṣabri Ḥāfiẓ in the official newspaper of the Iraqi Ba'th party cautions against the dangers of the Jews taking over the study of modern Arabic literature. Warning the Arabs against this "infiltration by Zionism", Ḥāfiẓ writes that Israel has found that "the Jews of Iraqi origin are the most proficient in the knowledge of the Arabic language; this is because the Jews in Iraq were able to assimilate into Arab society, while they failed in Egypt, North Africa, Yemen and elsewhere. This is why Jews in Iraq knew Arabic well, whereas the Jews in Egypt spoke a jargon in which Arabic words were mingled with foreign words and constructions". (Ṣabri Ḥāfiẓ in al-Thawra, Baghdad, 16 January 1977). The ultimate compliment indeed!

Until 1932, as long as the British Mandate was in force, Zionist activity was still legal and money was raised openly for charitable purposes in the Holy Land, albeit on a small scale. There was also some purchase of land, again on a comparatively small scale. A variety of reasons may account for this: caution had become second nature, scepticism about the viability of such investments which were charitable rather than commercial, but principally the rootedness in the country. The end of the Mandate coincided with the rise of Nazi Germany and with the growth in the country of elements which were actively inimical to Zionism and not too favourably inclined to Jews as such. The Jewish community in Iraq naturally came to fear these elements and to realise more and more that events in Europe might have repercussions in their country. Nervousness taught them even greater caution.

To emphasise this need for caution, however, does not and need not imply that they were hiding Zionistic tendencies. On the contrary. By and large they were not interested in the movement. The religious among them did not necessarily connect the Return to Zion

283

with political ideology or with the immediate realisation of their Messianic hope. The notables could see the problems involved in Zionism and its realisation. The younger generation, those educated in the twenties and thirties, were educated in schools which emphasised Iraqi nationalism. It is not strange that they felt patriotic and proud of their own and their country's achievements. It is to be stressed that Iraq was founded after the First World War on the basis of Arab nationalist theory. Arab nationalism viewed Zionism as an inimical movement which established itself in Palestine in order to gain gradual control of the lands between the Nile and the Euphrates. It was therefore — by definition — impossible to be a patriotic Iraqi and a Zionist at the same time. This became very sharp in the thirties as in later decades.

This being the case, how then could the exodus of 120 000 people have taken place in 1950–51? If it was not the expression of Zionist fervour, what else could it have been? The answer is reasonably clear. There was the looting and massacre of Jews — the *farhūd* —of June 1941, a traumatic experience which had a lasting effect particularly on young people. Their unease made them realise that they could no longer leave decisions concerning their future in the hands of their elders. After the events of 1941, moreover, and right through the war, Palestinian Jews employed in the British Army in various capacities started to arrive in Iraq. There was an organised policy on their part to make contact with the Jewish community and to educate the youngsters in Hebrew and in Zionism. The most famous of these men was undoubtedly Enzo Sereni. (His assessment of the community has been published in *Pe'amim* (1981).) The internal political situation was by no means less important. There was significant unrest in the country, particularly after the end of the war. The year 1948 was particularly disturbed. Negotiations for the Portsmouth Treaty were underway, which was to put the relations between Iraq and Great Britain on a basis of equality, to end the special privileges of the British in Iraq and to establish a military alliance. There was widespread agitation by the opponents of Saleh Jabr and Nuri al-Said on the grounds that the Treaty had been entered into without proper consultation and that it was really perpetuating British privileges in Iraq. The leftists jumped on the bandwagon; among these there was a number of Jews who felt that for the first time they could play an active part in the national struggle. Nuri al-Said dealt very harshly with them.

The foundation of the State of Israel was almost simultaneous with these events. The reaction of the Jews in Iraq, as Anwar Shā'ūl — whom we shall discuss later — put it, was "a mixture of spiritual thirst, bewilderment, watchful anxiety and visions of a repetition of the massacre of 1941". The consequences were immediate and sweeping. There were unprovoked denunciations of Jews as Zionists and communists; the Criminal Code had already declared Zionism and communism serious criminal offences. Jewish employees were dismissed from government posts, and a ban on travel abroad together with the imposition of massive cash guarantees (acceptable only in cases of special emergencies) were practised indiscriminately against Jews. There was perhaps for the first time in the history of the community a shrinkage in commercial activity, with consequent massive unemployment among Jews. Events were daily taking a more and more nasty turn. Terror was the rule. The public hanging in 1949 of the millionaire Shafīq Adas was the final proof that there could be no protection from official persecution. Numbers of young people started fleeing the country — mostly via Iran, which became the perfect haven on the way to the Holy Land. The Law of Denaturalisation was passed in 1950, and against all expectations, the majority of Jews — 120 000 — left the country under very harsh and humiliating conditions. The several thousand who remained saw the official name of the community change from the "Israelite" to the "Mosaic" community.

Valuable evidence about the conditions facing the Jews at that time and later is to be found in the autobiography of the well-known lawyer, poet and journalist, Anwar Shā'ūl, published in Arabic in Jerusalem in 1980 *(Qiṣṣat ḥayātī fī wādī al-ra-rāfidain)*. Born *c.* 1905, Shā'ūl emigrated to Israel in 1971. He had a very traditional religious upbringing in the southern city of Ḥilla among a predominantly Shi'ite population. He also had a most solid grounding in the study of Arabic and the Muslim culture of the country. When his family moved to Baghdad in 1917 he became very involved in the literary life of the capital. He published *al-Ḥāṣid,* a literary magazine, from 1924 until 1929, was editor of a Jewish weekly *al-Miṣbāh,* and worked in various communal Jewish organisations.

On the occasion of the foundation of the Hebrew University in Jerusalem in 1925, Shā'ūl, then a teacher in a Jewish secondary school, *al-Madrasa al-waṭaniyya,* wrote a poem, "Salute to the Hebrew University", extolling the efforts through which both peoples — Arabs and Jews — would have a better future. The poem was inscribed in decorative script by a well-known master of Arabic calligraphy and was adorned with the Iraqi flag in one corner and the Star of David in the other. Shā'ūl sent the framed poem to Jerusalem and received many complimentary letters from all over the world. However, on his arrival in Jerusalem in 1971, he conducted a fruitless search for the poem, despite assurances from his friend, the educationist and poet Ezra Haddad, that he had seen it hanging at the University during a visit in the early 1930s. Anwar could recall only four verses of the poem and these he reprinted in his autobiography.

Anwar Shā'ūl refers more than once to his Jewish identity. His motto had always been: To every man his religion; religion is between man and God; one's country is a matter of public concern *(li kuli insān dīnuhu wal-dīn lil-lāh wal-waṭan lil-jamī').* In order to explain why he did not leave Iraq at the time of the general exodus, he describes the Law of Denaturalisation of 1950 *(qānūn tasqīt al-jinsiyya al-'irāqiyya)* as an earthquake which shook Iraq and the Jews in particular. It did not occur to him to register for denaturalisation and emigration, he wrote, not for lack of awareness concerning the terrible situation, nor because of his satisfaction with the existing conditions, but purely because of his deep attachment to his land and to his country.

Shā'ūl was, of course, one of the most literate men in the country and was involved for most of his life with Arabic literary movements and with the literary life of Iraq. It is not surprising therefore that he used his pen to defend the position of the Jews. Referring to the mid-1930s, when Yāsīn al-Hāshimī was Prime Minister, he describes how his own situation changed as well as that of the community. Certain papers had begun to publish insinuations and attacks against the Jews, who had come to be known as "Yāsīn al-Hāshimī's prey"; a few were even hunted down and murdered in the streets of Baghdad.

In a meeting at Ezra Daniel's house at which the Chief Rabbi and other eminent Jews were present, it was disclosed that prominent members of al-Hāshimi's government had suggested to the notables of the Jewish community that they publish, both individually and as a group, declarations to affirm that they were loyal both to their country and to their government's policy — and that there existed no connection whatever between them and Zionist activities. The following day, and on successive occasions, Iraqi dailies published declarations from a number of Jews confirming their patriotism, their deep-seated Iraqi consciousness and their total detachment from anything which "smelt of Zionism" — *(ibti'āduhum min kulli mā yushammu fīhi rā'ihatu al-ṣahyūniyya)*. The signatories were the Chief Rabbi Sasson Khaduri, Anwar Shā'ūl, Ezra Ḥaddād and Menashe Za'rūr. "You can smell in him the odour of Zionism" became a charge on which Jews were convicted during the show trials in al-Mahdāwī's court of the late 1950s.

From this brief survey it is clear that the Holy Land became a negative force in the life of the Jewish community in Iraq. In conclusion, therefore, a few points should be made. On coming to Israel, the Iraqis quickly discovered that they had to face an uphill battle in order to take their rightful place in Israeli society. They soon discovered that Israel was built on Zionism as much as it might be the Promised Land *(arḍ al-mī'ād)* and that Zionist credentials were the most important criteria in gaining status. In the writing of the history of the community in Israel there is thus a tendency to overstress the existence of Zionist activity in Iraq and to blow it out of all proportion. This, in my view, does a disservice to a community which has had a very long and varied history, the interest of which is out of all proportion to the relatively minor Zionist activity which occurred during the last few years of its existence but which now seems to occupy the centre of the stage.

23 Judaism and Zionism in the Holy Land

Elie Kedourie

To begin at the beginning, as this beginning is described in the Bible and traditionally accepted by successive generations of Jews, the Land of Israel was bestowed on the children of Israel according to a covenant. This covenant, entered into on Mount Sinai, obligates the sons of Israel as a whole, as well as each individual Jew, to obey the divine commandments. In return the children of Israel are promised perpetual enjoyment of divine favour: their enemies will be powerless against them, they will multiply and enjoy prosperity and plenty.

This account may be similar to many which were generally familiar and acceptable to Antiquity — accounts based on the notion that the group is protected by its tutelary deity on condition that the deity is worshipped and propitiated. But between the outlook of pagan Antiquity and that which is articulated in the Bible, the differences are significant and far-reaching. In pagan Antiquity there is a tight, indeed unbreakable, connection between rule and religion — a religion which is in effect simply ancestor-worship. In this religion king and priest are the same, and have to be the same. Frequently also the ruler himself is a god. What is most remarkable about the biblical scheme is that within the polity of the children of Israel there is disjunction and often outright opposition between political power and religious authority. This disjunction and opposition is spoken of in many places in Scripture. One of its most striking expressions is found in I Samuel VII: 10–18, where the elders apply to Samuel to give the children of Israel a king. God tells Samuel, who had been rather taken aback by this request, to accede to it, "for they have not rejected thee, but they have rejected me, that I should not reign over them." Samuel then proceeds to give the elders a list of all the fearful things which the people may expect at the hands of a king. This they will find out by and by, and then "ye shall cry out in that day because of the king which ye shall have chosen you, and the Lord will not hear you in that day".

This scepticism about, mistrust of, politics and political power had further far-reaching consequences when the Jewish polity suffered shipwreck at the hands of the Assyrians, and many centuries later at the hands of the Romans. In pagan Antiquity, because the tie between religion and rule was so tight, the group (as well as the individual) had no defence, no inner defences, against political disaster. Political defeat was the defeat of the group's tutelary god. Built into the Jewish outlook, however, was the certainty that God was infinitely greater than any local or temporary political arrangement, and that politics was perpetually under judgement. Assyrians and Romans were no more than instruments of divine punishment — punishment which the children of Israel drew upon themselves for having disobeyed the covenant to which they were a party. As Deuteronomy XXVIII:64 declares, the consequence of transgression is that "the Lord shall scatter thee among all people, from one end of the earth even unto the other".

The young Hegel, whose interests were chiefly historical and theological, speculated on the reasons for the ruin of the classical world, and on the supersession — on the face of it so unlikely and so astonishing — of the ancient religions of the polis and civitas by Christianity, a religion in all ways alien to the peoples who were converted to it. He came to the conclusion that the reason for this prodigious outcome was the rise of a remote, heavy-handed despotism in the shape of the Roman Empire — a despotism which transformed citizens into subjects, thus emptying of all meaning the civic religions of the polis which imparted cohesion and solidarity to the citizen body, and gave the individual citizen the certainty that the city and its government was veritably flesh of his own flesh. Hegel held that it was this etiolation of the civic religion brought about by Roman despotism which created spiritual hunger which, in spite of what he then believed to be its radical unsuitability for a healthy social and political life, Christianity came to satisfy.

We may think that Hegel was mistaken in making Roman despotism responsible for destroying the spiritual mainsprings of the classical world, and more precisely in attributing to policital vicissitudes such transcendental importance. For the catastrophes which the Jewish polity underwent in 586 BCE and in 70 CE were, on any reckoning, much worse than the daily monotonous grind of heavy-handed Roman rule. Yet these catastrophes did not mean the supersession or ruin of Judaism, which has remained a living religion under the most unpropitious, indeed the cruelest of circumstances. Against the young Hegel we may hold that civic religion, and the worship of tutelary deities are, inherently and inevitably, brittle things which any political failure may irremediably shatter.

After the catastrophe of 70 CE the Jews were dispersed and powerless. The rabbis who considered themselves the heirs of the Prophets and the Prophetic tradition, kept together, in a most remarkable — indeed a unique — achievement, a people devoid of territory and political power, dispersed over wide regions, and subject to a variety of regimes. They maintained and amplified the Jewish self-view which has its roots in the Bible. In this self-view, dispersion and suffering are the result of transgression, while pardon and restoration await repentance. The restoration is that of the Promised Land, and of a polity again governed according to divine prescriptions under the kingship of the House of David, the anointed of the Lord. The rabbis added other elements to the traditional self-view: that the restoration would take place in God's own good time; that speculation about the time of its occurrence, i.e. about the coming of the Anointed One, was forbidden; and that the Jews must not go up to the Land in a column — i.e. that the restoration must not be the outcome of forcible human action. Not only this, but also many eminent rabbinical authorities deemed that it was not a religious duty to live or seek to settle in the Land. In this, they disagreed with the views of Yehuda Halevy and Nachmanides, now much better known. They did so on the score that salvation was easier outside than within the Land; that exile itself was a substitute for the Temple sacrifices which could no longer be carried out; and that political conditions in the Land were now such as to make a life of study and religious observance difficult in the extreme.

With the European Enlightenment which in due course spread among the Jewries of Central and Eastern Europe (who constituted the majority of Jews in the world), there came a new Jewish self-view. According to this outlook, the Jews were simply a group among other human groups all sharing in the irresistible and inevitable ascent of humanity from superstition to enlightenment. Jews had the right to partake in the rights and duties of citizenship on an equality with their fellow-citizens. This outlook is encapsulated in the injunction to be a man abroad and a Jew at home. It is obvious that the traditional notions of transgression and punishment, exile and restoration are very far removed from this new outlook. But about a century and a half after this outlook had begun to spread, a great shock was administered to it by the rise of Hitler and the setting up of the death-camps by a state hitherto believed to be in the vanguard of civilisation. Such a phenomenon is utterly inexplicable in terms of the Enlightenment scheme.

The Jewish self-view inspired by the Enlightenment was at the opposite pole from the assumptions, the categories and the mind-set of rabbinical Judaism which had hitherto provided the norms of belief and behaviour for Jews everywhere. A dialogue between them was bound to be a *dialogue de sourds*. It was, however, otherwise with another modern development within the Jewish world. This development, because it was intimately involved with traditional beliefs and attitudes, in a way in which the Enlightened self-view could not, was bound to have profound and far-reaching consequences for Judaism, in the same way perhaps as the destruction of the Jewish polity by the Romans had had for Jews and Judaism everywhere — consequences which have reverberated over the centuries.

This new development is also deeply indebted to European ideas. It is Zionism, which is a variant of the European doctrine of nationalism. In this self-view the Jews are a nation defined by their history, and as such entitled to live, and to govern themselves, on their own historic national territory. Like the Enlightenment Jewish self-view this, too, was incompatible with the traditional self-view. In Zionism, it is not a matter of transgression, repentance and return. Again, in requiring Jews to be active in setting up a national Jewish state in the Land of Israel, Zionism goes against the rabbinical teaching that the people must not go up to the Land in a column. The disagreement, at times outspoken and at others muted, has never been resolved. The state of Israel, which embodies the Zionist vision, depends on the existence of Jews. Jews are what they are because in some sense or another they subscribe to Judaism. In Judaism, the triple notion of transgression, repentance and restoration is central — and this notion applies not only to individuals but also to the group as a whole. And it is clear that the state of Israel is not that restoration of which repentance is the essential prerequisite.

In any case, Zionism does depend on the existence of Jews and Judaism, while Jews and Judaism cannot but be profoundly and lastingly affected by the rise and spread of Zionism and the fortunes of the state of Israel where (as at the time of the destruction of the Second Temple) lives a minority — albeit a substantial one — of the Jewish people. In synagogues outside Israel a blessing of the state and its inhabitants is recited on every Sabbath and feast-day, which ends by declaring that out of Zion shall come forth the Law and the word of the Lord from Jerusalem. It is obvious that the Zion and the Jerusalem of which the blessing speaks are not the earthly Zion, or the capital of the state of Israel. There is, thus, tension between the actual reality and the aspiration which the blessing expresses — an aspiration central to the Messianic promise in Judaism. Somehow or another, this tension has to be faced and articulated. Since we do not see how the earthly Jerusalem can approximate, in any foreseeable future, to the heavenly one, it is the religious discourse of Judaism which has to accommodate, live with, and even perhaps draw strength from this tension. Here, then, is an issue which did not have to be faced when the traditional self-view came to be confronted with the rival self-view stemming from the Enlightenment. Now the tension has to be faced.

The existence of the state of Israel faces Jewish religious thought with another new situation. It is that of the existence of an independent Jewish political authority. However it came about, the state of Israel does not prescribe a set of religious beliefs and practices as a condition of citizenship. And Israeli society (its Jewish majority at any rate) is not of a kind to accept such tests of citizenship. The context of rabbinical thought, however, has been a traditional society in which the tastes, inclinations and behaviour of individuals by and large conformed to norms which were generally unquestioned. Now, however, there is a new situation: an extensive Jewish society in Israel — which is a Jewish state in some sense or another — the members of which entertain an infinite variety of tastes and opinions. Can rabbinical thought reformulate itself so as to take account of the fact that here is a Jewish society and a Jewish government unlike anything with which it had to deal for now coming on to 2 000 years? It seems necessary that it should. Not to do so would expose it to the considerable dangers inherent in an utter separation between the realm of the sacred and that of the secular. It would create insoluble and unbearable paradoxes. Would Jewish religious discourse have enough inventiveness to cope with an unprecedented situation?

The two religions to which Judaism can be said to have given birth, namely Christianity and Islam, have had, by reason of their historical experiences, to face this problem, and it is instructive to see how they have dealt, or failed to deal, with it. Islam, to take the simpler and more straightforward case, has in effect failed to do so. Fairly soon after the establishment of Islamic empires, the Muslim divines were driven by the reality of unrestrained despotism to emphasise the religious duty of obedience to the ruler, whether bad or mad, and to teach that to him whose hand is heavy — to him who has the power — obedience is due. From what can be called this impasse, Muslim political thought has not yet emerged. But the ruler to whom obedience was due was a Muslim ruler, and his Muslim subjects by and large shared the same universe of discourse, fully accepting the truth and authority of the Revelation and the necessity of ordering their lives according to its prescriptions. This remained the case until, so to speak, yesterday. But Muslim society has become increasingly exposed to foreign ideas, and in many parts of the Muslim world the unspoken consensus long taken for granted has ceased to hold. But Islamic religious thought has been unable to formulate a teaching suitable to an Islamic society in which men — and women — choose to follow their own individual preferences. Islamic religious thought has not been able to devise a doctrine which makes a place for Islam in a modern society open to all manner of influences and innovations. On the contrary, fundamentalism so-called which has triumphed in Iran, and is now the predominant influence in legislation and judicial arrangements in Pakistan, is predicated on a return to a presumed pristine condition when Muslim society will again function exactly as it did at the time of the Prophet and his immediate successors. We may wonder whether, things being what they are, such a dream can ever become reality.

As for Christianity, its Eastern branch has never evolved a doctrine which goes beyond the belief that rule and religion are twins, that the king is both ruler and guardian of orthodoxy, or which can deal with a society in which uniformity of belief does not obtain. Indeed the assertion of uniformity and its necessity, was the work of the Byzantine emperors. It is in Western Christianity that we find the most successful attempts to come to terms, doctrinally, with a society marked by diversity of belief, and in which government is committed neither to a single set of beliefs nor to its enforcement. But this took a very long time to come about.

To start with, there was the medieval ideal of a *respublica christiana* where unity between people, church and ruler was supposed to obtain. The Reformation followed with the idea of a godly prince who was to enforce religious belief and extirpate unbelief. But to enforce and extirpate requires the prince to use power, and the ways of power are necessarily sinful. Recourse therefore must be had to what English seventeenth-century divines called the holy pretence, in order to justify power by the hallowed ends which it purports to pursue. But in the religious wars of the Reformation the pretence came to be seen through, and religion became discredited. Religiously speaking, the Peace of Augsburg which put an end to religious conflict in Central Europe by decreeing that the religion of the subject had to be the same as that of prince, was the peace of the grave. Belief was now more than ever a matter of state, subject to calculations of strategy, utility and convenience. Hence the increase, among Western thinking classes, of cynicism and scepticism, and the increasing doubts on all sides about the feasibility of enforcing uniformity of belief. And out of this scepticism about officially enforced religion there arose the ideal of "a free church in a free state". It is an ideal which seems best fitted to a society populated by individuals aware of their own specific individuality and attached to their freedom of choice and of conscience. The ideal has acquired full reality only very recently and in only a few countries.

Such then, are the possibilities which the historical record shows Islam and Christianity, grappling with social and political tension in their societies, have explored. Which way rabbinical thought, grappling with the particular tensions produced by the existence of Israel and its modern society, will go, remains to be seen.